MW01294280

This book explores the full range of social, economic, religious, and cultural contacts between England and the German city of Cologne during the Central Middle Ages, *c.* 1000 to *c.* 1300.

A wealth of original archive material reveals an extensive network of English and German emigrants who were surprisingly successful in achieving assimilation into their new homeland. From beguines to English sterling, pilgrims to emigrants, crusaders and merchants to teachers, there existed a complex world of Anglo-German associations. The book therefore maintains the thesis that the Anglo-German nexus should be given a higher profile in current historiography on the Middle Ages, and that the book should stand as a contribution towards the reconfiguration of medieval history away from the boundaries created by modern political and intellectual categories. It will also encourage historians to reconsider their basic assumptions about what constituted "medieval Europe."

JOSEPH P. HUFFMAN is Associate Professor of European History, Messiah College, Pennsylvania.

Cambridge Studies in Medieval Life and Thought

FAMILY, COMMERCE, AND RELIGION
IN LONDON AND COLOGNE

Cambridge Studies in Medieval Life and Thought
Fourth Series

General Editor:
D. E. LUSCOMBE
Leverhulme Personal Research Professor of Medieval History, University of Sheffield

Advisory Editors:
R. B. DOBSON
Professor of Medieval History, University of Cambridge, and Fellow of Christ's College

ROSAMOND MCKITTERICK
Professor of Early Medieval European History, University of Cambridge, and Fellow of Newnham College

The series Cambridge Studies in Medieval Life and Thought was inaugurated by G. G. Coulton in 1921; Professor D. E. Luscombe now acts as General Editor of the Fourth Series, with Professor R. B. Dobson and Professor Rosamond McKitterick as Advisory Editors. The series brings together outstanding work by medieval scholars over a wide range of human endeavour extending from political economy to the history of ideas.

For a list of titles in the series, see end of book.

FAMILY, COMMERCE, AND RELIGION IN LONDON AND COLOGNE

Anglo-German emigrants, c. 1000 – c. 1300

JOSEPH P. HUFFMAN

CAMBRIDGE
UNIVERSITY PRESS

PUBLISHED BY THE PRESS SYNDICATE OF THE UNIVERSITY OF CAMBRIDGE
The Pitt Building, Trumpington Street, Cambridge, United Kingdom

CAMBRIDGE UNIVERSITY PRESS
The Edinburgh Building, Cambridge CB2 2RU, UK
40 West 20th Street, New York NY 10011–4211, USA
477 Williamstown Road, Port Melbourne, VIC 3207, Australia
Ruiz de Alarcón 13, 28014 Madrid, Spain
Dock House, The Waterfront, Cape Town 8001, South Africa

http://www.cambridge.org

First published 1998
First paperback edition 2002

Typeface Bembo 11/12 pt.

A catalogue record for this book is available from the British Library

Library of Congress Cataloguing in Publication data
Huffman, Joseph P., 1959–
Family, commerce and religion in London and Cologne:
Anglo-German emigrants, c. 1000–c. 1300 / Joseph P. Huffman.
p.   cm. – (Cambridge studies in medieval life and thought)
Includes bibliographical references and index.
ISBN 0 521 63292 7
1. London (England) – Relations – Germany – Cologne.
2. Cologne (Germany) – Relations – England – London.
3. London (England) – Emigration and immigration – History.
4. Cologne (Germany) – Emigration and immigration – History.
5. London (England) – Social life and customs.
6. Hamburg (Germany) – Social life and customs.
7. London (England) – Commerce – Germany – Cologne.
8. Cologne (Germany) – Commerce – England – London.
9. London (England) – History – to 1500.
10. Germans – England – London – History.
11. British – Germany – Hamburg – History.
12. Great Britain – Church history 1066–1485.
I. Title. II. Series.
HF3520.L65H84 1998
303.4′824210435514–dc21   97-52659   CIP

ISBN 0 521 63292 7 hardback
ISBN 0 521 52193 9 paperback

CONTENTS

Preface page ix
List of abbreviations xii
The wards of medieval London xv
The parishes and districts of medieval Cologne xvi
Anglo-Cologne family genealogies xvii

Introduction 1

Part I The historical background: Anglo-German commercial foundations and the city of Cologne

1 The London guildhall and Cologne's rise to dominance
in the eleventh and twelfth centuries 9
2 The rise of the Hansa towns and the decline of Cologne's
dominance in the thirteenth century 23
3 Anglo-German currency exchange: Cologne and English
sterling 41
Appendix: Schreinsbücher *manuscript entries* 57

Part II Anglo-Cologne family, property, and inheritance ties

4 The formation of individual and family identity in
medieval Cologne: property and surnames 67
5 *Anglicus in Colonia*: the social, economic, and legal status
of the English in Cologne during the twelfth and
thirteenth centuries 82
6 Cologne families with English connections: the Zudendorps 128
7 Cologners in England 162

Contents

Part III Anglo-German religious and cultural life

8 Confraternities, expatriate monks, pious legends, and pilgrims   199
9 Clerics, canon law, crusaders, and culture   217
   Conclusion: A reappraisal of the Anglo–German nexus   240

   Appendix: The archbishops of Cologne   243
   Select bibliography   244
   Index   269

PREFACE

Mention of my research in the Cologne city archive during a recent conversation with a prominent historian of medieval France elicited the following response "Cologne my, but that is so far east!" Such is the common *mentalité* among most medievalists who concentrate their attention on the traditional Anglo-French historiographical paradigm. This book is my response to that conversation.

For the majority of English-speaking historians of medieval Europe, whose education and research have been centered on Anglo-French concerns, medieval Germany evokes images of life more akin to early-modern Germany after the Thirty Years War: an economically backward region of Europe devastated by warfare, constantly harassed by famine and disease, where the middle class lagged far behind their Anglo-French counterparts, and where political polycentrism and the lack of a strong centralized government assured this curious collage of principalities a status of underdevelopment and cultural sterility. In this vision, Cologne is more conceptually "east" in the mind of my colleague than the geography of Europe even allows, and thus not part of western Europe properly understood.

Happily, this was not the Germany of the Central Middle Ages. Indeed, Alfred Haverkamp has rightly argued that Germany was the most affected and transformed of all the regions of medieval Europe by the rapid changes occurring in European society during this period. Germany not only constantly received the cultural and economic impulses from the western European and Mediterranean regions, but also came to serve a mediating role between these regions and the north and east of Europe.[1] Medieval Germany therefore began moving

---

[1] Alfred Haverkamp, *Medieval Germany (1056–1273)*, 2nd edn., trans. Helga Braun and Richard Mortimer (Oxford, 1992), p. 352. Timothy Reuter, "Past, present and no future in the *regnum Teutonicum*," *The Perception of the Past in Twelfth-Century Europe*, ed. Paul Magdalino (London, 1992), p. 17 has also asserted that: "A further point needs to be made about comparisons: the

inward from the periphery and merging with the currents of western European and Mediterranean civilization during the Central Middle Ages (eleventh to thirteenth centuries). This being the case, Germany is an especially suitable vantage point from which to evaluate the trends and culture of this period, as well as to consider the growing ties of the larger western world with central Europe during this period of expansion.[2] The setting aside of former historical and historiographical boundaries established by earlier political historians seems eminently appropriate at the close of the twentieth century, and therefore it is time that Germany is grafted more soundly onto the historiography of the medieval West. This study is intended to contribute to such a needed integration, which bridges both modern political as well as intellectual boundaries through a distinctly interregional approach.[3] Hence we shall make a geographical shift away from the traditional Anglo-French focus found in most English-speaking scholarship. Instead, the much-neglected realm of medieval Germany will be considered and integrated into Anglo-French historiography by considering its fascinating contacts with England.

My hope, therefore, is that this book may stimulate its readers to reconsider the paradigms we Anglophones have traditionally used to define medieval Europe. I could think of no better way of achieving this than offering a study of the multifarious ties that linked the Rhineland and the English realm together, since it would employ familiar English sources and yet introduce the possibilities of German sources to a wider audience. From beguines to sterling, pilgrims to emigrants, crusaders to teachers, we shall discover a world of Anglo-German commercial, social, religious, and cultural associations. The picture of medieval life which emerges from these should give us pause to reconsider the boundaries we tend to create in our own visions of the past.

Such a project would have been impossible without the generous support of scholars, colleagues, foundations, and friends. I thank the Deutscher Akademischer Austauschdienst for the generous research

---

twelfth-century *regnum Teutonicum* was a mainstream European country and partook of most of the developments found in France and England."

[2] Hagen Keller, *Zwischen regionaler Begrenzung und universalen Horizont: Deutschland im Imperium der Salier und Staufer, 1024–1250*, Propylaen Geschichte Deutschlands, 2 (Berlin, 1986), p. 49: "Gemeinabendländische Entwicklungstendenz und regionale Sonderbildung, Vereinheitlichung und Differenzierung griffen so ineinander, daß eine Geschichte Deutschlands zum Spiegel für die abandländische Geschichte im Hochmittelalter werden kann."

[3] For a creative comparative approach to studying the relationship between the state and society that seeks to bridge regional histories, see James Given, *State and Society: Gwynedd and Languedoc under Outside Rule* (Ithaca, 1990).

fellowship which made the archival work possible. For further writing and research grants that enabled me to complete the book I thank both Westmont College and Messiah College. My warmest appreciation goes to Dr. Manfred Groten and Dr. Joachim Deeters of the Historisches Archiv der Stadt Köln, whose knowledgeable and kind assistance made my time in Cologne most enjoyable and productive. I extend particular thanks to Professor Scott L. Waugh, the late Professor Robert L. Benson, Dr. Gerhart B. Ladner, and Dr. Bengt Löfstedt of University of California at Los Angeles (UCLA) for their wise counsel and example of sound scholarship, and to Professor Dr. Odilo Engels and the Historisches Seminar of the University of Cologne for further advice and assistance.

In England the archivists of the Public Records Office, the Corporation of London Records Office, the Guildhall Library, the Institute of Historical Research at the University of London, and the Norfolk Record Office all have my gratitude for unfailing guidance through the primary and secondary sources available. I especially want to thank Dr. Derek Keene of the Centre for Metropolitan History for his enthusiastic encouragement of my project and his insights into the London sources, and to Dr. Colin Taylor of the Museum of London for help with the CLRO sources. I am also indebted to the many librarians at the UCLA University Research Library and the Interlibrary Loan Offices of UCLA and Messiah College for providing me access to many foreign and rare publications.

All this being said, however, the greatest debt is owed to my wife, Peggy. She has endured the travails of my early academic years with a confidence in me and a belief in our future that has more than once carried me beyond what I myself could trust confidently. To her go my deepest thanks and I dedicate this book to her, for although the abovementioned people have in several ways been my Virgil through the Inferno and Purgatorio of this project, Peggy has always been my Beatrice.

ABBREVIATIONS

Annalen	*Annalen des Historischen Vereins für den Niederrhein, insbesondere die alte Erzdiözese Köln*
Böhmer	J. F. Böhmer, *Regesta Imperii* (Vienna, Cologne, and Graz, 1870–1984); vol. III: part 1 revised by N. von Bischoff and Heinrich Appelt (1951); vol. III: part 2 revised by Tilman Struve (1984); vol. IV: part 2 revised by Ferdinand Opll (1980); vol. IV: part 3 revised by Gerhard Baaken (1972–79); vol. V: parts 1–3 revised by Julius Ficker and Eduard Winkelmann (1881–1901); vol. V: part 4 revised by Paul Zinsmaier (1983); vol. VI: part 1 revised by O. Redlich with appendix by C. Brühl (1969); vol. VI: part 2 revised by Vincent Samanek (1933–48)
CCHR	*Calendar of the Charter Rolls Preserved in the PRO*, 6 vols. (London, 1903–27)
CCLR	*Calendar of Close Rolls Preserved in the PRO*, 19 vols. (London, 1900–38)
CFR	*Calendar of Fine Rolls Preserved in the PRO Volume I: 1272–1307* (London, 1911)
CLR	*Calendar of Liberate Rolls Preserved in the PRO*, 6 vols. (London, 1916–64)
CLRO	Corporation of London Records Office
CPR	*Calendar of Patent Rolls Preserved in the PRO*, 10 vols. (London, 1894–1913)
CRC	*Chronica regia Coloniensis (Annales Maximi Coloniensis)*, ed. Georg Waitz, *MGH SS rer. Germ.*, 18 (Hanover, 1880; rpt. 1978)

Abbreviations

Curia Regis Rolls	*Curia Regis Rolls of the Reigns of Richard I, John and Henry III Preserved in the PRO*, 16 vols. (London, 1938–79)
DA	*Deutsches Archiv für Erforschung des Mittelalters*
EHR	*English Historical Review*
Ennen/ Eckertz	*Quellen zur Geschichte der Stadt Köln*, ed. L. Ennen and G. Eckertz, 6 vols. (Cologne, 1860–79)
HGB	*Hansische Geschichtsblätter*
HUB	*Hansisches Urkundenbuch*, 11 vols. (Halle, Leipzig, Weimar, and Munich, 1876–1939); vols. I–III ed. Konstantin Höhlbaum (1876–86); vols. IV–VI ed. Karl Kunze (1896–1905); vol. VII ed. H. G. Runstedt (1939); vols. VIII–XI ed. W. Stein (1899–1916)
JKGV	*Jahrbuch des Kölnischen Geschichtsvereins*
LUB	*Codex Diplomaticus Lubecensis. Lübeckisches Urkundenbuch*, Verein für Geschichte und Althertumskunde, 11 vols. (Lübeck, 1843–1905; rpt. Osnabrück, 1976)
MGH Const	*Monumenta Germaniae Historica: Constitutiones et acta publica imperatorum et regum*
MGH DD	*Monumenta Germaniae Historica: Diplomata*
MGH Leges	*Monumenta Germaniae Historica: Leges* (folio)
MGH SS	*Monumenta Germaniae Historica: Scriptores* (folio)
MGH SS rer. Germ.	*Monumenta Germaniae Historica: Scriptores rerum Germanicarum in usum scholarum separatim editi*
MIÖG	*Mitteilungen des Instituts für Österreichische Geschichtsforschung*
MPCM	Matthew Paris, *Chronica majora*, ed. Henry Richards Luard, RS, 57, 7 vols. (London, 1872–73; rpt. 1964)
MPHA	Matthew Paris, *Historia Anglorum sive historia minor*, ed. Frederic Madden, RS, 44, 3 vols. (London, 1866–9; rpt. 1970)
MSAK	*Mitteilungen aus dem Stadtarchiv von Köln*
Munimenta	*Munimenta Gildhallae Londoniensis: Liber Albus, Liber Custumarum et Liber Horn*, ed. Henry Thomas Riley, RS, 12, 3 vols. in 4 (London, 1849–62)

NF	Neue Folge
NS	New series
PGRG	Publikationen der Gesellschaft für Rheinische Geschichtskunde
PR	Pipe Roll Society
PRO	Public Record Office
REK	*Die Regesten der Erzbischöfe von Köln im Mittelalter*, 4 vols. PGRG, 21 (Bonn, 1901–15); vol. I ed. Friedrich Wilhelm Oediger (1954–61); vol. II ed. Richard Knipping (1901); vol. III: i–ii ed. Richard Knipping (1909–13); vol. IV ed. Wilhelm Kisky (1915)
RS	Rerum Britannicarum Medii Aevi Scriptores (Rolls Series)
Rymer	*Foedera, conventiones, litterae etc.*, ed. George Holmes, 2nd edn. (London, 1727–35)
Shirley	*Royal and other Historical Letters Illustrative of the Reign of Henry III*, ed. Walter W. Shirley, RS, 27, 2 vols. (London, 1862–8)
TRHS	*Transactions of the Royal Historical Society*
UGN	*Urkundenbuch für die Geschichte des Niederrheins*, ed. Theodor Josef Lacomblet, 4 vols. (Düsseldorf, 1840–58)

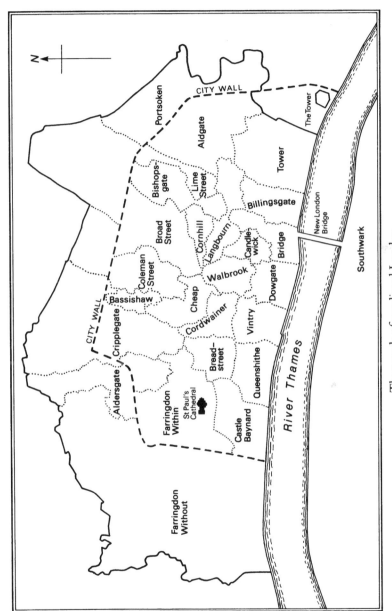

The wards of medieval London

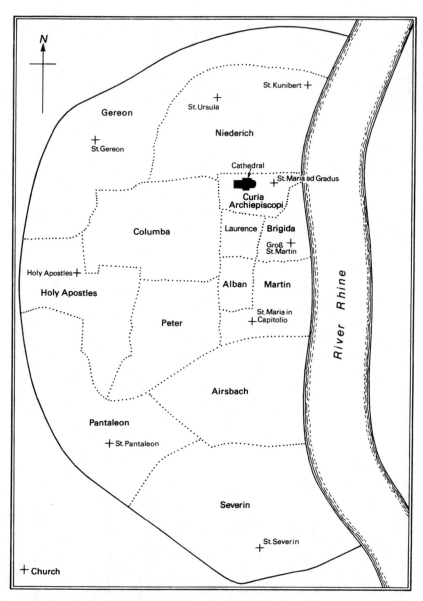

N

St. Kunibert +

St. Ursula +

Gereon

Niederich

+
St. Gereon

Cathedral
Curia
Archiepiscopi

+ St. Maria ad Gradus

Columba

Laurence | Brigida

Groß +
St. Martin

Holy Apostles +

Holy Apostles

Alban | Martin

St. Maria in
+ Capitolio

Peter

Airsbach

River Rhine

Pantaleon

+ St. Pantaleon

Severin

St. Severin
+

+ Church

The parishes and districts of medieval Cologne

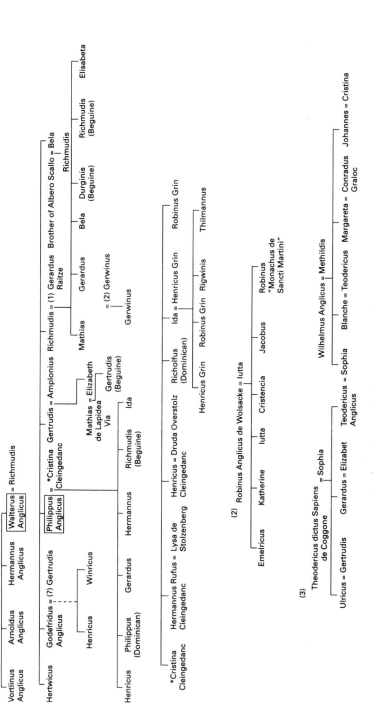

Anglo–Cologne family genealogies (Anglicus)

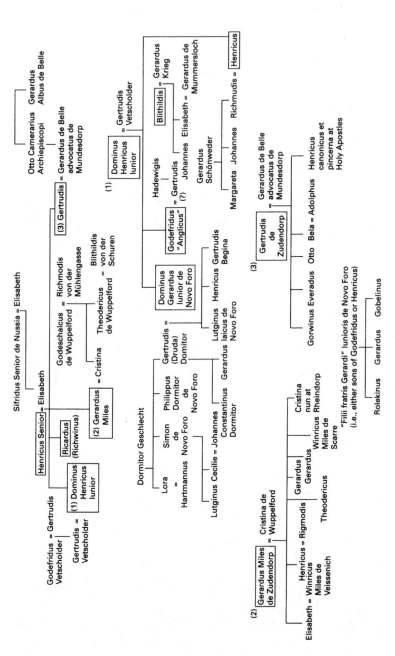

Anglo-Cologne family genealogies (Zudendorp)

INTRODUCTION

Relations between the English and German realms have received very limited attention thus far among historians, in marked contrast with the traditional historiography of Anglo-French and German–Italian relations. Of course, these traditional constellations obviously exist with good reason. The Norman Conquest and the subsequent English involvement in French continental holdings on the one hand, or the preoccupation of the German emperors in Italy and their resultant conflicts with the papacy on the other, explain why the history of the Central and Later Middle Ages has been written along these two main geopolitical axes. Nevertheless, activity between England and Germany represented a vital and at times no less influential interregional relationship, which has not received its due attention under such a primarily geopolitical framework.

Previous research on Anglo-German relations has emphasized either political alliances or commercial exchange. These two spheres of research have been almost wholly the domain of German-speaking scholars, who have viewed England rather narrowly in the context of either its political involvement in papal–imperial conflicts and its cultivation of anti-French allies among the German princes, or its place in the development of the German Hansa. Since political history has been eclipsed by social history in the past thirty years, little new scholarship has appeared to revise older studies that present Anglo-German relations as a series of alliance schemes more akin to the late nineteenth and early twentieth-century Europe than to political conditions of the Middle Ages. Furthermore, the overwhelming majority of the research in economic history concentrates on the Hanseatic era in the Later Middle Ages, so that little work has been devoted to Anglo-German relations during the *Vorhansezeit* – that is, from *c.* AD 1000 to 1300.[1] Of course, the dearth of

[1] A recent example of this trend is T. H. Lloyd's *England and the German Hanse, 1157–1611.*

I

quantifiable evidence on trade in the earlier period accounts for the emphasis on the Later Middle Ages. The historiography on the pre-Hanseatic period, however, stands in the shadow of the *Hansezeit* and has not been considered in the broader context of exchange between the regions and without reference to later developments. The written history of the *Vorhansezeit*, like the political histories of the nineteenth and early twentieth centuries, is often characterized by later categories not belonging to its own era.

Aside from a few notable endeavors,[2] virtually nothing new on the Anglo-German connection has appeared in recent years. A conference held in 1987 at the German Historical Institute in London, entitled "Germany and England in the High Middle Ages: a comparative approach," was intended to create momentum among medievalists for the cultivation of this open field. Yet, except for Karl Leyser's impressive research the exhortation has received little response to date for the crucial period of the Central Middle Ages. It seems incredible that 1987 was the first time English and German medievalists met to consider the merits of such cooperative research, yet this was the case.[3] It then took nine years for a volume to appear as a result of the conference.[4] The articles therein are splendid summaries of the state of research on literacy, kingship and warfare, Jewish and crusading history, and the history of urban communities, manors, and social mobility. Yet

---

(Cambridge, 1991) which, although beginning its study in 1157, actually emphasizes almost exclusively the fourteenth through sixteenth centuries. See also John D. Fudge, *Cargoes, Embargoes, and Emissaries: The Commercial and Political Interaction of England and the German Hanse, 1450–1510* (Toronto, 1995).

[2] Julia Barrow, "Cathedrals, provosts and prebends: a comparison of twelfth-century German and English practice," *Journal of Ecclesiastical History* 37:4 (October 1986), pp. 536–64 and "Education and the recruitment of cathedral canons in England and Germany 1100–1225," *Viator*. 20 (1989), pp. 118–37; C. Stephen Jaeger, *The Envy of Angels. Cathedral Schools and Social Ideas in Medieval Europe, 950–1200* (Philadelphia, 1994); and selected portions in Veronica Ortenberg's *The English Church and the Continent in the Tenth and Eleventh Centuries: Cultural, Spiritual, and Artistic Exchanges* (Oxford, 1992) are valuable recent contributions. A comparative effort in the area of urban historical geography is worthy of note as well: Dietrich Denecke and Gareth Shaw, eds., *Urban Historical Geography. Recent Progress in Britain and Germany*, Cambridge Studies in Historical Geography, 10 (Cambridge, 1988), though Brian Graham concludes: "Finally, there is an awareness of the insular parochialism of much previous [British] work and ideas and rather belatedly more attention is being paid to continental studies, both as comparisons and contrasts. Oddly, however, the revisions and reevaluations persist in their isolation of each other" (p. 38).

[3] Alfred Haverkamp (Trier), Hanna Vollrath (Bochum) and Karl Leyser (Oxford) were the organizers of the symposium (July 1–4, 1987): "This conference seems to have been the first opportunity for British and German medieval historians to meet in order to discuss German and English history in this way." See the *Bulletin of the German Historical Institute of London* 10 no. 2 (May, 1988), pp. 23–6.

[4] Alfred Haverkamp and Hanna Vollrath, eds., *England and Germany in the High Middle Ages* (Oxford, 1996).

typically these articles review English and German historiographical issues in isolation from one another, and leave the reader to do the comparative work. In particular, there is not one study of any actual relations *between* the English and German realms. In fact, the English and German historiographical traditions have developed so independently of one another that they often employ two parallel systems of citation for primary sources, which further complicates any attempt to synthesize the body of secondary literature.[5] This unfortunate situation, along with a much more unfortunate Anglo-German history in the twentieth century, may help to account for the lack of interest in such research but it does not reflect the actual status of the primary sources themselves, which are rich in material concerning the multifaceted relations between these regions.

Little needs to be said about the sizeable body of documents surviving from the English realm in the period from the eleventh to the early fourteenth century, as its value and usefulness has been demonstrated over and over again. Despite the lack of a highly developed royal administration in Germany a large amount of primary source material survives virtually untapped, if one knows where to look. A major source of available data can be found in the records of German cities, and most significantly in the municipal documents of the largest and most important of these cities – Cologne. Therefore, Cologne has been chosen as our case study, based on its vast archival holdings as well as on its close relationship with the English kingdom. While Cologne enjoyed relations with England unequaled by other German cities during this period, a study of its contacts will confirm the value of comparative, interregional research and serve as an exhortation to consider similar research elsewhere in Germany and England.

The city of Cologne serves as an excellent case study for applying the methodology described above. Its highly developed relationship with England rested on two firm foundations: the traditionally pro-English policies of its archbishops and the privileged legal and economic position held by Cologne merchants and citizens in the English realm. Cologne was a natural point of contact for the English, situated as it was along the Rhine–Thames trading route and on the eastern frontier of

---

[5] This is best seen in the practice of German scholars citing English sources from the excerpts in *MGH SS* volumes 27 and 28 (entitled "Ex rerum Anglicarum scriptoribus") rather than from the standard complete editions as found in the English Rolls Series. In addition the use of separate charter books and *Urkundenbücher* (e.g. Rymer's *Foedera* and Böhmer's *Regesta Imperi*) has created many problems in the consistent dating of documents. Most recently, Ferdinand Opll's *Friedrich Barbarossa*, Gestalten des Mittelalters und der Renaissance (Darmstadt, 1990) makes no use of Karl Leyer's extensive scholarship.

France. The powerful position of the city's archbishops as regional princes made it all the more important.

The Cologne archbishops accumulated a number of honors and powers which led to their ultimate political dominance over the lower Rhine region. Many of these ecclesiastical lords were imperial chancellors, and they had exercised the right to crown the king-elect at Aachen since the pontificate of Archbishop Heribert (999–1021); thus they played a leading role in all royal elections. In addition to their superior ecclesiastical authority throughout northwest Germany they also exercised imperial regalian rights. Close ties had existed between the archbishopric and the German monarchs since the pontificate of Bruno I of Saxony (953–65), the brother of Emperor Otto I. The emperor not only appointed his brother to the Cologne see, but also made Bruno the duke of Lotharingia. From this time on, therefore, the Cologne archbishops were both secular and ecclesiastical princes. As *principes imperii* they were heavily involved in the emperors' Italian policies (several died there on imperial campaigns) and bore the title of archchancellor of Italy from 1031. A few even exercised royal authority in Germany as regents, such as Anno II (1056–75) during part of the minority of Henry IV, or Engelbert I (1215–25) during the almost permanent absence of Frederick II from Germany. Engelbert was also the guardian of Frederick's son Henry. Their regional political power as *Landherr* was ultimately solidified when, as a reward for military assistance to Emperor Frederick Barbarossa against Duke Henry the Lion in Saxony, Archbishop Philip I was given the ducal dignity and lands of Westphalia in 1180. Over time these powerful ecclesiastical princes developed close ties with the English royal house and therefore acted as diplomatic middlemen in virtually all political contacts between England and the empire during this period.[6]

The second foundation of the unique relationship between Cologne and England, one certainly in concert with the first, was the dominance of the Cologne merchants in Anglo-German commerce. Cologne merchants were a powerful economic force in Germany, and beneficiaries of a long tradition of royal privileges in England which exempted them from exactions and local legal authority. These grants were in turn reconfirmed by every English king during this period. They also possessed their own guildhall in London, from which all other German merchants had to operate if they wished to participate in English trade. The Cologne merchants thus held a virtual monopoly over German

---

[6] For a study of Anglo-Cologne diplomacy see J. Huffman, *A Social History of Medieval Diplomacy: Anglo-German Relations (1066–1307)* (Ann Arbor, 1999).

trade with England until the late thirteenth century, when Cologne was gradually replaced by Lübeck as the dominant power within the newly emerging Hanseatic League, and the London guildhall was subsumed into the larger Hanseatic "Steelyard" complex.

Economic historians have sketched this early commercial dominance of Cologne merchants. Yet a wealth of data survives which reveals the specific activities of Cologne citizens in England and, perhaps more surprisingly, of the English in Cologne. Hence the social history approach of this study adds considerably to the fleshing out of economic interaction between the regions.

Furthermore, there are hitherto unexploited sources which reveal interregional relations on levels other than the economic and political. Canterbury and Cologne were major pilgrimage sites that received visitors from both sides of the English Channel. Early monastic prayer brotherhoods and emigrant clergy further strengthened this cross-Channel religious and cultural network. Finally, although Cologne did not found a university until 1338, there is also evidence of intellectual relations between the regions. Such English scholars as the canon lawyer Gerard Pucelle and the great philosopher Duns Scotus spent time teaching in Cologne, and the latter was buried there in 1308. There is evidence of students from Cologne at Oxford and Cambridge, and still other expatriate Cologners who held prebends in England. All this we shall be exploring in the coming pages.

Relations between medieval England and Germany were surely rich and varied, and at times as influential as the Anglo-French and German–Italian axes; in fact all three axes were often deeply intertwined. In order to keep this particular study to an appropriate length, we shall focus primarily on the evidence of interactions between English and German emigrants from London and Cologne. This fascinating inter-section of peoples will allow us to combine regional and interregional history in a manner that provides a more comprehensive view of the dynamics of medieval life, and at the same time integrates at least one region of Germany more fully into western European society. By doing this we have all the tools necessary to reevaluate earlier paradigms of medieval life in Germany as essentially localized and disconnected from the developmental patterns of western Europe.

Part I

The historical background: Anglo-German commercial foundations and the city of Cologne

THE LONDON GUILDHALL AND COLOGNE'S RISE TO DOMINANCE IN THE ELEVENTH AND TWELFTH CENTURIES

The most enduring dynamic uniting Germany with England during the Central Middle Ages was commerce along the Rhine–Thames corridor. Hence we must first consider the emergence and evolution of this economic nexus in order to set the context for our subsequent researches into emigrant populations at both ends of the corridor.

Commercial contacts existed between England and the eastern Frankish realm at least as far back as the era of Charlemagne,[1] yet not until around the year 1000 do we find a specific reference to such activity. King Aethelred II's "Institutes of London" mention the presence of "homines imperatoris qui veniebant in navibus suis" among the foreign merchants in the city.[2] There has been much speculation about the identity of these "men of the emperor." Koppmann supposed that Cologne merchants were the principal figures along with others from the Westphalian cities of Dortmund, Soest, and Münster,[3] while Kellenbenz expected merchants from Cologne, Tiel, Deventer, and Utrecht[4] and Dollinger believed they were merchants from Cologne, Tiel, and Bremen.[5] The full passage in Aethelred's

---

[1] Charlemagne's letter to King Offa of Mercia (757–96), in which the emperor promises protection to English merchants and pilgrims passing through his territories, has been described as the "earliest commercial treaty" between England and Germany, yet no other evidence survives which indicates the extent of this activity: A. Weiner, "Early commercial intercourse between England and Germany," *Economica* 11 (1922), p. 127.

[2] *HUB*, I, pp. 1–2 no. 2; Johann Martin Lappenberg, *Urkundliche Geschichte des Hansischen Stahlhofes zu London* (Hamburg, 1851; rpt. Osnabrück, 1967), p. 1 no. 1; *Ancient Laws and Institutes of England*, ed. B. Thorpe (London, 1840), pp. 127–8; *Die Gesetze der Angelsachsen* ed. Felix Liebermann (Halle, 1903–16; rpt. 1960), I, p. 234; *The Laws of the Kings of England from Edmund to Henry I* ed. and trans. A. J. Robertson (Cambridge, 1925), p. 72.

[3] *Hanserecesse. Die Recesse und andere Akten der Hansetage von 1256–1430. 1: 1256–1370* ed. Karl Koppmann (Leipzig, 1870), p. xxxvi: "Diese Leute des Kaisers waren insbesondere wohl die später ausschliesslich genannten Kölner."

[4] Hermann Kellenbenz, "Der Aufstieg Kölns zur mittelalterlichen Handelsmetropole," *JKGV* 41 (1967), p. 8.

[5] Philippe Dollinger, *Die Hanse* (Stuttgart, 1966), pp. 5–6 (the English edition is cited hereafter).

statutes reads: "Et homines imperatoris, qui veniebant in navibus suis, bonarum legum digni tenebantur, sicut et nos," which indicates that the German merchants enjoyed legal rights comparable to those of the English. This was a privileged status for foreign traders. The *Leges Edwardi Confessoris* also allude to traditionally good trading relations between Germany and England during the Anglo-Saxon era.[6]

By the early eleventh century Cologne had emerged both economically and politically as a leader among the cities of Germany.[7] The city had never been completely abandoned after the decline of the Carolingian world, since it remained an administrative center and the seat of an archbishop. During the course of the eleventh century its merchants established long-distance trading ties to southern and eastern Germany as well as to the northwest and beyond. The city owed such commercial growth and prosperity primarily to its central location on the Rhine, western Europe's largest internal waterway,[8] and it soon became the major port for an ever-increasing amount of goods passing through the Rhineland. Eventually three fairs were held annually: at Easter, at the feast of St. Peter in Chains (August 1), and at the feast of St. Severin (October 23) which would last for three to four weeks each.[9] Thus by the end of the eleventh century Cologne dominated trade in Germany.[10] William of Malmesbury assures us that Cologne's reputation as the German city most blessed with prosperity and power was known in England when he wrote in the early twelfth century.[11]

Edith Ennen, "Europäische Züge der mittelalterlichen Kölner Stadtgeschichte," *MSAK* 60 (1971), p. 12 follows Dollinger, asserting that the merchants were from Tiel and Cologne.

[6] Martin Weinbaum, "Stahlhof und Deutsche Gildhalle zu London," *HGB* 33 (1928), p. 48; *Die Gesetze der Angelsachsen*, ed. Liebermann I, p. 658.

[7] Edith Ennen, "Kölner Wirtschaft im Früh- und Hochmittelalter," in *Zwei Jahrtausende Kölner Wirtschaft*, ed. Hermann Kellenbenz, Rheinisch-Westfälisches Wirtschaftsarchiv zu Köln (Cologne, 1975), I, p. 113: "Eine Reihe von Nachrichten bezeugt uns, daß Köln um 1000 einer der bedeutendsten Marktorte des deutschen Reiches mit einem vorbildlichen Marktbrauch war."

[8] Cologne benefited also from the fact that the Rhine empties into the sea by way of several branches and therefore no port could develop at the lower Rhine which would dominate foreign and local trade along the river.

[9] E. Ennen, "Kölner Wirtschaft im Früh- und Hochmittelalter," I, pp. 113, 149.

[10] M. M. Postan, E. E. Rich, and Edward Miller, eds., *Cambridge Economic History* (Cambridge, 1963), II, pp. 233–4: "By the end of the eleventh century Cologne had already become an emporium of trade and industry. Its two fairs [sic] – one at Easter and the other in August – were already well-established, and so also was its fame for wealth and power"; Dollinger, *The German Hansa*, p. 14: "It is . . . true that in all essentials Cologne initiated urban life in north-west Germany." Hugo Stehkämper, *England und Köln. Beziehungen durch die Jahrhunderte in archivalischen Zeugnissen. Ausstellung im Historischen Archiv der Stadt Köln Mai–Juni 1965* (Cologne, 1965), p. 10a: "Der Ausganspunkt des deutschen Englandhandels war im Mittelalter Köln."

[11] William of Malmesbury, *De gestis pontificum Anglorum*, ed. N. E. S. A. Hamilton, RS, 52 (London, 1870; rpt. 1964), p. 425: "Colonia est civitas maxima, totius Germaniae metropolis, conferta mercimoniis, referta Sanctorum patrociniis."

Significant industrial production developed in the city, resulting in linen textiles, cloth, yarn, thread, and metal goods. Cologne and the neighboring royal city of Aachen also functioned as the Rhenish emporium for the manufacture and sale of woolen textiles during this period.[12] Rhenish cloth, manufactured from a mixture of English and German wool, was cheaper than the Flemish variety and thus widely used throughout the region.[13] Edith Ennen has suggested that evidence of English wool in Cologne goes back to as early as the year 1000.[14]

Trade, however, was the most important source of economic growth and power. To the north Cologne merchants transported wine (their major export product),[15] metal goods (especially weaponry), and luxury goods purchased from the Italians, and they returned home bringing wool from England and the Low Countrie; as well as raw metals and fish. German grain was also shipped to England during times of famine.[16]

Trade with England quickly became the major preoccupation of Cologne merchants. Geography also played an important role here, because the mouths of the Rhine and Thames rivers are almost directly

---

[12] Hans Pohl, "Zur Geschichte von Wollproduktion und Wollhandel im Rheinland, in Westfalen und Hessen vom 12. bis zum 17. Jahrhundert," *La lana come materia prima i fenomeni della sua produzione e circulazione nei secoli XIII-XVII: atti della "prima settimana de studio" (18–24 aprile 1969)*, Istituto Internazionale di Storia Economica "F. Datini" Pubblicazioni Serie II: atti delle "settimane di studio" e altri convegni 1 (Florence, 1974), p. 92–3: "Neben Aachen war Köln die bedeutendste Stätte der Wollverarbeitung im rheinischen Raum . . . Köln war im übrigen neben Aachen das wichtigste Zentrum des Wollhandels, das nicht nur rheinische, westfälische und hessische Wolle in die Niederlande, z. B. Antwerpen, und Nordfrankreich exportierte, sondern auch aus den Niederlanden, etwa Antwerpen, und auch direkt aus England Wolle einführte." No doubt Aacheners and Cologners collaborated in exporting wool from England.

[13] *Die Kölner Schreinsbücher des 13. und 14. Jahrhunderts*, ed. Hans Planitz and Thea Buyken, PGRG, 46 (Weimar, 1937), p. 4: "Das Textilgewerb gab der größten Zahl von Menschen Arbeit und Brot. Kölner Tuch, aus meist deutscher Wolle gewebt, war billiger als das flandrische, das englische Wool verarbeitete; es war daher zum Massenverbrauch geeignet und besonders im Osten weit verbreitet. Auch Wolldecken, Garn, Leinen, Hanf und Seide wurden in besonderen Spezialitäten in großer Menge hergestellt."

[14] E. Ennen, "Kölner Wirtschaft im Früh- und Hochmittelalter," p. 137: "Wir berichteten vom Import englischer Wolle um 1000. Die Wollweberei muß sich im 11. Jahrhundert zum qualifizierten Exportgewerbe entwickelt haben."

[15] Ibid., I, pp. 113–14: "Auch der Weinhandel spielt schon eine Rolle; Köln lag im Mittelalter am Nordrand des rheinischen Weinanbaugebiets; der Weinanbau im Siebengebirge und in der Ville war damals umfangreich. Die Badorfer und Pingsdorfer Amphoren, deren Scherbau in Skandanavien bis Haithabu und Birke, in England in Canterbury und in Hamwich-Southampton gefunden wurden, haben sicher dem Export von Wein gedient."

[16] Arnold fitz Tedmar, *De Antiquis legibus liber sive cronica Maiorum et Vicecomitum Londoniarum*, ed. Thomas Stapleton, Camden Society, 34 (London, 1846), p. 37: "Hoc anno [1257] agricultura deficit; qua deficiente, fames secuta est ita, quod homines de villis confluebant ad Civitatem pro cibo acquirendo, qua, fame convelescente, multa milia hominum perierunt; et multa plura milia occubuissent fame, nisi bladum venisset tunc temporis de Alemannia."

opposite each other at either end of the English Channel.[17] The Cologners brought Rhenish wine, weaponry and metalwork, luxury cloth and linen, precious gold and silver objects, spices, wax, fustian, and grain in exchange for wool, raw metals like tin, and commodities like lard and bacon.[18] London was the natural location for their activities in England, but they soon branched out into all the port cities along the eastern and southern coasts.

London, for its part, had also been expanding since the latter years of Alfred the Great's reign (870–99).[19] William Page credits King Edgar (959–75) with establishing the wine merchants of Rouen on the west side of Dowgate (known appropriately as the Vintry) and the merchants of Cologne on the east side of Dowgate in an effort to expand the port city's trade.[20] We cannot, however, place the Cologne guildhall in London with certainty at this early date.

William of Malmesbury indicates that the German merchants were in the majority among the foreign merchants who were visiting both London and York by his day, but he gives no particulars about their urban origins.[21] Another contemporary source is also vague on this point: the *Ley as Lorengs* or Law of the Lorrainers, dated around the year 1130.[22] These regulations for foreign merchants coming to London from Lorraine do not specify in any more detail who the merchants of Lorraine were except mentioning that they sold wine. Yet some have concluded that Cologners were intended here, since Lower Lorraine included the region to the south and west of Cologne.[23]

[17] Joachim Deeters, *Die Hanse und Köln. Ausstellung des Historischen Archivs der Stadt Köln zum 8. Hansetag der Neuzeit in Köln im September 1988* (Cologne, 1988), p. 22.

[18] Christopher Brooke and Gillian Keir, *London 800–1216: The Shaping of a City* (Berkeley and Los Angeles, 1975), p. 267: "First of all, they brought wine, and it seems likely that the English taste for Hock preceded by a century their dedication to Claret, although the name Hock is nothing like so venerable and the German wines, the 'Rhenish,' were eclipsed by the French in the twelfth and thirteenth centuries, in the fourteenth and fifteenth centuries little German wine came to England."

[19] Ibid., pp. 19–29.

[20] William Page, *London: Its Origin and Early Development* (London, 1923), p. 137. It does appear certain that the Rouen wine merchants were located at Dowgate before the Norman Conquest: Derek Keene, "New discoveries at the Hanseatic Steelyard in London," *HGB* 107 (1989), p. 18.

[21] William of Malmesbury, *De gestis pontificum Anglorum*, p. 140: "Haud longe a Rofa quasi xxtivque miliaris est Lundonia civitas nobilis. Opima civium divitiis, constipata negotiatorum ex omni terra et maxime ex Germania venientium commertiis," and p. 208: "Secundae post Cantuariam dignitatis est Eboracum, urbs ampla et metropolis, elegantiae Romanae preferens inditium. A duabus partibus Husae fluminis edificata includit medio sinu sui naves a Germania et Hibernia venientes." This history was completed in 1125.

[22] *HUB*, III, pp. 388–92 no. 602; *Munimenta*, II, 1, pp. 61–3 and II, 2, pp. 528–31; Mary Bateson, "A London municipal collection of the reign of John," *EHR* 17 (1902), pp. 495–502; *Die Gesetze der Angelsachsen*, ed. Liebermann, I, p. 674.

[23] Eleonora Carus-Wilson, "Die Hanse und England," *Hanse in Europa. Brücke zwischen den*

The *Ley as Lorengs* appears to have been based on Aethelred's Laws of *c.* 1000[24] and in fact the Lorrainers are referred to as the "men of the emperor" in the last paragraph.[25] We learn in this last clause that the German merchants (presumably including those from Cologne) were at this point allowed to dwell in the city, with the exception of merchants from Tiel and Bremen.[26] Therefore it seems most likely that Cologne merchants began to reside in London at the latest from *c.* 1130 onward, although they had already been frequenting the city on trading ventures for some time.[27]

We do not find specific references to the activities of the Cologne merchants in England until the reign of Henry II (1154–88), when a series of royal charters of liberties began which continued down to the reign of Edward I (1272–97). From the reign of Henry II to that of King John (1199–1216) the Cologners thereby enjoyed an almost monopolistic control over German trade with England by virtue of these privileges and through control of a guildhall in London. Benefiting greatly from Welf-Plantagenet dynastic ties, the Cologne merchants dominated Anglo-German trade during the twelfth and early thirteenth centuries. In almost every case the privileges granted by the English kings to the Cologners were the result of Anglo-German diplomatic activity, and thus they help to explain the strong support which the Welf Otto IV received from the citizens of Cologne, as well

Märkten 12.-17. Jahrhundert (Cologne, 1973), p. 87: "So war London durch die Männer von Lothringen mit der großen Handelsstraße verbunden, die durch Europa von Konstantinopel über die Donau an den Rhein führte. Unter diesen 'Lothringern' waren die Bürger von Köln deutlich führend"; Dollinger, *The German Hansa*, pp. 5–6 uses this document to date the period in which Cologne merchants began to dwell in London.

24 *Munimenta*, II, 1, pp. xxxv–xxxvi.

25 Here follows Riley's translation (*Munimenta*, II, 2, p. 531): "That they may lodge within the walls of the city of London, wherever they please; except those of Tiesle and of Brune; and those of Anwers shall not pass London Bridge, if they do not wish to be ruled by the law of London. If they have mercery, they may sell a quarter of cummin, and a dozen of fustian, and half [that quantity]. And the tron by which they weigh, ought to be one of twenty-two cloves."

26 Dollinger, *The German Hansa*, p. 6 renders "Brune" as Bremen, while Riley, *Munimenta*, II, 1, pp. xxxix renders it as Bruurren in Gelderland.

27 P. H. Sawyer, "The wealth of England in the eleventh century," *TRHS* 5th series 15 (1965), pp. 145–64 asserts that England's wealth explains the many raids and conquests the island suffered during the eleventh century, and that this wealth came through the reception of German silver in exchange for English wool. No doubt Cologne merchants were central in this process, since much silver from the Hartz mountains passed through Cologne for minting and was then transferred to England to purchase wool. See also P. D. A. Harvey, "The English trade in wool and cloth, 1150–1250: some problems and suggestions," in *Produzione commercio e consumo dei panni di lana nei secoli XII-XVII: atti della "seconda settimana di studio" (10–16 aprile 1970)*, Istituto Internazionale di Storia Economica "F. Datini" Pubblicazioni Serie II: atti delle "settimane di studio" e altri convegni 2, ed. Marco Spallanzani (Florence, 1976), pp. 369–76.

as the city's subsequent allegiance to the rival Staufen Frederick II in
1235 when he married the English princess Isabella.[28]

At some point during the years 1173 to 1175 Henry II issued two
privileges to the Cologne merchants which contain important information. The first grant extended protection to the merchants and their
goods throughout England as well as to their guildhall in London.[29]
The second grant allowed them to sell Rhenish wine in London at the
same price that the French merchants charged for their wine.[30]

Before examining the charters themselves we must address the issue
of their dating, since it has been the source of disagreement between
German, English, and French scholars. J. M. Lappenberg, in his
ground-breaking 1851 study of the German Hansa's origins, dated these
two documents to the year 1157. He did so by concluding that the
witness Richard de Lucy could only have been present during the years
1154–62, and that in this space of time the king was at Northampton
only in 1157. All subsequent German editions and studies on the
Cologne guildhall and the later German Hansa have used Lappenberg's

[28] Hildegard Thierfelder, *Köln und die Hanse*, Kölner Vorträge zur Sozial- und Wirtschaftsgeschichte, Heft 7 (Cologne, 1970), p. 4: "Die reiche Privilegierung der Kölner Kaufleute in
England hatte neben wirtschaftlichen auch politische Gründe. Der König erhoffte sich im 12.
und 13. Jahrhundert durch gute Beziehungen zum Erzbischof von Köln eine Unterstützung
gegen den Kaiser, später gegen Frankreich, woraus die Stadt Köln ihren Vorteil zog."

[29] *Receuil des actes de Henri II roi d'Angleterre et duc de Normandie concernant les provinces et les affaires de
France*, ed. Léopold Delisle and Élie Berger, Chartes et diplômes relatifs à l'histoire de France, 7
(Paris, 1909), II, pp. 116–17 no. 540; Lappenberg, *Urkundliche Geschichte des Hansischen Stahlhofes
zu London*, pp. 3–4 no. 2; *Ennen/Eckertz*, I, p. 544 no. 68; *HUB*, I, p. 8 no. 14; *UGN*, I, p. 365
no. 523 (dated 1154–89); *Quellen zur Geschichte des Kölner Handels und Verkehrs im Mittelalter*, ed.
Bruno Kuske PGRG, 33 (Bonn, 1917) Part I, p. 2 no. 3: "Henricus, Dei gratia Rex Anglorum,
et dux Normannorum et Aquitanorum, et Comes Andegavorum, justiciis, vicecomitibus et
omnibus ministris suis Anglie, salutem. Precipio vobis quod custodiatis et manuteneatis et
protegatis homines et cives Colonienses sicut homines meos et amicos, et omnes res et
mercaturas suas et possessiones, ita quod neque de domo sua Londoniensi neque de rebus neque
de mercaturis suis aut aliquibus aliis ad eos spectantibus injuriam aliquam vel contumeliam eis
faciatis neque fieri permittatis, quia [ipsi] et omnia sua sunt in custodia et protectione mea; et
ideo firmam pacem habeant, faciendo rectas consuetudines suas; et nullas exigatis ab eis novas
consuetudines vel rectitudines quas facere non debeant nec facere solebant. Et si quis super hoc
maligne forifec[er]it, plenam eis inde sine dilatione justiciam fieri faciatis. Testibus: Ricardo de
Luci, Willelmo filio Adelini dapifero. Apud Norhampton[am]." I have used Delisle's transcrip-
tion both here and below.

[30] *Receuil des actes de Henri II roi d'Angleterre et duc de Normandie*, ed. Delise and Berger, II, p. 117
no. 541; Lappenberg, *Urkundliche Geschichte des Hansischen Stahlhofes zu London*, p. 4 no. 3;
Ennen/Eckertz, I, p. 544 no. 69; *HUB*, I, p. 8 no. 13; *UGN*, I, pp. 364–5 no. 522a (dated
1154–89); *Quellen zur Geschichte des Kölner Handels und Verkehrs im Mittelalter*, ed. Kuske I, p. 1
no. 2: "Henricus Dei gratia Rex Anglorum, et Dux Normannorum, et Aquitanorum, et comes
Andegavorum, vicecomitibus et ballivis suis Lundonie, salutem. Concedo ut homines Colonienses vendant vinum suum ad forum quo venditur vinum Francigenum, scilicet sextarium pro
III denariis. Et ideo prohibeo ne ipsi inde disturbentur, nec aliquis super hoc injuriam eis faciat
vel contumeliam. Testibus: Ricardo de Luci et Willelmo filio Adelini dapifero. Apud
Norhampton[am]."

1157 dating and much has been made of such an early date for the Cologne guildhall's existence.[31] Most studies in English have almost universally accepted this dating.[32]

Travers Twiss challenged the 1157 date as early as 1881 at a lecture given in Cologne.[33] He asserted that the proper date was 1164, when Henry II was also at Northampton, and tied the charters to the negotiations between the English court and Rainald of Dassel (then archbishop of Cologne) for a double-marriage union between the Plantagenet, Staufen, and Welf dynasties amid the papal schism. Twiss also concluded that the second charter, which granted to the Cologners privileges identical to those enjoyed by the Rouen wine merchants, was an intended strike against French interests in the face of the Becket dispute.[34] Konstantin Höhlbaum rightly showed, however, that Rainald did not meet with Henry II until April of 1165.[35] Höhlbaum saw Henry II's charters instead as a part of the delicate negotiations surrounding Barbarossa's September 1157 Würzburg court. Henry II sent envoys there to deliver the so-called "submissive letter" to the emperor, by which the Plantagenet monarch carefully rejected the emperor's request to return a prized relic taken by Henry's mother, the empress Matilda, upon her return from the empire as a widow.[36] With this solid

---

[31] In addition to the above-mentioned German sourcebooks, see Hans Hartmeyer, *Der Weinhandel im Gebiete der Hanse im Mittelalter*, Volkswirtschaftliche und Wirtschaftsgeschichtliche Abhandlungen NF, 3 (Jena, 1905), p. 10; E. Ennen, "Kölner Wirtschaft im Früh- und Hochmittelalter," I, p. 143; Dollinger, *The German Hansa*, p. 186; Karl Wand, "Die Englandpolitik der Stadt Köln und ihrer Erzbischöfe im 12. und 13. Jahrhundert," *Aus Mittelalter und Neuzeit. Festschrift zum 70. Geburtstag von Gerhard Kallen*, ed. Josef Engel and Hans Martin Klinkenbert (Bonn, 1957), p. 77; Kellenbenz, "Der Aufstieg Kölns zur mittelalterlichen Handelsmetropole," p. 9; Deeters, *Die Hanse und Köln*, p. 22 and Hugo Stehkämper, "England und die Stadt Köln als Wahlmacher König Ottos IV," *Köln, Das Reich und Europa. MSAK* 60 (1971), p. 225 for example.

[32] Gwyn Williams, *Medieval London. From Commune to Capital*, University of London Historical Studies, 11 (London, 1963), p. 13; Weiner, "Early commercial intercourse between England and Germany," p. 127; Lloyd, *England and the German Hanse*, p. 15 for example.

[33] Travers Twiss, *On the Early Charters Granted by the Kings of England to the Merchants of Cologne*, The Ninth Annual Conference for the Reformation and Codification of the Law of Nations (London, 1881).

[34] Stehkämper, "England und die Stadt Köln," p. 225 note 45 also argues that these privileges were directed against France.

[35] Konstantin Höhlbaum, "Kölns älteste Handelsprivilegien für England," *HGB* 3 (1882), pp. 45–6.

[36] Although Twiss' linking of the "submissive letter" and these royal charters was incorrect, it is still of major importance to note an oft-overlooked phrase in the letter's famous clause: "Sit igitur inter nos et populos nostros dilectionis et pacis unitas indivisa, commertia tuta, ita tamen, ut vobis qui dignitate preminetis, imperandi cedat auctoritas, nobis non deerit voluntas obsequendi." The words "commertia tuta" indicate the mutual desire for safe trade between Germany and England and reveal the importance of German trade with the English at this early date. Thus this letter, so often employed in discussions of political theory and practice, has relevance for economic history as well. For specifics on the so-called "submissive letter" see

refutation of Twiss' thesis, the 1157 date became henceforth the accepted one.

Subsequently Léopold Delisle more accurately identified the dating of these two charters, but only recently has this been recognized.[37] Delisle's investigation into the careers of the two charter witnesses reveals that Richard de Lucy was viceroy in England during the years 1169, 1172 to 1174, and 1179, and that the second witness, William fitz Adelm, served Henry II in the office of steward (*dapifer*, as he is referred to in the charter) from 1173 to 1175. Hence, although Delisle generously spreads the possible years for these charters to 1172–9, it is safe to say that 1173–5 is an accurate dating, and not Lappenberg's early date of 1157. Of course, this pushes forward the first verifiable evidence of the Cologne guildhall by sixteen years, yet the guildhall could easily have existed many years before the privileges of 1173–5.[38]

Were there political motives for Henry II's issuance of such valuable privileges to the merchants of Cologne in 1173–5? The possibility exists, but it can only be inferred circumstantially. By 1173 Henry II had survived the Becket debacle and had thereby become a supporter of Pope Alexander III by necessity. Furthermore, Louis VII and Frederick Barbarossa had begun a *rapprochement* with the hope of resolving the papal schism. Henry might have feared such a constellation of continental power, while he still enjoyed positive relations with northern Germany because of dynastic ties with Duke Henry the Lion of Saxony (who had married his daughter Matilda) and commercial ties with Cologne. Or perhaps the charters are simply evidence of an effort to stimulate a growing and mutually beneficial economic relationship

Hans Eberhard Mayer, "Staufische Weltherrschaft? Zum Brief Heinrichs II. von England an Friedrich Barbarossa von 1157," *Festschrift Karl Pivec*, ed. Anton Haidacher and H. E. Mayer, Innsbrucker Beiträge zur Kulturwissenschaft, 12 (Innsbruck, 1966), pp. 265–78; rpt. in *Friedrich Barbarossa*, ed. G. Wolf, Wege der Forschung, 390 (Darmstadt, 1975) and Karl Leyser, "Frederick Barbarossa, Henry II and the hand of St. James," *EHR* 40 (1975); rpt. in *Medieval Germany and Its Neighbours (900–1250)* (London, 1982), pp. 215–40.

[37] *Receuil des actes de Henri II roi d'Angleterre et duc de Normandie*, ed. Delise and Berger, Introductory volume pp. 434–35, 478; II, pp. 116–17. Keene, "New discoveries at the Hanseatic Steelyard in London," pp. 15–25; Manfred Groten, *Köln im 13. Jahrhundert. Gesellschaftlicher Wandel und Verfassungsentwicklung*, Städteforschung: Veröffentlichungen des Instituts für vergleichende Städtgeschichte in Münster, Reihe A: Darstellungen, Band 36 (Cologne, Weimar, and Vienna, 1995), p. 14; Brooke and Keir, *London 800–1216*, p. 267; and Natalie Fryde, "Arnold fitz Thedmar und die Entstehung der Grossen Deutschen Hanse," *HGB* 107 (1989), pp. 27–42 have recently employed Delisle's dating.

[38] The appearance of a Cologne merchant named Berengar in the Pipe Rolls for Lincolnshire during the years 1176 to 1177 coincides with the dating for these first royal charters of privilege (*Pipe Roll 23 Henry III*, PR, 26, p. 117). Certainly Cologners were active in England before the granting of these privileges, as the discovery in London of Rhenish pottery from the eleventh century has confirmed: A. Vince, "Saxon and medieval pottery in London: a review," *Medieval Archaeology* 29 (1985), pp. 25–93, esp. 39, 42, 86.

between England and Cologne, with no geopolitical implications necessarily contained therein.

At least this is the most obvious message found in the content of the charters themselves. In the first charter the sheriffs and bailiffs of London are ordered to give perpetual protection to the "homines et cives Colonienses sicut homines meos et amicos." No new exactions could be placed on them without their consent as long as they continued to pay the traditional dues. In addition to these remarkable words of royal protection for foreigners, we also find the first mention of the Cologne guildhall in London (*domo sua Londonensi*), the existence of which obviously antedated the issuance of the royal privileges. This hall of the Cologne merchants became the headquarters for German merchants in England, and the Cologners maintained a monopolistic control over it. They shared the benefits of their privileges with the towns of Westphalia and the Rhineland, which joined the guild in order to trade in England and which most probably had to provide substantial payments for this privilege.[39] No other group of German merchants enjoyed such extensive privileges in England, and the guildhall itself is a unique institution. This hall was recognized by royal authority as a legal organization and its members thereby enjoyed corporate protection in a foreign land. In addition the guild members had their own alderman, who served as the community's legal representative in negotiations with the city of London and the crown. The Cologne guildhall would see no equal among the German merchants for almost another hundred years.

Recent construction work at the Cannon Street underground station has resulted happily in the discovery of the remains of the Cologne guildhall, and we are now more informed about its size and layout.[40]

---

[39] Luise von Winterfeld, "Das Westfälische Hansequartier," *Der Raum Westfalen* (Münster, 1955) II, 1, p. 266: "Diese Kölner Hanse . . . war die älteste aller deutschen Hansen in England und besaß die weitgehendsten Privilegien. Da sie anfänglich Monopolcharakter trug, mußten alle anderen deutschen Kaufleute, die in England Handel treiben wollen, sich in die Hanse der Kölner Englandfahrer aufnehmen lassen"; Karl Kunze, "Das erste Jahrhundert der deutschen Hanse in England," *HGB* 6 (1889), p. 130: "In ihrer Gildhalle am Ufer der Themse, dem Keim des späteren hansischen Stahlhofes, sassen sie auf eigenem Grund und Boden und erfreuten sich mannigfacher Privilegien als eine Hanse, eine staatsrechtlich anerkannte Genossenschaft. Zu ihnen gehörten die Kaufleute vom Niederrhein und ohne Zweifel auch aus Westfalen, Landschaften, welche mit Köln ein zusammengehöriges Handelsgebiet darstellen. Die Führung aber unter den Deutschen gebürt unbestritten den Kölnern." Deeters, *Die Hanse und Köln*, p. 22: "Die Stellung Kölns in London wurde vorbildlich für weitere deutsche Kaufleute, die mit England Handel treiben wollten. Die Kölner bildeten dort eine eigene 'hanse,' zu der Nicht-Kölner nur schwer, d. h. wohl nur gegen hohe Geldzahlungen, Zutritt fanden."

[40] For a photo of the excavation site see John Clark, *Saxon and Norman London* (London, 1989), p. 35. For details of the excavation, see Keene, "New discoveries at the Hanseatic Steelyard in London," pp. 15–25 with a map on page 17.

The guildhall was located along the Thames river, to the east side of Dowgate. This location no doubt reflects the Cologners' trade in wine, since the Rouen wine merchants were located to the west side of Dowgate (an area soon known as the Vintry). This site was one of the most developed and busiest parts of the London waterfront, which says a great deal about the wealth and importance of the Cologne merchants.[41] The guildhall was 10.3 meters wide (from east to west) and about 30 meters in length (from north to south). The building's interior was divided by an arcade running north–south, leaving one aisle measuring 3 meters in width and the other 6.4 meters. The arcade itself was supported by square bases with a plain chamfer; two of these bases and a part of a third one were discovered, built out of skillfully cut stone from Caen and Surrey, and measured 0.9 meters on each side. The external walls were constructed of chalk and gravel while the upper portion of these walls was fashioned from rough stone brought from Kent. The use of Caen stone indicates that the guildhall was of high quality, since such stone had been imported for use on royal buildings since the eleventh century.[42] In addition to storage facilities, the building had space for residential and social purposes on the first floor.[43] Based on this recently discovered evidence, the guildhall was an impressive and expensive building, which dominated German activity in London.[44]

The second charter granted the Cologne merchants the right to sell their Rhine wine at the same price as that charged by the Rouen merchants (i.e. 3 pence for a pint). Some historians have concluded that

[41] Yet another proof of the value placed on Cologne as a commercial partner appears in 1205, when the archbishop of Canterbury sent a ship under royal protection to Cologne in order to purchase his own Rhine wine: *Rotuli litterarum patentium in turri Londinensi asservati. 1:1 Ab anno MCCI ad anum MCCXVI*, ed. Thomas Duffus Hardy (London, 1835), I, p. 51: "Rex etc. omnibus ballivis portuum maris et omnibus fidelibus suis ad quos etc. Sciatis quod dedimus licenciam venerabili patri nostro in Christo H. Cant. Archiepiscopus quod mittat hac vice unam navem in partes Coloniensis propter vina. Et quod navis illa libere et sine impedimento possit ire et redire per potestatem nostram. Et prohibemus ne quis navem illam vel homines illam ducentes in aliquo impediat. Teste me ipso apud Oxon." (March 28, 1205).

[42] H. M. Colvin, ed., *The History of the King's Works I: The Middle Ages* (London, 1963), p. 491. The Rouen merchants located nearby were possible sources for the Norman stone.

[43] Keene, "New discoveries at the Hanseatic Steelyard in London," p. 21: "Parts of the building were certainly used for residential or other social purposes since the structure incorportated a large, stone-lined latrine bonded into the outer face of the western wall and incorporating a buttress to that wall. These activities probably took place in the large room at first-floor level, the guildhall proper, where the men of Cologne would have held their feasts and business meetings."

[44] Ibid., p. 21: "So far as it is possible to tell, the building occupied the full width of the property controlled by the Germans at this time." Brooke and Keir, *London 800–1216*, p. 267: "evidently it was the men of Cologne who formed the backbone of the German colony in England from the eleventh century for many to come."

Henry II was trying to damage the Rouen merchants, who brought much wine from the Capetian region around Paris. This would, however, have injured merchants from a territory that was under Henry's lordship (Normandy), so this seems rather unlikely as an explanation. The most plausible account is simply that the Cologners, along with their Westphalian compatriots, had by this point achieved a significant position among the foreign merchants in London and the privileges were a sign of this, as well as of the value placed on the growing Anglo-German commercial connection in general. So important did Henry II consider Cologne's trading relationship that he extended royal protection over its citizens to his continental lands as well in July 1175.[45] Here he refers to the Cologners as "homines et fideles mei."

The Cologne merchants gained further advantage as diplomatic ties were strengthened between the Plantagenets and the archbishops of Cologne, who were by this time the most powerful princes in northern Germany. As part of his efforts to obtain release from imprisonment at the hands of Henry VI after the Third Crusade, Richard I had turned to Archbishop Adolf of Cologne among other Rhenish princes and assured himself of their support in the ransom negotiations through an offer of feudal rents.[46] Adolf fulfilled his end of the bargain and played a major role in negotiating Richard's release from captivity in 1194. He also accompanied Richard as far as Antwerp on the king's return trip home – a journey which included a festive reception in the cathedral city of Cologne. Richard did not stop at rewarding the archbishop with

---

[45] *Receuil des actes de Henri II roi d'Angleterre et duc de Normandie*, ed. Delisle and Berger, II, pp. 46–7 no. 495 (dated May–November 1175); Lappenberg, *Urkundliche Geschichte des Hansischen Stahlhofes zu London*, pp. 4–5 no. 4 (dated June 1175); Ennen/Eckertz, I, p. 571 no. 86; HUB, I, p. 16 no. 25; UGN, I, p. 365 no. 522b (dated 1154–89): "Henricus, Dei gracia rex Anglorum, et dux Normannorum et Aquitanorum, et comes Andegavorum, justiciis, vicecomitibus et omnibus ministris et fidelibus suis Francis et Anglis terre sue, salutem. Precipio vobis quod custodiatis et manuteneatis et protegatis cives et mercatores et homines Colonienses, et omnes res et possessiones suas, ubicunque ad vos venerint in terram meam, sicut meas proprias, ita quod nullam injuriam vel contumeliam eis faciatis nec fieri permittatis, quia homines et fideles mei sunt, et ipsi et omnia sua sunt in manu et custodia et protectione mea. Et si quis super hoc maligne forisfecerit, plenariam eis inde sine dilatione justiciam fieri faciatis. Testibus: R. Wyntoniensi et Hugone Dunelmensi episcopis, Johanne decano Saresb[er]iensi, Willelmo Aldelini. Apud Wudestok[am]." Twiss, *On the Early Charters Granted by the Kings of England to the Merchants of Cologne*, p. 9 has more closely dated the charter to July 1175, and Konstantin Höhlbaum, "Kölns älteste Handelsprivilegien für England," pp. 44–5 agreed to this emendation of Lappenberg's June 1175 dating.

[46] For more on Adolf's role in Richard's release see A. L. Poole, "Richard the First's alliances with the German princes in 1194," in *Studies in Medieval History Presented to F. M. Powicke*, ed. R. W. Hunt, W. A. Pantin, and R. W. Southern (Oxford, 1948), pp. 90–9, and Albert Schreiber, "Drei Beiträge zur Geschichte der deutschen Gefangenschaft des Königs Richard Löwenherz," *Historische Vierteljahrschrift* 26 (1931), pp. 268–94.

the rent, however. While sojourning in Louvain on his journey home the king issued a charter which extended the most expansive privileges yet. He freed the Cologne merchants from paying a yearly assessment of 2 shillings for their guildhall, and also freed them from paying any other local dues throughout England. Furthermore, they were given the liberties of attending all fairs, buying and selling anywhere, and of the right to exercise their own customs.[47] We learn from this charter that the Cologne merchants had been customarily paying the English crown a 2-shilling fee each year. Perhaps this was a payment given in exchange for Henry II's original grants of liberties. It would certainly not be the last time that the Cologne merchants sought and obtained a confirmation of their liberties in England from a new monarch.[48]

The connection between Anglo-Cologne diplomatic activity and royal grants of liberties which set Cologne merchants apart from all other German merchants reached its zenith in the reign of King John. From 1198 to 1215 Cologne became a bulwark of support for the royal candidacy of his nephew, the Welf Otto IV, in the *Thronstreit* between Staufen and Welf claimants.[49] Archbishop Adolf of Cologne and

---

[47] *Ennen/Eckertz*, I, p. 605 no. 109; *HUB*, I, p. 22 no. 40; Lappenberg, *Urkundliche Geschichte des Hansischen Stahlhofes zu London*, p. 5 no. 5; *UGN*, I, p. 378–79 no. 542; Kuske, *Quellen zur Geschichte des Kölner Handels und Verkehrs im Mittelalter*,. PGRG, 33 (Bonn, 1917), I, p. 3 no. 7; *REK*, I, p. 296 no. 1472: "Richardus Dei gracia Rex Anglie, Dux Normannie, Acquitanie et Comes Andegavie archiepiscopis, episcopis, abbatibus, comitibus, baronibus, justiciariis, vice-comitibus, ministris et omnibus ballivis et fidelibus tocius Anglie salutem. Sciatis, quod nos quietos clamasse dilectos nostros cives de Colonia et mercandisam suam de illis duobis solidis, quos solebant dare de Gildhalla sua Londoniensi et de omnibus aliis consuetudinibus et demandis, que pertinent ad nos in Londonia et per totam terram nostram in Anglia. Concessimus eciam eis salvum ire et salvum venire in totam terram nostram et quod libere possint ire ad ferias per totam terram nostram et emere et vendere et in villa Londoniensi et alibi. Quare volumus et firmiter precipimus, quod predicti cives de Colonia prenominatas libertates et liberas consuetudines habeant per totam terram nostram Anglie. Testibus Henrico duce de Lovanio, Gaufrido de Sey, Thoma filio Bernardi, Wilhelmo de Stagno, Wilhelmo de Sancte Marie Ecclesia. Datum per manum Willelmi Elyensis episcopi apostolice sedis legati, cancellarii nostri, apud Lovanium, 16. die Februarii anno quinto Regni nostri." Twiss and Höhlbaum agree that the proper date is February 16, not the February 6 date that some sourcebooks cite (cf. *Ennen/Eckertz*).

[48] For some reason Kellenbenz, "Der Aufstieg Kölns zur mittelalterlichen Handelsmetropole," p. 9 ascribes this grant as reward for ships which the Cologners supposedly provided to Richard I for his crusade: "Für die drei Schiffe, die sie für den Kreuzzug von Richard Löwenherz ausrüsteten, befreite der König ihr Haus von London von allen Ausgaben." Equally unfounded is Kurt Knoll's assertion: *London im Mittelalter*, Wiener Beiträge zur englischen Philologie, 56 (Vienna and Leipzig, 1932), p. 95: "Es war dies [i.e. the charter of liberties] der Dank des englischen Königs für die Kölner geldliche Beihilfe zu seiner Befreiung."

[49] Otto IV was the son of the Welf Duke Henry the Lion, who had married Henry II's daughter Matilda. For details on Otto IV's royal election and kingship with regard to Cologne see Hugo Stehkämper, "Der Kölner Erzbischof Adolf von Altena und die deutsche Königswahl (1195–1205)," in *Historische Zeitschrift Beiheft* NF 2, ed. Theodor Schneider, Beiträge zur Geschichte des mittelalterlichen deutschen Königtums (Munich, 1973), pp. 5–83; Stehkämper, "England und die Stadt Köln," pp. 213–44; and Jens Ahlers, *Die Welfen und die Englischen*

Richard I cooperated diplomatically to secure the election of the Welf Otto in 1198, and after the sudden death of the Lionheart his brother John took on the mantle of patron for their Saxon nephew. John often appealed to the Cologne citizens to remain loyal, reminding them of their privileges in his kingdom.

Initially John had been reticent to aid his nephew, claiming that the provisions of the Peace of Le Goulet prevented him from such activity. In 1202, however, after he had become embroiled in war with Philip II over Aquitaine, John decided to support Otto's increasingly successful efforts to secure his disputed title over the German kingdom. He hoped by this to revive Otto's promise of military aid against France. In this setting John wrote to the citizens of Cologne and thanked them for supporting the Welf and exhorted them to continue to be loyal.[50]

But by 1204 Otto had lost the support of the archbishop of Cologne as well as of other important princes from the lower Rhine. In the face of this bleak situation John issued another letter to the citizens of Cologne, which again exhorted them to defend Otto's kingship. As an incentive he confirmed their privileges in England, yet he did not renew the exemption from paying customary dues. The Cologne merchants may have pressed for a confirmation of Richard's charter by the new king, since later that year another royal confirmation of their rights in England was promulgated.[51] Yet John continued to require them to pay customary dues, and made the liberties contingent on their support of Otto: "quamdiu ipsi fuerint in fidelitate Regis Othonis nepotis nostri." No more clearly do we find the political and economic aspects of Anglo-Cologne relations linked than here. John left no room for doubt about how the Cologners could maintain their rights in his kingdom: continue to sustain his nephew.

Not until 1213, after the Staufer Frederick II had been crowned in Mainz and both John and Otto were under papal excommunication, did John finally confirm his brother's charter in full, excepting the

Könige 1165–1235, Quellen und Darstellungen zur Geschichte Niedersachsens, 102 (Hildesheim, 1987).

50 *Rotuli litterarum patentium in turri Londinensi asservati*, ed. Hardy, I, p. 11; *HUB*, I, p. 31 no. 59; Lappenberg, *Urkundliche Geschichte des Hansischen Stahlhofes zu London*, p. 6 no. 6; *Böhmer*, V, 2, p. 1584 no. 10652. The date of the letter is June 4, 1202.

51 *Rotuli litterarum patentium in turri Londinensi asservati*, ed. Hardy, I, p. 48; *HUB*, I, p. 34 no. 69; Ennen/Eckertz, II, p. 16 no. 11; Lappenberg, *Urkundliche Geschichte des Hansischen Stahlhofes zu London*, p. 6 no. 8; *Böhmer*, V, 2, p. 1588 no. 10674: "Rex etc. omnibus etc. Sciatis quod dedimus licenciam hominibus Coloniensis quod salvo et secure veniant et redeant per totam terram nostram Anglie cum vinis et aliis merchandisis suis faciendo inde rectas et debitas consuetudines quamdiu ipsi fuerint in fidelitate Regis Othonis nepotis nostri" (Tewkesbury, December 25, 1204).

customs rights of the city of London.[52] The situation was extremely dangerous for the two monarchs. England was nervously awaiting a threatened French invasion and Otto was fighting merely to save his ancestral Saxon lands in Brunswick and Lüneburg. So the support of Cologne was essential. It took such exigencies to move John to renew his brother's charter of privileges to the Cologne merchants.

Although the Plantagenet–Welf collaboration showed its political impotence for the last time at Bouvines in 1214, the merchants of Cologne derived from it a powerful economic advantage in German trade with England. By their allegiance to the Welf cause they had maintained their preeminent position among those German merchants trading with England,[53] and led the way in advancing the importance of Anglo-German commercial relations.[54] The eleventh and twelfth centuries were Cologne's centuries as far as German trade with the English is concerned.

---

[52] *Rotuli litterarum patentium in turri Londinensi asservati*, ed. Hardy, I, p. 194; *Ennen/Eckertz*, II, pp. 46–7 no. 41; *HUB*, I, p. 43 no. 109 and III, pp. 395–6 no. 605; Lappenberg, *Urkundliche Geschichte des Hansischen Stahlhofes zu London*, pp. 8–9 no. 15; Böhmer, V, 2, p. 1599 no. 10766: "Johannes Dei gratia Rex Angliae, Dominus Hibernie, Dux Normannie, Aquitanie et Comes Andegavie archiepiscopis, episcopis, abbatibus, comitibus, baronibus, iusticiariis, vicecomitibus, ministris et omnibus ballivis et fidelibus suis totius Anglie salutem. Sciatis nos quietos clamasse dilectos nostros cives de Colonia, et mercandisam suam de illis duobus solidis, quos solebant dare de gildehalla sua in Londonia, et de omnibus aliis consuetudinibus et demandis, que pertinent ad nos in Londonia et per totam terram nostram in Anglia. Concessimus etiam eis salvum venire in totam terram nostram, et quod libere possint ire ad ferias per totam terram nostram et emere et vendere et in villa Londoniensi et alibi, sicut carta domini regis Ricardi fratris nostri, quam inde habent, rationabiliter testatur, salva libertate civitatis nostre Londoniensi. Quare volumus et firmiter precipimus, quod predicti cives de Colonia prenominatas libertates et liberas consuetudines habeant per totam terram nostram Anglie, sicut supradictum est. Testibus Gerardo filio Petri comitis Essex, W. marescalco comite Pembroc, W. de Ferrar comite Dereby, Wilhelmo Briwere, Hugone de Gurnaco, Thoma de Santforde. Datum per manum magistri Picardi de Marisco, archidiaconi Richemundensis et Northumbrie apud Corff" (July 24, 1213). This charter is substantially the same as Richard I's original, and informs us that the Cologners had used the original charter to argue successfully after all this time that they deserved such rights. Twiss, *On the Early Charters Granted by the Kings of England to the Merchants of Cologne*, pp. 13–16 has shown that the proper date for this charter was 1213, although the Cologne Grosses Privilegienbuch of 1326 contains duplicate copies for the years 1210 and 1213: see Höhlbaum, "Kölns älteste Handelsprivilegien für England," pp. 43–4. This duplicate has been included in *HUB*, I, p. 37 no. 84.

[53] E. Ennen, "Europäische Züge der mittelalterlichen Kölner Stadtgeschichte," pp. 1–48.

[54] Weiner, "Early commercial intercourse between England and Germany," p. 133: "the extension of our [i.e. English] foreign trade and the benefits that accrued from it are among the many substantial advantages that the country has reaped from the memorable struggle of John against the internal and external forces that finally overcame him. Foreign commerce was now recognized as a necessary branch of national activity, worthy of the notice even of the feudal barons. One of the articles of the barons presented by them to the king on June 15th of 1215 demanded security for merchants travelling on business."

Chapter 2

THE RISE OF THE HANSA TOWNS AND THE DECLINE OF COLOGNE'S DOMINANCE IN THE THIRTEENTH CENTURY

The long reign of Henry III saw a gradual erosion of Cologne's privileged position in the face of increasing competition from other German cities. The leaders in this development were the merchants from Baltic port cities, particularly Lübeck, who developed an east–west trading artery in contrast to the older north–south channel of the Rhine. The new Baltic trade of the "Easterlings," as the merchants from this region became known, would overshadow Cologne by the end of the thirteenth century and serve as the basis for the future Hanseatic League. Although Cologne would still play a major role among the Hanseatic towns, it would no longer be the dominant power exercising virtually monopolistic control over Anglo-German commerce.

The Easterlings entered into German overseas trade during the early thirteenth century. Lübeck, established as a permanent town only in 1158–9, became the leader among the Baltic towns, which included Visby, Rostock, Stralsund, Elbing, Riga, and other inland towns in Saxony.[1] Initially the merchants of these towns did not make the sea journey around Jutland, as it was considered too long and dangerous. Instead they traversed the isthmus from Lübeck to Hamburg and thence onward to Flanders and England. This proved to be a difficult and expensive means of transporting goods and so the volume of trade between the Baltic and England was relatively low. By the second half of the thirteenth century, however, the Easterlings pursued regular sea travel from the Baltic to the North Sea and thus became serious competitors to Cologne and its Westphalian partners.

Naturally the Cologne merchants looked unhappily upon the growing numbers of Baltic merchants in England. Seeing them as

---

[1] For a fuller account of the Hansa towns see Dollinger, *The German Hansa*, pp. 38–42 and more particularly Lloyd, *England and the German Hanse*.

intruders and dangerous competitors, the Cologne guildhall members treated them with much contempt. So much so, in fact, that the Lübeckers obtained an imperial charter of Frederick II against them in 1226.[2] Among other liberties awarded to the burghers of the city, a clause appears in the charter which freed them by imperial authority from the exactions placed on the Lübeckers by the merchants of Cologne, Tiel, "et eorum socii." This is clearly a reference to those members of the Cologne guildhall in London. It appears therefore that the guild members were forcing payments from the Lübeckers for the right to trade in England. It is doubtful that this clause had any force in England, since the emperor's writ held no force in the English kingdom, yet it was a sign of things to come. This charter signals the beginning of the era in which the Baltic towns obtained royal privileges rivaling those of Cologne.

Already the traditional monopolistic liberties of the Cologners were being questioned in 1220. A Pipe Roll entry for this year indicates that the merchants paid thirty marks to retain seisin of the guildhall.[3] Martin Weinbaum may be correct in assuming that this payment was the result of a *Quo Warranto* proceeding.[4] The Cologne merchants must have sought confirmation of their ancient rights from the new monarch, Henry III (1216–72), in the face of new competition by the north German merchants,[5] since they were issued a patent letter promising royal protection in 1231. Once again, however, they were expected to pay established dues in exchange for this privilege.[6] It is apparent by this time that the Cologners were losing their unique status in England.

---

[2] *Historia Diplomatica Friderici Secundi* ed. J. L. A. Huillard-Bréholles (Paris, 1852–61), II, 2, pp. 625–9; *LUB*, I, pp. 45–8 at p. 46 no. 35; *HUB*, I, p. 64 no. 205: "Insuper burgenses Lubicenses predicti euntes quandoque in Angliam, ab illo pravo abusu et exactionis onere, quod Colonienses et Telenses et eorum socii contra ipsos invenisse dicuntur omnino absolvimus, illum penitus delentes abusum, sed illo iure et conditione utantur, quibus Colonienses et Telenses et eorum socii uti noscuntur" (June 1226).

[3] *Pipe Roll 4 Henry III*, PR NS, 47, p. 136: "Cives Colonie reddunt compotum de xxx marcis pro habenda saisina de gildhalla sua in Londonia, in thesauro liberaverunt et quieti sunt."

[4] Weinbaum, "Stahlhof und Deutsche Gildhalle zu London," pp. 49–50.

[5] In a gesture both showing kinship ties and the growing role of Saxon merchants in England, Henry III took the merchants of the lands of Duke Otto of Brunswick (which included the Lübeckers) under his royal protection on November 10, 1230: *Rymer*, I, p. 317; *Böhmer*, V, 2, p. 1641 no. 11087. On the same day the merchants of the count of Flanders were also taken under royal protection: *Rymer*, I, pp. 316–17.

[6] *CPR Henry III*, II, p. 431; *HUB*, I, p. 81 no. 241: "Rex suscepit in salvum et securum conductum omnes cives et mercatores de Colonia, et concessit eis quod salvo et secure veniant per totam potestatem regis cum rebus et mercandisis suis ad negociandum inde, et salvo morentur et salvo recedant, faciendo etc. sine termino" (April 17, 1231).

The marriage of Frederick II to the English princess Isabella in 1235 served as the last occasion on which the Anglo-Cologne diplomatic connection benefited Cologne merchants economically. No doubt in reward for Archbishop Henry of Cologne's assistance in the journey of Isabella into Germany, Henry III confirmed the ancient charter originally issued by Richard I and subsequently renewed by John (while retaining John's reservation of London's liberties).[7] Henry III even announced this to the bailiffs of the market of Hoyland in a charter dated the same day, which suggests that the Cologne merchants were in need of royal protection from exactions imposed there.[8] Once again, just as under King John, the Cologners were able to reassert their ancient liberties of avoiding traditional tolls in England. Since this charter is virtually identical with Richard I's original and John's subsequent confirmation, the merchants must have once again used the original charter as evidence for their rights. In fact, they were so anxious to assert their ancient liberties that they ascribed Henry II's original charter of 1175, complete with witnesses Richard de Lucy and William fitz Aldelm, to Henry III.[9]

Although Henry III's confirmation of his grandfather's original grant

---

[7] *CCHR Henry III*, I, p. 214; *Ennen/Eckertz*, II, p. 152 no. 149; *HUB.* I, p. 89 no. 268; Lappenberg, *Urkundliche Geschichte des Hansischen Stahlhofes zu London*, p. 12 no. 26; *Böhmer*, V, 2, p. 1654 no. 11172: "Henricus Dei gracia Rex Anglie, Dominus Hibernie, Dux Normannie etc. Sciatis nos quietos clamasse pro nobis et heredibus nostris dilectos nostros cives de Colonia et mercandisam suam de illis duobus solidis, quos solebant dare de Gildhalla sua Londoniensi, et de omnibus aliis consuetudinibus et demandis, que pertinent ad nos in Londonia et per totam terram nostram in Anglia. Concessimus etiam eis salvum ire et salvum venire in totam terram nostram et quod libere possint ire ad ferias per totam terram nostram et emere et vendere et in villa Londoniensi et alibi, salva libertate civitatis nostre Londoniensi. Quare volumus et firmiter precipimus pro nobis et heredibus nostris, quod predicti cives de Colonia prenominatas libertates et liberas consuetudines habeant per totam terram nostram Anglie, sicut supradictum est. Hiis testibus: venerabili patre Waltero Caerleolensi episcopo, Willelmo de Ferariis, Gilberto Basset, Waltero de Bello Campo, Hugone Dispenser, Waltero Marescallo, Galfredo Dispenser, Bartholomeo Pech, Bartholomeo de Sankeville et aliis. Datum per manum venerabilis patris Radulphi Cycestrensis episcopi cancellarii nostri. Apud Davyntre octavo die Novembris, anno regni nostri vicesimo" (Daventry, November 8, 1235).

[8] *CPR Henry III*, III, p. 130; *Ennen/Eckertz*, II, pp. 152–3 no. 150; *HUB*, I, p. 89 no. 269; *Quellen zur Geschichte des Kölner Handels und Verkehrs im Mittelalter*, ed. Kuske, I, p. 6 no. 17; *Böhmer*, V, 2, p. 1654 no. 11173: "Henricus Dei gracia Rex Anglie, Dominus Hibernie, Dux Normannie, Aquitanie et Comes Andegavie, universis ballivis ferie Hoylandie salutem. Sciatis, quod suscepimus in protectionem et defensionem nostram omnes mercatores Colonienses, res, mercandisas et omnes possessiones suas et ideo vobis mandamus, quod manuteneatis, protegatis et defendatis predictos mercatores, res, mercandisas et omnes possessiones suas, non inferentes eis aut inferri permittentes molestiam, iniuriam, dampnum aut gravationem, et si quid eis fuerit forifactum, id eis sine dilatione faciatis emendari. In cuius rei testimonium has literas nostras patentes eis fieri fecimus. Teste me ipso apud Davyntre octavo die Novembris, anno regni nostri vicesimo" (Daventry, November 8, 1235).

[9] *Ennen/Eckertz*, II, p. 153 no. 151.

was occasioned by the Staufen–Plantagenet marriage,[10] it also served to combat aggressive actions being taken against the Cologners by the king's subjects.[11] We have already seen Henry III issue a notice to the bailiffs of Hoyland (probably at the request of Cologne merchants who were experiencing trouble there), and in December of the same year a royal command was sent to the bailiffs of Yarmouth to obey the November 8 promulgation and to return 53 shillings 4 pence which were taken unjustly from the Cologners there. The merchants had apparently raised *clamor iteratus* concerning this matter before the royal court.[12] Surely the merchants took advantage of the diplomatic circumstances surrounding Isabella's marriage and obtained royal intervention, yet additional pressure was still needed the following year to resolve the conflict in Yarmouth.[13]

Even with the increasing competition of the Easterlings, it appears that to this date the Cologners and their Westphalian partners had maintained the monopoly of trade privileges and were still legally distinguished from the other German merchants.[14] But the decade of the 1230s saw the end of this economic dominance as the Easterlings finally gained their own royal charters of liberty in England. In 1237 Henry conferred protection on the merchants from Gotland (Visby) and

---

[10] Ennen, "Europäische Züge der mittelalterlichen Kölner Stadtgeschichte," p. 35; Weiner, "Early commercial intercourse between England and Germany," p. 138: "This continued favour shown towards this city, upon whom the competition of its rivals was now pressing heavily, must be attributed to the unshaken loyalty with which it supported the Hohenstaufen emperor, who this year married the king's daughter Isabella."

[11] T. H. Lloyd, *Alien Merchants in England in the High Middle Ages* (New York, 1982), p. 130.

[12] *CCLR Henry III*, III, p. 216; *HUB*, I, p. 90 no. 271: "Rex baillivis suis de Gernemuth' salutem. Sciatis nos quietos clamasse per cartam nostram pro nobis et heredibus nostris dilectos nostros cives de Colonia de omnibus consuetudinibus et demandis que pertinent ad nos per totam terram nostram Anglie, et concessimus eis salvum ire et salvum venire in totam terram nostram, et quod ii libere possint ire ad ferias per totam terram nostram et emere vendere in villa Londoniensi et alibi, salva libertate civitatis nostre Londoniensi. Et ideo vobis precipimus quod predictas libertates et quietancias predictis civibus a nobis concessas libere et sine impedimento habere permittatis, liii solidos et quatuor denarios quos nuper a predictis civibus contra easdem libertates cepistis, ut dicitur, eisdem civibus sine dilatione reddi facientes, ita quod clamor iteratus ad nos non debeat inde pervenire" (December 12, 1235).

[13] *CCLR Henry III*, III, p. 399: "Mandatum est ballivis de Jernemowe quod si, occasione libertatum quas habent homines de Colonia per cartam predecessorum regum Anglie, vel per cartam regis, quibus hucusque usi sunt, aliquid eis abstulerint contra libertates predictas, id ei [sic] reddi faciant" (*CCLR Henry III*, II, p. 453 dated 1236).

[14] In 1234 Henry III instructed the authorities in London not to exact murage from any Germans until they had counsel with him about the matter. In this command two groups of German merchants are differentiated: "de terra regis Alemannie vel archiepiscopi Coloniensis" (*CCLR Henry III*, II, p. 453). In 1244 the guildhall was still known as that of the Cologners, not the Germans: *The London Eyre of 1244*, ed. Chew and Weinbaum, London Record Society, 6 (London, 1970), p. 111 no. 262; *Munimenta*, I, p. 241 and III, p. 448: "Item bladum quod applicuerit inter guteram de Gyldhalle Colonensium et sokam archiepiscopi Cantuariensis non solet mensurari per aliud quarterium quam per quarterium de soka Regine."

exempted them from customs dues on all items they bought or sold in England.[15] On August 26, 1238 – if it is not a forged charter – the king also extended to the merchants of Lübeck and other Easterlings those liberties which the Germans of other cities (meaning those of the Cologne–Westphalian guildhall) had traditionally possessed, and promised them exemption from confiscation in case of shipwreck.[16] At this point in time the formation of the Hanseatic League was under way among the Baltic trading towns: Lübeck and Hamburg established a confederation in 1241 and in 1259 a similar treaty was arranged between Hamburg and Bremen. In the same year Lübeck, Rostock, and Wismar united to fight piracy. Cologne also entered into such a confederation when it joined with Bremen in 1258. The days of independent control were fading for the Cologners.[17] The merchants of Hamburg were also able to obtain trading privileges and royal protection in England by 1252.[18]

This process of unification among the German merchants had an impact on the fate of the Cologne guildhall. As early as 1251 we have mention of an "alderman of the Germans" – a certain Arnold fitz Tedmar – whose career we shall consider at length later.[19] Hence the Germans were by this time considered a legal corporation in England with a spokesman on their behalf before the municipal and royal officials. The merchants of Lübeck, leaders among the new Baltic towns

---

[15] *LUB*, I, p. 84 no. 77 (March 20, 1237).

[16] *HUB*, I, p. 97 no. 292; *LUB*, I, pp. 86–7 no. 80: "Henricus Dei gratia Rex Anglie etc. consulibus et burgensibus civitatis Lubicensis amicis nostris karissimis salutem. Ad nostram notitiam iam pervenit, quod mercatores civitatis vestre et mercatores civitatum Alemannie aliunde [i.e. other Easterlings from the Wendish towns] cum mercimoniis suis regnum nostrum cupiant frequentare, dummodo per nos et incolas regni nostri pacifice et civiliter admittantur. Quapropter tam vobis quam mercatoribus aliarum civitatum Alemannie tenore presentium volumus notum, quod omnibus et singulis mercatoribus supradictis regnum nostrum frequentare volentibus, per nos et nostros exhibere volumus graciam et favorem et omnes consuetudines et libertates, quibus mercatores Alemannie usi sunt temporibus predecessorum nostrorum regem Anglie; volentes etiam, ut si contigerit naves vestras in partibus nostris periclitari et de tali nave periclitata aliquis homo vivus evaserit et ad terram venerit, omnia bona et catalla in illa navi contenta remaneant quorum prius fuerunt, nec ex eo, quod Wreccum dicitur, veris dominis extorqueantur" (Westminster, August 26, 1238). See *Hanserecesse*, ed. Koppmann, p. xxvii. There is the real possibility that this charter for Lübeck is a forgery: A. von Brandt, "Das angebliche Privileg Heinrichs III. von England für Lübeck. Ein ergänzender Hinweis zu den Fälschungsmethoden des Lübecker Syndikus Dreyer," *HGB* 71 (1952), pp. 84–8, esp. pp. 87–8. In any case the charter to the Gotland community is real and signals the rise of the Baltic towns and the origins of the Hanseatic League.

[17] Weiner, "Early commercial intercourse between England and Germany," pp. 139–40.

[18] *HUB*, I, p. 160 no. 444 (October 25, 1252).

[19] *HUB*, I, p. 132 no. 405; *LUB*, I, pp. 163–4 no. 177, where Arnold appears as a witness to the settlement between two London merchants and the merchants of Lübeck concerning damage the latter inflicted on the goods of the Londoners at Copenhagen. Arnold's name appears as "Arnaldo Thedmar, aldermanno Teutonicorum."

in much the same way as Cologne had been among the Westphalian towns, were gradually replacing the Cologners as the predominant power at the London guildhall. We see this in two charters from the years 1257 and 1260.

In the former the Lübeckers were granted trading privileges in England at the request of Richard of Cornwall, who had recently been elected King of the Romans and was at the time in the midst of his first trip into Germany. Naturally he needed the support of the northern German towns, and so his brother Henry III granted to the Lübeckers liberty from royal prises for seven years. The final sentence of this grant indicates that the merchants of Denmark and Brunswick had also received the same charter.[20] King Henry included a condition to the privileges that looks very much like King John's grant to the Cologners on behalf of Otto IV: these liberties were to be in force only as long as the German merchants remained loyal to Richard of Cornwall.

The second charter, dated June 15, 1260, reveals even more clearly the shift in emphasis at the London guildhall.[21] Here Henry III issued a confirmation of the ancient mercantile privileges for Germans at the request of his brother Richard of Cornwall, yet important alterations had been made in the charter. The liberties, once the sole possession of

---

[20] Lappenberg, *Urkundliche Geschichte des Hansischen Stahlhofes zu London*, pp. 12–13 no. 27; *LUB*, II, pp. 20–1 no. 27; *HUB*, I, no. 506; *Böhmer*, v, 2, p. 1737 no. 11810: "Henricus, Dei gracia Rex Angliae, Dominus Hiberniae, Dux Normanniae, Aquitainae, et Comes Andegaviae, omnibus ballivis suis salutem. Sciatis nos ad instantiam dilecti et fidelis fratris nostri Ricardi, comitis Cornubiae, in regem Romanorum electi, suscepisse in protectionem et defensionem nostram et salvum et securum conductum nostrum burgenses de Lubeke in Alemannia cum omnibus rebus et mercandisis, quas in regnum nostrum deferent vel facient deferri. Et eis concessimus, quod de omnibus rebus et mercandisis suis nihil capiatur ad opus nostrum vel alterius contra voluntatem eorundem, sed libere vendant et nogocientur inde in regno praedicto, prout sibi viderint expedire. Et ideo vobis mandamus, quod dictis burgensibus vel eorum nunciis in veniendo in terram nostram cum rebus et mercandisis suis, ibidem morando et inde recendendo, nullum inferatis aut ab aliis inferri permittatis impedimentum aut gravamen. Nec eos contra quietantiam praedictam vexetis aut ab aliis vexari permittatis. In cuius rei testimonium has literas nostras fieri fecimus patentes, per septennum durantes, dum tamen iidem burgenses interim bene et fideliter se habuerint erga praefatum electum, fratrum nostrum . . . Hec litera duplicata est, pro burgensibus et mercatoribus Dacis, Brunswig et Lubek" (Westminster, May 11, 1257). All but Lappenberg incorrectly date this charter in the year 1258.

[21] *HUB*, I, pp. 193–4: no. 552; *LUB*, I, p. 231 no. 250; *Böhmer*, v, 2, p. 1744 no. 11867a: "Henricus Dei gratia Rex Anglie etc. Sciatis, quod ad instantiam serenissimi principis Ricardi Romanorum Regis karissimi fratris nostri concedimus mercatoribus regni Allemannie, illis videlicet qui habent domum in civitate nostra Londoniensi, que gildehalla Teutonicorum vulgariter nuncupatur, quod eos universos et singulos manutenebimus et servabimus per totam regnum nostrum in omnibus eisdem libertatibus et liberis consuetudinibus, quibus ipsi nostris et progenitorum nostrorum temporibus usi sunt et gavisi, ipsosque extra huiusmodi libertates et liberas consuetudines non trahemus nec trahi permittemus aliquatenus. In cuius rei testimonium presentes literas nostras patentes eis duximus concedendas" (Westminster, June 15, 1260). This letter was issued two days before Richard departed for Germany: Weiner, "Early commercial intercourse between England and Germany," p. 143 note 6.

the Cologners and their Westphalian associates, had now been extended to all merchants *regni Allemannie*. In addition, the guildhall is no longer referred to as the guildhall of the Cologners alone but as the *gildhalla Teutonicorum*. The language of the charter states that the Germans (no reference is made to the Cologners) were in possession of the guildhall. The fact that a much later copy of this charter located in the Cologne Stadtarchiv has inserted the phrase:

concedimus mercatoribus regni Germanie, illis videlicet civibus de Colonia, qui habent domum in civitate nostra Londonia, que gildehalle Teutonicorum vulgariter nuncupatur[22]

suggests that the Cologne merchants were not pleased with the transfer of their traditional liberties to all German merchants of the newly named *gildhalla Teutonicorum*. Lübeck's emerging leadership within the guildhall could be inferred from the fact that the original copy of this charter resides in the Lübeck archives.[23]

This transformation of the "guildhall of the Cologners" to the "guildhall of the Germans" complete with its own alderman is further confirmed by the appearance of Arnold fitz Tedmar in a charter of the same year.[24] He, along with the members "mercatorum Allemanie in Angliam veniencium," purchased a rent of 2 shillings from a piece of land lying east of the guildhall itself. Arnold was no doubt involved in his role as the alderman of the Germans. Once again we have the guildhall referred to as that of the Germans. This purchase was part of the merchants' efforts to expand, since the original guildhall property could no longer hold the growing German population of merchants now that the Easterlings had joined.

The German merchants, along with other foreigners, found it difficult to exercise their liberties in England during the years of the Montfort regime. Margaret of Flanders,[25] and the burghers of

---

[22] *Ennen/Eckertz*, II, p. 417 no. 397 dated incorrectly as June 15, 1259.

[23] Stadtarchiv von Lübeck, Anglicana no. 4. The charter contains a damaged yet intact royal seal and the inscription "Carta domini Henrici regis Anglie" on the reverse side. An English copy survives also: British Museum Cottonian MS. Vespasian B VIII, fo. 86.

[24] *HUB*, I, pp. 190–1 no. 540; Lappenberg, *Urkundliche Geschichte des Hansischen Stahlhofes zu London*, p. 13 no. 28 (dated 1260): "Sciant presentes et futuri, quod ego Wilhelmus filius Wilhelmi Reyneri quietas clamavi et presenti carta mea confirmavi Arnulpho filo Thedmaro aldermanno mercatorum Allemanie in Angliam veniencium et eisdem mercatoribus duas solidatas annui et quieti redditus, quas per annum recipere solebam de quadam particula terre cum pertinenciis in latere orientali gildhallie eorum, quam habent Londonie in parrochia omnium sanctorum."

[25] *HUB*, I, p. 211 nos. 603–4 (August 31 and November 10, 1264).

Hamburg[26] and of Cologne[27] all wound up appealing for royal protection for their citizens in England. The Cologners wrote a very personal letter to the king, which shows great sympathy for the difficulties Henry endured during the Barons' Revolt. They also gained the assistance of their archbishop in the appeal for redress on behalf of Hermann of Cologne, who had been despoiled of his goods at Winchelsea to the cost of more than one hundred marks.[28] In fact, Archbishop Engelbert wrote directly to the barons for assistance in this matter. The Battle of Evesham was, therefore, a most beneficial event for these merchants.

No sooner was the Dictum of Kenilworth promulgated (October 31, 1266) than the royal chancery began issuing new privileges to foreigners. At this point another major shift occurred among the German merchants in England. At the request of his kinsman, Duke Albrecht of Brunswick, Henry III published three charters that gave great advantage to the Easterlings. He granted an independent Hansa for the merchants

---

[26] *HUB*, I, p. 212 no. 606 (*c.* 1264).

[27] *HUB*, I, pp. 211–12 no. 605; *Shirley*, I, p. 488 no. 404; *Diplomatic Documents Preserved in the Public Record Office. Volume I: 1107–1272*, ed. Pierre Chaplais, (London, 1964), p. 272 no. 398; *Böhmer*, v, 2, p. 1756 no. 11970: "Serenissimo domino Henrico Dei gracia Regi Anglie illustri, judices, scabini, consilium ceterique cives in Colonia, paratissimum cum omni devocione et reverencia in omnibus obsequium. Vestre dominacioni significamus quod de vestris adversitatibus quamplurimum dolemus, attamen vestre magnificencie immensas referimus graciarum actiones eo quod nostri concives mercatores cum mercimoniis eorum in terra vestra hucusque a vestra regia auctoritate sine omni gravimine fuerunt protecti et conservati. Nunc autem ex ostensione et gravi querimonia dilecti concivis nostri Hermanni latoris presentium intelleximus quod ipse veniens cum bonis suis in vestram jurisdictionem et quod vestri cives de Winkilse [Winchelsea] ipsum bonis suis spoliaverunt ad estimationem centum marcarum et amplius, exceptis dampnis inde habitis. Quare vestre magnificencie affectuosis precibus supplicamus humiliter et devote quatinus intuitu Dei et justicie ac precum nostrarum interventu id efficere dignemini, ut ipsi bona sua restituantur ei non occasione premissa aliqua dissensio inter vestros et nostros oriatur, tantum pro nobis in hac parte facientes ut exinde vestram regiam majestatem commendare valeamus, et si nulla restitucio ipsi fieri poterit, tunc ipsum in jure suo deserere non possumus quin ipsi ut in vestris hominibus recuperare valeat assistere debeamus" (April 13, 1265).

[28] Chaplais, *Diplomatic Documents Preserved in the Public Record Office*, pp. 271–2 no. 397: "Engelbertus Dei gracia sancte Coloniensis ecclesie archiepiscopus, sacri imperii per Italiam archicancellarius, dilectis sibi viris eximie strenuitatis . . . summo justiciario et baronibus Anglie, salutem cum sincera in Domino caritate. Ex gravi querimonia dilecti civis nostri Colon' Herimanni presencium exhibitoris accepimus quod, cum ipse cum mercibus suis negociandi cause partes Anglie adiisset, opidiani de Winkelse cum bonis suis et mercibus ad estimacionem centum marcarum sicut idem noster civis asserit contra justiciam spoliarunt preter dampna que sustinuit exinde. Rogamus igitur vos cum ea qua possumus attencione studiose requirendo quatinus operam efficacem, consilium et auxilium ad hoc adhibere curetis, ut dictus noster civis bonorum suorum solucionem et restitucionem integraliter consequatur, ut idem apud vos et mercatores Anglie teneamur in grata graciarum vicissitudine promereri et ne ipse noster civis exinde contra mercatores Anglie juste occasionis materiam habeat querelandi cum in juris sui prosecucione deesse non possumus nec debemus" (April 13, 1265).

of Hamburg,[29] freed the Lübecker merchants from arrest for debts and from royal prise[30] and then granted them their own Hansa as well.[31] Now the merchants of Lübeck and Hamburg, having benefited from Henry III's largess on the occasion of Duke Albrecht's marriage to the count of Montferrat's daughter at Windsor,[32] no longer needed to remain within the Cologne Hansa. They now could establish their own separate Hansas "eodem modo, quo burgenses et mercatores Colonie hansam suam habent."[33] This was a rather confusing situation, with three separate German associations operating and competing against one another within England. Kunze has suggested that Cologne remained dominant in London, while Lübeck and Hamburg were active along the eastern coast.[34] Yet lacking evidence to the contrary we still must

[29] *HUB*, I, pp. 218–19 no. 633; *Hamburgisches Urkundenbuch*, ed. J. M. Lappenberg, (Hamburg, 1842; rpt. 1907), I, pp. 579–80 no. 706; *Böhmer*, V, 2, pp. 1761–2 no. 12015: "Henricus Dei gracia etc. omnibus ballivis et fidelibus suis, ad quos presentes littere pervenerint, salutem. Volentes ad instanciam nobilis viri A. ducis Bruneswyk, mercatoribus ipsius ducis de Haumburg gratiam facere specialem, concedimus eisdem mercatoribus pro nobis et heredibus nostris, quod ipsi habeant hansam suam per se ipsos per totam regnum nostrum imperpetuum. Ita tamen, quod ipsi mercatores faciant nobis et heredibus nostris consuetudines inde debitas et consuetas. In cuius rei testimonium has litteras nostras eisdem mercatoribus fieri fecimus patentes" (Kenilworth, November 8, 1266).

[30] *HUB*, I, p. 219 no. 635; *LUB*, II, p. 32 no. 39: "Concessimus eciam burgensibus et mercatoribus predictis, quod de mercandisiis suis in terram et potestatem nostram venientibus nullam prisam fieri faciemus ad opus nostrum, nisi ipsis vel suis servientibus statim inde rationabiliter satisfecerimus, salvis tamen inde nobis debitis et antiquis prisis nostris" (Oxford, December 27, 1266).

[31] *CPR Henry III*, VI, p. 23; *HUB*, I, p. 220 no. 636; *LUB*, I, pp. 279–80 no. 291; *Böhmer*, V, 2, p. 1762 no. 12021: "Concessimus insuper, quantum ad nos pertinet, burgensibus et mercatoribus praedictis, quod ipsi habeant hansam suam reddendo inde quinque solidos eodem modo, quo burgenses et mercatores Colonie hansam suam habent et eam temporibus retroactis habere et reddere consueverunt" (Westminster, January 5, 1267).

[32] *Annales Londonienses*, ed. William Stubbs, RS, 76: 1 (London, 1882), p. 76: "venit in Angliam dux de Brundeswico cum magna familia variisque indumentis divaricata, et die omnium sanctorum [November 1] filiam marchionis [Adelheid, daughter of the count of Montferrat] cum domina regina commorantem apud Wyndelshore celebri festo duxit in uxorem."

[33] Weiner, "Early commercial intercourse between England and Germany," p. 145 explains the meaning of the term Hansa: "Firstly, it was used to signify 'a mercantile tribute or exaction, as a fee payable upon entering the Gild merchant;' secondly, it seems to have denoted 'the right to exact money requisitions or presentations from the brethren as well as from the gildsmen trading in the town;' its third use was often synonymous with the term 'guild merchant' with all its privileges and advantages attributable to that institution. It is probable that the German grantees derived all three benefits from it. In other words they exacted entrance fees from newcomers to compensate them for their initial outlay and trouble involved in obtaining it; a definite contribution from all members to defray the expenses of maintenance of the Guildhall, and lastly, it formed the basis of their trading rights in the kingdom."

[34] Karl Kunze, "Das erste Jahrhundert der deutschen Hanse in England," *HGB* 6 (1889), pp. 135–6. A certain Simon de Stavere appears as "burgensis Lennensis ac aldermannus Romani imperii apud Lennen" *c.* 1271 (*LUB*, I, pp. 310–11 no. 329; *HUB*, I, p. 247 no. 701). Here he writes a letter informing the city council in Lübeck of his progress in gaining a confirmation of the city's liberties in England, and both Kunze and Lappenberg see this as evidence for Lynn as

assume that the London guildhall had not only a common alderman but also members from three separate Hansas within its walls.

With the creation of two new Hansas under the leadership of Lübeck and Hamburg the ancient monopoly on English trade held by the Cologners had finally been broken.[35] Hanseatic cities like Lübeck could lodge a successful plea for its citizens to Queen Eleanor for help against the king's royal officials during the summer of 1272.[36] They asked her to move the king to release the Lübeckers who had been arrested at the Boston market for trading illegally with Flanders. The queen proved to be both responsive and effective, and the merchants were quickly pardoned.[37]

The complexities of three German Hansas proved to be unmanageable for the German merchants as well as for the London government, and the three were eventually assimilated into one German Hansa that became known as the Hanseatic Steelyard. This process of amalgamation appears in the dispute over the upkeep of Bishopsgate. In 1275 an inquest was held to discover who had the responsibility for the maintenance and defense of the gate, but the result was only confusing testimony by Londoners.[38] The witnesses from Billingsgate (the ward of

the location of the Lübeck Hansa. No location, however, has been suggested for the Hamburg Hansa.

[35] *Hanserecesse*, ed. Koppmann, p. xxvii: "Bisher also war England die deutsche Kaufmannwelt unter der Vorortschaft Kölns vereinigt, wie die flandrische Kaufmannschaft unter der Führung von Brügge: die Privilegien König Heinrichs für Hamburg und Lübeck zerbrechen diese Einigung; statt bei der Kölnischen Hanse können die Kaufleute der mit Hamburg oder Lübeck näher verbundenen Städte bei einer der neuen Hansen um ihre Aufnahme nachsuchen." Weiner, "Early commercial intercourse between England and Germany," p. 146: "the monopoly so long enjoyed by Cologne was now shattered. Hitherto the Rhine city alone had possessed a permanent habitation in England, and although its merchants allowed others to share their good fortune on the payment of an entrance fee of five shillings, it had exercised a controlling influence over them which they must have found unpalatable. Henceforth all three compete for supremacy until all three amalgamate and are known as the 'Hanse,' with Lübeck as the leader."

[36] *HUB*, I, p. 248 no. 705; *LUB*, II, p. 707 no. 1007.

[37] *CCLR Henry III*, XIV, p. 516; *HUB*, I, p. 248 no. 707; *LUB*, II, pp. 33–4 no. 42 (August 16, 1272). Merchants of Cologne, Dortmund, and Brunswick were also released.

[38] *Rotuli hundredorum temp. Henri III et Edw. I in turri Londinensi et in curia receptae scaccarii Westmonastariensi asservati*, ed. W. Illingworth and J. Caley (London, 1812–18), I, pp. 416, 428, 431; *HUB*, I, p. 262 no. 747; Lappenberg, *Urkundliche Geschichte des Hansischen Stahlhofes zu London*, p. 14 no. 29: "Veredictum warde Wolmari de Essex: Item iurati dicunt, quod Teutonici sunt liberi in civitate sicut et cives ejusdem pro porta, que vocatur Bissopesgate, quam sumptibus ipsi eorum in bono statu et competenti sustentare deberent, et nichil faciunt ad maximum dampnum et dedecus domini regis et civitatis. Item dicunt quod Teutonici non sustinent portam, que vocatur Bisshopesgate, quam bene sustentare deberent, pro qua liberi sunt in civitate ad grave dampnum civitatis. Warda Philippi le Taillur: Item porta de Bisshopesgate, quam gentes Danorum antiquitus solebant sustinere et debebant pro libertate, quam habebant in civitate Londoniensi, nunc per defectum ipsorum vel potius ballivorum civitatis fere corruitur ad terram ad magnum periculum civitatis."

Wolmar of Essex[39]) claimed that it had been the responsibility of the Germans to care for the gate, and that they had not been fulfilling their obligation in return for their liberties in the city. Yet the witnesses from Bishopsgate ward itself (the ward of Philip the Tailor[40]) testified that the Danes were responsible for the upkeep of the city gate.

Christopher Brooke explains this confusion by asserting that the Germans had gradually replaced the Danish trade during the twelfth century, having moved into the parish of St. Clement Danes and taken on the upkeep of Bishopsgate by 1225.[41] Martin Weinbaum has surmised that the Germans were charged with servicing the gate as a punishment for supporting the Montfortian faction in London.[42] But a better explanation can be found in the conflict between the Cologne–Westphalian and Easterling elements within the London guildhall. As a sign of the growing dominance of the Easterlings in the guildhall by this time, the building itself began to be referred to as "the hall of the Danes." As Derek Keene has shown, this name was an inaccurate term used for those German "Easterling" or "Wendish" merchants coming from the regions around Lübeck who traveled through the lands of the king of Denmark.[43] The same confusion about, and yet differentiation of, these "Danes" and the Cologners occurs in an entry from this period in the *Liber Albus*.[44]

[39] Alfred B. Beaven, *The Aldermen of the City of London* (London, 1908–13), I, pp. 22, 375.

[40] Ibid., I, pp. 33, 374; II, p. 159.

[41] Brooke and Keir, *London 800–1216*, pp. 267–8.

[42] Weinbaum, "Stalhof und Deutsche Gildhalle zu London," p. 51: "Vor allem aber scheint die Verpflichtung der Deutschen Hanse, das Bischofstor instandzuhalten und zu verteidigen, entweder aus der unruhigen Reformzeit Simons de Montfort zu stammen, oder sie ist gewissermaßen die Strafe der Hansen für ihre Parteinahme zugunsten der Londoner Oligarchie; denn sie wird erst 1275 in den Hundertschaftsrollen zum ersten Male erwähnt."

[43] Keene, "New discoveries at the Hanseatic Steelyard in London," p. 23: "By 1275 another name, 'the hall of the Danes' (Dennishemanneshalle and variants) was also being used for the same establishment [as the gildehalle or aula Teutonicorum: see CLRO Hustings Rolls 11: 63 and *Munimenta*, I, p. 243 (Liber Albus)]. As the references in 1275 to their responsibility for the upkeep of Bishopsgate show, the 'Danes' in London at this time were identical with the wider group of German traders. Scandinavian merchants had probably traded in London since the tenth century, and were certainly present there with merchants from Bremen early in the twelfth century, but the name 'hall of the Danes' probably has no connection with this earlier Scandinavian presence. It is more likely to have been adopted in the thirteenth century because the dominant group among the Germans using the hall now comprised the men of Lübeck and other towns who traded through territory controlled by the king of Denmark and, indeed, had once been subject to him. One early fourteenth-century reference to the guildhall describes it as that of the merchants of Cologne and Germany (Alamania), but the increasing dominance of the merchants involved in Baltic trade is revealed by yet another name, 'Easterlings Hall' (Esterlingeshalle), which from the 1340s onward was regularly used to denote the property."

[44] *Munimenta*, I, p. 229: "De la ferme des Coloniens, cestassavoir de la saille des Deneis, est pris par an xl soulz; cestassavoir, a le Pask et a le Fest, pur avoir lour court et lour attachiementz." Translation from III, pp. 63–4: "For the ferm of the people of Cologne, that is to say, for the

Therefore the confusion of the witnesses actually concerned whether the Germans of the Cologne Hansa or the Germans of the Lübeck and Hamburg Hansas were required to repair and defend Bishopsgate in exchange for their liberties in London. We know that the Cologners were never obligated to such service, yet the merchants from Lübeck and Hamburg did owe customary dues in exchange for their royal privileges.[45] This issue actually goes back to June 16, 1234, when Henry III, at the time work was being done on the city's wall, instructed the mayor and sheriffs of London not to demand murage payments from the German merchants until they had taken counsel with him over the matter.[46] The issue concerned the merchants "de terra regis Alemannie," yet a distinction was made between "mercatoribus de terra regis Alemannie vel archiepiscopi Coloniensis." This suggests that, although the Cologne–Westphalian merchants were traditionally free from such customs as murage, the other Easterling merchants had never been granted such a liberty and thus were being pressed to contribute to the repair of the city's walls. If so they may have been assigned Bishopsgate at this time, while the Cologners were not a part of the assignment because of their ancient liberties dating back to Richard I's reign. Henry III probably ordered the London officials to hold off pressing the issue in 1234 because of marriage negotiations with Frederick II, yet the Cologners may also have complained that they were not to be included among the Easterlings in this matter. It is likely then that the use of the terms "Danes" and "Germans" reflects the Londoners' confusion about which Hansas the various Germans belonged to and thereby what their privileges and obligations actually were.

Hall of the Deneis, forty shillings are received per annum; at Easter and at the Feast [of St. Michael], that is to say, for holding their own court and having their own attachments in their court, without aid of the sheriffs."

[45] The grants which awarded Lübeck and Hamburg their respective Hansas still respected the obligations due in the city of London. The Hamburg merchants received their Hansa "ita tamen, quod ipsi mercatores faciant nobis et heredibus nostris consuetudines inde debitas et consuetas" and the merchants of Lübeck theirs from the king "quantum ad nos pertinet," suggesting that they had certain obligations in London outside of this grant. These conditional clauses sound very much like the "salva libertate civitatis nostre Londoniensis" clause in the 1213 and 1235 charters which the Cologners fought successfully to have dropped from subsequent confirmations of Richard I's original grant of liberties. Hence the Cologners could argue that they did not owe such services based on Richard's original charter, while the other Germans had no such provisions in their charters.

[46] *CCLR Henry III*, II, p. 453: "Pro mercatoribus de terra regis Alemannie. Mandatum est majori et vicecomitibus Londonii, quod occasione domini regis facta ad claudendum civitatum London, nullam capiant consuetudinem vel exigant de mercatoribus de terra regis Alemannie vel archiepiscopi Coloniensis, set exactionem illam ponent in respectum, donec dominus rex ad partes illas venerit et cum predictis majore et vicecomitibus locutus fuerit" (June 16, 1234).

34

This lack of clarity led to no resolution of the matter and a second inquest was ordered by Parliament into the dispute between the "mercatores Alemannie" and the citizens of London in 1279.[47] The Hundred court investigated this time within Dowgate ward, where the Germans and their guildhall were located, and the witnesses declared:

quod mercatores Alemannie tenent unam Gihaldam et clamant libertatem per regnum Anglie occasione dicte Gihalde et habent. Pro qua quidem Gihalda tenentur edificare portam de Bissopesgat et dictam portam sustinere et non sustinent. Per quod dominus rex potest admittere civitatem suam si guerra eveniret.[48]

The determination of the inquest was that the Germans, the "Danes" no longer being mentioned, owed service to Bishopsgate in exchange for their guildhall. Did this now mean Germans from all three Hansas? Apparently the matter remained in dispute. Certainly the merchants from Cologne would have argued that they were not to be included with the other Germans when determining murage dues in the city because of the liberties which Richard I had granted them. The members of the Hamburg Hansa would have shown a similar concern for being identified with the Wendish merchants.

While the case was being mediated the German merchants obtained a confirmation by Edward I of Henry III's 1260 charter.[49] This grant did not free them from the Bishopsgate case, however, as it promised privileges only "quantum in nobis est," suggesting again that they had obligations within the city of London. Yet Edward's confirmation was probably issued within the context of this case, for seven months later a

---

[47] *HUB*, I, p. 287 no. 832 (April 1279).

[48] PRO Hundred Rolls Tower Series, fo. 15 (Warda de Douuegate).

[49] *HUB*, I, p. 305 no. 890; *LUB*, I, pp. 380–1 no. 421; *Calendar of the Letter-Books Preserved among the Archives of the Corporation of the City of London at the Guildhall. Volume III: Letter Book C*, ed. Reginald Sharpe (London, 1901), p. 41; *Rymer*, II, p. 161 (incorrectly dated 1280): "Edwardus Dei gratia rex Anglie etc. Omnibus, ad quos presentes littere pervenerint, salutem. Cum celebris memorie dominus Henricus rex, pater noster, dudum per litteras suas patentes, quas inspeximus, ad instanciam bone memorie Ricardi, Romanorum regis, avunculi nostri, concesserit mercatoribus regni Alemannie, illis scilicet, qui habent domum in civitate Londoniensi, que Gildehalle Teutonicorum vulgariter nuncupatur, quod eos universos et singulos manuteneret, et servaret per totum regnum suum in omnibus eisdem libertatibus et liberis consuetudinibus, quibus ipsi suis et progenitorum suorum temporibus usi fuerunt et gavisi, ipsosque extra huiusmodi libertates et liberas consuetudines non traheret nec trahi aliquatenus permitteret, prout in litteris predictis prefatis mercatoribus inde confectis plenius continentur: Nos eisdem mercatoribus gratiam illam continuari volentes, ipsos mercatores manuteneri et servari volumus in omnibus eisdem libertatibus et liberis consuetudinibus, quibus ipsi nostris et progenitorum nostrorum temporibus usi sunt et gavisi, ipsosque extra huiusmodi libertates et liberas consuetudines non trahemus nec quantum in nobis est trahi aliquantenus permittemus. In cuius rei testimonium has litteras nostras fieri fecimus patentes" (Westminster, November 18, 1281).

negotiated settlement was reached between the German merchants and the Londoners through royal intervention.[50]

The agreement was reached between the mayor of London, Henry Waleys, and representatives of the "mercatores de hansa Alemanie" in the presence of the Barons of the Exchequer. As the charter indicates, the Londoners continued to assert that the Germans had been obligated to repair and defend Bishopsgate *longo tempore*, but the Germans disputed this claim. At the suggestion of the lord mayor and burghers King Edward called the case before the Exchequer and threatened to revoke the Germans' privileges if the investigation confirmed their responsibility for the gate. Under these circumstances the German merchants relented and a settlement was reached. Their representatives promised "pro se et pro omnibus mercatoribus et sociis suis de hansa predicta [hansa de partibus Alemannie] quibuscumque et quandocumque confluentibus" (hence without distinctions as to their origins in Germany) to keep Bishopsgate in repair and defended *omni tempore*, and they gave 240 marks for the initial repairs.[51] In return they were asked only to pay for one-third of the future expenses for the gate and their privileges in the city were confirmed. The privileges mentioned were: freedom from murage charges elsewhere along the city wall, the right to sell grain in the city, and the retention of their own alderman. The alderman, however, was to be a citizen of London and after his election he was to appear before the mayor and swear an oath to maintain the laws of the city.

The representatives of the German merchants included, in addition to their alderman Gerard Merbode of Dortmund,[52] three men from

---

[50] *Munimenta*, I, pp. 485–8 (Liber Albus); *HUB*, I, pp. 308–10 no. 902; *Calendar of the Letter-Books Preserved among the Archives of the Corporation of the City of London at the Guildhall. Volume III: Letter Book C*, ed. Sharpe, p. 41; Lappenberg, *Urkundliche Geschichte des Hansischen Stahlhofes zu London*, pp. 14–15 no. 31 (June 1282).

[51] Although Edward I's Carta Mercatoria freed all foreign merchants from murage payments, in 1305 the German Hansa was released only from an entrance fee for passing through Bishopsgate since they were still under obligation to maintain the gate: *Munimenta*, II, 1, pp. 112–13 (Liber Custumarum): "Die Martis proxima post festum Sancti Michaelis, anno regni regis Edwardi, filii regis Henrici, xxxiiio, per Johannem le Blount majorem, aldermannos, et vicecomites, consideratum est et concessum, quod Alemanni de Hansa, mercatores Alemanniae, sint quieti de ii solidos, ingrediendo et exeundo cum bonis suis ad portam de Bisshopesgate, eo quod onerantur de custodia et reparatione portae praedictae, etc. Et solverunt pro irrotulatione ii solidos vi denarios."

[52] Merbode's ancestor may have been a namesake from Dortmund who is mentioned in a settlement between Count Engelbert of Mark, Archbishop Engelbert II of Cologne, and the city of Soest on May 1, 1265 (*UGN*, II, pp. 230–1 no. 551; *REK*, III, 2, p. 25 no. 2325). The count promised that: "bona quoque Merbodonis dicti de Tremonia, qui in Anglia nuper decessit, apud Tremoniam deponentur, et cuicumque per ius fuerint adiudicata, illi sine contradictione alterius debent integraliter assignari et super bonis huiusmodi in Anglia requirendis nos una cum prefato domino archiepiscopo et oppidanis Susaciensibus destinabimus patentia nostra scripta."

Dortmund, one from Hamburg, one from Münster, and one from Cologne. These were clearly members from the Cologne–Westphalian group, yet only one "hansa de partibus Alemannie" is mentioned in the agreement. For this reason scholars have generally cited this event as the moment when the three Hansas of Cologne, Lübeck, and Hamburg were united into one Hansa.[53] It simply proved too disadvantageous and confusing to maintain three separate organizations, and a reconciliation between the competing parties – apparently as a result of the seven-year dispute over Bishopsgate – brought about one German Hansa in London under the authority of an elected alderman.

The predominance of members from the original Cologne–Westphalian Hansa in the negotiations must mean that the German merchants as a whole were trying to use Cologne's ancient rights from Richard I in order to avoid murage payments. They probably emphasized that all German merchants frequented only one guildhall and not that they were members of three different Hansas. That the representatives of the Hansa spoke for all German merchants regardless of their specific origins suggests that the rights of the old Cologne Hansa were no longer considered separate from the other Germans. In any case the defense failed, and even the Cologners' old Hansa rights were not recognized, probably because a single Hansa had existed by this time and older distinctions were no longer valid.

The Cologne merchants tried one last time to affirm their earlier rights apart from the Easterlings' subsequent liberties, but King Edward only confirmed Henry III's charter of 1235, which retained John's condition: "salva libertate civitatis nostre Londoniensis."[54] Hence the

---

[53] Dollinger, *The German Hansa*, p. 40; Kunze, "Das erste Jahrhundert der deutschen Hanse in England," p. 136; E. Ennen, "Kölner Wirtschaft im Früh- und Hochmittelalter," I, pp. 180 and 187; E. Ennen, "Europäische Züge der mittelalterlichen Kölner Stadtgeschichte," p. 44; *Munimenta*, I, p. xcvi; Deeters, *Die Hanse und Köln*, p. 23; Lloyd, *England and the German Hanse*, pp. 20–1.

[54] *Munimenta*, II, 1, pp. 66–7; *CCHR*, II, pp. 381–3; *Calendar of the Letter-Books Preserved among the Archives of the Corporation of the City of London at the Guildhall. Volume III: Letter Book C*, ed. Sharpe, p. 50; *HUB*, I, p. 371 no. 1070: "Rex archiepiscopis, episcopis, abbatibus, prioribus, comitibus, baronibus, justiciariis, vicecomitibus, praepositis, ministris, et omnibus aliis bailivis et fidelibus suis, salutem. Inspeximus chartam, quam bonae memoriae dominus Henricus, rex, pater noster, fecit civibus de Colonia, in haec verba – 'Henricus Dei gratia, etc. archiepiscopis, etc. Sciatis nos quietum clamasse, pro nobis et heredibus nostris, dilectos nobis cives de Colonia, et mercandisam suam, de illis duobus solidis quos solebant dare de Gildhala sua Londoniarum, et de omnibus aliis consuetudinibus et demandis quae pertinent ad nos in Londoniis, et per totam terram nostram in Anglia. Concessimus etiam eis, salvum ire et salvum venire in totam terram nostram, et quod libere possint ire ad ferias per totam terram nostram, et emere et vendere, et in villa Londoniarum et alibi, salva libertate civitatis nostrae Londoniarum. Quare volumus, et firmiter praecipimus, pro nobis et haeredibus nostris, quod praedicti cives de Colonia praenominatas libertates et liberas consuetudines habeant per totam terram nostram Angliae, sicut praedictum est. Hiis testibus, venerabili patre Waltero Karleolonsi episcopo, et aliis. Datum

Cologners were now considered members of the German Hansa with no absolute freedom from London customs such as they had enjoyed from Richard I. While they were successful with John and Henry III in removing this clause and thus maintaining their unique status among the Germans, with Edward I they were classified with the other "mercatores de Alemannie." Their unique status among the Germans, fading as it was under the competition of the Easterlings during Henry III's reign, was finally lost during the reign of Edward I.

As Edward I began to build his anti-French coalition scheme with German princes he issued another charter of royal protection over the German merchants, in which he called them all to sail into his kingdom to pursue trade.[55] Here he made no distinctions between the German merchants, but treated them as members of the same Hansa. In a 1299 dispute between the German merchants and the mayor and sheriffs of London the king renewed Henry III's privileges of the "mercatores regni Alemannie, illos scilicet, qui sunt de gilda Teutonicorum et de haunca Alemannie in Londonia."[56] The Cologners are no longer mentioned in regard to their old guildhall, which was now the property of the single German Hansa.[57] The completion of the process of Cologne's amalgamation into the German Hansa is confirmed in

per manus venerabilis patris, Radulphi Cecestrensis episcopi, cancellarii nostri, apud Davyntre, octavo die Novembris, anno regni nostri vicesimo.' Nos enim, quietam clamationem et concessionem praedictas ratas habentes et gratas, eas, pro nobis et haeredibus nostris, quantum in nobis est, praedictis civibus de Colonia concedimus et confirmamus, sicut charta praedicta rationabiliter testatur. Hiis testibus: venerabili patre Roberto Bathoniensi et Wellensi episcopo cancellario nostro, Edmundo comite Cornubiae consanguineo nostro, Walter de Bello Campo senescallo hospitii nostri, Ricardo de Bosco, Walter de la Haye et aliis" (Langley, July 28, 1290).

[55] *HUB*, I, p. 389 no. 1128: "Rex etc. universis et singulis mercatoribus, rectoribus navium et marinellis Alemannis ac aliis quibuscunque, ad quos presentes littere pervenerint, salutem. Quia corditer affectamus, quod mercatores cum navibus, rebus er mercimoniis suis negociaciones exerceant et commodum suum inde faciant, prout sibi magis viderint expedire, vos affectuose rogamus, quatinus in regnum predictum cum navibus, rebus et mercimoniis vestris applicetis ad negociandum et commodum vestrum inde faciendum ibidem, ut predictum est. Vos enim cum navibus, marinellis, famulis, rebus et mercandisis quibuscunque in veniendo in regnum predictum, ibidem morando et inde redeundo in salvum et securum conductum nostrum suscepimus per presentes inhibentes universis et singulis ballivis et fidelibus nostris, ne vobis in personis seu rebus vestris quibuscunque inferant vel quantum in eis est inferri permittant injuriam, molestiam, dampnum, impedimentum aliquod seu gravamen. Et hoc similiter proclamari fecimus patentes quamdie nobis placuerit duraturas. Teste rege apud Bristoll, 26. die Septembris" (1293).

[56] *HUB*, I, pp. 443–4 nos. 1314, 1315, 1317 (August 1299).

[57] Weinbaum ("Stahlhof und Deutsche Gildhalle zu London") has argued that two distinct guildhalls existed – one for the Cologners and one for the Easterlings. This view has found no support either in archaeological evidence or among other scholars: see Keene, "New discoveries at the Hanseatic Steelyard in London," pp. 22–3; M. M. Postan, E. E. Rich, and Edward Miller, eds., *Cambridge Economic History* (Cambridge, 1963), p. 273; Brooke and Keir, *London 800–1216*, p. 268 note 2: "The problem has been discussed whether there was originally one or two guildhalls – one for the men of Cologne, one for the rest of the German traders. The

Edward I's comprehensive charter for all foreign merchants issued in 1303, known as the *Carta Mercatoria*.[58] Here all German merchants are lumped together without distinction as those of *Alemannia*.

The days of Cologne's monopoly over Anglo-German trade, begun in the eleventh century, were now over: the future of Anglo-German trade belonged to the Hanseatic League under the leadership of Lübeck. This did not mean that the Cologners were unable to maintain a leadership position within the Hansa,[59] but their earlier authority faded as Lübeck came to dominate the Hansa. Medieval tensions between Cologne and Lübeck over leadership within the Hansa have continued among modern German historians of local history: some assert that the origins of the Hansa came from Cologne[60] and some argue that the Hanseatic mother city was really Lübeck.[61]

The end of Cologne's unique commercial relationship with England came at roughly the same time as its unique diplomatic ties with the island were fading, and so it is fitting to end this portion of the present background study with the *Carta Mercatoria* of 1303. Diplomatic and commercial relations continued between England and Cologne throughout the remainder of the Middle Ages. Yet they never again rivaled the era of the eleventh to thirteenth centuries, when Cologne was the linchpin of Anglo-German commercial relations. From the late thirteenth century onward Cologne was only one among many German cities which had highly developed ties with England.

We have yet to consider what role the English merchant or expatriate played in Cologne, and this is because no comparable series of charters

---

evidence is inconclusive [this was written before the excavation at Cannon Street], but a single hall (no doubt many times altered and adapted) seems the more likely answer."

[58] *Munimenta*, II, 1, pp. 205–11; *HUB*, II, pp. 14–18 no. 31 (February 1, 1303). A Cologne merchant named Hildebrand Schönwetter is listed among those to whom Edward I owed 500 marks (*HUB*, I, p. 446 no. 1325 dated November 21, 1299). All the merchants listed here are considered members of the one German Hansa. See Stuart Jenks, "Die *Carta Mercatoria*: Ein 'hansisches Privileg,'" *HGB* 108 (1990), pp. 45–86.

[59] Several of the Hansa's aldermen during the fourteenth and fifteenth centuries were Cologners. See Horst Buszello, "Köln und England (1468–1509)," *Köln, Das Reich und Europa. MSAK.* 60 (1971), pp. 431–68; Karl Engel, "Die Organisation der deutsch-hansischen Kaufleute in England im 14. und 15. Jahrhundert bis zum Utrechter Frieden von 1474," *HGB* 19 (1913), pp. 477 ff. and Friedrich Schulz, *Die Hanse und England von Eduards III. bis auf Heinrichs VIII. Zeit*, Abhandlungen zur Verkehrs- und Seegeschichte, 5 (Berlin, 1911), pp. 189–91.

[60] Deeters, *Die Hanse und Köln*.

[61] Detlev Ellmers, "Die Entstehung der Hanse," *HGB* 103 (1985), p. 10: "Nicht die Kölner Hanse in England war der entscheidende Ansatzpunkt für die Entstehung der Deutschen Hanse, sondern ein Vorgang, der mit der Gründung Lübecks 1159 ebenso zusammenhing wie mit der 1161 endgültig abgesicherten Etablierung der Genossenschaft der Gotland besuchenden Deutschen" and p. 40: "Lübeck ist nicht irgendwann das Haupt der Hanse geworden, sondern war von Anfangen Ausgangspunkt und Basis der Hanse." There is not a little civic pride mixed into this debate.

was issued to foreign merchants by the archbishops of Cologne. Regulations for commerce by foreigners in Cologne were issued by Archbishop Conrad of Hochstaden in 1257[62] and again in 1259,[63] but they do not mention Englishmen or women specifically. Hence we shall rely heavily on Cologne municipal records to discuss the English in the prosopographical studies of Part II. Now that we have established the historical background undergirding our social history of Anglo-German emigrants during the Central Middle Ages, let us look more closely at the role currency exchange played in this interregional nexus. We shall find some surprising ways in which English sterling linked Cologners to England.[64]

---

[62] *UGN*, II, p. 237 no. 436; *REK*, III, 1, p. 268 no. 1994.

[63] *UGN*, II, pp. 261–3 no. 469; *REK*, III, 1, pp. 276–7 no. 2053; *HUB*, I, pp. 182–5 no. 523 (May 7, 1259). Cologne was given staple rights in 1259.

[64] As we shall see, Kunze's comment ("Das erste Jahrhundert der deutschen Hanse in England," p. 140): "Zwar ein eigener aktiver Handelsbetrieb fehlte den Engländern jener Zeit nicht ganz: längst war der englische Kaufmann in Brügge wie in Köln ein gern und häufig gesehener Gast" is more true than he realized.

Chapter 3

ANGLO-GERMAN CURRENCY EXCHANGE: COLOGNE AND ENGLISH STERLING

Currency exchange is a significant kind of interregional activity in Europe. It can serve not only as evidence of expanding economies and trade, but also as a signifier of a growing social and cultural inter-connectedness between European regions. One expects to find such evidence existing, for example, between regions like England and France or between the Italian cities and the Levant from the eleventh to thirteenth centuries. Traditionally these early corridors of urban and commercial expansion identified by historians (one could also mention other centers of activity like Champagne and the Low Countries) have generally not included a highly developed economic nexus between Germany and England before the Hanseatic era. Yet there was such a vital corridor of activity, which emerged quickly after the deleterious effects of the Viking invasions were shaken off. The central role in the growth of this Anglo-German commercial exchange was played by the city of Cologne and its inhabitants. As early as the late tenth century there is evidence that Cologne and England were becoming tied to a growing commercial nexus. They would thereby be directly and equally affected by the ebb and flow of currency within northern Europe as a whole.

Let us establish the backdrop for our study by briefly reviewing the gradual interpenetration of the English and Cologne currencies during the eleventh and twelfth centuries. With the increasing prosperity of both Ottonian Germany and Anglo-Saxon England during the late tenth century came an increase in the circulation of coinage. The discovery of silver at Goslar in the Harz Mountains in the decade of the 960s increased the flow of specie markedly, but it was the expansion of markets during this period which drew the silver from its mountain fastness and spread it throughout Saxony.[1] The simultaneous growth of

---

[1] Peter Spufford, *Money and Its Use in Medieval Europe* (Cambridge, 1988), p. 77.

41

markets and mints throughout Germany resulted in Otto I (936–73) having this new silver made into coins at various mints.

From Saxony much silver was transported westward, reaching the Rhineland first, not only reviving the old royal mint at Cologne but also making it the most prolific in Germany.[2] Large amounts of new silver also stimulated coin production in the Meuse valley, in Frisia, and even in England. Only a very small amount of silver, however, passed into France, where little minting was being done in the late tenth and early eleventh centuries. The Frisian merchants were the primary agency by which Saxon silver entered England at this time. P. H. Sawyer's thesis of a major English wool trade in the eleventh century which drew German silver to the island fits well with the evidence in Germany.[3]

Since southern and eastern England had already had active mints for centuries, the silver from Germany was not circulated as foreign specie but rather minted into English coin.[4] Anglo-Saxon monarchs maintained strong central control over the mints and refused to allow foreign currency into the country. Thus it was silver bullion which entered England, and an increase in the number of active English mints emerging at this time parallels those of Saxony and the Rhineland.

Pamela Nightingale has shown another important aspect of the growing commercial links between England and Germany during the eleventh century.[5] King Cnut of England (1016–35) instituted a reform of weight-standards for English coinage that replaced the Carolingian pound with the mark weighing 216g (thus a penny weighed 1.5g). By the end of the eleventh century the Rhineland, Normandy, and Flanders had all joined England and Scandinavia in instituting this Anglo-Danish currency reform. Cologne, as the commercial leader of the Rhineland, had instituted the new standard by the second half of the eleventh century.[6] No doubt this was done for

---

[2] Ibid., p. 85.

[3] Sawyer, "The wealth of England in the eleventh century," pp. 145–64.

[4] Aethelstan's edict against the circulation of foreign coinage in 930 was often repeated by later kings: see Dorothy Whitelock, ed., *English Historical Documents* (London, 1955), I, p. 384.

[5] Pamela Nightingale, "The evolution of weight-standards and the creation of new monetary and commercial links in northern Europe from the tenth century to the twelfth century," *Economic History Review* 2nd series 38 no. 2 (May, 1985), pp. 192–209. See also P. Nightingale, "The ora, the mark and the mancus: weight-standards and the coinage in eleventh-century England," *The Numismatic Chronicle* 143 (1983), pp. 248–57 and 144 (1984), pp. 234–48.

[6] Nightingale, "The evolution of weight-standards," p. 200: "Although Cologne was a prolific mint in the eleventh century, there is no evidence that the mark was used by the merchants of Cologne before the second half of the century. It was then satisfied by a payment of 144 pence, and since the penny was struck to a standard of c. 1.5g there can be little doubt that Cologne had adopted Cnut's standard of 216g . . . it seems clear that by the end of the eleventh century, England, Normandy, Flanders, Scandanavia, and the Rhineland enjoyed a common weight-

commercial reasons,[7] and once again we find the Anglo-Cologne connection as part of the growing commercial integration of northern Europe in the eleventh century. Such uniformity made currency exchange, and thereby all commercial activities, much easier and so contributed greatly to stimulating trade between the regions.

The expanding trade network fueled by German silver experienced a major contraction by the late eleventh century, however, when the Saxon silver mines began to decline. By the 1070s an era of economic contraction and shortage of currency set in that would last until the 1160s. The impact of this decline in silver production was felt keenly in Cologne, which had been the principal bullion market of northwestern Europe for Goslar silver. Unlike many other Ottonian mints the archiepiscopal mint at Cologne did not close, yet it produced very little currency during the century from the 1070s to the pontificate of Archbishop Philip of Heinsberg (1167–91). Likewise in England as the supply of new silver was cut off a recession resulted from a lack of demand for wool.[9] Further exacerbating the situation was the enormous drain on silver coinage caused by the Crusades. Not only the costs of transportation and foodstuffs for individual crusaders but also the cost of maintaining the new principalities in the Holy Land drew vast amounts of currency southward and eastward.

This silver famine was eventually relieved by the discovery of new silver veins in Freiberg in the 1160s. Freiberg would sustain output of

standard in the mark of 216g." See also Walter Hävernick, *Der Kölner Pfennig im 12. und 13. Jahrhundert*, Vierteljahrschrift für Sozial- und Wirtschaftsgeschichte, Beihefte 18 (Stuttgart, 1930; rpt. Hildesheim, 1984).

[7] Bruno Kuske, "Köln. Zur Geltung der Stadt, ihrer Waren und Maßstäben in älterer Zeit (12.–18. Jahrhundert)," *JKGV* 17 (1935), p. 113: "Feststehen dürfte, daß der Handel der Kölner Kaufleute ausschlaggebend für das Aufkommen der neuen Mark als Edelmetallgewicht gegenüber dem alten Karolingerpfund gewesen ist. Diese Mark bürgerte sich mindestens seit dem 12. Jahrhundert unter nordischen Einfluß ein und zwar wurde diese den Kölnern wohl namentlich über England vermittelt, wo sie mit Normannen und Dänen besonders in London ständig zusammen kamen."

[8] I am following Hävernick's assertions in *Der Kölner Pfennig im 12. und 13. Jahrhundert* as well as Spufford's in *Money and Its Use in Medieval Europe*, although there is some dispute about the extent to which the Cologne mint declined in production during this period. That the weight of the coins was slowly diminished, however, is generally agreed upon: see Peter Ilisch, "Die Schatzfunde von Werlte und Remscheid," *Fernhandel und Geldwirtschaft. Beiträge zum deutschen Münzwesen in sächsischer und salischer Zeit*, ed. Bernd Kluge, Berliner Numismatische Forschungen NF, 1: Römisch-Germanisches Zentralmuseum Monographien, 31 (Sigmaringen, 1993), p. 161. A similar significant increase in the productivity of Barbarossa's imperial mint at Aachen also occurred in the 1170s: J. Menadier, "Die Aachener Münzen," *Zeitschrift für Numismatik* 30 (1913), pp. 321–422.

[9] Spufford, *Money and Its Use in Medieval Europe*, p. 97 estimates that the number of circulating pennies in England dropped from approximately 20 million in the year 1000 to only 10 million by around 1158. Thus the cumulative effect was a remarkable halving of the currency available in England.

silver until *c.* 1300, and it was joined by similar finds in central Europe to fuel the expanding economy of the late twelfth and thirteenth centuries.[10] Silver was even found in England at Beer Alston (Devonshire) in 1262. Although German miners were brought in and later the Frescobaldi took over the mine, it proved too expensive and unproductive to maintain. Yet it did for a time add to the expansion of English coinage in the thirteenth and fourteenth centuries.[11]

This revived silver supply led quickly to a new generation of coins in the late twelfth and thirteenth centuries, but they were products of a differing system of minting than before. The so-called era of regional pfennigs had begun in Germany, which mirrored the fragmented system of feudal mints in France. As a result of the Investiture Struggle imperial control over German bishops – many of whom administered imperial mints – was weakened. These mints were therefore appropriated by both secular and ecclesiastical princes and coins were increasingly produced with varying quality.[12] Hence the value of pfennigs depended on the place of production: the new Freiberg silver had thus entered a politically fragmented Germany and the result was the growth of regional currencies.

Amid the multiplicity of coins coming from feudal mints in Germany, the mint at Cologne proved to be exceptional in quality. While other German coins remained debased throughout the twelfth and thirteenth centuries (some had begun this slide as early as the tenth and eleventh centuries) the Cologne pfennig retained its weight and fineness. Revitalized with Freiberg silver, the archiepiscopal mint produced vast numbers of Cologne pfennigs, and the high quality of the specie made it the dominant coin in the Rhineland – from Frankfurt to the North Sea – throughout the thirteenth century.[13]

Meanwhile in England the newly established Norman kings had

[10] Other primary silver mines were at Freisach (Carinthia), Iglau (on the border of Bohemia/Moravia), and the Hungarian mine of Schemnitz. The Italians also had discovered silver at Monteri (Tuscany).

[11] Spufford, *Money and Its Use in Medieval Europe*, pp. 124–7.

[12] Julia Barrow, "German cathedrals and the monetary economy in the twelfth century," *Journal of Medieval History* 16:1 (March, 1990), p. 25: "Overall there were 215 mints in Germany in 1197, 106 of which were in church ownership and only 28 in royal control; of the 106 ecclesiastical mints, 61 were in episcopal hands."

[13] Spufford, *Money and Its Use in Medieval Europe*, p. 195: "The new silver of Freiberg can thus be seen . . . in the pfennigs of Philip of Heinsberg as Archbishop of Cologne. The pfennigs that he had minted there in the 1170s were the first to be struck at Cologne in considerable quantities since those of St. Anno in the 1070s. As early as 1174 it was possible for Philip of Heinsberg to mortgage the income from his mints for a year for 1000 marks. Dr. Elisabeth Nau has suggested that this implies an annual output of at least 13,000 marks, reckoning on a maximum seigniorage of 1 shilling per mark. In terms of actual coins struck this meant a minimum of 2 million pfennigs a year. From negligible activity to 2 million pfennigs a year is a remarkable

maintained centralized control over the Anglo-Saxon royal mints. After the brief period of feudal mints under Stephen's confused reign, the Angevin king Henry II reformed the mints in order to reestablish both royal authority and the high standards of English coinage. He was aided in this by the increasing quantities of silver available in England from the 1170s – much of which had passed through Cologne from Freiberg – and thereby coin production in England also rose dramatically from the 1180s onward. Thus by the middle of the twelfth century the strongest and most widely accepted coinages in northern Europe were the Cologne pfennig and the English sterling, both of which had maintained their original weight and purity after the long years of economic stagnation.[14]

Henry's reform of English currency in 1158 reveals yet again the important commercial link between England and Cologne. The new English cross-and-crosslets coinage issued in this year was based no longer on the old Roman weight-standard but rather on the French troy weight.[15] This meant that the English monetary or "Tower" mark now weighed 233g and the sterling penny about 1.46g. The Flemish assumed the troy standard also because of their growing French and English commercial contacts. More significantly, the Cologne mint began to use the Tower mark as its standard mark by 1170[16] because of expanding commercial ties with England.[17] Cologne increased the size of its mark from 12 shillings to 13 shillings and 4 pence, while keeping the individual pfennigs the same weight. Linking the fineness of their coins to the English standard made exchanging currency on a par with the sterling possible. Thus the two most valuable coins in northern Europe were kept virtually identical in weight and purity throughout this period.

Because foreign coins were not allowed to circulate legally in England, we have little direct evidence of the flow of Cologne currency

transformation, and surviving coins suggest that the high level of mint activity that began so suddenly in the 1170s continued unabated at Cologne until the end of the thirteenth century."

[14] Ibid., p. 105: "Taking a view right across Europe, the heaviest coinages on the eve of the great expansion of the late twelfth century were the sterling pennies of England and the pfennigs of Cologne weighing 1.4 grams each, of silver 92% fine."

[15] No doubt Henry's continental revenues were collected in troy-weight coins, and so the king was regularizing the currency throughout his lands.

[16] Hävernick, *Der Kölner Pfennig im 12. und 13. Jahrhundert*, pp. 48–51.

[17] Nightingale, "The evolution of weight-standards," p. 207: "The weight-standards of Cologne also show the effect of the monetary changes in England. By 1170 Cologne had adopted as its magna marca the English Tower mark of 160 sterlings weighing 233g. In 1157 and 1175 Henry II granted special trading privileges to Cologne merchants in England, and it appears that Cologne adopted the Tower mark because the fineness and slightly heavier weight of its pennies meant that they could be exchanged in England on par with the sterling."

to the island.[18] But the presence of the English sterling penny in the Rhineland and Westphalian regions can clearly be demonstrated. Indeed its high value led to some interesting activities on the part of German merchants and mints.

English sterling circulated widely enough in the Low Countries and northern Germany by the early thirteenth century to become an accepted means of exchange, even rivaling the regional standard, the Cologne pfennig.[19] Its form was copied by many princes of the region: the duke of Brabant, and the counts of Flanders, Holland, and Luxembourg to name the most important, all imitated the English sterling.[20] Some of these were honest coins in weight and fineness and easily distinguishable as derivatives independent from genuine English sterlings, but there also existed fraudulent copies lacking in either weight or fineness and produced only for the profit of the issuer. Throughout the thirteenth century imitation sterlings were deliberately struck on the continent rather than being sent across the channel to England as whole silver ingots.[21]

The cities of lower Saxony, the Netherlands, and Westphalia in particular were quite active in imitating the English sterling. Already in the eleventh century Stade fashioned its coin after the English penny, and thereafter virtually identical derivatives appeared in Lüneburg, Goslar, Dortmund, and Deventer.[22] In 1210 the Westphalian episcopal

[18] There is very little Cologne or Westphalian material that has been found in England except for Westphalian imitative issues in small amount. The Vintry material, though not yet properly listed, contains only three pieces of Cologne or Westphalian provenance (two of these being cut halves). I gratefully acknowledge my debt to Dr. Barrie Cook of the British Museum, Dept. of Coins and Medals, for this information. See also Ian Stewartby, "German imitations of English short-cross sterlings," *The Numismatic Chronicle* 155 (1995), p. 221.

[19] Hävernick, *Der Kölner Pfennig im 12. und 13. Jahrhundert*, pp. 108–9, esp. p. 109: "Allmählich [in the Low Countries during the thirteenth century] wird aber der denarius coloniensis durch die Konkurrenz des Sterlings zurückgedrängt sein" and Peter Berghaus, "Das Münzwesen," in *Hanse in Europa. Brücke zwischen den Märkten 12.–17. Jahrhundert. Ausstellungskatalog des Kölnischen Stadtmuseums 9. Juni–9. Sept. 1973* (Cologne, 1973), p. 74: "In seinem Wert entsprach er [English sterling] fast genau dem weithin beliebten Kölner Pfennig, dessen Währungsregion sich wohl beiderseits des Niederrheins erstreckte und auch bis nach Westfalen hinein reichte, der aber auch gern für weiträumige Geldtransaktionen benutzt wurde und sich bis nach Ungarn hin verfolgen läßt."

[20] For a survey of the eras of sterling circulation see Peter Berghaus, "Die Perioden des Sterlings in Westfalen, dem Rheinland und in den Niederlanden," *Hamburger Beiträge zur Numismatik* 1 (1947), pp. 34–53 and Peter Berghaus, *Westfälische Münzgeschichte des Mittelalters*, 2nd edn., Landesmuseum für Kunst und Kulturgeschichte (Münster, 1986).

[21] Spufford, *Money and Its Use in Medieval Europe*, p. 162 note 1. Ian Stewartby's article, "German imitations of English short-cross sterlings," documents very well the sizeable volume and skillful craftsmanship of these forgeries, and concludes: "many of [these] until recently have deceived modern numismatists almost as successfully as they must have deceived their medieval users" (209).

[22] Berghaus, "Das Münzwesen," p. 73.

town of Münster minted a derivative of an English short-cross sterling that even bore on one side the inscription HENRI ONLUNDE. (Henri of London, that is, an English master minter).[23] Soon thereafter Henri's name was replaced with MONASTERIUM, and derivative short-cross types were also minted at Herford, Schwalenburg, Vlotho, Wiedenbrück, and Wildeshausen. A similar variety was minted at Dortmund, whose style in turn was copied by Arnsberg, Bentheim, Hamm, Herford, Iserlohn, and Schüttorf. Still others were fashioned at Osnabrück, Pyrmont, Lippstadt, and Lemgo, on whose coins even the logo LONDON CIVTAS appeared.[24]

The actual circulation of short-cross sterlings in the Low Countries, Westphalia, and the Rhineland was very limited, according to evidence found in both hoards and documents.[25] Yet in Westphalia (rather than the Low Countries, as the above-mentioned mints indicate) imitations were plentiful, especially during the 1230s to 1240s.[26] The equivalent value of the sterling and the Cologne pfennig helps explain this, since those Westphalian mints which produced derivative imitations operated on the heavy Cologne weight-standard and yet wished to avoid the political and legal ramifications of copying the coinage of the powerful archbishop.[27] Hence they chose the familiar and reliable sterling as an exemplar. The close integration of the sterling and Cologne pfennig during the short-cross period is also illustrated by the fact that sterlings are always found in the company of Cologne pfennigs in German hoards, and even in those as far away as Croatia and Romania.[28]

The 1247 English coinage reform, which replaced the short-cross with long-cross sterlings, reduced such imitations from Westphalia, though the short-cross variety continued to be produced for some years thereafter along with Scottish and Irish sterling imitations.[29] Few long-

---

[23] Ibid., p. 76.   [24] Ibid., p. 76.

[25] G. P. Gittoes and N. J. Mayhew, "Short-cross sterlings from the Rotenfels hoard," *British Numismatic Journal* 53 (1983), p. 23; W. Jesse, "Der Münzfund von Hildesheim vergraben um 1260," *Hamburger Beiträge zur Numismatik* 2 (1948), pp. 16–48.

[26] Ian Stewartby, "German imitations of English short-cross sterlings," pp. 210–11: "most of the better short-cross copies come from Westphalia."

[27] N. J. Mayhew, "The circulation and imitation of sterlings in the Low Countries," *Coinage in the Low Countries (800–1500)*, ed. N. J. Mayhew, B.A.R. International Series, 54 (Oxford, 1979), p. 55 and Gittoes and Mayhew, "Short-cross sterlings from the Rotenfels hoard," p. 24. The earliest coins of Lemgo, for example, imitated the Cologne pfennig in the early thirteenth century, but by the 1230s sterling had become the standard for imitation: H. Ihl, *Die Münzprägung der Edelherrn zur Lippe. Münzstätte Lemgo* (Lemgo, 1991), pp. 13–14.

[28] Gittoes and Mayhew, "Short-cross sterlings from the Rotenfels hoard," p. 22 and Appendix 2; N. J. Mayhew and B. H. I. H. Stewart, "The sterling element in the 1898 Ostrovo hoard," *The Numismatic Chronicle* 144 (1984), pp. 173–79; and Peter Ilisch, *Münzfunde und Geldumlauf in Westfalen im Mittelalter und Neuzeit* (Münster, 1980), p. 37 note 197.

[29] Ihl, *Münzprägung*, p. 16.

cross derivatives were minted in western Westphalia once the circulation of the real English sterling rapidly expanded there by the middle of the century.[30] Instead, the center of long-cross derivative production shifted to Brabant and other territories of the Low Countries, with no intentionally deceptive copies produced.[31] The long-cross style was copied in the eastern Westphalian cities of Bielefeld, Vlotho, Lemgo, and Helmarshausen, and clearly to the point of forgery in Lippstadt.[32] These forgeries were produced as a source of income for the small mints[33] and eventually for use in long-distance trade with England. Weighing on average about 10 percent less than the English sterling, they assured the bearer a positive balance of trade.[34]

While imitation may be the sincerest form of flattery, the additionally insincere practice of overstriking Westphalian derivative sterlings with counterfeit English dies – complete with the names of different English mints on their reverses – was apparently a common practice. These overstrikes are evidence that English money was widely used in the region by at least 1205.[35] Probably these forgeries were struck for use in England, and were employed to avoid losses in currency exchange. It appears that some German mints even took to including coins of English type as part of their regular production in order that overstriking could be avoided altogether.[36]

Such a growth in copying sterlings obviously caused great difficulties in England by the midpoint of the thirteenth century. Edward I's new

---

[30] For a more detailed history of this region's economic relations with England see Emil Dösseler, *Südwestfalen und England: mittelalterliche und frühneuzeitliche Handelsbeziehungen* (Münster, 1989).

[31] Mayhew, "The circulation and imitation of sterlings in the Low Countries," p. 57.

[32] Paul Weweler, "Lippische Sterlinge," *Festschrift zur Feier des 25jährigen Bestehens des Vereins der Münzforscher und Münzfreunde für Westfalen und Nachbargebiete*, ed. K. Kennepohl (Münster, 1938), pp. 41–53 and Ihl, *Münzprägung*, p. 18.

[33] Mayhew, "The circulation and imitation of sterlings in the Low Countries," p. 57: "It has to be remembered that when sterlings were struck in remote areas, their manufacture was an important business in itself. We are so used to looking at coins as evidence of trade that we forget their manufacture and marketing was a trade in itself . . . Forgeries seem to have been produced mostly in areas with little economic importance of their own. Such backwaters attracted silver only by offering accurate sterling copies at substantially less than sterling prices."

[34] Ihl, *Münzprägung*, p. 18.

[35] Ian Stewart, "Some German coins overstruck with sterling types," in *Lagom. Festschrift für Peter Berghaus zum 60. Geburtstag am 20. November 1979* (Münster, 1981), p. 208. The presence of English money in the region may have been the result of John's subsidy of 6,000 marks in support of Otto IV in 1207, much of which made its way to Cologne: see S. Rigold, "The trail of the Easterlings," *British Numismatic Journal* 26 (1949), p. 39.

[36] Stewart, "Some German coins overstruck with sterling types," p. 210: "A foreign merchant buying English wool would have suffered an exchange loss if he used German coin, even though it was of the same standard as the English, since foreign coins were not permitted to circulate in England and so had to be reminted. It would therefore have been to his advantage to pay in English coin or, if he did not have it, to pay in coin of English type designed to deceive the recipient. He would thereby save the loss on exchange."

penny in 1279 and recoinage of over £250,000 of foreign silver from 1299 to 1302 eliminated a whole series of these crockards and pollards, but many others continued to circulate until the middle of the four-teenth century.[37] In 1299 Edward I was even moved to order the sheriffs of London to prevent German merchants from unloading foreign goods, falsely labeled as German wares, by night or to sell them without prior inspection. This was done not only to prevent the German merchants from avoiding toll charges but also to stop the importation of *mala moneta*.[38]

The merchants of Cologne, many of whom had metallurgical skills because of their involvement with the episcopal mint (the most productive mint in Germany), were apparently notorious for such counterfeiting. Cologne artisans were widely known for their work as both goldsmiths (the street Untere Goldschmied still remains in Cologne today) and coin manufacturers. Some enterprising expatriates brought this skill with them to England and employed it in the importation and manufacture of forged English coins.

In 1252, for example, three Cologners were charged with forgery and were cast into the Tower of London, but their ingenuity apparently aided them also in finding an undetermined means of escape.[39] The same charge was leveled against Gocelin of Cologne, who publicly confessed before the London Eyre in 1276 that he was a forger. He was smart enough, however, to take sanctuary in St. Paul's Cathedral beforehand and was thereupon allowed to abjure the English realm.[40] The Red Book of the Exchequer even contains a distinction made during the reign of Henry III between *Colonnenses legales* and *Colon-nenses falsi*, with the former worth twice as much as the latter.[41] The imitating and/or forging of English pennies was thus so widespread in the districts of Cologne and Westphalia by the early thirteenth century that even Otto IV – the nephew of the Plantagenet kings Richard and John and the Welf claimant to the imperial throne – had such coins

---

[37] Mavis Mate, "Monetary policies in England 1272–1307," *British Numismatic Journal* 41 (1972), pp. 34–79; Mayhew, "The circulation and imitation of sterlings in the Low Countries," pp. 54–8 and *Sterling Imitations of Edwardian Type* (London, 1983). A total of just over 60 million Edwardian-types were minted as a result.

[38] *Munimenta*, II, 1, pp. 196–7; *HUB*, I, pp. 439–40 no. 1306 (May 26, 1299).

[39] *CCLR Henry III*, VII, p. 277: "Rex perdonavit Johanni de Plessetis comiti Warr' et constabulario Turris Lond' excapium Jordani de Colon', Johannis de Colon', Hereberti de Colon', nuper detentorum in gaiola predicte Turris pro fabricacione false monete" (November 14, 1252).

[40] *The London Eyre of 1276*, ed. Martin Weinbaum, London Record Society, 12 (London, 1976), p. 4 no. 11: "Gocelin de Colon' took sanctuary in the church of St. Paul's, London, confessed that he was a forger of money and abjured the realm before the chamberlain and sheriffs. No chattels."

[41] *The Red Book of the Exchequer*, ed. Hubert Hall, RS, 99 (London, 1896; rpt. 1965), III, p. 979.

struck, as did his rival Frederick II after the Staufer's victory over Otto.[42] Lord Stewartby has even identified a German short-cross imitation which shares enough common features with a coin from the first Ribe hoard reading *Sancta Colonia* to conclude that they were possibly produced by the same die-sinker.[43]

With the high popularity and availability of the English pennies in northern Germany by the middle of the thirteenth century, it should not be surprising to find the sterling in Cologne. In fact, coinage from all over Germany as well as from England, France, Italy, and Hungary passed through the city during this time.[44] Hävernick accurately dated the regular appearance of the English sterling in the city by at least the 1260s (that is, in the long-cross period).[45] But what is surprising is the extent to which the English sterling was used as payment for local and even intra-familial property transactions. Archival documentary evidence for this activity does not appear until the 1260s, yet by that time sterling pennies appear to have been as acceptable as the Cologne pfennig as a means of payment within the city itself.

In one of the most remarkable passages of the municipal Schreinsbücher,[46] for example, a beguine confirmed before a parish court in 1266 that she had sold her interest in a quarter part of her familial house to her sister in exchange for a yearly rent (*census*) of 1 mark and 6 pence, which was to be paid in English pennies (**1**).[47] What use a Cologne beguine would have had for English currency remains unclear, but this was not an isolated case.[48] In 1297 Peter de Houberg transferred his ownership of a house to his two brothers, with the provision that either he or his brothers would in the future purchase the *domus* above this house from beguines who were dwelling there. The buying price set by the beguines was "infra 60 marcas vel 50 marcas novorum Angliensium

[42] Rigold, "The trail of the Easterlings," pp. 31–55.

[43] Stewartby, "German imitations of English short-cross sterlings," p. 233.

[44] *Die Kölner Schreinsbücher des 13. und 14. Jahrhunderts*, ed. Planitz and Buyken, pp. 15*–16*. Until 1258 merchants arriving in Cologne had to take their silver to the archiepiscopal mint for exchange, but thereafter this monetary-exchange monopoly was abandoned by the archbishops and foreign currency was allowed to circulate in the city: Hävernick, *Der Kölner Pfennig im 12. und 13. Jahrhundert*, pp. 21–3.

[45] Hävernick, *Der Kölner Pfennig im 12. und 13. Jahrhundert*, p. 132.

[46] The *Schreinsbücher* are the municipal records maintained by the parish courts during this period, and are so called since they were placed in a box or chest (*Schrein* or *scrinium*) for safe keeping. See Manfred Groten, "Die Anfänge des Kölner Schreinswesens," *JKGV* 56 (1985), pp. 1–21.

[47] Bold numbers in brackets refer to entries in the appendix to this chapter (pp. 57–63).

[48] Concerning the very large beguine population in Cologne see Johannes Asen, "Die Beginen in Köln," *Annalen* 111 (1927), pp. 81–180; 112 (1928), pp. 71–148; 113 (1929), pp. 13–96; Frederick Stein, "Einige Bemerkungen zu J. Asens 'Die Beginen in Köln,'" *Annalen* 178 (1976), pp. 167–77; Frederick Stein, "The Religious Women of Cologne 1120–1320" (unpublished dissertation: Yale University, 1977).

denariorum vel tantum pagamenti" (**2**). Once again we have a case of rather entrepreneurial beguines whose currency activities tied them to an economy far beyond the walls of their beguinage. Incidentally, the use of the adjectives *novorum* and *bonorum* appear in descriptions of the English sterling from 1286 onward, which must refer to the coinage reforms of Edward I in 1279 and 1299 as well as the proliferation of sterling imitations by this date.

It was a common practice in Cologne to sell a house in exchange for a yearly rent (*census*) to be drawn from the dwelling, with the rent always paid in Cologne currency. Yet there is a case in 1277 in which Walter the Carpenter was expressly asked to pay his rent in English pennies (**3**). Walter and his wife sold the house shortly thereafter, but the rent was continued to the original owner in English pennies (**4**). In order to liquefy their assets for investment purposes Cologne merchants would also often mortgage houses in exchange for a yearly rent. Such transactions appear in the court documents which request payment in English money (**5**). Even the local clergy sought payment in sterling (**6**). Frequently these mortgages carried a clause which allowed the original owner to redeem the mortgage through a future lump-sum payment. These redemption payments are also recorded in English currency (**7**). Not only did Cologners mortgage their houses, they also mortgaged rents from houses. Here too we find English sterling used as redemption money, even though the original rent was paid in Cologne currency (**8**).

Both the mortgaged rent of 1292 (**8**) as well as another property transaction in 1287 (**9**) contain puzzling references to English *monnaie noire*. *Monnaie noire* was generally debased continental coinage (*niger denarius* as opposed to *albus denarius* or *monnaie blanche*) which only circulated within the city of its origin for small-scale purchases of daily necessities, and had little value even for exchange between the city and its surrounding countryside.[49] However, unlike most other European countries at the time, all English money was of fine silver.[50] Perhaps these references to "nigrorum Angliensium [bonorum] denariorum" are two independent scribal errors; however, they might also refer to the farthings and half-pennies that Edward I had minted in 1279 and 1280, which served the same purpose in England as *monnaie noire* did on the continent. Henricus Quattermart appears in the 1292 transaction as the purchaser, and his merchant family was one of the most wealthy and powerful patrician dynasties in Cologne. The Quattermart merchants

---

[49] Spufford, *Money and Its Use in Medieval Europe*, pp. 379, 386–7.
[50] I thank E. M. Besly for this clarification.

were very active in Anglo-Cologne trade and thus would have found use for such coins during their frequent stays in the port cities of England.[51] If this latter scenario is correct, the acceptability of these petty foreign coins hundreds of miles away from their original provenance is most peculiar and hard to explain. The impossibility of exchanging foreign pennies (the modern equivalent of *monnaie noire*) in one's own country these days after returning from a holiday trip abroad reminds us of the unique status English coinage apparently enjoyed in Cologne.

English currency also appears in estate settlements between Cologne family members. In a mutual agreement in the year 1274, a dower was established for Arnold de Muntabure's wife Elizabeth of 100 marks to be paid in English pennies (**10**). In another case a son received a house from the estate of his deceased father, but in exchange he had to pay the executors 50 marks of English sterling in order to take possession of the dwelling (**11**). Finally, in a rather complicated series of entries, we find another disposition of property among family members (**12**). Hubert Grin and his wife Cristina received yearly payments from Hubert's brothers, John and Ludolf, for their respective one-third shares in the family house known as Bergerhausen,[52] and these payments were made in English currency. John and Ludolf (and their respective families) were able to redeem these rents within five years by paying a large lump sum of money, again in English pennies. Ludolf redeemed his 30-shilling rent (or 1 mark, 18 shillings) in two installments during the next two years, and John redeemed his 1-mark rent in one payment within the same time frame. The fact that Cologne families used English currency for exchanges *between themselves* shows the remarkable extent to which the sterling was accepted in Cologne. The reverse was never the case in London or England in general.

We are fortunate that some of the passages in the Schreinsbücher also include exchange equivalencies between English, Cologne, and other currencies. In 1286 a rent of 18 Cologne shillings was allowed to be redeemed either by English pennies or the *gros tournois* (**13**). Here we learn that the English penny was accepted in Cologne at the standard rate of 3 sterlings to the *gros tournois*.[53] There are also entries which indicate the ratio between sterlings and Cologne pfennigs. In 1292

---

[51] For a prosopographical reconstruction of the Quattermart family see Friedrich Lau, "Haus Quattermart zu Köln," *Annalen* 20 (1869), pp. 218–48, and Friedrich Lau, "Das Kölner Patriziat bis zum Jahre 1325," *MSAK* 26 (1895), pp. 134–6.

[52] For the genealogy of this family see Lau, "Das Kölner Patriziat bis zum Jahre 1325," *MSAK* 25 (1894), p. 381.

[53] Mayhew, "The circulation and imitation of sterlings in the Low Countries," p. 56 indicates this as the standard rate of exchange in the Low Countries.

Theoderic de Kalle and his wife mortgaged two houses to a cathedral canon for 75 marks of Cologne pfennigs, and were able to redeem the mortgage after six years either with 75 marks of Cologne pfennigs, or with English pennies at an equal exchange, or with the *gros tournois* at 3 pfennigs to one French coin (**14**). Once again the exchange ratio of the *gros tournois* was 3:1, and the English penny was accepted on a par with the Cologne pfennig. Similar passages with a 1:1 exchange ratio between Cologne and English currency also occur elsewhere; however, they contain the phrase *de gratia* or *cum gratia*, which may indicate that this was an exceptional favor being done (**15**).

The most convincing evidence that the English penny was accepted in the city on a par with the Cologne pfennig comes from July 26, 1275.[54] On this date the municipal government of Cologne borrowed 1,530 marks in English pennies from nine merchants and gave them the *Malzpfennig* tax as collateral until the loan was repaid by installments. The government officials promised as well that if the Cologne pfennigs used in repaying the loan were of lesser value than the original English sterling they would make up the difference. Hence this entire transaction of the Cologne municipal government was based on English currency, which was treated as equal to the Cologne pfennig.[55] We also discover that there was a sizeable amount of English currency on hand among the Cologne merchant families to make such a loan.

Two passages from the 1290s give additional information concerning the value of the English sterling among other German currencies. In 1293 Lambert de Botyn purchased half of the *domus Blankenberg* for a rent of four marks, which was to be paid by various individuals. One person was to pay a yearly rent of 2 marks either from Cologne pfennigs or the *gros tournois* at the usual 3:1 ratio, or pfennigs from Schwäbish Hall (known as the Heller)[56] at a 4:1 ratio, or English pennies again at

---

[54] *Ennen/Eckertz*, III, pp. 80–2 no. 109: "1530 marcas sterlingorum bonorum et legalium, duodecim solidis pro marca qualibet computatis . . . et quamdiu denarii monete coloniensis peiores fuerint quam sterlingi, defectum valoris supplebimus et ad valorem sterlingorum reducemus."

[55] Most of the nine Cologne merchants (Daniel Jude, Bruno Hardevust, Matthew de Speculo, Cuno de Cornu, Franco de Cornu, Theoderic de Cerva, Gerard Quattermart, Henry Quattermart, and Philipp Quattermart) came from patrician families who had commercial ties with England and appear in English sources. Hence they would have had plenty of English sterling on hand. Cf. Hävernick, *Der Kölner Pfennig im 12. und 13. Jahrhundert*, p. 46 note 38: "Die Gleichheit vom englischen Sterling und Kölner Denar ist wiederholt bezeugt."

[56] "Der Heller" from Schwäbish Hall circulated as widely as Bohemia and Cologne in the late thirteenth century and was commonly used as a half-pfennig since it contained half as much silver as the Cologne pfennigs. Concerning the "Heller" and its circulation in the Rhineland see Hävernick, *Der Kölner Pfennig im 12. und 13. Jahrhundert*, pp. 161, 183, 194–201; E. Nau, "Münzen und Geld in der Stauferzeit," *Zeit der Staufer*, ed. R. Haußherr (Stuttgart, 1977), III, p. 97; F. von Schrötter, ed., *Wörterbuch der Münzkunde* (Leipzig, 1930; rpt. 1970), pp. 259–61;

the same rate as the Cologne pfennigs (**16**). In 1298 John de Kannus and his wife Druda mortgaged half of a house and half of an adjacent apple orchard, which were to be redeemed by the feast of Pentecost for 200 marks of Cologne pfennigs. This was a very expensive piece of real estate (**17**). John and Druda could also use other currency at the following exchange rates: 7 Cologne pfennigs to the *gros tournois*, or 2 black *gros tournois* for every Cologne pfennig, 1 English sterling for 9 Cologne farthings,[57] the Heller of Schwäbish Hall at equal value, or 1 Brabantiner for 7 Cologne farthings. These exchange rates are favorable to foreign currency from France or Brabant, but the ratio between the English penny and the Cologne pfennig favors the pfennig. Agreements reached concerning foreign currency were negotiated at varying rates and probably reflect the commercial interests and regional activities of the recipient of the payments. In this latter case we may have found a merchant whose commercial interests were directed more toward France and Brabant than England.

But we can say that the English sterling was consistently accepted at a 1:1 ratio to the Cologne pfennig. Given the 1275 *Malzpfennig* transaction, we also know that this was the case even before the defeat of the archbishop by the burghers of Cologne in the Battle of Worringen (1288), which had a negative impact on the stability of the *denarius Coloniensis*. We can also certainly conclude that the English penny enjoyed a remarkable circulation in Cologne and was as acceptable a means of exchange as the Cologne pfennig itself. There was enough English currency in Cologne as early as 1214 for Archbishop Adolf of Altena to send 500 marks to Rome "bonorum novorum et legalium sterlingorum" instead of Cologne coinage.[58]

The extensive use of English currency in Cologne and its environs raises the question: how did all this currency get there? Trade with England alone cannot completely account for such volume, as German merchants returned from the island with more English goods than sterling. The flow of silver specie actually went in the opposite direction, namely to England as payment for the export goods. German merchants certainly received English coins as payment for the goods they brought there, but much of this was used to purchase English wool and other items since foreign currency could not circulate on the island

---

and N. Klußendorf, *Studien zu Währung und Wirtschaft am Niederrhein vom Ausgang der Periode des regionalen Pfennigs bis zum Münzvertrag von 1357*, Rheinisches Archiv, 93 (Bonn, 1974), pp. 182–8.

[57] Farthings (*quadrans*) and half-pennies (*obolus*) were also minted for local use in Cologne at least from 1150 onward: see E. Ennen, "Kölner Wirtschaft im Früh- und Hochmittelalter," I, p. 144.

[58] *UGN*, II, pp. 24–5 no. 47; *REK*, III, 1, p. 23 no. 124 (February 1214).

kingdom. The lengths individuals went to in order to imitate, forge, and overstrike currency to make it appear like English sterling suggests that German merchants' desire for the sterling outstripped their own ability to obtain it in sufficient amounts as individuals. There was, therefore, an additional impetus to the spread of English currency in the Low Countries and Germany: the political payments of the English monarchs.

Throughout the twelfth and thirteenth centuries a series of massive payments were sent from the English kingdom to Germany as a result of political and diplomatic initiatives. When we add up the amounts of silver sent from England into Germany alone because of (1) the 1114 marriage of the emperor, Henry V, and the English princess, Matilda,[59] (2) Richard I's ransom,[60] (3) Richard's pensions to German princes after his release,[61] (4) the financial support of the Welf Otto IV by both his uncles, Richard I and John of England,[62] (5) the 1235 marriage of the emperor, Frederick II, and the English princess, Isabella,[63] (6) Richard of Cornwall's quixotic kingship in Germany,[64] and (7) Edward I's anti-French alliance project with German princes from 1294 to 1298,[65] we get the ponderous total of over £355,000 or some 532,500 marks of silver. If this amount were actually paid in sterling, (some was surely paid in bullion) it would have totaled 85.2 million pennies. This is a very conservative estimate, and of course it does not take into consideration inflation during the nearly two hundred years covered here; yet the sheer number of pennies that were sent helps to explain why English currency was circulating so thoroughly in northern Germany and the Low Countries. Since English sterling was of such

[59] 10,000 marks (£6,667).

[60] 150,000 marks (£100,000). See Heinrich Fichtenau, "Akkon, Zypern und das Lösegeld für Richard Löwenherz," *Archiv für Österreichische Geschichte* 125 (1966), pp. 11–32.

[61] Approximately £4,000. This figure cannot be accurately determined since the surviving financial records are spotty for this period. It is particulary uncertain whether rents were always paid annually or continued after Richard's death. This amount is based on Austin L. Poole's article, "Richard the First's alliances with the German princes in 1194," and other evidence of payments.

[62] At least £40,000 and certainly more. John spent some 40,000 marks of silver (over £26,000) to pay for the Bouvines campaign alone: see Hugo Stehkämper, "Geld bei deutschen Königs-wahlen des 13. Jahrhunderts," in *Wirtschaftskräfte und Wirtschaftswege 1: Mittelmeer und Kontinent. Festschrift für Hermann Kellenbenz,* ed. Jürgen Schneider (Bamberg, 1978), p. 110 and Georges Duby, *Le Dimanche de Bouvines* (Paris, 1973), p. 39.

[63] 30,000 marks (£20,000).

[64] 28,000 marks (£18,667) for his election, and untold amounts for his perambulations through Germany and for gifts to the German nobility (we are unable to include these payments in our calculation but Richard was said to have poured out this money like water): N. Denholm-Young, *Richard of Cornwall* (Oxford, 1947), p. 89; Stehkämper, "Königswahlen," pp. 96–8.

[65] At least £165,000 alone in Germany. For the additional payments to the Low Countries and elsewhere, see Michael Prestwich, *Edward I* (Berkeley, 1988), pp. 399–400.

high quality it was not melted down for reminting, but rather was used over and over again as a means of exchange. Therefore its circulation in Germany was long-lived.[66]

These vast English subsidies flowed in the opposite direction from the regular movement of silver from Germany into England. In fact the English kingdom enjoyed such an overwhelming advantage in the balance of trade – namely, silver in exchange for wool and other exports – that it could not only afford such expenditures but could also recover from such drain of silver in a very short period of time.[67] Therefore these diplomatic investments functioned as an impetus for renewed circulation of the German silver which had come to England, and as such they played a significant role in the economy of silver in northern Europe.

So did the city of Cologne, the leader among German cities in the realm of interregional commercial relations with England in the pre-Hanseatic period. The unique economic ties between the two can be seen in several ways. Cologne was the central and directing force behind the early development of Anglo-German trade, and continued to play an important role (though no longer unique) during the Hanseatic era. Its merchants enjoyed unparalleled monopolistic trade privileges in England, which were not equaled by other German merchants until the middle of the thirteenth century. They thereby played a key role in the return of sterling specie to England, along with various continental imitations. The uniform weight and purity of the English sterling and the Cologne pfennig, along with the coordinated weight-standards of their respective mints, made these two coins the most acceptable and circulated currency within the northern commercial world. They shared common areas of circulation and their forms were copied by others in the Low Countries, Rhineland, and Westphalia. The use of English coins in Cologne, even for payments between local family members, the clergy, and religious individuals, and for petty cash transactions shows just how closely interwoven the economies of the city and England were. Both the flow of German silver into England in exchange for wool and other goods, and the reciprocal outflows of this silver from England as a result of political payments functioned as a major stimulus to the growing northern European economy and circulation of specie. Both streams of silver passed through Cologne at one point or another. Commercial activity

---

[66] Spufford, *Money and Its Use in Medieval Europe*, pp. 160–1.

[67] Ibid., p. 391: "Many of these very sterlings, exported for political reasons, returned to England by way of trade, unfortunately accompanied by large numbers of their continental imitations."

had so interpenetrated and linked England and Germany before the Hanseatic era that bootleg versions of the sterling were a widespread phenomenon and a devout beguine could be assured that her inheritance stipend was based on sound foreign currency. Such was the fabric of this significant interregional nexus.

Appendix: Schreinsbücher *manuscript entries*

(1) Historisches Archiv der Stadt Köln (hereafter HASK) Schreinsbuch 1 Saphiri (St. Martin parish), fol. 25r: "Notum sit tam futuris quam presentibus, quod Agnes dicta de Fossa Porta acquisivit sibi iure hereditario erga sororem suam Aleidim, becginam, quartam partem domus et aree, que dicitur ad Fossem Portam, site ex opposito cappelle sancte Norburgis pro annuo censu unius marce et sex denariorum Angliensium denariorum [*sic*] solvendorum in festo pasche vel infra quatuor septimanas postea ad longius: tali captione, quod si dicta Agnes dictum censum aut eius heredes in dicto termino non persolverint Aleidi, becgine predicte, alia quarta pars dicte hereditatis dicte Agnetis cedet sorori sue Aleidi cum sua prescripta quarta parte libere et absolute et sine aliqua contradictione. Actum anno Domini 1266."

(2) HASK Schreinsbuch 17 Eckardi A (St. Martin parish), fol. 24r: "Notum sit, quod Petrus dictus de Houberg tradidit et remisit Johanni et Frederico fratribus, cognatis suis, domum et aream sitam ex opposito ecclesie Sancti Martini, que vocatur domus Corduwenarii, ante et retro subtus et superius, prout ibi jacet et sicut in sua habebat proprietate: ita quod ipsi Johannes et Fredericus fratres predictam domum iure et sine contradictione optinebunt, potestate tamen predicto Petro reservata istud mutandi in vita sua, si voluerit. Actum anno Domini 1297. Et sciendum, quod, si predictus Petrus non comparaverit domum unam beckinis commorantibus super predicta domo Corduwenarii ad manendum infra 60 marcas vel 50 marcas novorum Angliensium denariorum vel tantum pagamenti, tunc predicti fratres Johannes et Fredericus eam comparabunt pro denariis supradictis ad manendum eisdem, et antea non exibunt beckine predicte, potestate tamen reservata predicto Petro istud mutandi in vita sua, si voluerit." The text is also published in *Die Kölner Schreinsbücher des 13. und 14. Jahrhunderts*, ed. Hans Planitz and Thea Buyken, PGRG, 46 (Weimar, 1937), p. 439 no. 1634.

(3) HASK Schreinsbuch 299 Lata Platea (Airsbach), fol. 30r: "Notum, quod Welterus Carpentarius et Aleydis uxor sua acquisiverunt sibi domum unam cum area hereditarie sitam ex opposito cimiterii sancti Johannis iuxta domum vocatam ad Latam Ianuam superius erga

Johannem dictum Schalle et Engilradem uxorem suam singulis annis pro xv solidis Angliensium denariorum, medietatem in festo Omnium Sanctorum vel post infra quatuor septimanas sine captione solvendam. Quod si adinplere [*sic*] ipse Welterus et Aleydis predicti neglexerint dictum censum non solvendo terminis predictis, mittentur dicti Johannes Scallo et uxor sua in proprietate hereditatis predicte per sentenciam scabinorum, ita quod iure et sine contradictione obtinebunt" (1277).

(4) HASK Schreinsbuch 299 Lata Platea (Airsbach), fol. 33r: "Notum, quod Gobelinus de Henerischem et Methildis uxor sua emerunt sibi domum unam cum area sitam supra Latam Plateam ex opposito cimiterii Sancti Johanni iuxta domum vocatam ad Latam Ianuam superius erga Walterum Carpentarium et Aleydis uxorem suam, prout Welterus et Aleydis uxor sua predicti habuerunt in sua proprietate et possederunt. Salvis Johanni dicto Schallo et Engilradi uxori sue xv solidis singulis annis solvendis Angliensium denariorum."

(5) HASK Schreinsbuch 299 Lata Platea (Airsbach), fol. 31r: "Notum, quod Johannes dictus Abelline et Methildis uxor sua inpignoraverunt domum suam cum area sitam super Latam Plateam iuxta domum Compostere superius versus Sanctum Johannem Philippo Rufo dicto Hartvust pro septem marcis Angliensium denariorum solvendis in festo beati Johanni Baptiste" (1277).

(6) HASK Schreinsbuch 299 Lata Platea (Airsbach), fol. 29v: "Notum, quod Arnoldus sacerdos inpignoravit sive exposuit duas domus sitas sub uno tecto in platea Lata iuxta domum Widonis superius versus Sanctum Johannem Hermanno de Cluele et Henrico de Leopardo pro quinquaginta marcis Angliensium denariorum infra festum beati Martini nunc venturum redimendis" (1277).

(7) HASK Schreinsbuch 290 Porta S. Pantaleonis (Airsbach), fol. 36v: "Notum, quod Hermannus et Theodericus, fratres, filii Engelberti Ligatoris Vasorum, emerunt sibi tertiam partem domus et aree site in platea Filtrorum iuxta domum vocatam Muntabur, que fuit mansio Engelberti predicti, erga Nicolaum, fratrem ipsorum, et Gertrudem, uxorem suam, tali conditione, quod, si Nicolaus predictus tertiam partem predictam retinere voluerit, quod illam reabebit a festo beati Johannis Baptiste ad sex anno pro 13 marcis Angliensium denariorum. Si vero reabere noluerit, tunc Hermannus et Theodericus, fratres predicti, dabunt Nicolao, fratri ipsorum predicto, 5 marcas Anglienses et retinebunt tertiam domus et aree predicte absque omni contradictione" (1275). The text is also published in *Die Kölner Schreinsbücher*, ed. Planitz and Buyken, pp. 202–3 no. 837.

(8) HASK Schreinsbuch 80 De super muros (St. Alban parish), fol.

10r: "Notum sit tam presentibus quam futuris, quod Henricus dictus Quattermart et Aleydis uxor sua, emerunt sibi erga Tilmannum dictum de Irco et Engilradem uxorem suam marcam unam census Coloniensium denariorum de quarta parte domus et aree vocate ad Gigantem site in Bovenmure, tali conditione, quod predicti Tilmannus et Engilradis reemere poterunt predictam marcam pro sedecim marcis nigrorum Angliensium denariorum cum censu predicto infra festum beati Remigii proximum futurum vel infra quator septimanas postea. Quod si non fecerint, habebunt predicti Henricus Quattermart et Aleydis uxor sua unam marcam Coloniensium denariorum hereditarii census solvendam de quarta parte domus predicte eisdem singulis annis in festo beati Remigii vel infra quator septimanas postea sine captione. Quod si dictum censum predicto termino solvere neglexerint, predicta quarta pars domus et aree predicte ad ipsos Henricum et Aleydem uxorem suam devolvetur libere et absolute divertere poterunt, quocumque voluerint. Datum crastino beatorum apostolorum Symonis et Jude [October 29] anno Domini 1292." The text is also published in *Die Kölner Schreinsbücher*, ed. Planitz and Buyken, p. 339 no. 1311.

(9) HASK Schreinsbuch 290 Porta S. Pantaleonis (Airsbach), fol. 50r: "Notum sit, quod Constantinus de Ecclesia Lisolfi et Rigmudis uxor sua emerunt sibi erga Everardum predictum et Gertrudem, filiam suam, et Wilhelmum, maritum eius, contra quemlibet nonam partem domus et aree dicte Juliacum site in Ripa pro quinque marcis et sex solidis nigrorum bonorum Angliensium denariorum tali apposita condicione, quod predicti Everardus et Gertrudis, filia sua, et Wilhelmus, maritus eius, reemere poterunt pro quinque marcis et sex solidis predictorum denariorum et pro sex solidis datis ad scribendum infra festum beati Johannnis Baptiste proximum futurum. Quod si non fecerint, cedent predicte due nove partes hereditatis predicte predictis Constantino et Rigmudi libere et absolute et divertere poterunt quocumque voluerint. Datum anno Domini 1287 in vigilia beati Gregorii."

(10) HASK Schreinsbuch 315 Generalis (Airsbach), fol. 6r-v: "Notum, quod Arnoldus dictus de Muntabure et Elizebet [*sic*] uxor sua, que quondam fuit filia Henrici dicti Schoneweder, inter se concordaverunt, quod ipsa Elizabet predicta dedit Arnoldo marito suo predicto liberam potestatem omnes hereditates quas ipse habet Arnoldus et de cetero est habiturus et omnia mobilia que habet et est habiturus divertendi, ad quamcumque voluerit manum, sine omni contradictione. Et si Arnoldus decessit sine prole, tunc ipsa Elizabet uxor sua predicta habebit in bonis ipsius Arnoldi centum marcas Angliensium denariorum et ultra nichil, nisi sit de ipsius Arnoldi predicti bona et libera voluntate. Si vere Arnoldus et Elizabet uxor sua inter se prolem vel proles genuerint, ipse Arnoldus habebit liberam potestatem dandi uni puere et alteri minus de bonis suis pro sua voluntate. Set si Arnoldum predictem contingat ingredi viam universe carnis et Elizabet Arnoldum supravivat et ad secundas nuptias transire noluerit, tunc ipsa Elizabet sedebit cum pueris suis et utetur bonis puerorum quamdiu sedere et esse voluerit cum pueris ipsius. Et si pueri ipsius Elizabet in vita ipsius decesserint, tunc ipsa Elizabet predicta habebit centum marcas Angliensium predictas tantum pro sua portione et omnia alia sua bona mobilia et hereditates . . . omnes habebit potestatem liberam divertendi, ad quamcumque voluerit manum et si bona sua alicui in vita sua non . . . gaverit seu donaverit, cederet ad proximos suos heredes" (1274).

(11) HASK Schreinsbuch 168 Campanarum (St. Columba parish), fol. 36v: "Item notum, quod Ingebrandus de Wederhane, filius Ingebrandus, et Druda uxor eius tradiderunt et remiserunt Johanni, fratri ipsius Ingebrandi, domum cum area, ante et retro suptus [*sic*] et superius, que quondam fuit mansio Alberti dicti Kolnere sitam in Platea Sancti Columbe omni iure, quo ipsi eam habent. Ita si ipse Johannes infra festum nativitatis Domini proximo nunc venturum quinquaginta marcas bonorum Angliensium denariorum non pagaverit sive persolverit Franconi de Cornu, Hildegero dicto Schoneweder, Franconi de Reno et Ingebrandi fratri suo, executoribus testamenti quondam Ingebrandi de Wederhane, quod dicta domus omni iure, quo ipsi Ingebrandus et Druda eam habent, ad dictos executores testamenti sit libere sit libere [*sic*] devoluta, quod divertere possit, quocumque voluerint. Actum . . . anno Domini 1300."

John apparently did not come into his inheritance until three years later, when he was able to make the payment to the executors: HASK Schreinsbuch 168 Campanarum (St. Columba parish) fol. 39v: "Notum, quod, quia Johannes, filius quondam Ingebrandi de Wederhane, reemit sibi erga Franconem de Cornu, Hildegerum Schoneweder, Franconem de Reno et Ingebrandi fratrem ipsius pro quinquaginta marcis bonorum Angliensium denariorum domum, que quondam fuit Alberti dicti Kolnere sitam in Platea Sancti Columbe cum area, ante et retro subtus et superius, ita quod eandem domum, prout iacet, omni iure, quod prius habuit, optinebit et divertere poterit, quocumque voluerit. Salvo censu hereditario. Actum crastino beate Katherine anno Domini 1303."

(12) HASK Schreinsbuch 162 Lata Platea (St. Columba parish), fol. 73v: "Notum, quod predicta divisione concordatum, quod Johannes dictus Grin predictus cum uxore sua Richmude solvent singulis annis hereditarie dicto Huperto Grin et Cristine eius uxori de sua tercia parte domus et curie de Berghusen predicte contigue capelle sancti Apri

unam marcam Angliensium denariorum solvendam singulis annis in festo nativitatis beati Johannis Baptiste, quatuor septimanas post sine captione. Quod si neglexerint, quod ipsa tercia pars ipsorum Johannis et Richmudis dicte domus et curie ipsis Huperto et Cristine libere sit devoluta, quod divertere poterunt, quocumque voluerint. Et sciendum, quod ipsi Johannes et Richmudis dictam marcam Angliensium infra V annos, qui currere incipient in festo nativitatis beati Johannis Baptiste, reemere poterunt cum xvIII marcis denariorum Angliensium. Actum ut supra. Notum, quod Ludolphus Grin et pueri sui solvent hereditarie dicto Huperto Grin et Cristine eius uxori de sua tercia parte domus et curie de Bergerhusen, videlicet media tercia parte, xxx solidos Angliensium singulis annis in festo nativitatis beati Johannis Baptiste, quatuor septimanas post sine captione. Ita si ipsum terminum neglexerint, ipsa tercia pars predicta ad ipsos Hupertum et Cristinam eius uxorum libere devolvitur, quod divertere possunt, quocumque voluerint. Et sciendum, quod ipsi Ludolphus et pueri sui ipsos xxx solidos infra quinque anno, qui currere incipient in festo nativitatis beati Johannis Baptiste, reemere poterunt cum quadriginta quinque marcis denariorum Angliensium. Actum ut supra" (1301).

HASK Schreinsbuch 162 Lata Platea (St. Columba parish), fol. 76v: "Notum, quod Ludolphus dictus Grin et pueri sui reemerunt sibi erga Hupertum dictum Grin et Cristinam eius uxorem xvIII solidos bonorum Angliensium denariorum de triginta solidis Angliensium, pro quibus tercia pars ipsorum Ludolphi et puerorum suorum curie et domus de Bergerhusen fuerat et est obligata. Ita quod ipsi Ludolphus et pueri sui optinerunt et diviserunt ipsorum xvIII solidos, quocumque voluerint. Actum crastino Symonis et Jude anno ut supra" (1302).

HASK Schreinsbuch 162 Lata Platea (St. Columba parish), fol. 77v: "Notum, quod Johannes dictus Grin de Bergerhusen et uxor eius Richmudis reemerunt sibi erga Hupertum dictum Grin et Cristinam eius uxorem unam marcam Angliensium denariorum, quam eis solvere consueverunt de tercia parte domus et curie de Bergerhusen sitam versus sanctam Apram in Lata Platea. Ita quod ipsi Johannes [dictam expugned] et Richmudis dictam marcam in dicta domo et curia, seu tercia parte earundem, optinebunt et divertere poterunt, quocumque voluerint liberam et solutam. Acto anno Domini 1303."

HASK Schreinsbuch 162 Lata Platea (St. Columba parish), fol. 77v: "Notum, quod Ludolphus dictus Grin et pueri sui reemerunt sibi erga Hupertum dictum Grin et Cristinam eius uxorem unam marcam Angliensium denariorum de triginta solidis Angliensium denariorum, pro quibus tercia pars curie et domus de Bergerhusen fuit obligata. Ita quod ipsi Ludolphus et pueri sui dictam marcam in dicta tercia parte et curie et domus de Bergerhusen optinebunt et divertere poterunt, quocumque voluerint. Actum ut supra" (1303).

(13) HASK Schreinsbuch 299 Lata Platea (Airsbach), fol. 36r: "Item notum sit, quod idem Wilhelmus et Agnes (uxor) sua reemere poterunt predictos decem et octo solidos Coloniensium denariorum hereditarii census erga Henricum dictum Eszmenger et Hildegundem uxorem suam, infra festum beati Johannis Baptiste proximum nunc futurum vel infra sex septimanas postea sine captione pro decem et nonem marcis novorum Angliensium denariorum vel quolibet magno Turonense semper computato pro tribus novis Angliensibus denariis. Quod si reemerint, solvent predicto Henrico et Hildegundi expensas factas ab eis secundum veritatem circa hereditatem predictam. Datum anno Domini 1286 in die beati Lamberti [September 17]." This text is also published in *Die Kölner Schreinsbücher*, ed. Planitz and Buyken, p. 361 no. 1379.

(14) HASK Schreinsbuch 324 Wetschatz (Airsbach), fol. 9r: "Notum sit, quod Theodericus dictus de Kalle et Hadewigis, uxor sua, posuerunt in pignore Hermanno dicto Scherfgin, canonico Resensi, domum vocatam Kalle sitam in Buttegasse et domum vocatam Bickilsten sitam in Lata Platea cum omni iure, sicut eas habebant in eorum proprietate, pro 75 marcis Coloniensium denariorum alborum et ponderosorum. Tali apposita conditione, quod predicti Theodericus et Hadewigis, uxor sua, predictas duas domus redimere potuerunt transactis sex annis continuis proximis et non prius pro predictis 75 marcis Coloniensium denariorum vel novorum Angliensium denariorum vel magnorum Turoniensium denariorum de Francia, quolibet magno Turonensi denario pro tribus denariis Coloniensibus computato" (Febuary 1, 1292). The text is also published in *Die Kölner Schreinsbücher*, ed. Planitz and Buyken, p. 624 no. 2136.

(15) HASK Schreinsbuch 168 Campanarum (St. Columba parish), fol. 28r: "Item notum, quod Johannes dictus de Porta et Druda uxor eius predicti acquisiverunt sibi erga Johannem, Richmudim et Belam, fratrem et sorores dicte Drude, aliam dimidietatem domus predicte, que fuit mansio Henrici Stillekin patris eorundem, et aree, ante et retro subtus et superius, pro viginti et septem solidis Coloniensium denariorum – seu bonorum Angliensium de gratia in festo nativitate beati Johannis quatuor septimanas post sine capcione singulis annis solvendis. Tali capcione, quod si dictum terminum neglexerint, dicta dimedietas simul cum alia dimidietate, quam dicti coniuges ad hoc obligaverunt, ad prefatos pueros Johannem, Richmudim et Belam libere devolventur sine contradictione, quocumque voluerint, divertende. Actum anno Domini 1293 in crastino nativitatis beati Johannis Baptiste."

HASK Schreinsbuch 179 Clericorum (St. Columba parish), fol. 50v:

"Item notum, quod Wilhelmus et Greta uxor eius acquisiverunt sibi erga Thilmannum dictum Cleyngedanc et Durginim eius uxorem medietatem unius domus et aree, ante et retro subtus et superius, prout iacet in cymiterio beate Margarete et retro, protendit ex opposito murum urbis, pro xv solidis bonorum Coloniensium denariorum vel Angliensium cum gratia solvendis singulis annis: XIII solidis in festo nativitatis beate Virginis et VIII solidis in festo annuntiatoris" (1300).

(16) HASK Schreinsbuch 179 Clericorum (St. Columba parish), fol. 40v: "singulis annis duas marcas Coloniensium denariorum alborum iusti ponderis debiti, seu magno Turonense pro tribus denariis Coloniensium, quatuor Hallensibus pro uno denario Coloniensium, seu novo Angliensium pro Coloniensium denariorum numerandis" (1293).

(17) HASK Schreinsbuch 168 Campanarum (St. Columba parish), fol. 34v: "Item, quod Johannes dictus Kannus et Druda uxor eius tradiderunt et remiserunt Franconi de Cornu militi et Philippo dicto Quattermart medietatem domus dicte Walkinberg site in termino campanarum, que fuit ansedil quondam Gerardi de Gluele et E. uxoris eius, prout iacet cum area, ante et retro suptus [sic] et superius et ex iusta cadere potest divisione; item medietatem pomerii siti ex opposito dicte domus, salvo censu hereditario utriusque iure suo. Ita tamen, quod ipsi Johannes et uxor eius Druda vel pueri sui vel Herbordus, frater dicti Johanis [sic], medietatem dicte domus et medietatem dicti pomerii infra festum Pentecosten reemere poterunt et in illa die pentecosten tota cum duocentis marcis denariorum Coloniensium usualium, videlicet grosso Turonense pro septem denariis, novo Angliense pro nonem quadrantibus, uno Hollense pro denario, duobus nigris Turonensibus pro uno denario, uno Brabantino pro septem quadrantibus. Ita [sic] scripti Johannes et uxor eius vel pueri sui vel Herbordus, frater dicti Johannis, medietatem dicte domus et pomerii infra festum Pentecosten non reemerint, ut dictum est, quod ad ipsos Franconem et Philippum sint libere devoluta, quod divertere possint, quocumque voluerint, salvo censu hereditario. Et sciendum, quod ipse Franco et Philippus dictas medietates domus et pomerii ipsi Johanni et D. vel pueris eorum vel Herbordo predictore remittere poterunt, cum eas reemerint ut est dictum, absque eorum uxoribus, que eis super hoc dederunt potestatem. Actum sabbato post oculi anno Domini 1298."

Part II

Anglo-Cologne family, property, and inheritance ties

The historical context of the Central Middle Ages has now been set. Cologne's preeminent place in the flourishing of Anglo-German commercial relations is undoubted, and served as a foundation for all other interregional contacts between Cologners and the English. Now we turn to the equally intensive and interesting social relations between these two communities. The surviving records reveal some remarkable activities of both Cologners in England and the English in Cologne. In both cases these began at a very early date. We begin with the English in Cologne, since their social relations have hitherto remained unreconstructed from the municipal records of the city. The new prosopographical information that emerges requires a revision of the generally accepted view that, while the Germans emigrated and traveled to England for commercial purposes, the English did not establish equivalent personal contacts in Germany until much later in the Hanseatic era. We shall then look in more detail at the nature of Cologner activity in England in order to complete our comparative study of Anglo-German expatriate communities. In all this the extent of integration between German and English communities proves surprisingly great.

Chapter 4

THE FORMATION OF INDIVIDUAL AND FAMILIAL IDENTITY IN MEDIEVAL COLOGNE: PROPERTY AND SURNAMES

INHERITANCE AND PROPERTY-HOLDING CUSTOMS IN MEDIEVAL COLOGNE

Before a consideration of the evidence on English activity in Cologne, we must say a few words concerning the inheritance and property-holding customs of the city during the Central Middle Ages. An understanding of these customs will make much more intelligible the subsequent prosopographical studies of English families in Cologne, and of the Cologne families that pursued activities in England.[1]

Evidence for the economic and social life of Cologne is contained in the voluminous collection of folios known as the Schreinsurkunden. Begun in the early twelfth century, these municipal documents were originally a collection of entries on individual leaves of parchment (Schreinskarten), which were then replaced sometime between the years 1220 and 1240 by large codices (Schreinsbücher). The entries on these folios contain transactions concerning landed property such as the sale, conveyance, and mortgaging of houses and parcels of land, the distribution of inheritances, and bequests of such properties to religious houses. In addition there are contracts concerning rents, easements, property settlements, dowries, legacies, testaments, gifts, and transfers of property between family members. This rich source of information not only allows the geographical plotting of a family's properties in the city,

---

[1] The appropriate studies on this subject are: Hans Planitz, "Das Grundpfandrecht in den Kölner Schreinskarten," *Zeitschrift für Rechtsgeschichte (germanische Abteilung)* 54 (1934), pp. 1–88; *Die Kölner Schreinsbücher*, ed. Hans Planitz and Thea Buyken, pp. 6–17; Hermann Conrad, *Liegenschaftsübereignung und Grundbucheintragung in Köln während des Mittelalters*, Forschungen zum Deutschen Recht, 1: 3 (Weimar, 1935); Clemens Graf von Looz-Corswarem, "Hausverkauf und Verpfändung in Köln im 12. Jahrhundert," *Zwei Jahrhunderte Kölner Wirtschaft*, ed. Hermann Kellenbenz, Rheinisch-Westfälisches Wirtschaftsarchiv zu Köln (Cologne, 1975), I, pp. 195–204. For an excellent study of Cologne's urban institutions of government see Paul Strait, *Cologne in the Twelfth Century* (Gainsville, 1974).

but also the prosopographical reconstruction of entire families and their social and economic connections.

Originally the Schreinsurkunden served only as an additional witness to transactions which were enforced by the memory of those who participated in the affair. However, by around 1200 they became the constitutive legal record of transactions and could be used as evidence in court – in fact the actual court decisions were then inscribed in these books. The parish *Amtleute* preserved the documents in a chest (*scrinium, Schrein*) in the parish churches, hence the name, while the archiepiscopal *scabini* (*senatores*, or jurors) kept their own similar collection. The Schreinsurkunden tell us a great deal therefore about the landholding and inheritance practices of the city.

The land law of Cologne (*Bodenrecht*) protected private property *(ius proprietatis)*, and assured that the nearest heirs possessed an equal right of inheritance (*Wartrecht*). Therefore children inherited directly, unless they renounced their legal claim to the property (*effestucatio*) in favor of other family members. Landed property was held in common by both married partners, yet the surviving spouse only retained usufruct of a portion of the property as a pension while ownership passed to the children. According to Cologne land law each child, irrespective of gender, received an equal portion of their parents' property. This could lead to extremely small inheritance portions in a large family, for example when six children inherited their one-sixth portion and then seven children of one of these six original siblings later inherited one-seventh of their parent's portion, thus leaving each grandchild with a one-seventh part of one-sixth of a house. Such mathematical night-mares could theoretically continue throughout subsequent generations. In actuality, however, an elder sibling (or a third party) would gradually buy up each inheritance portion and restore a unified owner-ship of the house, parcel of land, rent, or whatever the inheritance might be.

Often the children would transfer their inheritance portions to the widowed parent (in most cases the wife) in order to provide for their parent's maintenance. The widow, once she held legal ownership, could then liquidate properties to obtain an income. When the marriage produced no children the surviving spouse had outright ownership. There are a number of cases in which a widowed woman brought her children to court in order for them to legally transfer the family's property into her hands in preparation for its sale. In addition, family members would transfer properties among themselves as gifts or purchases, and so the records allow us to identify virtually all family members over several generations and what properties each held.

The mortgaging of houses and of rents from properties was a popular practice among the patrician merchants in Cologne as a quick means of raising capital for trading ventures. The city's mortgage law (*Grundpfandrecht*) allowed for this practice, which circumvented the forbidden business of usury and at the same time allowed the owner to extract wealth from his properties without losing ownership of them.[2] Mortgages were usually arranged for a short period of time, usually a year or less.[3] During this period the creditor could reside in the house and enjoy usufruct of the property. Once the mortgage was redeemed, the original owner regained usufruct of the property. If he was late in making the established redemption payment (or payments) a penalty was imposed; and if he remained in default on the loan after this, the property was forfeited into the hands of the creditor. But whenever the creditor chose to sell this forfeited property the former owner held the right of repurchasing it, so as to recover his real estate. All sorts of property were mortgaged in this way, from houses (and portions thereof) to rooms, movable goods, merchants' booths and tables, and so forth. Payments on these mortgages were usually made in money, although there are many cases in which payments were made in kind (chickens, swine, salt, and pepper for example).

Another means of extracting a steady income from one's estate for investment capital while avoiding the loss of direct ownership was through rental agreements. A sizeable amount of income could be assembled by renting out a number of properties, from single rooms to entire houses. The renters in turn enjoyed the right of dwelling in these properties and could even bequeath this right to others. The owners would often sell or mortgage these rents to other parties in order to raise additional capital, so a house could have one owner of the property and several other owners of its rents. Ownership of the various rents was continually bought, sold, or mortgaged by whoever possessed them, and was legally separate from the ownership of the building itself. Hence one could sell or mortgage the house without affecting the ownership of the rents, and vice versa. In all cases the owner of the building held the option of buying back all of the rents he/she had sold. Raising capital through a series of rents was safer than mortgaging the entire property, whereby one risked foreclosure and complete loss of ownership. The only limitation was that it proved a slower means of accumulating money for further investment.

---

[2] von Looz-Corswarem, "Hausverkauf und Verpfändung in Köln im 12. Jahrhundert," I, p. 196.

[3] There were cases, however, in which the time period was extended over a number of years.

Family, property, and inheritance ties

To participate in these types of community transactions one had to be at least twenty years of age, or be represented in court by a legal guardian (*tutor, mundiburnus*). Women actively participated in these landholding practices and were often before the court seeking confirmation of such arrangements. All disputes arising from these types of settlements, as well as the legal constituting of these transactions, were adjudicated in the parish courts (*Schöffengericht*) and then inscribed in the Schreinskarten and later in the Schreinsbücher. These entries were thereafter used as legally binding documents when future disputes or mutually agreed upon revisions were adjudicated.

The Schreinsurkunden are also filled with testaments enrolled by husbands. These wills often indicate that the husband's settlement of his estate was made with the cooperation and consent of his wife, who was provided for along with the children of the marriage. One might be surprised by the extent of female initiative and participation in these legal proceedings, and especially so when they were members of English expatriate families. The details of familial property dealt with in the testaments do not stop at real estate, but include moveable goods right down to the kitchen utensils.

Such were the property holding and inheritance customs of Cologne during the eleventh to thirteenth centuries, which served as the basis for all property transactions in the city. As such they will help elucidate the following prosopographical studies of various English families in Cologne and their activities as recorded in the Schreinsurkunden.

THE FORMATION OF ENGLISH SURNAMES IN COLOGNE

Cologne has long been known for the creative and humorous surnames borne by members of its medieval patrician class. Names like Overstolz, Hardevust, Schönweder, Gir (*Gier, avarus*), Cleingedank (*subtili mente* or *parvi mentes*), and Ungemaz (*immoderatus*) to name but a few, perhaps indicated unique family characteristics exhibited in their shrewd business practices. With such attention to creating surnames based on a personal characteristic (even to the extent of surnames like Jungfrau), one has to ask how foreigners were identified – especially in legal documents like the Schreinsurkunden. In particular, what should we make of the numerous references to individuals and families styled *de Anglia* and *Anglicus*? A brief linguistic study is necessary to answer these fundamental questions.

Although the presence of expatriate English in Cologne has been noted by historians in the past, no systematic investigation ever resulted.[4] This is curious, because there are numerous entries in the Schreinsurkunden which document the activities of families styled *Anglicus* or *de Anglia*. The daunting number of folios to be read in order to extract all entries mentioning these families and the uncertainty concerning the toponymic name *Anglicus* has kept any scholar thus far from attempting this task. The first problem required a lengthy time spent in archival work, which has now been done.[5] The second problem, which has caused not a little confusion, requires detailed consideration in order to clear up a few misconceptions.

The adjectival surname *Anglicus* is a less well-defined surname than the toponymic *de Anglia*, a clearer indicator of one's origins, and therefore has been interpreted by scholars to mean different things. In the case of such families in Cologne the name has previously been taken to mean a Cologne family that had English trading ties. One need only recall Bede's legendary account of St. Gregory's mission to England to consider another confusion possible because of the play on the words *anglicus/anglus* and *angelicus/angelus*.[6] In fact the same double meaning occurred in the German language of the time[7] and even survives today in contemporary German.[8] Some of the modern dictionaries of

[4] Stehkämper, *England und Köln*, p. 10: "Im 12. und bis zur Mitte des folgenden Jahrhunderts beherrschten die Kölner den englischen Fernhandel fast ungestört . . . Umgekehrt lassen sich auch im Köln des 12. Jahrhunderts – laut Schreinskarten – nicht wenig Engländer nachweisen." Also E. Ennen, "Kölner Wirtschaft im Früh- und Hochmittelalter," I, pp. 124–6: "Viele Kölner Einwohner waren neu zugezogen oder wohnten erst in der zweiten oder dritten Generation in dieser Stadt. Aus unvollständigen Unterlagen hat Hektor Ammann eine Karte über die Zuwanderung nach Köln im 12. Jahrhundert entworfen; das Bild, das sie bietet, stellt ein Minimum der Reichweite und Dichte des bürgerlichen Einzugsbereichs dar . . . Mehrfach erscheint der Zuname »von England« oder »Engländer«, einmal erscheint ein Mann aus Ipswich . . . Dieser Herkunftsbereich stimmt überein mit den Ergebnissen der Handelsgeschichte Kölns im gleichen Zeitraum, ja, er ergänzt unsere noch unvollständige Kenntnis der damaligen Kölner Handelsbeziehungen."

[5] For the period under study here I consulted the unpublished Schreinskarten and all of the Schreinsbücher folios from the beginning to *c.* 1310. This was composed of roughly 2,700 folios, on which were approximately 36,000 entries.

[6] Bede, *Venerabilis Bedae Historia Ecclesiastica Gentis Anglorum*, ed. Joseph Stevenson, Publications of the English Historical Society (London, 1838; new edn. 1964), I, p. 97: "Rursus ergo interrogavit, quod esset vocabulum gentis illius; responsum est, quod Angli vocarentur. At ille, 'Bene,' inquit, 'nam et angelicam habent faciem, et tales Angelorum in coelis decet esse coheredes.'"

[7] Karl Schiller and August Lübben, *Mittelniederdeutsches Wörterbuch* (Bremen, 1875), I (A–E), p. 663: "engelsch, adj. angelicus. Darna wart en sang gesungen van den engelnschen tungen . . . engelsch, engels, adj. anglicus. De enghelschen Koplude . . . eyn enghels schip . . ." and August Lübben, *Mittelniederdeutsches Handwörterbuch* (Leipzig, 1888), p. 96: "engelsch, englisch (angelicus und anglicus)."

[8] Harold T. Betteridge, *Cassell's German-English Dictionary* (New York, 1978), p. 186: "²englisch, adj. (Poet.) angelic(al); (Eccl.) der englische Gruß, the Annunciation, Angelic Salutation, Ave Maria."

medieval Latin follow this dual meaning for *Anglicus*,[9] while others attribute various additional meanings.[10] A few more specialized dictionaries, however, render *Anglicus* clearly as denoting a person of English origin.[11]

Studies of surnames have been done that also confirm *Anglicus* as a toponymic surname indicating someone's English heritage.[12] In no cases are non-English persons mentioned who bear the surname *Anglicus*. Benjamin Z. Kedar's brief summary of views concerning toponymic surnames concludes, "As a rule, however, surnames of this type may be considered to denote the origin of the bearer, or of his immediate ancestors."[13] He cautions, however, that toponymic names ending in -us (e.g. *Anglicus*) are less certain to have been a legal proof of origin than those with the preposition *de* (i.e. *de Anglia*).[14] So where does this adjectival form *Anglicus* appear as a surname in the sources?

Anglicus can be found in English sources too often to count: it appears from Domesday Book[15] to the Curia Regis, Hundred, Assize, Patent, and Coroners Rolls to name just a few places.[16] In many cases they are

---

[9] Albert Blaise, *Dictionnaire Latin-Français des Auteurs de Moyen Age* (Turnholt, 1975), p. 47: "I. anglicus, pour angelicus II. anglicus, des Angles, des Anglais" or J. W. Fuchs, *Lexicon Latinitatis Nederlandicae Medii Aevi* (Amsterdam, 1971), Fasc. 1 (A–B), col. A347: "anglicus, vid. angelicus." Oddly J. F. Niermeyer, *Mediae Latinitatis Lexicon Minus* (Leiden, 1984) does not include an entry for "anglicus."

[10] Albert Sleumer, *Kirchenlateinisches Wörterbuch* (Limburg, 1926), p. 110: "Anglicus, englisch; pellis anglica = englisches Leder" or Otto Prinz, *Mittellateinisches Wörterbuch* (Munich, 1967), I (A–B), p. 642: "Anglicus -i m. (Anglia) genus nummi Britannici – englisches Geldstück" – this repeats Charles Du Fresne, sieur Du Cange, *Glossarium and scriptores media et infima Latinitatis* (Frankfurt am Main, 1710), I, p. 252 and Laurentius Diefenbach, *Supplementum Lexici Mediae et Infimae Latinitatis conditia Carolo Dufresne Domino Du Cange* (Frankfurt, 1857), p. 35.

[11] Wilhelm Beelmans, *Wörterbuch für den Rheinischen Sippenforscher*, Hilfsbücher zur westdeutschen Familien- und Sippenforschung, 2 (Cologne, 1939), p. 14: "Anglicus, a, um, Anglus, a, um – Engländer"; or Marianus Plezia, *Lexicon mediae et infimae Latinitatis Polonorum*, Academia Scientarum Polona (Cracow/Warsaw/Wroclaw, 1953–8), p. 516: "Anglicus, -a, -um (Anglia) angielski, qui ex Anglia est"; or R. E. Latham, *Revised Medieval Latin Word List* (London, 1965), p. 20: "Anglicus a. 1087–c. 1450 = English, Englishman"; or R. E. Latham, *Dictionary of Medieval Latin from British Sources* (London, 1975), I (A–B), pp. 85–6: "Anglicus, English, Englishman, Englishwoman . . . 1087: sic permixte sunt nationes, ut vix decerni possit hodie, de liberis loquor, quis Anglicus quis Normannus sit genere (Dial. Scac. I 10B)."

[12] For example Gösta Tengvik, *Old English Placenames*, Nomina Germanica. Arkiv für Germansk Namnforskning utgivet av Jöran Sahlgren, 4 (Uppsala, 1938), p. 130: "Lat. anglicus (anglus) 'Englishman (English),' perhaps equivalent to OFr engleis 'English' . . . the reduced variant anglus . . . Anglicus might be opposed to Normannus 'Norman' "; and C. L'Estrange Ewen, *A History of Surnames of the British Isles. A Concise Account of their Origin, Evolution, Etymology and Legal Status* (London, 1931), p. 144: "A possible explanation of this description is that Englishmen going abroad, acquired the name and afterwards returning to their native land, retained it. Anglois and Anglais are common in France and N. Italy."

[13] Benjamin Z. Kedar, "Toponymic surnames as evidence of origin: some medieval views," *Viator* 4 (1973), p. 123.

[14] Ibid., p. 127.   [15] Tengvik, *Old English Placenames*, p. 130.

[16] L'Estrange Ewen, *A History of Surnames of the British Isles*, p. 144.

recorded in the context of activity on foreign soil or with foreigners. For example, a certain Henricus Anglicus de Cadamo (Caen) was transporting wine on behalf of the bishop of Saintes in 1226;[17] in 1230 Johannes Anglicus was among the "homines Galonis senescalli de Nauntes";[18] in 1211 a Walterus Anglicus was given funds for a trip to Normandy on behalf of the king;[19] and in 1198–9 a certain *magister* Garinus Anglicus was the archdeacon of the diocese of Rouen while Rodbertus Anglicus and Herbertus Anglicus were witnesses to charters of St. Evroul in Normandy.[20] Several bearers of the surname were employed by European monarchs: Willelmus Anglicus de Rothomagensi (Rouen) was given license to bring grain to England by royal edict;[21] Emperor Frederick II employed Gualterus Anglicus and son Wilhelmus Anglicus as falconers;[22] and Hugo Anglicus was a financial administrator in Palermo.[23] The surname also appears often in the transnational affairs of the church: Johannes Anglicus, the Provincial of the Franciscans in Provence, served as papal nuncio in negotiations for papal revenues due from England in 1247.[24] These are only a miniscule sample of the numerous *Anglicus* entries to be found in European sources that have a connection to areas beyond the English island. Taken as a whole the surname functions as a conscious signifier of an expatriate Englishman in the context of relations with a foreign land or a foreign person. As early as the laws of King Aethelred for the city of London a legal distinction between the English and foreigners was made by the use of the adjectival surname, in this case concerning anyone accused of either falsifying money, using false money, or stealing a coin stamp: "Et si aliquis eorum accusetur, sit Anglicus sit transmarinus, ladiet se pleno ordalio."[25] This use of the name to indicate one's status

[17] *CPR Henry III*, II, p. 59: "Mandatum est omnibus baillivis portuum maris et aliis baillivis suis, quod navem Henrici Anglici de Cadamo, carcatam vinis venerabilis patris Xanctoniensis episcopi, quam Henricus Buchard arestavit apud Sanctum Matheum, in quocumque portuum inventa fuerit, sine dilatione reddi faciant Petro Noel, clerico predicti episcopi litteras domini regis deferenti, cum omnibus vinis in ea inventis et captis, ducendis in Angliam quo voluerit, accepta securitate ab ipso Petro et illis, qui navem illam ducunt, quod cum nave illa et cum vinis in ea contentis alibi non divertent quam in terram Anglie, et quod vina illa alibi non vendent."

[18] Ibid., p. 327.

[19] *Rotuli de liberate ac de misis et praestitis regnante Johanne*, ed. Thomas Duffus Hardy (London, 1844), p. 156: "Waltero Anglico eunti in Norm. in nuntium domini Regi 1 M. per episcopum Winton."

[20] *Calendar of Documents Preserved in France* ed. J. Horace Round, (London, 1899), p. 222.

[21] *Rotuli selecti ad res Anglicas et Hibernicas spectantes, ex archivis in domo capitulari Westmonasteriensi depromti*, ed. Joseph Hunter (London, 1834), pp. 29–30.

[22] *Böhmer*, V, 1, p. 530 no. 2857.

[23] *Böhmer*, V, 1, p. 513 no. 2664; V, 1, 545 no. 3075.

[24] *Böhmer*, V, 2, p. 1310 no. 7850.

[25] *Die Gesetze der Angelsachsen*, ed. Liebermann, I, p. 234; *The Laws of the Kings of England from Edmund to Henry I*, ed. Robertson, pp. 74–5.

in relation to foreigners fits well with Ewen's theory about the formation of the surname.[26]

For our purposes the most crucial question is: to what extent did the surname *Anglicus* appear in Germany – and in Cologne in particular – between the eleventh and thirteenth centuries? One could continue to cite such well-known men who bore the surname as the canon lawyer Alanus Anglicus[27] and the philosopher/translator Alfredus Anglicus de Sareshel.[28] But was there anyone with the surname, definitely known as an Englishman, who lived in Germany? The answer is yes. Bartholomaeus Anglicus, an English Franciscan who studied in Paris, was active as a teacher at the Franciscan school in Magdeburg around 1230–45.[29] We owe our knowledge of him to his well-known nineteen-volume encyclopedia entitled *De proprietatibus rerum*, in volume 15 of which he describes the Rhine region in great detail.[30] He also describes the county of Kent and Scotland in similar intimate detail in the short chapter 35, perhaps giving a hint of his local English origin. There was never any confusion in Germany or elsewhere concerning the English heritage of the author of this very popular work.

In addition there are many entries in German sources that employ the term *Anglicus* to mean "an Englishman" or "English." Here we cannot present an extensive study but only a representative sample of the widespread occurrence of the surname *Anglicus* in German sources. Manfred's letter to the Romans in May 1265 uses the appellation in the

[26] See note 12 above.

[27] Josef Höfer and Karl Rahner, *Lexicon für Theologie und Kirche* (Freiburg, 1957), I, pp. 265–6: "einer der bedeutenderen klass. Kanonisten. Aus Wales stammend, hat er wohl in Bologna studiert, dann vielleicht in England kanon. Recht gelehrt." He was certainly a teacher at the beginning of the thirteenth century in Bologna and was probably a Dominican.

[28] James K. Otte, "The life and writings of Alfredus Anglicus," *Viator* 3 (1972), pp. 275–92. Alfredus was a major translator of Arabic and Aristotelian texts; he flourished around the years preceding and following 1200 and he probably spent time in Spain. Dr. Otte makes the following conclusions based on Alfredus' surname (p. 281): "Finally, the very form in which Alfred's name appears in the manuscripts – Alfredus Anglicus – proves that he was an Englishman. But, what is more important in our consideration, it proves conclusively that Alfred spent some time in a place other than England."

[29] Höfer and Rahner, *Lexicon für Theologie und Kirche*, II, pp. 9–10: "einer der ersten Enzyklopädisten des MA, gg. Ende des 12. Jh. in Alt-Engl., wahrsch. aus dem adligen Geschlecht de Glanville (lange mit einem Namensgenossen [1360] verwechselt); war Bacclaureus bibl. von Paris, als er 1231 ans Magdeburger Ordensstudium kam. Schrieb die naturwiss. orientierte, viel gelesene Enzyklopädie *De proprietatibus rerum* (wohl 1240–50 beendet)." For the text see *On the Properties of Things: John Trevisa's Translation of Bartholomaeus Anglicus' De proprietatibus rerum. A Critical Text*, ed. M C. Seymour et al., 3 vols. (Oxford, 1975–88).

[30] Josef Giesen, "Köln im Spiegel englischer Reiseschriftsteller vom Mittelalter bis zur Romantik," *JKGV* 18 (1936), pp. 202–3; Anton E. Schönbach, "Des Bartholomaeus Anglicus Beschreibung Deutschlands gegen 1240," *MIÖG* 27 (1906), pp. 54–90.

context of various nationalities.[31] The *Annals of Marbach* record the death of the Venerable Bede in the year 731 using the surname: "Beda presbyter, natione Anglicus, doctor eximius, migravit ad Dominum."[32] The *Annales S. Vincentii Mettensis* call the Norman conquest of England the *Bellum Anglicum*.[33] And in Frederick Barbarossa's letter to Abbot Erleboldus of Stablo concerning the anti-Alexandrine oath allegedly taken by the English envoys in 1165 he repeatedly refers to the Henry II as *Rex Anglicus*.[34]

Closer to home, the venerable *Chronica regia Coloniensis* contains many instances of this surname. The marriage of the Emperor Henry V with Matilda, the daughter of King Henry I of England, is recorded:

Ibi apud Leodium dominus rex Anglici regis filiam honorifice ut regem decet sponsam suscepit,[35]

and

Altera die post epiphaniam, collectis totius regni principibus, nuptias filiae regis Anglici ingenti cum gloria consummat.[36]

In a rather excessive claim made in the joy of imperial victory over Milan in 1161 the chronicler writes,

Scripsit etiam idem rex Greciae regibus Turchiae, Babiloniae, Persidis et Comaniae, nuncians illis, quod Romanus imperator terram suam et illorum occupare intendat, si de Mediolano finem faciat. Idem timebant reges Hispanus, Barcilonensis, Francigena et Anglicus. Sic enim scripserunt eis Ruolandus et cardinales eius, excitantes odium imperatori.[37]

An interesting juxtaposition of *Anglia* and *Anglicus* occurs elsewhere, as the chronicler asserts that imperial intervention brought about a truce between the English and the French in 1187:

---

[31] *MGH Const.* II, p. 565: "Quis Germanicus, quis Yspanus, quis Anglicus, quis Francus, quis Provincialis, quisve cuiuslibet generis, nacionis nobis nolentibus tibi Rome poterit dominari et tui regiminis salubriter ministrare officium ac regimen tui populi et senatus?"

[32] *Annales Marbacenses*, ed. Hermann Bloch, MGH SS rer. Germ., 9 (Hanover, 1907; rpt. 1979), p. 5.

[33] *MGH SS*, III, p. 158. The *Annales Laubiensium* (*MGH SS*, IV, p. 20) contain the following entry for the year 1064: "Willelmus rex Anglicam terram invasit."

[34] *MGH Const*, I, pp. 319–20 no. 225; *Die Urkunden Friedrichs I. 1158–1167*, ed. Heinrich Appelt, *MGH DD*: Die Urkunden der Deutschen Könige und Kaiser, 10: 2 (Hanover, 1979), pp. 401–2 no. 483. "Rex Anglicus" is also used in a similar letter to the cathedral chapter, clerics, and ministerials of the bishopric of Passau, found in Gunther Hödl and Peter Classen, eds., *Die Admonter Briefsammlung*, MGH Epistolae: Die Briefe der Deutschen Kaiserzeit, 6 (Munich, 1983), pp. 151–2.

[35] *CRC*, p. 49.

[36] *CRC*, p. 53. So do the *Annales Corbeienses* (*MGH SS*, III, p. 8): "Nupsit Heinricus V cum maximo regni tripudio filiae Anglici regis."

[37] *CRC*, p. 108.

Regis Angliae Heinrici filius Richardus, mari transmisso, terram regis Francorum Philippi cum copiis suis invasit; unde [idem] rex Francorum opem Friderici Romanorum augusti asciscit; pro cuius metu Anglicus, treugis datis, ab incepto desistit.[38]

Here the name functions clearly as an adjectival appellation indicating Richard's ethnic origin – as exactly as would the surname *de Anglia* or title *Rex Angliae*. *Anglicus* also makes a curious appearance in a letter from Count Hugo of Saint Paul to Duke Henry of Louvain recounting the events of the fourth crusade in 1203, which was later placed into the Cologne chronicle. Here the count tells of how a crusading army was deflected from their plans to reach Jerusalem by Alexius III and headed instead for Constantinople. During the campaign they attacked a heavily fortified castle, in which Englishmen were found among other foreigners as mercenaries:

Inde perreximus ad quandam turrim fortissimam, que Galatha nuncupatur . . . In turri siquidem sepedicta erant sarianti Anglici, Pisani, Ieveniani, Dachi, ad eam servandam et protegendam constituti, qui exibant turrim et introibant sicut et quando volebant ad sagittandum nostros.[39]

This major Cologne source uses the term *Anglicus* with clarity of meaning and always either in the context of the activities of Englishmen with people of other ethnicity. Indeed no confusion appears in the wider German sources concerning the meaning of the name.

This evidence, coupled with the comments of Hugo Stehkämper and Edith Ennen,[40] goes a long way toward clearing up the confusion about the use of the surname *Anglicus* in German and Cologne sources, which until now has been incorrectly explained. In the two fundamental prosopographical studies on Cologne families during the eleventh and the fourteenth centuries the surname has been connected with well-known Cologne patrician families under the unproven assumption that the name indicated the families' involvement in English trade.[41] While English commerce was most certainly a family business in many cases – and Cologners from major local families did bear the surname – the taking of the name *Anglicus* had nothing directly to do with this. In other cases the surname was simply incorrectly applied in these studies to Cologne patrician families, perpetuating the erroneous view that

---

[38] *CRC*, pp. 135–6.   [39] *CRC*, p. 205.   [40] See above note 4.
[41] Lau, "Das Kölner Patriziat bis zum Jahre 1325," *MSAK* 24 (1894), pp. 65–89; 25 (1894), pp. 358–81; 26 (1895), pp. 103–58 and Luise von Winterfeld, *Handel, Kapital und Patriziat in Köln bis 1400*, Pfingstblätter des Hansischen Geschichtsvereins, 16 (Lübeck, 1925). Their contributions to the understanding of the name *Anglicus* will be considered below in the individual cases where the surname occurs in Cologne families.

Anglicus indicated a nickname for families whose members engaged in English trading activities. A close consideration of the actual *Schreinsur-kunden* entries will end this confusion.

Sten Hagström's extensive study of Cologne surnames is also disappointing on this count,[42] primarily because the section covering a full discussion on *Wohnstätten-Beinamen* such as *Anglicus* was never completed.[43] When he does mention the surname it is with reference to an entry in a Schreinsbuch dated 1287, which he takes to be an example of the *Anglicus–Angelus* play on words.[44] Hagström suggests:

Ausgeschlossen ist nicht, dass in dem entsprechenden deutschen Beinamen z. T. ein Rufname steckt. Man beachte das Nebeneinander von Wolteri dicti Anglici und Wolterus dictus Angelus als Bezeichnungen für einen Genter Bürger.[45]

Yet Hagström neglected to refer to two other Schreinsbücher entries concerning the same legal case, which consistently mention a Wolterus *dictus Angelus*.[46] Hence this is nothing more than one instance of a scribal error in which *Anglicus* – a common surname in Cologne – was written by mistake and not the reverse. This occurs nowhere else in the Schreinsbücher and so neither constitutes a precedent for a non-English meaning of the surname *Anglicus* nor serves as evidence that *Anglicus* and *Angelus* were variants of the same surname.

The earliest internal evidence for the surname and its meaning of "Englishman" occurs in Schreinskarten entries concerning a certain Jewish family. The interregional connections of the various Jewish

---

[42] Sten Hagström, *Kölner Beinamen des 12. und 13. Jahrhunderts*, Nomina Germanica, 8 and 16, 2 vols. (Uppsala, 1949–80).

[43] Hagström (*Kölner Beinamen des 12. und 13. Jahrhunderts*, II, p. 89) had planned to discuss the surname *Anglicus* in the forthcoming third volume (Kapitel IV); but such a volume was never finished.

[44] 17 Eckardi A (St. Martin) fo. 21r no. 267: "Notum sit tam presentibus quam futuris, quod Johannes dictus Overstolz et Daniel dictus Judeus miles comparentes in figura judicii ostenderunt, quod Thomas, filius Johannis de Fovea, posuisset eis in pignore ex parte Johannis dicti Minne et Wolteri dicti Anglici, burgensium in Gindavo . . . Et dictavit sententia scabinorum, quod predicti Johannes dictus Minne et Wolterus dictus Angelus ad dictam medietatem conscribi deberent." Text published in *Die Kölner Schreinsbücher des 13. und 14. Jahrhunderts*, ed. Planitz and Buyken, p. 438 no. 1632. References to the unpublished Schreinskarten and Schreinsbücher will appear as they are recorded at the Cologne Stadtarchiv.

[45] Hagström, *Kölner Beinamen des 12. und 13. Jahrhunderts*, II, p. 89.

[46] 31 Vadimoniorum (St. Martin) fo. 5v no. 55: "Item notum sit tam presentibus quam futuris, quod Thomas, filius Johannis de Fovea et Margerete uxoris sue, posuit titulo pignoris Johanni dicto Overstolz de platea Reni et Danieli dicto Judeo militi ex parte Johannis dicti Minne et Wolteri dicti Angeli, burgensium in Gindavo." Text published in *Die Kölner Schreinsbücher des 13. und 14. Jahrhunderts*, ed. Planitz and Buyken, pp. 632–3 no. 2163; and 17 Eckardi A (St. Martin) fo. 21v no. 268: "Item notum sit tam futuris quam presentibus, quod Johannes dictus Minne et Wolterus dictus Angelus, opidani de Gindavo" (dated November 1287).

communities during this period have been well documented, and evidence indicating traffic between the Jewish communities in England and Cologne in particular survives amid reports of the calamitous pogroms of the crusades.[47] In Rabbi Ephraim of Bonn's *Book of Remembrance* the following is recorded in connection with the Second Crusade for the month of August 1146:

In the month of Elul, at the time when Radulf the priest – may God hound and smite him – arrived in Cologne, Simon the Pious, of the city of Trier, returned from England where he had spent some time. When Simon came to Cologne, he boarded the vessel to return to Trier. As he set out from Cologne to board the ship, he encountered worthless persons who had been defiled by the abominable profanation. They entreated him to profane himself [i.e. to be baptized] and deny the Living God. He refused, remaining steadfast in loving and cleaving to his God. Then came persons of brazen face who severed his head from his body by placing it in a winepress and then cast away his pure corpse.[48]

Ephraim records another outbreak on March 17, 1190, probably precipitated by the Third Crusade, which reveals an important connection between England and Cologne:

Später, im Jahre 951,[49] erhoben sich die Irrenden gegen Gottes Volk in der Stadt York in England. Es war am grossen Sabbat, in der Wunderzeit, die sich jetzt zur Bedrückung und Strafe umwandelte. Die Juden waren in das Gebetshaus geflüchtet, hoffend, sich dort schützen zu können . . . Die Feinde rissen die Häuser nieder, plünderten Gold und Silber und die vielen herrlich geschriebenen Bücher, die geschätzter als Gold und Geschmiede ihres gleichen an Pracht und Schönheit nicht hatten; sie brachten dieselben nach Cöln und anderen Plätzen und verkauften sie dort den Juden.[50]

---

[47] See Guido Kisch, *The Jews in Medieval Germany. A Study of their Legal and Social Status*, 2nd edn. (New York, 1970); Robert Chazan, *European Jewry and the First Crusade* (Berkeley, 1987); *Regesten zur Geschichte der Juden im Fränkischen und Deutschen Reiche bis zum Jahre 1273*, ed. J. Aronius (Hildesheim and New York, 1970); *Hebräische Berichte über die Judenverfolgungen während der Kreuzzüge*, ed. A. Neubauer, M. Stern, and S. Baer, Quellen zur Geschichte der Juden in Deutschland, 2 (Berlin, 1892); Schlomo Eidelberg, *The Jews and the Crusaders. The Hebrew Chronicles of the First and Second Crusades* (Madison, 1977) and for Cologne see Carl Brisch, *Geschichte der Juden in Cöln und Umgebung aus älterer Zeit bis auf die Gegenwart*, 2 vols. (Mülheim, 1879; Cologne, 1882); Adolf Kober, *Cologne*, transl. Solomon Grayzel, Jewish Community Series (Philadelphia, 1940).

[48] Eidelberg, *The Jews and the Crusaders*, pp. 122–3; German translation also in *Hebräische Berichte über die Judenverfolgungen während der Kreuzzüge*, ed. Neubauer, Stern, and Baer, p. 189. These Jewish persecutions apparently had no economic basis but occurred rather in the context of the Crusades (see E. Ennen, "Kölner Wirtschaft im Fruh- und Hochmittelalter," 1, p. 129).

[49] This dating is according to the Jewish calendar, which corresponds to the year 1190 of the Christian calendar. See Richard B. Dobson, *The Jews of Medieval York and the Massacre of March 1190*, Borthwick Papers, 45 (York, 1974).

[50] *Hebräische Berichte über die Judenverfolgungen während der Kreuzzüge*, ed. Neubauer, Stern, and Baer, pp. 204–5.

These horrible reports reveal the behind-the-scenes existence of economic and social ties between the Jewish communities in England and the Rhine region.[51]

A well-defined Jewish quarter emerged by this time in Cologne's St. Laurence parish, to which many Jews emigrated during the twelfth century.[52] The continuous resettlement of Jews during this century is clear in the case of Cologne,[53] since the immigrants kept evidence of their origin in their surnames.[54] Kober's study found 134 separate references of *Herkunftsnamen* among the emigrant Jews mentioned in the Schreinsurkunden up to 1349, of which 73 came from the regions around Cologne, Düsseldorf, Aachen, Koblenz, and Trier, and others from such regions as Westphalia, Hanover, Hessen, Baden, Thuringia, Bavaria, Switzerland, Belgium, and the Netherlands.[55] But there are only two surnames surviving which are *Landschaftsbezeichnungen*: namely, *Westfalus* and *Anglicus*.[56]

It is to this Jewish family with the surname Anglicus that we now turn. In four Schreinskarten entries dated *c.* 1135–59 for St. Laurence parish a certain *Joseph, filius Vives* or *Joseph Iudeus* appears, whose son is in turn named Vives.[57] We learn more about the origin of Joseph and his father Vives, however, in the next three entries. The most crucial entry is Vives' purchase of a house from a certain Vives of

---

[51] There was even a similarity between Starrs (quitclaim charters involving Jews) in Cologne and England: *Starrs and Jewish Charters Preserved in the British Museum* ed. Israel Abrahams, H. P. Stokes and Herbert Loewe (Cambridge, 1932), II, pp. cxxx–cxxxi: "The Cologne Starrs extend over the years 1235–1347 . . . [and] the Cologne procedure was analogous to that in England."

[52] Adolf Kober, *Grundbuch des Kölner Judenviertels 1135–1425*, PGRG, 34 (Bonn, 1920), p. 61: "In Köln ist die Zuwanderungsziffer der Laurenzpfarre während des 12. Jahrhunderts nach Bungers Berechnungen die zwei höchste von allen Stadtbezirken . . . im ganzen weisen die Kölner Schreinsurkunden des 12. Jahrhunderts von 482 Personen, deren Herkunftsort genannt ist."

[53] Ibid., p. 61, "Die Unsicherheit der äusseren Lage und die Verfolgungen haben die Juden im Mittelalter ihren Wohnsitz häufig wechseln lassen. Erst in zweiter Reihe bot ihre Berufstätigkeit hierfür die Veranlassung."

[54] Klaus Cuno, "Namen Kölner Juden," *Rheinische Heimatpflege*, NF, 11 (1974), p. 290: "Besonders Herkunftsnamen sind für Juden typisch und z. T. schon Familiennamen geworden." The same is true of Cologne Jewish families who resettled elsewhere in Germany but retained the surname that indicated their origin, for example: Kober, *Cologne*, p. 112, "Many Jews can be shown to have lived in Frankfurt at this time who bore the surname 'de Colonia.'"

[55] Kober, *Grundbuch des Kölner Judenviertels 1135–1425*, pp. 67–70; see also E. Ennen, "Kölner Wirtschaft im Früh- und Hochmittelalter," I, pp. 129–30. That Jewish merchants as well attended the three yearly fairs held in Cologne further confirms the picture of a very active and fluid traffic of Jews in the region.

[56] Kober, *Grundbuch des Kölner Judenviertels 1135–1425*, p. 197: "Die meisten Zusätze beziehen sich auf den Herkunftsort, der im allgemeinen mit 'de' eingeführt wird. Nur vereinzelt ist der Name des Herkunftsortes auch Eigenname geworden, wie Baseleir (Baselerus). Der Name des Herkunftslandes findet sich in Anglicus und Westfalus."

[57] St. Laurenzpfarre Karte 1 col. 7: no. 6; Karte 2 col. 2: no. 14; Karte 2 col. 3: no. 3; and Karte 2 col. 3: no. 4. These have been published in Hoeniger, *Kölner Schreinsurkunden des 12. Jahrhunderts*, I, pp. 220, 226, 227.

Koblenz.[58] Here the unmistakable toponymic surname *de Anglia* indicates the family's place of origin. Then two entries after this one we learn even more when Joseph sells his portion of the family inheritance,[59] and perhaps his sister Bela and her husband sell their portion.[60] In this second set of entries Joseph and his father Vives bear the surname *Anglicus*. This suggests that the surnames *de Anglia* and *Anglicus* were understood as synonymous, or at least that the prepositional form could evolve into the adjectival form after some time in Cologne. In any case it is clear that *Anglicus* had become a family name that indicated English origins and that was inherited over generations.[61]

This use of the surname is not reserved for Jews. In fact the above example is the only one which survives in Cologne sources for a Jewish family. Rather, the surname can also be found even in such circles as the Cologne Cathedral curia. On September 26, 1331 the following passage completed a charter of the parish church of St. Severin:

Acta sunt hec presentibus viris descretis magistro Wigardo de Juliaco advocato, Alberto Wogolonis, Johanne dicto Anglicus de Arwilre, notariis curie Coloniensis et Johanne de Lubcke clerico.[62]

and again on January 9, 1339 a certain Johannes dictus Anglicus notarized a charter with the canons of St. Maria ad Gradus in

---

[58] St. Laurenzpfarre Karte 2 col. 4: no. 3: "Notum sit vobis, qualiter Vives Iudeus de Anglia emit partem domus erga Vives de Confluentia, que sita est in platea contra domum Herimanni. Hec fiebat ei delegata (firsalt) coram civibus et iudicibus absque omni contradictione, unde tradidit testimonium, sicuti iure debuit, et ita aquisivit, quod iure obtinebat ad proprietatem suam et coheredes sui" (c. 1135–65). Text published in Hoeniger, *Kölner Schreinsurkunden des 12. Jahrhunderts*, I, p. 230.

[59] St. Laurenzpfarre Karte 2 col. 4: no. 5: "Notum sit tam futuris quam presentibus, quod Joseph Anglicus partem hereditatis, que attingebat in eum ex parte avi sui Vivi Anglici, reliquit eam liberam Alexandro Iudeo cognomine Suzekind de Werzeburch" (c. 1160–1200). Text published in *Kölner Schreinsurkunden des 12. Jahrhunderts*, ed. Hoeniger, I, p. 230.

[60] St. Laurenzpfarre Karte 2 col. 4: no. 6: "Notum sit tam futuris quam presentibus, quod Suzekind de Werzeburch et uxor sua Adeleidis vendiderunt Godelivo Iudeo de Andirnache et uxori sue Belen dimidiam partem domus et aree, que fuit Vivi Anglici, ita ut eorum propria sit" (c. 1160–1200). Text published in Hoeniger, *Kölner Schreinsurkunden des 12. Jahrhunderts*, I, p. 230.

[61] Cuno, "Namen Kölner Jüden," p. 290 has come to the same conclusion: "Handelt es sich bei Anglicus um einen Übernamen, kann man sicher hier von einem vererbten Übernamen, also einem Familiennamen, sprechen. Aber auch wenn Anglicus hier als 'Völkername', bei Juden entsprechend etwa 'Name, der die Herkunft aus dem Bereich eines Volkes ausdrückt', zu verstehen ist, wurde mit den zitierten Belegen ein jüdischer Familienname des 12. Jahrhunderts nachgeweisen. Dann für die vergleichbaren Stammesnamen gilt 'wohl . . . im allgemeinen, dass ein durch drei Generationen nachgewiesener Zusatz dieser Art als Familienname zu betrachten ist'. Anglicus ist daher einer der überhaupt nur vier 'aus dem in dieser Hinsicht interessanten älteren Material' ganz Kölns ermittelten Familiennamen nach der Herkunft, was bei dem doch relativ geringen jüdischen Bevölkerungsanteil besonders ins Auge fällt."

[62] *Die Urkunden des Pfarrarchivs von St. Severin in Köln*, ed. Johannes Hess (Cologne, 1901), p. 133.

Cologne.[63] This creates at first glance some consternation, since Johannes bears a combination of surnames indicating both English and German origins (Ahrweiler is a small city to the southwest of Cologne along the Ahr river). The conundrum may be explained, however, in a rather unspectacular manner. A look at the urban records of the city of Ahrweiler reveals that a certain Master Christian Anglicus was a member of the powerful *Schöffen* of the city a generation before this Johannes, and it is not difficult to imagine that a well-placed member of the Ahrweiler community or his relatives could get a son or relative placed in some position within the Cologne diocesan administration.[64] Such patrician status for an Englishman in the Rhine region is worthy of note and is indicative of the heretofore unnoticed evidence of the English in Germany during this period. Furthermore, it corroborates the fact that *Anglicus* served as a family name, which in this case could be coupled with a German toponymic name for those who were resettled on foreign soil. Such a combination of surnames has already crossed our path in the examples of Henricus Anglicus de Cadamo, Willelmus Anglicus de Rothomagensi, and Alfredus Anglicus de Sareshel.

In summary then, Anglicus consistently denoted a person of English ancestry. The surname apparently developed as a natural signifier of one's status in relation to foreigners or at least of the original status of one's forebears when living outside of England.[65] We now turn to the individual families in Cologne bearing this surname and consider the erroneous assumptions of earlier scholars about their identity as well as uncover the remarkable activities of such expatriate families through prosopographical examination.

---

[63] *Das Stift St. Mariengraden zu Köln. Urkunden und Akten (1059–1817)*, MSAK 57/58, ed. Anna-Dorothee von den Brincken (Cologne, 1969), II, pp. 40–1. This Johannes is referred to only as "Johanne de Arwilre, notariis curie Coloniensis" in a charter of November 20, 1337 of St. Gereon, in *Urkundenbuch des Stiftes St. Gereon zu Köln*, ed. P. Joerres (Bonn, 1893), pp. 368–9.

[64] *Inventar des Archivs der Stadt Ahrweiler (1228–1795)*, ed. Theresia Zimmer, Veröffentlichungen der Landesarchivverwaltung Rheinland-Pfalz, 5 (Koblenz, 1965), pp. 3–4 no. 7: "1307 April 16 Die Schöffen von Ahrweiler Rolevus Johannes Vernekorn; Gobel, Bruder des Vogtes; Meister Christian Anglicus; Gerhard, Bruder des Herrn Bruno; Meister Johann, Sohn des Rolinus, und Peter Cudel beurkunden."

[65] A rather remarkable use of the term *Anglicus* appears in the "Vita Norberti Archiepiscopi Magdeburgensis," *MGH SS*, XII, p. 684, where Norbert evaluates one of two novices: "Cumque considerasset [i.e. Norbert] alterum eorum [the novices] minus devotum in confessione, levem in verbis, inquietum in corpore, inconstantem moribus, tepidum in oratione, negligentem in obedientia, Anglicus enim erat." The chronicler of the *Annales de Waverleia*, p. 349 uses the term in the context of the xenophobic attitude of the Barons' Revolt under Henry III: "Tot alienigenae diversarum linguarum iam per plures annos miltiplici erant in Anglia, tot redditibus, terris, villis et caeteris facultatibus ditati, quod Anglicos, quasi se inferiores, maximo contemptui habebant."

Chapter 5

ANGLICUS IN COLONIA: THE SOCIAL, ECONOMIC, AND LEGAL STATUS OF THE ENGLISH IN COLOGNE DURING THE TWELFTH AND THIRTEENTH CENTURIES

The English appear in the earliest Cologne municipal sources, as in the case of Joseph and his father, Vives "Iudeus de Anglia." Indeed, since the Schreinskarten were first systematically kept, beginning in the 1130s, English citizens not only appear among their earliest entries but also were certainly present even before such documentation.[1] Vives' family was unfortunately living in Cologne during the anti-Jewish violence of 1146 surrounding the Second Crusade. Other families appear throughout the twelfth century, such as a certain Walterus Anglicus and his wife Guda, who mortgaged half of a house and its land to Guda's mother Gertrudis for 15 marks with a promise of repayment in 1189–90.[2] That the property was *iuxta Renum* in St. Martin's parish strongly suggests a mercantile background – something not unexpected for a foreigner, since the parish was the heart of the city's market quarter.[3] Moreover, their ownership of a house or portion thereof tells us something of the level of involvement in the civic life of Cologne already achieved by some English at this early date. Walterus probably had married a Cologne woman, since her mother lived in the city, and the mortgaging of their property in order to obtain capital is indicative of merchant activity in the city.[4] Although no certain connection can be made, this Walterus Anglicus may have been the ancestor of a later namesake who became one of the wealthiest Englishman in Cologne

---

[1] "Die Anfänge des Kölner Schreinswesens," pp. 1–21.

[2] St. Martin Karte 12 col. 6: no. 7: "Notum sit, quod Walterus (Anglicus) et uxor eius Guda exposuerunt matri sue Gertrudi dimidiam partem domus et aree iuxta Renum site pro 15 marc., ita ut, si in epiphania domini non solvatur, hereditas illa propria sit Gertrudis. Inde dedit testimonium." Text published in *Kölner Schreinsurkunden des 12. Jahrhunderts*, ed. Hoeniger, I, p. 190.

[3] E. Ennen, "Kölner Wirtschaft im Früh- und Hochmittelalter," I, pp. 131–4.

[4] See von Winterfeld, *Handel, Kapital und Patriziat in Köln bis 1400*; von Looz-Corswarem, "Hausverkauf und Verpfändung in Köln im 12. Jahrhundert," I, p. 196; and Planitz, "Das Grundpfandrecht in den Kölner Schreinskarten," pp. 1–88.

(the latter Walterus Anglicus will be a main focus of the remaining portion of this chapter).

A thoroughgoing involvement by the English in the urban life of Cologne is further confirmed by the appearance of Englishmen on three different citizen rolls of the city. Albreth Anglicus appears on the list for the entire city dated by Hoeniger as late twelfth-century,[5] and Adam de Gipswich [i.e. Ipswich] is recorded on a list for the parish of St. Martin dated *c.* 1159–69.[6] The third Englishman is someone on whom we may have additional information: Wilhelmus de Anglia. He appears on a citizen list for the entire city dated around the middle of the twelfth century,[7] and could be the same Wilhelmus who was a partner in selling a house with its land in the district of Niederich around the years 1135–58.[8] Or perhaps he was the Wilhelmus Anglicus who was active in St. Laurence parish at the end of the twelfth century. Within the years 1198 to 1206 a Wilhelmus Anglicus and his wife Hadewigis purchased half a house and its land,[9] and then mortgaged it.[10] They

---

[5] *Kölner Schreinsurkunden des 12. Jahrhunderts*, ed. Hoeniger, II, 2, p. 24 col. 6: no. 132.

[6] Ibid., I, 2, p. 61 no. 199.

[7] Ibid., II, 2, p. 18 col. 5: no. 12. Hermann Keussen, in his monumental work *Topographie der Stadt Köln im Mittelalter* (Bonn, 1910; rpt. Bonn, 1918; rpt. Düsseldorf, 1986), I, p. 57*, concludes that such place names did indeed indicate one's national origin: "Betrachtet man die Namen, welche in der Gildeliste (*c.* 1130/40–1170/80) und in den gleichzeitigen Bürgerlisten von St. Martin überliefert sind, so treten uns zahlreich die Herkunftsbezeichnungen . . . vor Augen. Leider ist die übergrosse Mehrzahl der Vornamen ohne jede besondere Kennzeichnung, ein Umstand, der andererseits es wieder fast zur Gewissheit macht, dass die vereinzelt beigefügten Ortsnamen auch als Herkunftsbezeichnungen aufgefasst werden müssen, zumal Familienname damals kaum schon vorkamen." He then continues, listing foreign merchants from throughout Germany, Austria, Belgium, the Netherlands, even Poland and Rome – but never once mentions the presence of the English.

[8] Niederich Karte 1 col. 7: no. 10: "Significamus posteris nostris, quod Albertus (clericus) domum cum statione ab Wilhelmo (Anglico) (et Herwico) sibi et suis heredibus comparavit coram civibus et iudicibus et vero testimonio." Text published in *Kölner Schreinsurkunden des 12. Jahrhundert*, ed. Hoeniger, II, 1, p. 59. *Statio* was a term used in the district of Niederich for land on which the house sat – i.e. "*area*" – (see Keussen, *Topographie der Stadt Köln*, I, p. 110*).

[9] St. Laurenz Karte 5 col. 7: no. 5: "Notum sit etc., quod Wilhelmus Anglicus et uxor eius Hadewigis emerunt dimidietatem domus et aree, ubicunque eis in divisione contigerit, erga Vugelonem et uxorem eius Liveradem, ita ut eorum propria sit." Text published in *Kölner Schreinsurkunden des 12. Jahrhunderts*, ed. Hoeniger, I, p. 275.

[10] St. Laurenz Karte 5 col. 7: no. 10: "Notum autem sit, quod Wilhelmus Anglicus et uxor eius Hadewig predictam hereditatem suam, que quondam fuit Vugelonis, inpignoraverunt officialibus, ita ut, si Iohannes et Cunradus, filii Hadewigis, super partem [*sic*] predicti pistrini eos attinentis non effestucaverint, hereditas Wilhelmi et Hadewigis respondeat." Text published in *Kölner Schreinsurkunden des 12. Jahrhunderts*, Hoeniger, I, p. 275. The bakery mentioned here was purchased in two parts by a widow named Richmudis in the prior two entries of this folio – nos. 8 and 9: "Notum sit etc., quod Richmudis, vidua Gerardi (filii advocati) comparavit sibi et heredibus suis dimidietatem pistrini (siti in Stezin) contra domum Cristinam, filiam Sibodonis, et suos heredes, ita ut eorum propria sit. (No. 9): Item notum sit, quod eadem Richmudis predicti pistrini dimidietatem emit sibi et heredibus suis erga Hadhewigem, filiam Henrici Bougin, et suos heredes, ita ut eorum propria sit." Thus the clause that Hadewigis' sons

apparently redeemed the house thereafter, as they subsequently sold it.[11]
Here again we find the typical Cologne commercial activity of investing
in and mortgaging property in order to raise capital. The evidence also
tells us something of Hadewigis' own family. She was evidently married
once before and had at least two sons. Her father is also mentioned,
suggesting that he too was a resident of Cologne. This looks like
another case of an Englishman who married into a local Cologne
family. In this context it should be noted that no Englishmen appear on
the surviving role of the merchant guild of St. Martin parish, which did
include foreign merchants but had no connection to the Cologners'
guildhall in London.[12]

The material on English families in Cologne becomes much more
plentiful as the Schreinsurkunden are developed further in their detail
and volume during the thirteenth century. Whereas the Schreinskarten
are not very useful in determining the actual location of property, the
Schreinsbücher that replace them have much more detailed descriptions
and thus allow us to plot the properties mentioned on the streets of
medieval Cologne.

The main family comprising this prosopographical study was perhaps
the wealthiest and best-placed family of all those we shall encounter.
The first we hear of them is with reference to their main dwelling,
which was simply known as the "domus Englant."[13] As we find out in

must forego their claims to the bakery was necessary because of the sale of it by "Hadhewigem,
filiam Henrici Bougin et suos heredes." Here we learn of Hadewigis' father, Henricus Bougin,
and it also appears that her sons Iohannes and Cunradus were children of a previous marriage
and so had claims to a property other than the house purchased earlier by Wilhelmus and
Hadewigis.

[11] St. Laurenz Karte 5 col. 6: no. 12: "Notum sit etc., quod Ludewicus et uxor eius Cristina
emerunt dimidietatem domus iuxta domum Cunradi (Renger) erga Wilhelmum Anglicum et
uxorem eius Hadewigim, que quondam fuit Vugelonis, ubicunque ei in divisione contingit, ita
ut absque contradictione Ludewici sit." Text published in *Kölner Schreinsurkunden des 12.
Jahrhunderts*, ed. Hoeniger, I, p. 274.

[12] Keussen, *Topographie der Stadt Köln*, I, p. 58*: "Der Zusammenschluss der fremden Elemente zu
einer Schwurvereinigung, zur Gilde, bot in jenen Zeiten die einzige Möglichkeit, sich rechtlich
als Gemeinschaft mit gemeinsamen Interessen und Zielen zu betätigen, dem einzelnen
Kaufmanne wie einer Mehrheit die Stütze zu geben, deren der Händler bedurfte sowohl bei
den gefahrvollen Wanderungen zu Lande, wie bei den schwierigen Fahren zur See, die zumal
mit dem englischen Handel verknüpft waren . . . Es erscheint zweifelhaft, ob die im Besitze der
Londoner Gildhalle befindliche Genossenschaft Kölner Kaufleute mit der Kölner Gilde im
Zusammenhang gebracht werden darf, ebenso ob die den Kölner Kaufleuten in England und in
Trier verliehenen Privilegien nur für die Gildgenossen galten." See also Heinrich von Loesch,
Die Kölner Kaufmannsgilde im zwölften Jahrhundert, Westdeutsche Zeitschrift für Geschichte und
Kunst, Ergänzungsheft 12 (Trier, 1904).

[13] 290 Porta S. Pantaleonis (Airsbach) fo.12r: "Notum sit, quod Aleidis, que filia fuerit Eckeberti
et Gerbernis, de morte patris sui proprietatem quinte partis domus site super pontem prope
domum, que Englant dicitur" (1212). Keussen, *Topographie der Stadt Köln*, I, p. 87*: "Ganz
durchweg wird in dieser älteren Zeit der Name des Hauses die Herkunft des Besitzers verraten,

subsequent entries, this house was located on Filzengraben in the district of Airsbach.[14] Airsbach may have been a center for weavers (cf. Weberstrasse), and perhaps Filzengraben took its name from the makers of felt hats, a product that was very popular in England.[15] Filzengraben later became the work center for the coopers (*ligatores vasorum*),[16] many of whose barrels held the Rhine wine which was such an important element in Cologne's trade with England.[17] Perhaps this family exported such goods to England.

We begin to get detailed information on the family members in two entries describing the division of the children's inheritance.[18] With the crucial middle portion marred on the first entry it is difficult to be certain what the business at hand was, but it appears that three brothers – Walterus, Hermannus, and Arnoldus – were acknowledging their brother Vortlinus' claim to his inheritance. The property is the same as that in Filzengraben and was originally possessed by the parents of these men. We know nothing of their parents – whether they were the first generation of emigrants to Cologne or not – it is with these sons that the family's history survives in the written record. As for the house, it retained the name "Engelant" but the interests of the sons lay elsewhere and the house passed at some point into the hands of another family. The last mention of the house in this family's possession occurs with the division of Vortlinus' portion among the other three brothers at his death.[19] At this point we see the rise to prominence of the brother Walterus Anglicus and his wife Richmudis, as they obtain full owner-

---

während später vielfach der vom Ortsnamen abgeleitete Hausnamen auf den neuen Besitzer überging." This is exactly the case with the "domus Engelant."

[14] Airsbach (or Oversburg) had been outside the city walls until an extension of the fortifications in 1106 annexed the district along with Niederich to the north. Both quarters were densely populated by many artisans and merchants, see Strait, *Cologne in the Twelfth Century*, p. 31. The actual location would have been Filzengraben II (see Keussen, *Topographie der Stadt Köln*, II, p. 10 col. b, 1 – all subsequent locations will be identified using Keussen's topography).

[15] E. Ennen, "Kölner Wirtschaft im Früh- und Hochmittelalter," p. 137: "Zum Textilgewerbe gehören die Hutmacher, deren Stände schon im 12. Jahrhundert erwähnt werden; auch die Hutmacherei wurde zum Exportgewerbe; um 1300 erscheinen die Kölner Filzhüte als besonderer Posten in einer Jülicher Zollrolle und werden in England gerne getragen."

[16] Keussen, *Topographie der Stadt Köln*, I, p. 162*.

[17] In Cologne the blending of *Handel* and *Handwerk* was widespread, hence the coopers were also directly involved in the wine trade, so some of them certainly had activities in England, see E. Ennen, "Kölner Wirtschaft im Früh- und Hochmittelalter," p. 139.

[18] 290 Porta S. Pantaleonis (Airsbach) fo. 21v: "Notum sit, quod Walterus Anglicus et uxor eius Richmudis et Hermannus et Arnoldus fratres sui . . . Vortlinum, fratrem suum, de domo et area et camera retro sita, que sita est apud pontem situm in platea Filtrorum [Filzengraben] et que fuit patris et matris sue. Inde Vortlinus dedit testimonium ut iure debuit" (c. 1222–56).

[19] 307 Veteris Portae (Airsbach) fo. 5v: "Notum, quod Welterus Anglicus et Hermannus et Arnoldus venerunt in presentiam scabinorum et iudicis et optinuerunt per sententiam scabinorum tres partes domus et aree de quatuor partibus, que eis accesserunt de morte Vortlini. Inde dederunt testimonium sicut iure debuerunt. Notum, quod predicte Hermannus et Arnoldus

ship of the house. Walterus alone will remain in the documentation and will amass several houses. At some unknown point thereafter, Walterus or his heirs sold the house or it passed to another family through marriage, since the next mention of it occurs in 1280, where the children of Godescalcus de Trappa and his wife Sophia inherit portions thereof.[20]

Detailed information survives for a second parcel of property that the sons inherited, called the "hereditas Anglicorum," located in St. Severin parish.[21] This entry is again a division by the three remaining brothers of Vortlinus' one-third portion of the family inheritance at his death. The family, whose main residence was probably at the "domus Engelant" in Airsbach, had been renting out some of this other property.[22] In fact, Arnoldus and Hermannus had already (prior to Vortlinus' death) sold their portions of a rent of 10 shillings 6 pence from an apple garden on some of this land to a certain Godefridus Hardevust, canon of the parish church of St. George in Airsbach.[23]

remiserunt Weltero et uxori sue Richmudi quicquid habuerunt in prescripta domo et area. Inde dederunt testimonium sicut iure debuerunt" (*c.* 1233).

20 290 Porta S. Pantaleonis (Airsbach) fo. 40r: "Notum, quod Alstradi, Hildegero, Gertrudi, Brunoni et Sophie, liberis Godescalci de Trappa et Sophie, cuilibet ipsorum cessit de morte parentorum suorum predictorum quinque partes duarum mansionum sitarum sub uno tecto in Wilzegraven ex opposito Muntabur. Ita quod iure etc. Notum, quod predictis quinque pueris Godescalci et Sophie cessit de morte parentum suorum predictorum, cuilibet ipsorum quinta pars domus et aree vocate Engelant iuxta pontem. Item cuilibet quinta pars camere site retro domum predictam vocatam Engelant. Ita quod iure et sine contradictione obtinebunt" (1280). The house continued to pass to members of this family at least until *c.* 1303 and yet retains the name "Engelant/Englant." See 290 Porta S. Pantaleonis (Airsbach) fos. 40r; 72r; 72v; and 79v. The family styled "de Trappa" (and "de Baculo") was an important patrician family in Cologne, with members among the Scabini and in the Richerzeche (Meliorat). As Friedrich Lau, "Das Kölner Patriziat bis zum Jahre 1325," pp. 151–2 has found, the family's main dwellings were in Airsbach: "Der haupttheil des Familienbesitzes lag in Airsbach, wo wohl auch der ursprüngliche Wohnsitz des Geschlechts zu suchen ist." The domus Englant was thus added to their central holdings in the area.

21 371 Per Totam Parochiam (St. Severin) fo. 9r: "Notum sit tam futuris quam presentibus, quod hereditas Anglicorum sita supra antiquum fossatum, tercia pars illius attingens Vortlinim, de morte ipsius ad alios tres fratres superstites, scilicet Walterum, Hermannum et Arnoldum, de morte Vortlini ad ipsos tres fratres devoluta est per sentenciam scabinorum, ipsis tres fratribus ad iudiciam est. Notum sit tam futuris quam presentibus, quod hereditas [*sic*] Anglicorum sita ab hereditate Gerardi Lupi versus Minores fratres Walterus Anglicus et Richmudis sine contradictione obtinebunt effestucantibus illis, qui de iure effestucare debuerunt" (*c.* 1233). The actual location of the *hereditas* "supra antiquum fossatum" would have been Katherinengraben I (see Keussen, *Topographie der Stadt Köln*, II, p. 185 col. a, c).

22 Per Totam Parochiam (St. Severin) fo. 11v: "Notum sit tam futuris quam presentibus, quod Henricus Hameschit et uxor eius Gertrudis manu coniuncta remiserunt Engilberto et Bele uxori sue totam partem hereditatis, quam ipsi ab Anglicis tenuerunt eo iure, quod tenetur predictis Anglicis" (*c.* 1233).

23 371 Per Totam Parochiam (St. Severin) fo. 2v: "Notum sit tam futuris quam presentibus, quod Arnoldus, Hermannus et Vorlienus [*sic*], fratres dicti Anglici, habent in area, que pomerium appellatur, supra antiquum fossatum retro immunitatem fratrum Minorum decem solidos et sex

Three things are of interest in this property settlement. Firstly, Vortlinus had apparently not sold his income to Godefridus; therefore, it is his portion of the apple garden that the three surviving brothers are dividing as inheritance. Secondly, Walterus is not mentioned as having any prior ownership of this property among the brothers. That may indicate that he was the youngest brother. And thirdly, the entry distinguishes between two parcels of property in the "hereditas Anglicorum": that located "supra antiquum fossatum" (known as Katherinengraben), which Walterus, Hermannus, and Arnoldus divided equally, and that located "ab hereditate Gerardi Lupi versus Minores fratres," which Walterus alone received. Keussen has listed both of these parcels on Katherinengraben, but the latter was actually located elsewhere. The "hereditas Gerardi Lupi" was situated at the intersection of Bozengasse (i.e. Buschgasse), Seyengasse, and Rosenstrasse – on the opposite side of the Franciscan cloister Sion from the apple garden on Katherinengraben.[24] Thus the second portion of the "hereditas Anglicorum" was somewhere south of there on Seyengasse. Unfortunately we do not learn what kind of property Arnoldus held here, but the entire share went to Walterus with the agreement of the other brothers.

Walterus added to his properties in the parish of St. Severin and the district of Airsbach during the next few years. His first acquisition was a house in St. Severin parish, which was perhaps adjacent to the "hereditas Anglicorum ab hereditate Gerardi Lupi."[25] A later inheri-

---

denarios annui census in nativitate sancte Marie vel in proximis octo diebus subsequentibus solvendos sine pena. Si autem tempus predicte solutionis neglectum fuerit, eadem area cum suis attinentiis ad illos, quos census annuus attingit, libere et absolute revertetur. Item notum, quod Arnoldus suam terciam partem et Hermannus suam terciam partem vendiderunt et remiserunt eo iure, ut supradictum est, Godefrido Hardevust, canonico ecclesie sancti Georgii, in quemcunque locum ei placuerit divertendi. Sciendum est, quod supradictus Godefridus supradictam hereditatem vel annuum censum, reservato sibi usufructu vite sue, donavit et remisit ecclesie sue sancti Georgii ea condicione, quod post mortem suam cedet ad opus prebende sacerdotalis, quam ibi creavit et ille sacerdos cottidie unam missam pro defunctis celebrabit nisi sit dies festus . . . chorum faciet tamquam canonicus et quicumque pro tempore fuerit de . . . prebendam idoneo debet confrere sacerdoti. Si autem Godefridus canonicus hoc factum suum mutare voluerit, liberam habebit potestatem" (pre-1235). *Ennen/Eckertz*, III, p. 206 no. 235 contains only a portion of this entry. Eventually Godefridus Hardevust sold 7 shillings of the *census* to the Franciscans of the monastery of Sion – 371 Per Totam Parochiam (St. Severin) fo. 2v: "Notum sit tam futuris quam presentibus, quod Godefridus canonicus sancti Georgii in Colonia vendidit et remisit monialibus conventus de Seine in Colonia septem solidos annui census, quos habebat iacentes retro immunitatem ipsarum monialium. Ita quod predicte moniales predictos septem solidos sine aliqua contradictione optinebunt" (pre-1230).

24 Keussen, *Topographie der Stadt Köln*, II, p. 198 col. a, a: " 'hereditas Gerardi Lupi in Bozengasse in fine illius platee, que de Atirstraze [Achterstrasse] descendit in Bozengasse' [i.e. Rosenstrasse] = dom. in fine Bozengasse contra Antiquam Portam."

25 371 Per Totam Parochiam (St. Severin) fo. 10v: "Notum sit tam futuris quam presentibus, quod Aleidis, vidua Marcmanni, vendidit et remisit Waltero Anglico domum et aream sitam in littore Reni inter domum Lamberti et hereditatem puerorum Franconis renunciantibus omnibus, qui

tance settlement for his heirs indicates property "in Bozengassen versus antiquam portam," which most likely meant Seyengasse, the extension of Bozengasse down to the Rhine. His brother Arnoldus had earlier obtained half of a field on Bozengasse,[26] but sold it directly to his nephew Philippus, a son of Walterus.[27] This was part of Arnoldus' inheritance in the area, the remainder of which Walterus subsequently received. Thus the purchase of the house was probably an effort to consolidate the family inheritance at this location.

In addition Walterus obtained half a house on Holzmarkt and a plot on nearby Holzgasse in Airsbach, to which we shall turn in the discussion of his heirs' inheritance. These properties were among the least expensive sections of real estate in the city, with St. Severin parish being the poorest of the parishes.[28] But Walterus also acquired two houses in the valuable merchants' quarter of St. Martin's parish, both being very near each other on Turnmarkt.

The first mention of property in St. Martin parish occurs as Walterus and Richmudis parcel out portions of one of the houses to other family members. This happened before the death of Vortlinus, hence before c. 1230, since all three of Walterus' brothers were given a quarter part of the house and its land.[29] Walterus also gave one-quarter of half of the house to a son, Hertwicus, who died shortly thereafter.[30] Having

renunciare debebant. Ita quod idem Walterus et Ricmudis [sic] uxor eius predictam hereditatem iure et sine contradictione obtinebunt" (pre-1235). Around the same time the sale of a "domum cum area sitam in littore Reni proxime domui Walteri Anglici" was recorded in Schreinsbuch 307 Veteris Portae (Airsbach) fo. 5r (c. 1235). The actual location was probably Seyengasse I.

26 307 Veteris Portae (Airsbach) fo. 11r: "Notum, quod Arnoldo Anglico cessit ex . . . dimidietas unius aree iacentis in Bozen[gassen]. . . attingit. Ita quod iure et sine contradictione obtinebit" (undated). Since this folio is unreadable in many portions the valuable information here is unfortunately no longer available. The formulaic entry here suggests that Arnoldus obtained this property by inheritance [i.e. "cessit ex morte . . ."].

27 307 Veteris Portae (Airsbach) fo. 11r: "Notum, quod Philippus, filius Walteri Anglici, emit . . . dimidietatem aree erga Arnoldum Anglicum" (undated). This Philippus, the son of Walterus Anglicus, was a large property holder in his own right and will be discussed at length below. He is important also because both Lau and von Winterfeld have incorrectly located him in the Hardevust family. A further entry below this one follows, "Notum, quod Walterus Anglicus dedit . . ." but the remainder is gone. Hence Walterus was a part of this series of transactions having something to do with his own house at this location.

28 von Looz-Corswarem, "Hausverkauf und Verpfändung in Köln im 12. Jahrhundert," pp. 200–1.

29 13 Wolberonis A (St. Martin) fo. 2v: "Notum sit tam futuris quam presentibus, quod Welterus Anglicus et uxor eius Richmudis contradiderunt et remiserunt quartam partem domus et aree site in littore Reni prope domum Vogelonis de Nusia versus plateam Reni [Rheingasse] Arnoldo, Vortlino et Hermanno, fratribus predicti Welteri, sicut in sua possidebant proprietate et ubicumque eis in particione acciderit. Et hoc eis officiales iure obtinebunt" (undated). The same description occurs c. 1235 for Turnmarkt V (see Keussen, *Topographie der Stadt Köln*, I, p. 86 col. a, 12).

30 13 Wolberonis A (St. Martin) fo. 8r: "Item notum sit tam futuris quam presentibus, quod Walterus Anglicus in figura iudicii per sentenciam scabinorum obtinuit quartam dimedietatis

regained this portion upon Hertwicus' death, Walterus then presented it to his next son, Godefridus Anglicus.[31] An entry immediately following this may be evidence that the house entered into Walterus' possession through marriage, since the son Godefridus inherited an additional sixth part of half of the house at the death of his mother.[32] Note also that Godefridus bore the surname *Anglicus*; the family name now passed to the next generation.

The second house owned on Turnmarkt is perhaps the most unique of them all. A Schreinsbuch entry dated 1268 mentions a "dimidietatem domus et aree site in littore Reni contiguam domui Welteri Anglici versus Engzegazin."[33] This house may originally have been the property of Walterus' parents and then passed down to their sons, since Walterus' son Godefridus purchased half of the house from his uncle Hermannus Anglicus,[34] and another son of Walterus, Philippus Anglicus (about whom we will have more to say below), purchased an eighth of this house *c.* 1261.[35] Note that by this time other merchants had at least partial ownership of the house, since Philippus Anglicus purchased his eighth part from a certain Gozwinus of Brussels. Either the property was

---

domus et aree site in littore Reni, que mansio fuit Walteri predicti, de morte filii sui Hertwici. Ita quod idem Welterus iure et sine contradictione optinebit" (undated). Since a *mansio* was a room, the house had at least eight rooms.

[31] 13 Wolberonis A (St. Martin) fo. 8r: "Item notum sit, quod Walterus Anglicus donavit et remisit Godefrido, filio suo, quartam predictem, que sibi cessit vel cedere posset de morte puerorum suorum [si per inopia retinere poterit written above the line], ante et retro subtus et superius, prout ibi iacet et ubicumque ipsum in particione attinget. Ita quod idem Godefridus iure et sine contradictione optinebit" (undated). Why the passage "de morte puerorum suorum" is in the plural is unclear based on the earlier entry; however, perhaps there was another deceased son who had previously had a legal claim on the property.

[32] 13 Wolberonis A (St. Martin) fo. 8r: "Item notum sit, quod Godefridus Anglicus predictus optinuit de morte matris sue proprietatem sexte partis dimidietatis prescripte, ubicumque ipsum in particione attingit, ante et retro subtus et superius, prout ibi iacet. Ita quod idem Godefridus iure et sine contradictione optinebit" (undated). Walterus and Richmudis had six children. It would thus appear that the other five-sixths of half of this house went to the other children as well.

[33] 448 II St. Martin (Schöffenschrein) fo. 4r. Encegassen = Sassenhofgässchen.

[34] 6a Vogelonis (St. Martin) fo. 21r: "Notum sit, quod Godefridus, Welteri Anglici filius, emit sibi dimidietatem domus et aree site in littore Reni prope domum Godescalci de Wuppervurde versus Engcegassen erga Hermannum Anglicum, patruum suum, ubicumque eum in particione attingebat et sic in sua possidebat proprietate. Ita quod iure et sine contradictione obtinebat" (undated).

[35] 1a Marcmanni (St. Martin) fo. 22v: "Item notum sit tam futuris quam presentibus, quod Philippus Anglicus et uxor sua Cristina emerunt sibi octavam partem domus et aree site in littore Reni proxime domui Godescalci de Wippilworde versus Enzzegazzin, ante et retro subtus et superius et circumquaque, prout ibi iacet et ubicumque ipsos in particione attingit, erga Gozwinum de Bruxellia et uxorem suam Richmudim, sicut in sua habebant proprietate. Ita quod dictus Philippus et uxor sua Cristina dictam hereditatem iure et sine contradictione obtinebunt" (*c.* 1261). Keussen, *Topographie der Stadt Köln*, I, p. 88 col. b, a–b places the house of Godescalcus de Wuppervurde on Turnmarkt "unbestimmt zwischen Bruchplätzchen und Rheingasse."

at one time jointly owned by members of the family, or perhaps the house was actually used as a storage facility for foreign merchants, particularly the English.

This speculation has its basis in the long-standing name of the house and the similarity of its appellation to the houses around it in this mercantile quarter. The parishes of St. Martin and St. Brigida were dominated by the merchant centers of Heumarkt and Altermarkt. In particular the southern end of the parish of St. Martin – namely the region ringing southern Heumarkt from the parish church of Klein St. Martin to the Kornpforte, Rheingasse, and around to Turnmarkt – was the center for foreign merchants and their storage facilities.[36] The names of the streets in this area reveal where the various foreign merchants dwelt: Strassburgergasse, Sachsenhof, Walengasse (*platea Gallicorum* – i.e. Wallonians from the Meuse region), and Friesengasse. The names of the houses themselves indicate the presence of foreigners: Haus Dinant, Haus Brüssel on the southwest side of Heumarkt for the Brabantiners, Haus Gent on the southeast corner of Heumarkt for the Flemish, Haus Basel at the beginning of Markmannsgasse. It is in this context that we discover the name given to the house of the family of Walterus Anglicus: the "turris Anglici." There are numerous entries in the Schreinsbücher beginning in the 1280s which refer to this building.[37]

---

[36] E. Ennen, "Kölner Wirtschaft im Fruh- und Hochmittelalter," p. 133: "Dieser Abschnitt des Marktviertels steht aber auch in nächster Verbindung mit dem Rhein; er ist Kaufmanns- und Hafenviertel und Hauptstapelplatz für die Waren der fremden Kaufleute." See also Keussen, *Topographie der Stadt Köln*, I, pp. 56–7*.

[37] 6a Vogelonis (St. Martin) fo. 36v: "Notum sit tam futuris quam presentibus, quod Constantinus, filius Gerardi fratris Vogellonis et Gertrudi uxoris sue, optinuit de morte fratris sui Gerardi dimidietatem dimidietatis turris site super Buchele, que quondam fuit Incgeldi, et dimidietatem duarum mansionum et duorum cubiculorum sub uno tecto dicte turri adiacendtium, sicut in sua habebat proprietate. Ita quod iure et sine contradictione" (next entry dated June 1286); 6a Vogelonis (St. Martin) fo. 43v: "Notum sit tam presentibus quam futuris, quod Wilhelmo, Philippo et Constantino, [ink smear – liberi?] quondam Philippi dicti Morart et Sophie uxoris sue, quilibet eorum cessit [ink smear – de morte?] parentum suorum predictorum terciam partem medietatis domus et aree site super Renum ex opposito turris Ingeldi iuxta domum Jacobi Rufi versus Enzcgassen" (undated); 27 Generalis (St. Martin) fo. 19r: "Item notum sit etc., quod Constantinus, filius Gerardi fratris Vogelonis et Ida uxor sua, acquisiverunt sibi hereditarie erga Vogelonem et Hermannum, fratres predictos, medietatem turris site super Bugele, que quondam fuit Ingeldi, per tribus marcas et tribus solidos Coloniensium denariorum" (1289); 448 II St. Martin (Schöffenschrein) fo. 4v: "medietas domus et aree site in parochia sancti Martini minoris ex opposito turris Ingeldi et . . . domum Jacobi Rufi, videlicet illas medietas, que sita est versus Marmansgassen super ordonem" was in the possession of Philippus Morart (*c.* 1293); 6 Vogelonis (St. Martin) fo. 43v: "Notum sit tam presentibus quam futuris, quod Tilemanus dictus de Lepore et Hadewigis uxor sue emerunt sibi erga Wilhelmum et Aleydem uxorem suam et erga Philippum et Constantinum tres supradictos, erga quemlibet eorum suam tertiam partem medietatis domus et aree site super Renum ex opposito turris Ingeldi iuxta domum Jacobi Rufi versus Enchegasse" (1293); 27 Generalis (St Martin) fo. 25r: "Item notum sit tam futuris quam presentibus, quod Hermannus, filius quondam Constantii filii Vogelonis et Elizabet uxoris sue, optinuit de morte Vogelonis fratris sui . . . Item optinuit

Hermann Keussen continues these references throughout the fifteenth century showing the forms of the building's name in both Latin and German, and on his own map of the parish he calls the building the "englischer Turm."[38] He also notes that the building was alternately called the "English House."[39] Yet he never deals with the role of this tower or the meaning of its name, saying only that the purpose of the Turnmarkt area was unclear.[40] Of course, this appellation could be just another house named after the family – such as the "domus Engelant" in Airsbach; however, the pattern of houses named after foreign merchant communities in this quarter allows the possibility that this was the storage center for any goods bought or sold by English merchants in Cologne, or perhaps even the place where those Cologne merchants who traded with England focused their joint ventures.[41]

We now turn to the extensive Schreinsbücher entries concerning the

medietatem trium marcarum et trium solidorum Coloniensium denariorum hereditarii census solvendorum singulis annis de medietate turris site super Bugele, que quondam fuit Ingeldi" (*c.* 1296); 27 Generalis (St. Martin) fo. 25v: "Notum sit tam futuris quam presentibus, quod Hermannus, filius quondam Constantii filii Vogelonis, tradidit et remisit post mortem suam Hermanno dicto Schoneweder avunculo suo . . . Item tradidit et remisit eidem tres marcas et tres solidos Coloniensium denariorum hereditarii census solvendorum singulis annis de medietate turris site super Buggel, que quondam fuit Ingeldi" (1296); 27 Generalis (St. Martin) fo. 29: "thurris . . . que quondam fuit Ingeldi"; 448 II St. Martin (Schöffenschrein) fo. 1v: "Gerardus Gyr, scabinus Coloniensis," gave to his son and wife "medietatem domus et aree site ex opposito turris Ingeldi in ordonem in parochia Sancti Martini et est illa medietas, que iacet versus Marcmansgassen" (1308); 448 II St. Martin (Schöffenschrein) fo. 3v: "domum cum area sitam in parochia Sancti Martini ex opposito turris Ingeldi proxime domui Jacobi Rufi versus Marcmansgazzin" owned by Godescalcus dictus Morart. Apparently at this time "Incgeldus" was the local German equivalent of "Anglicus" – see below note 38.

38 Keussen, *Topographie der Stadt Köln*, I, p. 84 col. b, 1 to p. 87 col. a, 18: "thurris in littore Reni, que voc. Incgeldi" [6b Löwenstein dated 1330]; "Turris Anglici ex opp. dom. ad Leporem" [8 Löwenstein dated 1395]; "der Englische Turm gegenüber dem Hs. zome Hasen bei der Stadt Mauer" [14 Wolberonis dated 1402 and 8 Löwenstein dated 1478]; "Der Turm auf dem Toirmarkt an der Stadt Mauer u. auf der Stadt Mauer gegenüber des Englischen Hs." [14 Wolberonis dated 1404]; "bei dem Engelschen Turme auf dem Buchell" [6b Löwenstein dated 1476]. The actual location was Turnmarkt IV.

39 Ibid., I, p. 85 col. a, 4–5: "1279 domus, que quond. fuit Walteri Anglici; 1359. dom. Anglici; 1409 Hs. gegenüber des Englischen Hs. auf des Rheins Ufer auf dem Thoermarkt mit seiner Hfst" [12b–14 Wolberonis]; "Hs. gegenüber dem neuen Hs. zome Thurne, u. ist genannt des Engelschen huys" [473 Scabinorum dated 1473]; "Hs. Brubachs huys nächst Engelschen huys gegenüber dem Stall des Hs. zome Torne" [472 Scabinorum dated 1427].

40 Ibid., I, p. 158*.

41 Ibid., I, p. 58*, where Keussen concludes: "Wie wir oben gesehen haben, sassen die Kaufleute, soweit sie aus entlegenen Gegenden gekommen waren, nach Landsmannschaften zusammen, hielten also nach dem Brauche des Mittelalters ihre nationale Sonderart aufrecht." Thus it is not too difficult to imagine that the English had their living quarters here and/or used this house as a center their trading activities. Since towers in Cologne did not serve as dwelling places (see I, p. 58*), a mercantile function for the tower seems likely, as it served no role in the defense of the city. Keussen again (I, p. 185* note 7): "Erst 1234 (I, p. 87 col. a, 14) wird der Engelsche Turm am Thurnmarkt mit Sicherheit zuerst erwähnt, und zwar noch ohne Bezugnahme auf die Stadtmauer."

heirs of Walterus Anglicus, where we learn of the significant social connections achieved by the family. We have already met three sons of Walterus: Hertwicus, Godefridus, and Philippus. As previously noted, Hertwicus was apparently the eldest son but he died quite young. Godefridus follows as the next eldest, yet he too died *c.* 1263[42] and so Philippus, the only remaining son, continued as the head of the next generation.

Philippus Anglicus has been misplaced by Lau and von Winterfeld as a member of the patrician Hardevust family; they suggest that he obtained the surname *Anglicus* because of his English trading activities.[43] Both scholars list him as a collateral member of the Hardevust clan, but admit that his connection to the *Geschlecht* cannot be ascertained. The confusion stems from one Schreinsbuch entry dated *c.* 1272, in which Philippus' wife is called, "Cristina, filia quondam domini Henrici dicti Kleyngedanc et Leticie uxoris sue, relicta quondam Philippi dicti Hardevust, qui vocabatur Anglicus."[44] This attribution of the name Hardevust to Philippus is simply a scribal error, since nowhere else is Philippus Anglicus called Hardevust. Indeed, this same transaction was recorded twice more in another Schreinsbuch, and in both cases (see below), although the dating differs, Cristina is simply called "relicta Philippi Anglici." Furthermore, Philippus Anglicus and his wife Cristina Cleingedanc appear regularly among the inheritance entries of the Schreinsbücher with Philippus indicated as the son of Walterus Anglicus. The best example of this is Schreinsbuch 307 Veteris Portae (Airsbach) fo. 26v, in which Philippus and his wife Cristina are listed among those children who obtained property "ex morte patris Welteri et matris eorum Richmudis." Later in the same entry "Cristina, quondam uxor Philippi Anglici," obtained with her children by Philippus a court settlement for the sale of this inheritance. There are almost fifty entries for the family of Philippus Anglicus and Cristina in the Schreinsbücher, some of which mention the same properties, that

---

[42] See below note 54.

[43] In a discussion on the Hardevust family and its founder Bruno, who apparently was involved in English trade, von Winterfeld, *Handel, Kapital und Patriziat in Köln bis 1400*, pp. 48–50 states: "Innerhalb seiner Familie war Bruno keine Ausnahme, wenn es auch Zweige gab, die sich nicht so glücklich entwickelten. Nach Konnubium und Beinamen scheinen fast alle Hardevust Kaufleute gewesen zu sein. So gab es einen Philippus H. dictus Anglicus (*c.* 1280)." Lau, "Das Kölner Patriziat bis zum Jahre 1325," p. 109 lists "Philippus H. dictus Anglicus" among the "Bruchstücke" of the Hardevust family and on page 104 states, "Die auf Tafel IV [Bruchstücke-Tafel] angeführten Personen gehören, wie es scheint, zum Theil anderen Familien an, die infolge von Verschwägerung mit den H[ardevust] den Namen der letzteren angenommen haben." Of course Philippus didn't marry into the Hardevust family, but rather into the Cleingedanc family. And his father Walterus never bore any surname except Anglicus.

[44] 449 II Generalis Alban (Schöffenschrein) fo. 1v.

Walterus Anglicus held. Since in the numerous entries concerning Philippus Anglicus and Cristina Cleingedanc only this one entry includes the name Hardevust, such a single entry was a scribal error involving one of the most common and important family names in Cologne. The name *Anglicus* does not indicate a Cologne merchant who pursued trading activities in England as von Winterfeld has suggested. We shall see similar errors made in the interpretation of the name *Anglicus* as we continue to consider such families.

These Schreinsbücher entries have also revealed that the family of Walterus Anglicus had successfully attached itself to a major Cologne patrician family by marriage, by virtue of Philippus Anglicus' marriage to Cristina Cleingedanc. The Cleingedanc family was a powerful patrician *Geschlecht* in Cologne, which first appears in municipal records during the second half of the twelfth century. There were many branches of the family, of which Cristina's was known as Rufus and dwelt in St. Laurence parish. The family was highly placed, with members in the college of *scabini* (*senatores* or *Schöffen* who administered cases of civil law and public order in archiepiscopal courts) and the *Richerzeche* (or *Meliorat*: a patrician gild of "the rich and powerful" that regulated all Cologne gilds).[45] Cristina's brother Henricus, who married into the patrician Overstolz family, was a *scabinus*. The Cleingedancs were heavily involved in jurisdictional conflicts with the archbishops, and Cristina's father Henricus Rufus was among five Cleingedanc members who were exiled along with twenty other burghers by the archbishop and his faction in 1259.[46] More will be said below concerning what property Cristina brought to the marriage with Philippus and the holdings amassed by Philippus himself. Let us turn now to a consideration of the other family members in addition to these sons.

Walterus Anglicus died sometime during the early 1250s, as Schreinsbücher entries listing his heirs' inheritance begin in this decade. The first series of texts gives us much information on the identities of the remaining members of the family. In the early years of the decade a certain Albero Scallo, described as "tutor Richmudis, filie fratris sue," came into court in the parish of St. Severin to obtain her inheritance.[47]

---

45 See Friedrich Philippi, "Die Kölner Richerzeche," *MIÖG* 23 (1911), pp. 87–112; Friedrich Lau, "Das Schöffenkollegium des Hochgerichts zu Köln bis zum Jahre 1396," *Mevissenfestschrift* (Cologne, 1895), pp. 107–30 and Paul Strait's chapter on urban institutions in *Cologne in the Twelfth Century*.

46 Lau, "Das Kölner Patriziat bis zum Jahre 1325," pp. 370–1; von Winterfeld, *Handel, Kapital und Patriziat in Köln bis 1400*, pp. 31–6.

47 379 Boesengasse (St. Severin) fo. 2v: "Notum sit tam presentibus quam futuris, quod Albero dictus Scalle, tutor Rigmudis, filie fratris sue, venit in presentiam iudicis aput Sanctum

Since this Richmudis was not yet of age (which was approximately twenty years),[48] she was represented by her uncle Albero. Albero Scallo was a well-placed Cologner who served as an *advocatus* and *Lehnsmann* of the archbishop.[49] He was married three times, his last wife being Cristina, the sister of Archbishop Wichbold.[50] His second wife, Duregin, was the niece of a certain Arnoldus dictus Ungevuch, who was involved in English trade and thereby quite wealthy.[51] This child Richmudis was a granddaughter of Walterus Anglicus and the daughter of a certain Bela. Both Bela and her husband were deceased by this time and so the husband's brother Albero was her guardian. Besides her the remaining "coeredes" are mentioned: we already know of Godefridus (who thus was still alive at the death of Walterus) and Philippus; the two daughters Gertrudis and Richmudis now complete this generation of the family.

In the following entries each of the four children as well as the granddaughter received their share of Walterus' property in St. Severin parish.[52] From the "hereditas supra antiquum fossatum" (i.e. Kather-

Severinum et obtinuit per sententiam scabinorum sibi fieri particionem in hereditate, que sita est in Bozengassen versus antiquam portam, sicut contingit inter ipsam et suos coeredes, scilicet Godefridum, Philippum, Gertrudem et Rigmudim, sorores eorundem. Ita quod predicta Richmudis et eius tutor obtinuerunt in particione tres mansiones sitas supra antiquum fossatum prope claustrum Seyne et quintam partem pomerii, que proxima est eisdem mansionibus; item cameram, que sita est prope hereditatem Mathie de Binge, que adiacet predicte G[odefridi] hereditati" (*c.* 1251). See Keussen, *Topographie der Stadt Köln*, II, p. 184 col. b, a.

[48] *Die Kölner Schreinsbücher des 13. und 14. Jahrhunderts*, ed. Planitz and Buyken, p. 15.

[49] *REK*, III, 2, p. 159 no. 3146 and p. 160 no. 3148. He is called "Albero Scallo dictus advocatus" in 178 Clericorum (St. Columba) fo. IV.

[50] A. Fahne, *Geschichte der Kölnischen, Jülichschen und Bergischen Geschlechter*, 2 vols. (Cologne, 1843–53), I, p. 377.

[51] 142 Wetschatz Generalis (St. Peter) fo. 13v for example. Much material survives about Arnoldus Ungevuch in Cologne and about his activities in English trade. Arnoldus was also related to the family of Waldeverus Advocatus, an important family in Cologne at this time – see Lau, "Das Kölner Patriziat bis zum Jahre 1325," pp. 88–9.

[52] 379 Boesengasse (St. Severin) fo. 3r: "Notum, quod predicta Richmudis et tutor eius obtinuerunt unam mansionem de duabus contiguis, que site sunt supra litus Reni versus portam antiquam prope hereditatem Cunonis. Ita quod predicta Rigmudis predictam hereditatem sine omni contradictione obtinebit, renuntiantibus et effestucantibus Godefrido et Philippo et Rigmudo et Gertrude supradicta hereditate.

Notum, quod Godefridus, filius Welteri Anglici, obtinuit in particione supradicte hereditatis duas mansiones contiguas sitas in Bozengassen prope hereditatem Philippi, fratris sui, et hereditatem sororis sue Rigmudis. Item obtinuit quintam partem pomerii retro adiacentis versus supradictas mansiones. Item sciendum, quod frater suus Philippus et sorores eius Rigmudis et Gertrudis et Rigmudis, filia sororis sue [i.e. Bela], effestucaverunt et renunciaverunt predictam hereditatem predicti Godefridi. Ita quod predictus Godefridus liberam habeat, in quemcumque locum voluerit, divertendi potestatem.

Notum, quod Philippus et uxor eius Cristina, frater Godefridi Anglici, obtinuit [*sic*] in particione inter ipsum et fratrem suum Godefridum et sorores suas Rigmudem, Gertrudem et cognatam suam, filiam sororis sue Bele R[ichmudim], duas mansiones contiguas proximas hereditati fratris sui predicti Godefridi versus antiquam portam. Item obtinuit quintam partem inengraben) each received one-fifth of the apple garden. There is also an additional piece of property on this street – here stated as three *mansiones* – which went to the granddaughter alone. She also received a small chamber (*camera*), perhaps a workshop, lying near the *hereditas* of her uncle Godefridus Anglicus. This mention of an existing inheritance for Godefridus suggests that the children of Walterus may have already received their portions of the *mansiones* and this entry concerned only the granddaughter at the death of her parents. If so, the size of Walterus' holdings on Katherinengraben would have been much larger than merely the apple garden as indicated in previous entries.

As for the *hereditas* on Bozengasse/Seyengasse (now including the house purchased by Walterus *c.* 1235), each heir received two *mansiones* from it excepting the granddaughter Richmudis, who obtained only one *mansio* – apparently the *mansio* contiguous to it was also given to the daughter Richmudis. We learn here something of the size of Walterus' property on Bozengasse/Seyengasse. It was comprised of ten *mansiones*, a rather sizeable piece of property. This *domus* or complex of *mansiones* on Bozengasse/Seyengasse was also called the "domus Anglici" in contemporary entries.[53] We also learn of the children of Richmudis and

partem [*sic*] pomerii retro adiacentis versus predictas mansiones. Item sciendum, quod predictus Godefridus, frater predicti Philippi, et sorores eius Rigmudis, Gertrudis et filia sororis sororis [*sic*] sue R[ichmudis] renunciaverunt et effestucaverunt predictam hereditatem predicti Philippi. Ita quod predictus Philippus predictam hereditatem sine omni contradictione obtinebit.

Notum, quod Rigmudis et pueri eius Mathias, Gorwinus, Gerardus, Bela, Durenge et Ricgmudis [*sic*] obtinuerunt in particione duas mansiones sitas in Bozengassen proximas claustro Seine et hereditati Godefridi, fratris eiusdem Richmudis. Item obtinuerunt quintam partem pomerii retro adiacentis versus predictas mansiones. Item sciendum, quod predicta Richmudis et pueri eius obtinuerunt unam mansionem de duabus mansionibus sitis supra litus Reni Beigene versus turrim [Kalkrasenturm (antiquam portam)]. Item sciendum, quod Godefridus, frater eius, Philippus, Gertrudis et Ricmudis, [*sic*] filia Bele sororis predicte Rigmudis, renunciaverunt predictam hereditatem. Ita quod predicta Rigmudis et eius heredes sine omni contradictione obtinebunt.

Notum, quod Getrudis et filia eius Elizabeth obtinuerunt duas mansiones contiguas sitas in Bozengasse proximas hereditati Philippi, fratris predicte Gertrudis, versus antiquam portam in particione cum quinta parte pomerii retro adiacentis versus predictam hereditatem. Sciendum etiam, quod Godefridus, Philippus, Ricmudis et Rigmudis, [*sic*] filia sororis sue, renunciaverunt unanimiter in supradictam hereditatem. Item predicta Gertrudis et Elizabeth predictam hereditatem sine omni contradictione obtinebunt" (*c.* 1251).

53 380 Drankgasse (St. Severin) fo. 1r: "Notum sit tam futuris quam presentibus, quod Theodericus Huno et uxor eius Methildis manu coniuncta vendiderunt et remiserunt dimidiam partem hereditatis sue site super litus Reni iuxta hereditatem Anglici versus turrim Winando et uxori sue Engilradi, aliam dimidiam partem predicte hereditatis Ide, matri predicte Engilradis, sicut in possessione sua habebant, ea condicione, quod liberam habeant potestatem, in quemcumque locum voluerit, divertendi" (*c.* 1251). 380 Drankgasse (St. Severin) fo. 2v: "Notum sit tam futuris quam presentibus, quod Cuno Molandinarius et uxor eius Metildis remiserunt libere filiis suis Cunoni et uxori sue Elizabet, Hildegero et uxori sue Elizabet duas mansiones cum areis sitas prope domum Anglici versus domum Minnevusch, ea condicione, ut liberam habeant, in quemcumque locum voluerint, divertenti potestatem" (*c.* 1251).

Gertrudis, about whose husbands there is more information in the passages below.

The inheritance entries for Walterus' property in St. Martin parish do not appear until 1263, roughly ten years after those for St. Severin parish. Much more detail about his children's families appears here. By this time Godefridus Anglicus had died and his sister Richmudis obtained his portion of the first house discussed on Turnmarkt.[54] She therefore owned portions of both halves of the house. We now discover that her husband was Gerardus "dictus Raze." Gerardus came from another major patrician family in Cologne known as Raitze. The first evidence of this *Geschlecht* occurs in the first third of the twelfth century when a certain Razo, from whom the family name developed, was a *ministerialis* for the church of St. Pantaleon. His son Hermannus was also a *ministerialis* for St. Pantaleon as well as a *scabinus* in the parish. Hermannus' son Henricus was not only a *scabinus* but an *Amtmann* of the *Richerzeche* (*Meliorat*) as well. Gerardus, the husband of Richmudis, was the grandson of this Henricus Raitze. Gerardus' brother Theodericus was a knight, a *scabinus* and a *Bürgermeister*, and was among those burghers who, along with the Cleingedanc family members, were exiled by the archbishop's party in 1259–60.[55] Hence this English family experienced the conflict between the archbishop and the Cologne patricians first hand through their ties to two families (Cleingedanc and Raitze) that lost the struggle.

Eight years later Richmudis sold her share in the house to Theodericus Raitze, the brother of Gerardus, only four months before he became a *Bürgermeister*.[56] The other sister Gertrudis gave her portion of

---

[54] 17 Eckardi A (St. Martin) fo. 9r: "Item notum sit tam futuris quam presentibus, quod Richmudis, filia Welteri dicti Anglici et Richmudis, comparavit in figura iudicii et per sententiam scabinorum optinuit de morte fratris sui Godefridi tertiam partem dimidietatis domus et aree site in litore [sic] Reni proxime domui Buzzonis versus plateam Reni, ante et retro subtus et superius, prout ibi dicta hereditas ibi iacet et sicut dictam hereditatem in sua habebat proprietate. Et ipsa remisit marito suo Gerardo. Ita quod dicta Richmudis et maritus eius Gerardus dictus Raze dictam hereditatem iure et sine contradictione obtinebunt. Actum anno Domini 1263.

Item notum sit, quod prefata Richmudis, filia Welteri dicti Anglici et Richmudis, comparavit in figura iudicii et per sentenciam scabinorum obtinuit de morte fratris sui predicti Godefridi terciam partem quarte partis alterius dimidietatis eiusdem domus supradicte, prout dicta hereditas ibi iacet et sicut dictus Godefridus dictam hereditatem in sua habebat proprietate. Ita quod ipsa [Richmundis (sic) crossed out] et ipsa Richmudis tradidit et remisit dictam hereditatem marito suo Gerardo. Ita quod ipsa Richmudis et maritus eius Gerardus dictam hereditatem iure et sine contradictione obtinebunt."

[55] Lau, "Das Kölner Patriziat bis zum Jahre 1325," pp. 137–8. Lau indicates with a question mark the marriage of Gerardus to a "Richmodis, Tochter von Welteri Anglicus." See also von Winterfeld, *Handel, Kapital und Patriziat in Köln bis 1400*, pp. 10–11.

[56] 17 Eckardi A (St. Martin) fo. 13v: "Item notum sit tam futuris quam presentibus, quod Theodericus dictus Raze comparavit sibi erga Richmudim, filiam Walteri Anglici et Richmudis,

the same house to her daughter Elizabeth and husband Mathias de Via Lapidea almost a year later, and the two purchased another third of the house back from Theodericus Raitze.[57] Now the house had passed out of the male line of the Anglicus family. No mention occurs anywhere of Philippus Anglicus possessing any portion of the house. In addition we learn the name of Gertrudis' husband, Amplonius, although no further information on his family is included.

The final two pieces of property left by Walterus Anglicus to his heirs were situated in the district of Airsbach and in the neighborhood of the original family house on Filzengraben. Inheritance entries for these do not occur in the Schreinsbücher until the 1270s, apparently because they were occasioned either by the sale of the property or simply by the grandchildren's claims. In the first entry concerning a half of a house on Holzmarkt a full list of Walterus Anglicus' grandchildren appears, with some interesting new data revealed.[58] Walterus' daughter Richmudis

et Gerardum maritum eius terciam partem dimidietatis domus et aree site in littore Reni prope domum Buzonis versus plateam Reni, ante et retro subtus et superius, prout ibidem iacet et sicut eam in sua habebant proprietate. Ita quod dictus Th. Raze dictam hereditatem iure optinebit, ubi eum in particione attingit.

Item notum sit etc., quod predictus Theodericus Raze emit sibi erga predictos Richmudim et Gerardum maritum eius terciam partem quarte partis alterius dimidietatis domus et aree supradicte, prout dicta hereditas ibidem iacet et sicut eam in sua habebant proprietate. Ita quod dictus Theodericus prescriptam hereditatem iure et sine omni contradictione optinebit. Actum anno Domini 1271 mense decembri."

[57] 13 Wolberonis A (St. Martin) fo.15v: "Notum sit tam futuris quam presentibus, quod Gertrudis, filia Walteri Anglici et Richmudis, optinuit de morte parentum suorum predictorum terciam partem domus et aree site in littore Reni prope domum Buzonis versus plateam Reni, ante et retro subtus et superius, prout ibidem iacet et sicut eam predicti parentes eius in sua habebant proprietate et ubi eam in particione attingit. Ita quod ipsa Gertrudis prescriptam hereditatem iure et sine omni contradictione optinebit.

Item notum sit, quod predicta Gertrudis, filia Walteri Anglici predicti, que quondam uxor fuerat Amplonii, donavit et remisit filie sue Elyzabeth et Mathie de Via Lapidea marito eius prescriptam terciam partem domus et aree predicte, ante et retro subtus et superius, prout ibidem iacet et sicut eam in sua habebat proprietate. Ita quod dicta Mathias et uxor sua Elyzabeth prescriptam hereditatem iure et sine omni contradictione optinebunt, ubi eos in particione attinget. Actum anno Domini 1272 mense Octobri."

17 Eckardi A (St. Martin) fo. 14r: "Item notum sit tam futuris quam presentibus, quod Mathias de Via Lapida et Elyzabeth uxor sua emerunt sibi erga Theodericum dictum Raze terciam partem mediatatis domus et aree site in littore Reni prope domum Buzonis versus plateam Reni, ante et retro subtus et superius, prout ibidem iacet et sicut ipse Th. Raze eam in sua proprietate. Ita quod dicti Mathias et Elyzabeth prescriptam hereditatem, ubi eos in particione attingit, iure et sine omni contradictione obtinebunt. Actum anno Domini 1272 mense Octobri." The daughter of Elizabeth and Mathias, named Gertrudis, was a Beguine who sold her inheritance to Hermannus Hardevust and his wife Gertrudis in 1311: 380 Drankgasse (St. Severin) fo. 23v.

[58] 307 Veteris Portae (Airsbach) fos. 26v–27r: "Notum, quod Richmudi et marito eius Gerwino, Gertrudi et marito suo Appollonio, Philippo et uxor eius Cristine, cuilibet eorum cessit de morte patris Welteri et matris eorum Richmudis tercia pars medietatis domus et aree site in Foro Lignorum iuxta domum Alexandri superius. Ita quod cuilibet predictorum suam terciam partem predictam medietatis domus et aree predicte, ubi eis in particione contingit, iure et sine

had married a second husband, a certain Gerwinus. A son of the same name can safely be said to be an offspring of this second union while another son named Gerardus probably came from her first marriage to Gerardus Raitze. At least two of her daughters, Durginis and Richmudis (and perhaps even Elizabeth), were beguines. The first mention of German beguines comes from Cologne, where they flourished.[59] The beguine movement was indicative of the developing bourgeois spirituality of the time and was strongly supported by the wealthy burgher families of Cologne. The English families in Cologne followed the religious practices of the Cologne burghers in an exemplary fashion. Eventually all heirs (including Cristina Cleingedanc, the widow of

contradictione obtinebunt. Notum, quod Mathie et uxori sue Beatrici, Gerwino, Elizabet, Richmudi et Durgine begginis, cuilibet eorum cessit de morte patris et matris Gerwini et Richmudi predictorum quinta pars tercie partis medietatis domus et aree predicte site in Foro Lignorum iuxta domum Alexandri superius. Ita quod cuilibet suam quintam partem domus et aree predicte, ubi eis in particionem [*sic*] attinget, iure et sine contradictione obtinebunt. Notum, quod Elizabet predicta venit in figura iudicii et obtinuit cum iuramento duorum proximorum ex utraque linea, quod iustam fecisset cum fratribus et sororibus suis predictis particionem de quinta parte tercie partis domus et aree predicte et quod aliam partem in alio loco eque bonam recepisset vel meliorem et decrevit sententia scabinorum, quod iure posset renuntiare. Item Elizabet predicta renunciavit super quinta parte domus et aree predicte ad manus Mathie, Gerwini, Richmudi et Durginis fratrorum et sororum predictorum. Ita quod cuilibet suam partem predictam, ubi eis in particionem [*sic*] contingit, iure et sine contradictione obtinebit.

Notum, quod Elizabet et marito suo Mathie cessit proprietas tercie partis medietatis domus et aree predicte de morte patris predicti et Gertrudis mater predicta dedit et remisit ipsis usumfructum. Ita quod iure et sine contradictione obtinebunt.

Notum, quod Cristina, quondam uxor Philippi Anglici, venit cum pueris suis Henrico, Philippo, Gerardo, Hermanno, Richmudis et Ida in figura iudicii et obtinuit iuramento duorum proximorum ex utraque linea, quod melius esset eis tercia pars domus et aree predicte vendita quam retenta et decrevit sentencia scabinorum, quod Cristina vendere posset et vendicio rata deberet et manere et firma. [Folio changes here to 27r]

Notum, quod Wolquinus et Richmudis uxor eius emerunt sibi erga Mathiam et Beatricem uxorem suam, Gorwinum, Richmudim et Durginam begginas terciam partem medietatis domus et aree predicte site in Foro Lignorum iuxta domum Alexandri superius eo iure, quo ipsi eam possidebant. Ita quod iure et sine contradictione, ubi eos in particionem contingit, obtinebunt. Item emerunt sibi [erga] Mathiam et Elizabet uxorem suam aliam terciam partem medietatis domus et aree predicte site ut supra. Ita quod iure et sine contradictione, ubi eos in particione contingit, obtinebunt. Item idem Wolquinus et uxor sua Richmudis predicti emerunt sibi proprietatem tercie partis medietatis domus et aree predicte erga Henricum, Philippum, Gerardum, Hermannum, Richmudim et Idam, liberos Philippi Anglici, et usumfructum erga Cristinam, puerorum predictorum matrem. Ita quod iure et sine contradictione obtinebunt" (1272). The actual location was somewhere on Holzmarkt 1. Keussen, *Topographie der Stadt Köln*, II, p. 24 col. b, b has "1235. dom. et ar. in littore apud Renum proxime domui Walteri Anglici superius" listed as "Holzmarkt I-IV westlich, unbestimmt."

59 E. Ennen, "Kölner Wirtschaft im Früh- und Hochmittelalter," pp. 165–66. See also Frederick Stein, "The Religious Women of Cologne 1120–1320"; Johannes Asen, "Die Beginen in Köln," *Annalen* 111 (1927), pp. 81–180; 112 (1928), pp. 71–148; 113 (1929), pp. 13–96; F. Stein, "Einige Bemerkungen zu J. Asens 'Die Beginen in Köln,'" *Annalen* 178 (1976), pp. 167–77.

Philippus Anglicus) sold their portions to a certain Wolquinus and his wife Richmudis, and the house passed out of the family's hands.

The final piece of property was located a stone's throw away from this house.[60] By the time of the entry only two children of Richmudis and Gerwinus appear to have survived, and no mention is made either of the death of Philippus Anglicus or his heirs. Yet there is abundant material for Philippus' family, to which we shall turn next. This final passage (no further mention occurs of this piece of property) concludes the evidence surviving for the generation of Walterus Anglicus.[61]

These entries, taken as a whole, have shed considerable light on the range of activities open to foreigners in Cologne. They have also suggested the thoroughgoing integration achieved by English expatriates in local Cologne life, an integration which subsequent material will further flesh out. These properties held in the district of Airsbach and the parishes of St. Severin and St. Martin are without exception along the shore of the Rhine, which strongly suggests a mercantile basis for the family's livelihood and would explain how they wound up in Cologne in the first place. The location for the majority of the property, which rings the foreign quarter of Heumarkt, and the probable function of the "English Tower" on Turnmarkt further confirm this. Not only did Walterus Anglicus accumulate a sizeable estate, but he also managed to establish impressive social ties in Cologne by marrying his children into the prestigious and powerful patrician families of Cleingedanc and Raitze. Unfortunately, we know nothing of Walterus' wife Richmudis, or perhaps yet another important link to a Cologne family could be shown (the same can be said for the brothers of Walterus, about whom there is nothing further). In addition, some of the family's daughters

---

[60] 307 Veteris Portae (Airsbach) fo. 29r: "Notum, quod Philippo, Richmudi et Gertrudis cessit de morte patris eorum Welteri dicti Anglici una area sita in Bossenrode [i.e. Holzgassen]. Ita quod Philippus et Cristina uxor sua, Richmudis et Gorswinus maritus eius, Gertrudis et Appollonius maritus eius, quilibet predictorum suam terciam partem aree predicte iure et sine contradictione obtinebit. Notum, quod Mathie et Gorswino cessit de morte Gorswini et Richmudis parentum suorum tercia pars aree predicte. Ita quod iure et sine contradictione obtinebunt. Notum, quod Elizabet cessit de morte Appollonii et Gertrudi parentum eius tercia pars aree predicte. Ita quod Elizabet et Mathias maritus eius iure et sine contradictione obtinebunt" (1277). The actual location was either Holzgasse I or II (see Keussen, *Topographie der Stadt Köln*, II, p. 21). Bossenrode = Holzgasse.

[61] There are in addition some vague references to a house owned by Walterus Anglicus: 447 Generalis (Schöffenschrein) fo. 88r: a house mentioned "site in littore Reni inter domum Danielis Iudei et domum Walteri Anglici" twice on this folio. Daniel Iudeus was a major political and economic figure in Cologne and a member of the patrician Jude family (see Lau, "Das Kölner Patriziat bis zum Jahre 1325," pp. 115–19 and von Winterfeld, *Handel, Kapital, und Patriziat in Köln bis 1400*, pp. 14–16). Also 447 Generalis (Schöffenschrein) fo. 71r: a house is mentioned "site in littore Reni inter domum . . . et domum Walteri Anglici." These could be any one of the houses he owned, as they were all along the shore of the Rhine.

entered into the religious life of Cologne, becoming beguines in the fashion of the daughters of Cologne burghers. Similar religious activity also occurs in the next generation among the male children in this family. All in all we have discovered the remarkable extent to which an English family had entered into the society and economy of Cologne. This degree of integration was continued by the only surviving son of the next generation, Philippus Anglicus.

The first independent reference to Philippus shows his involvement in a typical mercantile activity in Cologne – mortgaging property.[62] Here he loaned a certain Mathias 5 marks with Mathias' portion of his family inheritance in Neumarkt as collateral. Mathias was unable to redeem the loan in the allotted time, and Philippus sold a sixth of this property with three *mansiones* attached to it some time thereafter.[63] This is the only documented mention of the English in Holy Apostles parish, which had been added to the city along with Niederich and Airsbach in the extension of fortifications in 1106 and was still thinly populated. Neumarkt was probably used as a cattle market at the time.[64] But this transaction says something about the economic status achieved by the English – now they are lenders as well as mortgagers.

Philippus added to his inheritance in St. Severin parish around the time of his father's death.[65] He and his wife purchased two of three

---

[62] 211 Novum Forum (St. Aposteln) fo. 7r: "Notum sit etc., quod Mathias suam partem hereditatis site in Novo Foro iuxta Stellam, que sibi cessit de morte patris sui, obligavit cum concensu matris sue Philippo, filio Walteri Anglici, pro quinque marcis usque ad octavam pentecostes. Ita si ipse Mathias in termino statuto eandem partem eiusdem hereditatis non redemerit in termino prenominato, quod iustum est fieret; cum autem terminus redemptionis transierit et Mathias suam partem hereditatis prenominate non redemerit, per sentenciam scabinorum Philippus prefatus optinuit, quod in usus, quos voluerit divertere, poterit quicquid Mathias habuit in hereditate prememorata. Salvo tamen usufructu matri Mathie, tam in eadem hereditate quam in duabus mansionibus sitis pone ipsam" (*c.* 1250). Text published in *Die Kölner Schreinsbücher des 13. und 14. Jahrhunderts*, ed. Planitz and Buyken, p. 52 no. 222. The actual location was probably Neumarkt III (see Keussen, *Topographie der Stadt Köln*, I, p. 427 col. a, 1).

[63] 211 Novum Forum (St. Aposteln) fo. 12r: "Notum sit etc., quod Hermannus Kezzeler et uxor eius Richmudis emerunt erga Phylippum, filium Anglici, sextam partem domus prope Stellam, que quondam fuit Baldewini, et in tribus mansionibus iacentibus retro domum eandem. Ita ut communi manu vertant quicquid velint ad idem ius, quod habuerunt prescripti" (*c.* 1250–64). The scribe has for some reason left out the name of Philippus' father Walterus.

[64] Keussen, *Topographie der Stadt Köln*, I, pp.15*, 160*.

[65] 380 Drankgasse (St. Severin) fo. 9v: "Notum sit tam presentibus quam futuris, quod Philippus Anglicus comparavit et uxor eius Cristina erga Renzonem et uxorem eius Cunegundem duas mansiones contiguas de tribus mansionibus sitas super litus Reni prope hereditatem Adolfi Carpentarii, tali condicione, quod si predicti Philippus et uxor eius Cristina prolem genuerint, ipsorum sit. Si vero predictus Philippus sine prole discesserit, ad proximos heredes ipsius Philippi supradicta hereditas transeat in continenti et sic predicti Philippus et uxor eius Cristina predictam hereditatem sine omni contradictione obtinebunt, ut supradictum est et sicut predictus Renzo in sua possessione obtinebat" (*c.* 1251). For location see Keussen, *Topographie der Stadt Köln*, II, p. 184 col. b, b.

contiguous *mansiones*, which, although sounding peculiarly similar to the three *mansiones* his niece Richmudis inherited from Walterus Anglicus around the same time, were actually located on Bayenstrasse near his father's holdings on Seyengasse.[66] This purchase was kept distinct in the records from Philippus' portion of the apple garden and was identified as the "hereditas Philippi Anglici."[67] The terms of this purchase indicate that Philippus Anglicus and Cristina Cleingedanc had not yet conceived children. This would mean that his subsequent six children were either in or approaching their early twenties at his death in the early 1270s. He and his wife later purchased an hereditary rent of 24 pence in two separate transactions from the same location.[68] This rent would remain in the family for many years, eventually being passed down to their children. We have already seen that, in addition to these holdings, Philippus Anglicus also purchased half of a plot on Bozengasse/Seyengasse from his uncle Arnoldus and an eighth part of the "English Tower" on Turnmarkt. Philippus Anglicus, the eldest surviving male, was obviously trying to keep the family property intact by buying up portions that had been dispersed after the death of his father.

With regard to his own family, much material survives describing Philippus' children and the subsequent fate of his estate. At the death of Philippus his wife Cristina proceeded to sell his property, perhaps to maintain an income as a widow. She would eventually sell all of her

---

[66] Keussen, *Topographie der Stadt Köln*, II, p. 197 col. b, b: "dom. Adolfi Carpentarii inter Symon de Mitra et domum dominorum et fratrum de s. Katerina" was on Seyengasse I. Symon de Mitra's *hereditas* was located on Bayenstrasse II (Keussen, II, p. 175 col. b, b), and Adolfus Carpentarius' house was on Seyengasse.

[67] 380 Drankgasse (St. Severin) fo. 10v: "Notum sit tam futuris quam presentibus, quod Hermannus, clericus, quondam filius magistri Theoderici scolastici Sancti Georgii, tradidit et remisit convento Sancte Marie in Seyne aream iacentem supra litus Reni prope hereditatem Philippi Anglici in memoria anime sue sicut ipse in sua possessione a predicta ecclesia habebat. Ita quod predictus conventus dictam hereditatem sine omni contradictione obtinebit" (*c.* 1251–88).

[68] 380 Drankgasse (St. Severin) fo. 10v: "Notum sit tam futuris quam presentibus, quod Philippus Anglicus et uxor eius Cristina emerunt sibi erga Ricgolfum et uxorem eius Beatricem XII denarios Coloniense hereditarii census in hereditate, que sita super litus Reni iuxta aream Hermanni Dunze prope hereditatem Symonis de Mitra, de quibus sex denarii in festo beate Marie purificationis et sex in festo assumptionis beate Marie persolvent et octo dies sine pena habebunt. Si vero ex tunc persolvere negglexerint, predicti Philippus et uxor eius Cristina in proprietatem predicte hereditatis ascribentur" (*c.* 1251–88).

380 Drankgasse (St. Severin) fo. 10v: "Notum, quod predictus Philippus et uxor eius Cristina emerunt sibi erga dictum Rigolfum et uxorem eius Beatricem XII denarios Coloniense hereditarii census et hereditatem, que sita est super litus Reni prope hereditatem H. Dunze, de quibus sex denarii in festo beate Marie purificationis et sex in assumptione beate Marie persolvent et octo dies sine pena habebunt. Si vero ex tunc persolvere neglexerint, predicti Philippus et uxor eius Cristina in proprietatem predicte hereditatis ascribentur" (*c.* 1251–88). The actual location was probably Bayenstrasse I or II (see Keussen, *Topographie der Stadt Köln*, II, p. 175 col. b, b).

inheritance from the Cleingedanc side of the family as well. Evidence of liquidating assets to procure a steady income appears when Cristina sold Philippus' portion of the apple garden on Katherinengraben to a certain Godefridus Rufus and his wife Guderadis for an hereditary rent of 20 pence.[69] In this sale, her six children by Philippus are named: Henricus, Philippus, Gerardus, Hermannus, Richmudis, and Ida. In what was to be a standard practice for Cristina, she obtained the legal rights over Philippus' estate in court from her children and then sold the property – this procedure was necessary since the children were probably still minors, yet the legal heirs according to Cologne property law.

She followed the same procedure with the sale of the two contiguous *mansiones* at the intersection of Bayenstrasse and Seyengasse.[70] This passage lacks the son Hermannus, who had apparently died by this time. We also learn a valuable piece of information about Philippus' second

---

[69] 379 Boesengasse (St. Severin) fo. 6r: "Notum sit tam futuris quam presentibus, quod Cristina, uxor Philippi Anglici, venit in presentiam iudicis cum proximis utriusque linee puerum suorum iuramento interposito et obtinuit per sentenciam scabinorum, quod ad meliorem utilitatem factum sit dictam hereditatem, que sita sit iuxta hereditatem Adolfi versus antiquam portam, concedendi. Ita quod predicta Cristina predictam hereditatem liberam habebat concendendi potestatem, in quemcumque locum voluerit.

Notum, quod predicta Cristina tradidit et remisit aream sitam super litus Reni et concessit Godefrido Rufo et uxori sue Guderadi pro viginti denariis hereditarii census solvendis in festo pasche quatuor obdomadas sine pena. Si non dictum censum predicti Godefridus et uxor eius Guderadus dictum censum [*sic*] predicte Cristina et eorum heredibus predicto termino non persolvunt, predicta Cristina et eorum heredes in proprietate dicte hereditatis sine omni contradictione obtinebunt et predicti Godefridus et Guderadus liberam habebant, in quemcumque locum voluerint, divertendi potestatem" (undated). Whether Godefridus Rufus was a member of Cristina's Geschlecht is unknown. Lau has no such person included in his genealogy of the Cleingedanc family.

[70] 379 Boesengasse (St. Severin) fo. 6v: "Notum sit tam presentibus quam futuris, quod hereditas sita versus Seyne, videlicet due mansiones versus antiquam portam, devoluta est ex morte patris Philippi Anglici ad pueros suos, videlicet Henricum, Philippum, Gerardum, Ricgmudim [*sic*] et Idani. Ita predicti pueri dictam hereditatem sine omni contradictione obtinebunt. Salvo usufructu Cristine matris eorum quamdiu vixerit.

Notum, quod Henricus predictus tradidit partem suam ad manus matris sue Cristine. Item Philippus de consensu prioris sui ordinis Predicatorum tradidit et remisit partem suam Cristine matri sue.

Notum, quod Gerardus partem suam predicte hereditatis tradidit et remisit partem suam [*sic*] ad manus matris sue Cristine."

379 Boesengasse (St. Severin) fo. 7r: "Notum sit, quod predicta Cristina venit in presentiam iudicis cum duabus puellis, filiabus suis, Rigmudim et Idam [*sic*] apud Sanctam Severinum cum proximis utriusque linee puerorum suorum et obtinuit per sentenciam scabinorum iuramento interposito, quod ad meliorem utilitatem factum esset dictam hereditatem alienandi vel vendendi predictis puellis quam non factum esset. Et sic predicte puelle, videlicet Ricmudis et Ida, predictas suas partes dicte hereditatis tradiderunt et remiserunt ad manus matris eorum predicte Cristine et sic predicta [passage ends at this point].

Notum, quod predicta Cristina predictas duas mansiones tradidit et remisit Gerardo et uxori sue Blithildi de Hulreporte cum usufructu vite sue. Ita quod predicti Gerardus et uxor eius Blithildis dictam hereditatem sine omni contradictione obtinebunt" [Salvo iure Gerardi filii dictorum Philippi et Cristine, quod habet in dicta hereditate is erased] (undated).

son and namesake: he was a Dominican friar.[71] He gave his portion to Cristina "de consensu prioris sui ordinis Predicatorum." This is yet another sign of the integration of the family into Cologne life and probably resulted from ties to the Cleingedanc family, since Cristina's brother Richolfus was also a Dominican. In a subsequent entry we will find as well that the daughter Richmudis was a beguine.

Around the year 1288 Cristina sold even the rent obtained by the sale of the apple garden.[72] By this time another son, Henricus (probably the eldest), is missing from the list of children and thus perhaps deceased. We also see that Ida was now married, although her husband's name is lacking in the entry. Once again the children foreswore their claims to the inheritance and Cristina sold the rent back to Godefridus Rufus and Guderadis, who were therefore buying out all of the family's interest in the garden. About the year 1303 she sold the rent of 24 pence from the property on Bayenstrasse/Seyengasse as well.[73] Here only her daughter

---

[71] Gabriel P. Löhr, *Beiträge zur Geschichte des Kölner Dominikanerklosters im Mittelalter*, Quellen und Forschungen zur Geschichte des Dominikanerordens in Deutschland, 15/17 (Leipzig, 1920–2), II, p. 55 no. 105 mentions this renunciation of Philippus' inheritance, dating it "vor 1293 Okt. 8" and commenting: "Die Mehrzahl der Kinder scheint nach der eben erwähnten Eintragung (379 no. 77) verglichen mit 379 no. 68/9 noch minderjährig zu sein."

[72] 380 Drankgasse (St. Severin) fo. 14r: "Notum sit tam presentibus quam futuris, quod Philippus, Gerardus, Rigmudis et Ida, liberi Philippi dicti Anglici et Cristine uxoris sue, cuilibet eorum cessit de morte parentum suorum predictorum quarta pars viginti denariorum hereditarii census solvendorum de area sita super litus Reni, sicut in sua habebant proprietate. Ita quod quilibet suam quartem partem iure et sine omni contradictione optinebit.

Item notum sit, quod quilibet predictorum liberorum, videlicet Philippus, Gerardus, Rigmudis, Ida et maritus eius [blank], remisit et donavit matri sue Cristine suam quartam partem XX denariorum aree supradicte. Ita quod iure et sine contradictione optinebit.

Notum sit, quod Cristina, uxor quondam Philippi Anglici, vendidit et remisit Godefrido Rufo et uxori sue Guderadi viginti denarios hereditarii census, quos solvebant de area sita super litus Reni, sicut in sua habebant proprietate. Ita quod ipsi iure et sine contradictione optinebunt" (*c.* 1288). See above for the original sale of the field for the rent.

[73] At this time the house as well as the rent pertaining to it were sold: 380 Drankgasse (St. Severin) fo. 23r: "Notum sit, quod Adolfus cum Elizabet uxore sua et Elizabet, beckina, soror predicti Adolfi, cum manu . . [two dots here] plebani sui, quilibet eorum tradidit et remisit Engilberto, fratri suo, et Drude uxori sue suam terciam partem domus et aree predicte site super litus Reni iuxta hereditatem Hermanni dicti Dunze ex altera parte . . . ante et retro subtus et superius, prout ibi iacet et sicut in sua habebant proprietate et ubi eos ex recta particione attinget. Ita quod dictam hereditatem iure et sine contradictione obtinebunt et divertere potuerunt, quocumque voluerint. Salvo Philippo dicto Anglico et Cristine uxoris sue censu suo hereditario in hereditate predicta, sicut est prescriptum . . .

Notum sit, quod Henricus dictus de Heden et Lora uxor sua emerunt sibi erga Engilbertum et Drudam uxorem suam predictos tres solidos denariorum tempore . . . [from same house as above] Salvo Philippo dicto Anglico et Cristine uxori sue censu suo hereditario in dicta hereditate, sicut est prescriptum.

Notum sit, quod Arnoldus dictus Schurolf et Katerina uxor sua emerunt sibi erga Cristinam, relictam quondam Philippi dicti Anglici, et Rigmudim filiam suam duos solidos Coloniensium denariorum hereditarii census solvendos singulis annis de hereditate, que sita est super litus Reni iuxta aream Hermanni Dunze prope hereditatem Symoni dicti de Mitra duobus terminis, videlicet XII denarii in festo beate Marie purificationis et in festo assumptionis beate Marie

Richmudis remains as coheir. We know nothing further concerning the disposition of Philippus' property from the "English Tower," the field on Holzgasse, or the half of a field on Bozengasse/Seyengasse. Documentary silence on these properties suggests that they remained in the family.

In regard to the property Christina received from her own wealthy family there is much documentation. She inherited from her parents portions of and rents from four different houses. These were centered in the parishes of St. Martin and St. Laurence. In a rather involved series of entries dated May 1282 Cristina and her brother Hermannus received half of a quarter part of a house and its land called "Ad Turrim"[74] located on Sassenhof and an equal portion of another house and its land called "Munstere ad Lapideam Trappam" located on Klobengasse – both in the heart of the mercantile parish of St. Martin.[75] Cristina then

---

virginis vel infra octo dies postea sine captione quolibet predictorum terminorum. Ita quod, si dictum censum aliquo predictorum terminorum solvere negglexerint, predicti Arnoldus et Katerina uxor sua in proprietatem predicte hereditatis ascribentur et si predicta Cristina puerum aliorum habeat, qui renunciavit. Salvo iure suo in duobus solidis supradictis" (*c.* 1303).

[74] The tower implied in the name "Ad Turrim" may very well have been the English Tower, as the location of the house on Sassenhof was in the immediate vicinity of the English Tower on Turnmarkt.

[75] 6a Vogelonis (St. Martin) fo. 33v: "Notum sit etc., quod Hermannus et Cristina, liberi Henrici Cleingedanc et Leticie, quilibet eorum optinuit de morte parentum suorum predicorum unam medietatem unius quarte partis domus et aree site super Sasinhoven et vocate Ad Turrim. Item quilibet eorum optinuit unam medietatem quarte partis domus et aree site sub Lobiis vocate Ad Lapideam Trappam et Munstere, ante et retro subtus et superius, prout ibidem iacet et ubi ipsos in particione attinget et sicut in sua habebant proprietate. Ita quod iure et sine omni contradictione optinebunt. Et hoc testificatum est per scabinos de domo civium.

Item notum sit, quod predicta Cristina, comparens in figura iudicii cum proximis puerorum suorum utriusque Ide, Richmudis et Philippi, cum iuramento eorum et per sententiam scabinorum optinuit, quod particio dicte hereditatis, quam qui. . .? fecit cum predicto Hermanno, fratre suo, eisdem pueris eius, qui ad annos legitimos non pervenerant, melior ac utilior esset facta quam non facta.

Item notum sit etc., quod Henricus, Ida, Richmundis et Philippus, liberi dicte Cristine et Philippi Anglici, quilibet eorum optinuit de morte patris eorum predicti proprietatem unius quinte partis prescripte hereditatis, videlicet medietatis unius quarte partis domus et aree site super Sasinhoven vocate Ad Turrim et medietatis quarte partis dicte domus et aree site sub Lobiis et vocate Ad Lapideam Trappam. Ita quod iure et sine omni contradictione optinebunt.

Item notum sit etc., quod predicti pueri, videlicet Henricus, Ida, Richmudis et Philippus, liberi Philippi Anglici et Cristine predictorum, quilibet eorum donavit et remisit proprietatem suam quinte partis medietatis quarte partis domus et aree site super Sasinhoven vocate Ad Turrim Hermanno, filio Henrici Cleingedanc et Leticie, avunculo eorum, et uxori sue Elysabet. Ita quod iure et sine contradictione optinebunt. Et Cristina, mater dictorum puerorum, renunciavit et effestucavit super usufructu dicte hereditatis ad manus Hermanni et Elyzabet uxoris sue predictorum.

Notum sit, quod Gerardus, filius Cristine et Philippi Anglici, optinuit de morte patris sui predictam proprietatem unius quinte partis medietatis unius quarte partis domus et aree site super Sasinhoven vocate Ad Turrim, ante et retro subtus et superius, prout ibi iacet et sicut in sua habebat proprietate et ubi ipsum ex iusta particione attinget. Ita quod iure et sine contradictione optinebit.

obtained in court the right to pass this inheritance on to her children, of whom the only three mentioned are Ida, Richmudis, and Philippus. We have confirmation that these three were still minors, "qui ad annos legitimos non pervenerant." The children obtained a fifth part of Cristina's portion of both houses (in this entry the son Henricus is now included, suggesting that he was not a minor) and then they gave only their share in the house called "Ad Turrim" collectively to Cristina's brother Hermannus Cleingedanc and his wife Elizabeth. Independently of this, Cristina's other son, Gerardus, obtained his fifth portion of the house called "Ad Turrim," but he did not transfer it to his uncle. Rather, he sold it to Henricus Albus de Foro Ferri and his wife Elizabeth four years later.[76] The reason for this complex process in the settlement between Hermannus and Cristina was because her heirs' legal claims had to be addressed in the settlement. In return for giving her portion of the house "Ad Turrim" to Hermannus, he gave his share in the house called "Munstere ad Lapideam Trappam" to Cristina, to complete an even exchange.

Since the children retained their interest in the house "Munstere ad Lapideam Trappam," this grant by Hermannus now made the family's control a quarter of the house. Yet it appears that a close relationship between the two houses remained, as Cristina mortgaged this portion in May 1285 so that one of her sons might have some sort of interest in the house "Ad Turrim," now owned by Henricus Albus de Foro Ferri.[77]

Item notum sit etc., quod predicti Hermannus, filius Henrici Cleyngedanc et Leticie predictorum, et uxor sua Elyzabet donaverunt et remiserunt predicte Cristine, sorori eiusdem Hermanni, relicte Philippi Anglici, medietatem quarte partis domus et aree site sub Lobiis vocate Ad Lapideam Trappam et Munstere, ante et retro subtus et superius, prout ibidem iacet et ubi ipsam in particione attinget et sicut in sua habebant proprietate. Itaque iure et sine omni contradictione optinebit. Actum anno Domini 1282 mense Maio." It is worth noting here that the children obtained a fifth part of the inheritance in these proceedings, thus verifying that the brother Hermannus was indeed deceased by this time. The actual locations would have been Klobengasse II (see Keussen, *Topographie der Stadt Köln*, I, p. 43 col. a, 3 where "dom. Munstere ad lapideam Trappam sub Lobiis in angulo Aduycht" is mentioned) and probably Sassenhof III (see ibid., I, p. 72 col. b, I and 73 col. a, 4).

[76] 6a Vogelonis (St. Martin) fo. 34r: "Notum sit etc., quod Henricus Albus de Foro Ferri et Elizabet uxor sua emerunt sibi erga Gerardum, filium Cristine et Philippi Anglici, proprietatem unius quinte partis medietatis unius quarte partis domus et aree site supra Sasinhoven vocate Ad Turrim, ante et retro subtus et superius, prout ibi iacet et sicut in sua habebat proprietate et ubi ipsum ex iusta particione attinget. Ita quod . . . Actum anno Domini 1286 mense Martio." Hermannus Cleingedanc and Elizabeth sold the portion they received from Cristina's children also to Henricus Albus de Foro Ferri and Elizabeth at the time of its reception in May of 1282: 6a Vogelonis (St. Martin) fo. 33v. Thus it appears that Henricus was buying out the family's interest in the house.

[77] 31 Vadimoniorum (St. Martin) fo. 4r: "Item notum sit etc., quod Cristina, relicta Philippi Anglici, posuit tytulo pignoris Henrico dicto Albo de Foro Ferri et uxori sue Elyzabeth usumfructum quarte partis domus et aree site sub Lobiis vocate Ad Lapidam Trappam et Munstere tamdiu quousque [space] filius eius renunciet et effestucet ad manus manus [*sic*]

This was only a temporary arrangement, since Cristina sold her interest in the house to Gerardus Overstolz and his wife Alstradis (de Trappa) shortly thereafter.[78] Gerardus Overstolz was the father-in-law of Cristina's brother Henricus Cleingedanc, a former *vicecomes* of Cologne and an *Amtmann* of the *Richerzeche* (*Meliorat*).[79]

Cristina and her children also received a share in the Cleingedanc family house on Kleine Budengasse in St. Laurence parish. In her will the widow Gertrudis Overstolz (the sister-in-law of Cristina and the daughter of the above-mentioned Gerardus Overstolz) made religious contributions, leaving among them rents to two of Cristina's children.[80]

eorundem H[enrici] super decima parte quarte partis domus et aree site super Sasinhoven vocate Ad Turim. Quod si non fecerit, cum reversus fuerit, tunc idem Henricus et Elyzabeth tres solidos Coloniense singulis annis et quarta parte dicte domus et aree site sub Lobiis optinebunt tamdiu quousque renunciet (unam domum?) [very faded here] . . . Actum anno Domini 1285 mense Maio."

[78] This transaction was recorded three separate times in the Schreinsbücher, although at different dates: 449 II Generalis Alban (Schöffenschrein) fo. 1v: "Item notum sit, quod Cristina, filia quondam domini Henrici dicti Kleyngedanc et Leticie uxoris sue, relicta quondam Philippi dicti Hardevust [see discussion above about this appellation], qui vocabatur Anglicus, donavit et remisit domino Gerardo dicto Overstolz et Alstradi uxori sue quartam partem domus vocate Munstere site sub Lobiis, sicut eam habuit in sua proprietate. Ita quod iure et sine contradictione optinebunt et testificatum fuit ab officialibus parochie sancti Martini, quod ipsa Cristina potestatem habuit premissa faciendi" (undated).

447 Generalis (Schöffenschrein) fo. 68r: "Notum sit etc., quod Cristina, filia Henrici Cleyngedanc, relicta Philippi Anglici, tradidit et remisit Gerardo dicto Overstolz et Alstradi uxoris sue quartam partem domus et aree vocate Munstere sita sub Lobiis in angulo, ante et retro subtus et superius, prout ibidem iacet et ubi eos in particione attinget et sicut in sua habebant proprietate. Ita quod iure et sine contradictione optinebunt. Actum anno Domini 1287 mense junio et hoc testificatum est . . . officialibus parochie sancti Martini Minoris."

447 Generalis (Schöffenschrein) fo. 60r: "Notum sit etc., quod Cristina, relicta quondam Philipppi dicti Anglici, habens potestatem, donavit et remisit domino Gerardo dicto Overstolz, quondam vicecomiti, et domine Alstradi uxori sue quartam partem domus vocate Munstere sita sub Lobiis. Ita quod iure et sine contradictione optinebunt et ubi eos in particione attinget . . . anno Domini 1291 feria sexta ante palmas."

[79] Lau, "Das Kölner Patriziat bis zum Jahre 1325," p. 75.

[80] 99 Liber III de domo Milwirle (St. Laurenz) fo. 23r: "Item notum sit, quod supranominata Druda [Overstolz], quondam uxor Henrici Cleyngedanc predicti [son of Henricus and Leticia, mentioned in previous entry], tradidit et remisit post mortem suam illam marcam hereditariam supradictam, quam habet in medietate domus Henrici Cleynegedanc, Richmudi, becgine, filie Philippi Anglici et Cristine uxoris sue. Ita quod Herimannus Cleynegedanc [the uncle of Richmudis] et Lysa uxor eius solvent ipsi Richmudi, becgine predicte, de quarta parte domus Cleynegedanc predicte, quam supradicta Druda ipsis Herimanno et Lyse tradidit et remisit, dimidiam marcam hereditariam, tali condicione, quod si ipsi Herimanni et Lysa dictam dimidiam marcam aliquo anno post diem anniversarii dicte Drude vel infra quatuor septimanas sequentes non solverint, quod quarta pars domus Cleynegedanc supradicte cedet Richmudi, becgine antedicte, libere et absolute. Ita etiam quod Cristina, relicta dicti Philippi Anglici predicti, solvet sepedicte Richmudi, becgine filie sue, aliam dimidiam marcam hereditariam de alia quarta parte domus Cleynegedanc, quam sepedicta Druda ipsi Cristine tradidit et remisit, tali condicione, quod si ipsa Cristina dictam dimidiam marcam non solverit aliquo anno post diem anniversarii dicte Drude vel infra infra [sic] quatuor septimanas sequentes, quod aliqua quarta pars domus Cleynegedanc cedet Richmudi, becgine supradicte, libere et absolute.

Richmudis the beguine was to receive half a mark from both her uncle and her mother from their quarter parts of the house Cleingedanc. Philippus, along with his uncle Richolfus (both Dominicans) were to receive 3 shillings for their maintenance from four adjoining *mansiones*. The difference in the amounts given to the two religious siblings reflects the institutional support received by the Dominican Philippus and his uncle. Cristina had inherited a quarter of the family house[81] and had even sold a portion of the wall adjoining the back of the house, along with her brother and daughter Richmudis.[82] However, as with other properties Cristina and her daughter Richmudis finally transferred their

---

Item notum sit, quod supradicta Druda, relicta Henrici Cleynegedanc supradicti, post mortem suam de alia marca hereditaria, quam habet in quatuor mansionibus contiguis domui Ide supradicte, tradidit et remisit tres solidos hereditarios Richolfo, filio quondam Henrici Cleynegedanc senioris, et Philippo, filio quondam Ï ilippi Anglici, fratribus de ordine Predicatorum, quamdiu vixerint. Ita quod post mortem i sorum duorum fratrum dicti tres solidi hereditarii cedent domui et fratribus Predicatorum in C)lonia pro anniversario dicte Drude in perpetuum faciendo. Item ipsa Druda de eadem marcam post mortem suam tradidit und remisit tres solidos hereditarios conventui et monialibus in Dunewalde pro remedio anime sue." Löhr, *Beiträge zur Geschichte des Kölner Dominikanerklosters*, II, p. 49 no. 91 quotes this entry, names Druda as a member of the Overstolz family, and (continuing the error of Lau and von Winterfeld) states: "Philippus Anglicus gehört zu den Hardevust." Gertrudis continues (23v) giving 3 "solidos hereditarios domui et fratribus in Colonia beate Mariae de Monte Carmeli ob salutem et memoriam anime sue in perpetuum ibid faciendum" and 3 "solidos hereditarios [blank] filie Henrici Cleynegedanc senioris et filie Gerardi Overstolz Iunioris, fratris sui monialibus ad Martires." At their deaths the 3 solidi are to be given to the "abbatisse et conventui ad Martires ob salutem et memoriam anime sue ibid faciendum in perpetuum" (dated March 1288). The actual location of the house was on the corner of Kleine Budengasse III and Unter Goldschmied IV (see Keussen, *Topographie der Stadt Köln*, I, p. 198 col. a, 7 and p. 193 col. a, 11–12).

81 103 Liber IV de domo Kusini (St. Laurenz) fo. 17r: "Item notum sit, quod ex morte Henrici dicti Cleynegedanc, filii quondam Henrici dicti Cleynegedanc, cecidit supra Hermannum Rufum, fratrem dicti Henrici et uxorem suam Lisam, et supra Cristinam, sororem dicti Hermanni, supra quemlibet eorum quarta partis domus Ide Rufe. Ita quod quilibet eorum unam quartam partem dicte domus iure optinebit. Salvo censu hereditario de partibus predictis. Actum anno Domini 1296 crastino nativitatis beati Johannis Baptiste."

82 92 Per Totam Parrochiam (St. Laurenz) fo. 23r: "Item notum sit, quod Hermannus Rufus dictus Cleynegedanc, Lysa, uxor eius, et Cristina, soror dicti Hermanni, uxor quondam Philippi Anglici, tradiderunt et remiserunt Frederico de Stessa, Drude, uxori sue, et Brunoni de Stessa, fratri dicti Frederici, medietatem posterioris muri domus Ide Rufe, que dicitur Egtsterste Gevil versus Stessam a platea usque ad cameras retro. Ita quod dicti Fredericus et Druda uxor eius et Bruno edificia sua ponere possunt in medietatem dicti muri a fundo usque ad superioram partem dicti muri et suam facere voluntatem in medietate eiusdem muri. Ita etiam etiam [*sic*] quod dicti Fredericus, uxor eius et Bruno de cameris retro aquam suis expensis deducere debent. Et sciendum, quod Richmudis, filia Cristine predicte, predictam traditionem et remissionem ratam et gratam habuit et eam concensit omni iure, quo eidem Richmudi medietas predicti muri cadere potest. Salvo Frederico et uxori sue et Brunoni predictis cartis scrinii nostri et littera sigillata sigillo officiatorum nostrorum, que iacent in scrinio. Datum anno Domini 1297." Text published in *Die Kölner Schreinsbücher des 13. und 14. Jahrhunderts*, ed. Planitz and Buyken, pp. 419–20 no. 1569 with date of March 13, 1297. The name of the family house is often "Ide Rufe" in the entries, perhaps named after Ida, a matriarchal ancestor of the Rufus branch of the Cleingedanc family (see von Winterfeld, *Handel, Kapital und Patriziat in Köln bis 1400*, p. 33).

holdings in the house to her brother Hermannus Cleingedanc and his wife Elizabeth (or Lisa).[83] First, in 1298 Richmudis gave back to Hermannus the half-a-mark rent that he owed her for his portion of the house, as stipulated in Gertrudis Overstolz's will. Then, in 1300, Cristina gave her quarter part of the house and Richmudis her 6 shillings (coming from the other half-a-mark rent from Cristina's portion) to Hermannus. Now Hermannus had the full ownership of the family's portion in the house, saving a rent to a third party.

The final piece of property inherited by Cristina was located on the street named Am Hof in St. Laurence parish across from the cathedral.[84]

---

[83] 99 Liber III de domo Milwirle (St. Laurenz) fo. 32r: [Upper right portion of the entry reads: "De domo H. Cleynegedanc"] "Item notum, quod Richmudis, filia quondam Philippi Anglici et Cristine uxoris sue, tradidit et remisit avunculo suo Hermanno Rufo dicto Cleynegedanc et Lise uxori sue dimidiam marcam hereditarii census, quam ipsi Hermannus et Lisa p: :dicti solvebant singulis annis dicte Richmudi de quarte parte domus Ide Rufe. Ita quod ij :i Hermannus, avunculus predicte Richmudis, et Lisa predicti ipsam dimidiam marcam dicti census omni iure, quod ipsa Richmudis habuit, liberam habebunt. Hermannus et Lisa divertere potuerunt, quocumque voluerint. Actum vigilia Lucie anno Domini 1298."

   103 IV de domo Kusini (St. Laurenz) fo. 20r: "Item notum quod, Cristina, filia quondam Henrici dicti Cleynegedanc, tradidit et remisit quartam partem domus Ide Rufe cum area, ante et retro subtus et superius, prout iacet, apud Stessam, et Richmudis, filia predicte Cristine, tradidit et remisit sex solidos hereditarii census in predicta quarta parte dicte domus Hermanno dicto Cleynegedanc, fratro ipsius Cristine, et eius uxori eius [sic] Lise. Ita quod ipsi Hermannus et Lisa quartam partem dicte domus et ipsos sex solidos hereditarii census et dictam quartam partem dicte domus iure optinebunt et sic est dicta domus quondam Ide Rufe totaliter dictorum Hermanni et Lise eius uxoris. Salvo Agneti et Sophie, sororibus Hildegeri dicti Wickerode, iure suo. Actum anno Domini 1300 vigilia Urbani pape."

[84] 99 Liber III de domo Milwirle (St. Laurenz) fo. 34v: "Notum, quod ex morte Henrici dicti Cleynegedanc et Leticie eius uxoris devoluta est filiabus eorum Cristine, [eius marito Ph. Anglico inserted] et Ide, cuilibet eorum unius pueri partis in tribus sextis partibus duarum mansionum sitarum ex opposito Palacii versus Putzhove. Ita quod quilibet eorum suam pueri partem in dictis tribus sextis partibus dictarum duarum domorum iure optinebit et divertere poterit, quocumque voluerit. Salvo censu hereditario iure suo. Actum crastino . . . 1302. [This transaction was also recorded in another form elsewhere: 99 Liber III de domo Milwirle (St. Laurenz) fo. 39r: "Item notum sit, quod predicta Cristina, filia Domini Henrici dicti Clenegedanc et uxoris sue Leticie, obtinebit terciam partem in tercia parte in duabus mansionibus sitis inter Galiacores. Ita quod predicta Cristina terciam partem in tercia parte in duabus mansionibus predictis iure obtinebit. Salvo censu hereditario."]

   Item notum, quod ex morte Philippi Anglici devoluta est Richmudi, filie eius, [unius pueri partis crossed out] medietas de pueri parte parentum suorum de tribus sextis partibus duarum mansionum sitarum ex opposito Palacii versus Putzhof. Ita quod ipsa Richmudis dictam medietatem pueri partis optinebit. Salvo Cristine matre sue ususfructu et censu hereditario. Actum ut supra. Ipsa Cristina mater dictam scripturam ratam habente. Actum ut supra [no. 393 is like no. 391 – inheritance given to Henricus dictus Cleynegedanc, Hermannus dictus Cleynegedanc/Lisa].

   Item notum, quod ex morte predicti Henrici Cleynegedanc cecidit Hermanno et Lise uxori sue et Cristine, fratri et sorori ipsius Henrici predicti, cuilibet eorum medietas de pueri parte Henrici in tribus sextis partibus duarum mansionum sitarum ex opposito Pallacii versus Putzhove. Ita quod quilibet eorum medietatem dicte pueri partis iure optinebit et divertere poterit, quocumque voluerit. Salvo censu hereditario iure suo. Actum crastino . . . 1302.

   Item notum, quod predicta Cristina tradidit et remisit Hermanno, fratri suo predicto, et Lise

Cristina, along with her sister Ida and her brother Hermannus, received a portion of their father's inheritance at this location: three sixths parts of two *mansiones*. Her share was increased partially because of the death of her brother Henricus. In addition, her daughter Richmudis received a portion held by Cristina's husband Philippus Anglicus, who was by now long dead. Perhaps this portion was part of Cristina's dowry and thus in the legal possession of Philippus, apart from Cristina's inheritance. In any case Cristina, following the course of action taken numerous times already, transferred her portion to her brother Hermannus and his wife Elizabeth, as did other family members. Richmudis also gave up her portion, yet not to her uncle but rather to a certain Robinus Grin and his wife Bliza.

This Robinus Grin, a member of yet another major patrician family and bearing a very English-sounding Christian name, could be one of two possible Robinus Grins. A certain Henricus Grin, who was a *scabinus*, married as his second wife Ida Cleingedanc, who was the sister of Cristina and thus the aunt of Richmudis. This marriage produced a son named Robinus Grin. Henricus Grin also had a brother named Robinus. Hence Richmudis sold her share either to her uncle's brother or to her cousin (i.e. her aunt's son).[85] Continually in these later entries we find the daughter Richmudis as the only family member mentioned with legal claims to the property or inheritance of Cristina and Philippus Anglicus. It would seem then that she was the sole remaining heir by this time.

We have now reviewed the full presentation of this family's activities through two generations, in so far as the municipal Schreinsbücher

eius uxori suam medietatem de pueri parte propria ex morte Henrici fratris sui predicti, devoluta in tribus sextis partibus duarum mansionum sitarum ex opposito Palacii versus Putzhove. Ita quod ipsi Hermannus et Lisa medietatem dicte pueri partis in tribus sextis partibus duarum mansionum predicarum iure optinebunt et divertere potuerint, quocumque voluerint. Salvo censu hereditario. Actum ut supra. [The next entry records the death of Lisa (the wife of Hermannus), and her portion passed to her daughter Hadewigis/husband Mathias de Unicornu. In the following entry Mathias de Unicornu/Hadewigis transfer their portion also to Hermannus, the father of Hadewigis.]

Notum, quod Richmudis, filia quondam Philippi Anglici et Cristina eius uxoris, tradidit et remisit Robino dicto Grin et eius uxori Blize medietatem de pueri parte parentum suorum in tribus sextis partibus duarum mansionum sitarum ex opposito Palacii versus Putzhove. Ita quod ipsi Robinus et Bliza medietatem dicte pueri partis in tribus sextis partibus dictarum domorum iure optinebunt et divertere potuerint, quocumque voluerint. Salvo censu hereditario et salvo Cristine matri dicte Richmudis usufructu. Actum ut supra crastinum beati Severini anno Domini 1302." The actual location would probably have been Am Hof I (see Keussen, *Topographie der Stadt Köln*, I, p. 201 col. b, 7–10).

[85] Lau, "Das Kölner Patriziat bis zum Jahre 1325," p. 378 says of the family: "Die Zahl der Schöffen, welche dieser Familie entstammten, ist verhältnissmässig gross, ebenso sind einzelne Grin in der Richerzeche und dem Rathe nachweisbar. Die Wohnsitze der Familie waren weit in der Stadt zerstreut, besonders zahlreich war dieselbe in S. Columba ansässig."

entries allow.[86] The family of Philippus Anglicus continued down the road to integration into Cologne life begun by his grandfather's generation, developing marriage and kinship connections to a number of significant patrician families and with children who entered the religious life of the city. They also exhibited typical merchant activity in Cologne – mortgaging and investing in urban property. One could say that by now this expatriate English family was fully "colonized" and might even be considered German. If only we knew more about their mercantile activities. Did they become wealthy through trade with England and continue to maintain contacts there into the second and third generation? Since the pattern of foreigners resettling in Cologne as a result of their trading activity between their homeland and the city holds true in general, there is no reason to reject the notion that this family arrived in Cologne because of, and continued to rely on, trade with England. But this question requires further consideration of the other Englishmen and women in Cologne.

We are left to ponder the fact that by the end of the second generation of this family all male heirs who would have carried on the family name have disappeared – they had either died or perhaps relocated back to England. In fact, even the family's property was gradually sold off by Cristina after the death of Philippus, leaving no trail to follow of familial ownership in the Schreinsbücher. It looks as if Cristina returned to her Cleingedanc family as a widow and alienated all of her propertied wealth in order to sustain herself. Since the children had foresworn their claims to the estate we hear nothing more of them in the municipal records. Did they return to England or were they by this time more Cologner than English? We can never be certain of their relationship to England, since the type of sources which survive do not reveal such information. But we have discovered evidence that the English did in fact dwell in Cologne – and at an early date as well – and could flourish socially and economically.

In this context a certain beguine convent should briefly be mentioned, which was known as the "conventus Englant" on Antoniterstrasse in the parish of St. Peter. Established before 1303, Asen has stated that the origins of this convent are unknown, although perhaps members of the Wetterhahn and Schönwetter families were the founders.[87] The house was also called "zum Engel," but this appellation

---

[86] There is in addition one vague reference to "duas mansiones iuxta hereditatem Philippi Anglici" in 379 Boesengasse (St. Severin) fo. 3v.

[87] Asen, "Die Beginen in Köln," *Annalen* 113 (1928), pp. 73–5: "Die erste Erwähnung des K[onvent] Engeland findet sich 1303, sein Anfang ist unbekannt. Er befand sich in dem gleichnamigen Hause am Ende der Antonitergasse, wo der Römerkanal ein Stück zu Tage trat;

does not appear in the sources until the fifteenth century.[88] For two centuries it was consistently called "conventus Engelant," and such corruption of the name from *Engelant* to *Engel* over two centuries is quite possible, given the similarity between the two words in the German of the day.[89] This, coupled with the evidence concerning the various houses owned by the English called "domus Engelant," may suggest the patronage of the English, or at least of those Cologners who traded with the English, in the life of the beguine house. The English had many daughters who were beguines in Cologne; perhaps this was their domicile.

Unfortunately in the case of the four above-mentioned "fratres dicti Anglici," the surviving documentation does not indicate their occupation; but this is not the case with all the English in Cologne. There are many other families and individuals "dictus Anglicus" in the Cologne sources and we are able to ascertain the livelihood of some of them. This chapter, however, will only present one other family in detail (in addition to the family of Walterus Anglicus). This family is significant because we can determine the occupation of its father and because it gives us additional information about the integration of the English in Cologne.

Robinus Anglicus, the father of this family, bore the interesting surname "de Wolsacke." This name certainly reveals what profession Robinus pursued, and indeed one of his houses in the city was known as "domus de Wolsacke." We see virtually nothing of Robinus himself in the sources, but his widow Iutta is quite active. In 1286 they had entered in the parish register a mutual agreement concerning the authority of either person to dispose of their estate should one predecease the other.[90] Iutta's first legal action as a widow fortunately gives us a great deal of information about the family and its possessions.[91] Their properties were centered in the district of Niederich. The

---

hier hatten früher die fratres sacziti gewohnt. Im 15. und 16. Jahrhundert findet sich für den K[onvent] mehrfach die Bezeichnung zum Engel. Als Gründer kommen wahrscheinlich die Familien Wetterhahn und Schoneweder in Betracht; 1303 werden Hildeger Schoneweder und Ingebrand, Sohn des verstorbenen Ingebrand [de Wetterhane] als Provisoren genannt. 1307 gehörte das Haus Engeland und das dazu gehörige kleine Haus, in welchem sich der K[onvent] befand, dem Ingebrand, Sohn des Ingebrand Wederhane."

[88] Joseph Greving, "Protokoll über die Revision der Beginen et Begarden zu Köln im Jahre 1452," *Annalen* 7 (1902), p. 51 no. 60.

[89] Keussen, *Topographie der Stadt Köln*, I, p. 231 col. a, g–k.

[90] 447 Generalis (Schöffenschrein) fo. 66r: "Notum sit, quod Robinus Anglicus dictus de Wolsacke et uxor sua Iutta se convenerunt et concordaverunt, si quis eorum superviverit libere habet . . . suorum de bonis suis, que nunc habent vel in posteriam sunt hab[itura] . . . dare plus et alteri . . . pro sue libito voluntatis . . . alterius et carnali cupula . . . est datum IX . . . anno Domini 1286 mense Augusto."

[91] 276 Ordinationum (Niederich) fo. iv: "Notum sit unversis tam presentibus quam futuris, quod

first house mentioned, which, the text says, Iutta herself had built, was located on Unter Sachsenhausen near St. Maria Ablass.[92] In addition, Iutta had an hereditary rent of 7 shillings from a house and its land behind this house. This she had purchased from Theodericus de Porta, from whom she also obtained half of a second house of stone, which was located on Johannisstrasse.[93] All of this she willed to her daughters Iutta and Katherine, who were beguines. Then we come upon a most significant clause in the testament: the sisters were required to contribute yearly from the family estate one mark for the sustenance of their brother Robinus, who was a monk at Groß St. Martin's. We have already encountered English families in Cologne which had daughters among the beguines of the city, and even one case in which a son became a Dominican, but here we have a more remarkable situation. The Benedictine house of Groß St. Martin's was the preserve of only the children from the Cologne patrician and noble families, and yet the son of an English wool merchant has found his way into this select group of monks. This says a great deal about the social relations enjoyed by English families in Cologne. The monk Robinus de Wolsacke appears significantly at the head of the list of witnesses to a charter involving the archbishop dated October 7, 1319.[94]

In the following year the daughters returned their rights over the inheritance to their mother,[95] who six years later willed her movable

Iutta, relicta quondam Robini de Wolsacke, de bonis suis imobilibus [*sic*] sive hereditatibus, que et quas ipsa habet in sua proprietate, videlicet de domo sua, quam edificari fecit supra paludem ex opposito domus Linvali iuxta Sanctam Mariam ad Indulgentiam, item et de septem solidis hereditaris, quas habet de domo [et] area sitis retro dictam domum et emit erga Theodericum dictum de Porta, ususfructu Elizabet de Porta reservato, item et de medietate domus lapidee et eius aree site contra murum dominorum veteris montis, quam etiam emit erga Th[eodericum] de Porta, in quam etiam ipsa Elizabet habet ususfructum, ordinacionem fecit et constituit, dicte hereditates et bona, prout iacent et in sua tenuit proprietate, ad Iuttam et Katerinam, begginas, filias suas, si eam supervixerint, libere et sine contradictione devolvuntur. Ita quod divertere poterint, tali condicione, quod singulis annis de dicta hereditate Robino, filio ipsius Iutta, monacho ad Sanctum Martinum in Colonia, quamdiu ipse Robinus vixerit, unam marcam solvant et dent ad sustentationem eius. Actum et conscriptum anno Domini 1297 feria quinta post festum nativitatis beati virginis."

92 The location was Unter Sachsenhausen II (see Keussen, *Topographie der Stadt Köln*, II, p. 150 col. a, 20, 21, 23).

93 The location was Johannisstrasse I (see Keussen, *Topographie der Stadt Köln*, II, p. 92 col. a, 25–30). The house was near the court of the count of Altenberg.

94 *REK*, V, pp. 255–6 no. 1141.

95 276 Ordinationum (Niederich) fo. 1v: "Notum sit universis, quod Iutta et Katerina, beggina, sorores, filie quondam Robini dicti de Wolsacke et Iutta, ad huc viventes hereditatem ipsius a Iutta matre sua predicta donatam et remissam, videlicet domum sitam supra paludem, item proprietatem septem solidorum, item medietatis proprietatem domus lapide site contra murum curtis veteris montis, in omni . . . iure et condicione, quibus dicta mater ipsorum eandem hereditatem ipsis tradidit et remisit, rediderunt et remiserunt Iutte matri sue predicte. Ita quod ipsa mater prefata hereditatem teneat et divertat, sicut matris ante donationem eis factam. Et

goods to her children.[96] Here we learn of three more children: Emelricus, Cristencia, and Jacobus. The two beguine daughters made their own settlement concerning their goods as well.[97] There may be some other evidence concerning just what Iutta's movable goods were. Gerardus Scherfgin, a member of one of the most distinguished and wealthy patrician families in Cologne, held a rent and some property adjacent to the "domus Wolsacke."[98] In each reference the presence of a *coquina*, or kitchen, occurs.[99] Kitchens were often built as separate sections of the house,[100] and perhaps the household utensils were intended as the movable goods, along with any furniture.

In addition to these properties, Keussen has collected some later entries which refer to two other sites owned by Robinus Anglicus de Wolsacke. The first was a house on the street named Am Hof, which ran along the grounds of the cathedral, and the second was a house in the district of Eigelstein on Eintrachtstrasse, which Iutta subsequently sold and which was called "domus de Wolsacke."[101]

The Schreinsbuch entries for the de Wolsacke family, although brief

---

quod predicta Iutta sua mater effecta est, quod dicitur selfmundig, sicut patet per litteris plebanis sui Sancte Maria ad Indulgentiam in scrinio repositis. Actum et conscriptum anno Domini 1298 in octavis beati Remigii."

[96] 451 I Generalis (Schöffenschrein) fo. 26r: "Item notum sit, quod Iutta, relicta quondam Robini Anglici de Wolsacke, donavit et resignavit post mortem . . . liberis suis ab ipso Robino procreatis, videlicet Emelrico, Katerine, Iutte, Cristencie et Iacobo, omnia bona sua mobilia, que relinquit. Ita quod iure optinebunt. Datum anno Domini 1304 in vigilia beati Petri."

[97] 451 Generalis (Schöffenschrein) fo. 30r: "Item notum sit, quod Katerina et Iutta, becgine, sorores de Wolsacke, taliter inter se paraverunt, quecumque earum supervixerit aliam, quod bona sua, que relinquit, convertere poterit, in quamcumque manum voluerit. Datum anno Domini 1305."

[98] Lau, "Das Kölner Patriziat bis zum Jahre 1325," pp. 139–41.

[99] *Ennen/Eckertz*, III, p. 164 no. 198 is a disposition of Gerardus Scherfgin's estate in 1280, in which is mentioned: "Item 6 marcas Coloniense in domo et area vocata Wolsac excepta coquina." Then Heinricus Scherfgin (son of Gerardus) granted a house "sub coquina domus de Wolsacke" to a third party *c.* 1285–6 (III, p. 241 no. 278). And finally Heinricus Scherfgin and his wife Cristina gained ownership of a "cubiculum situm subtus trappam et coquinam domus vocata Wolsacke" (III, p. 304 no. 337).

[100] Keussen, *Topographie der Stadt Köln*, I, p. 102*.

[101] Ibid., II, p. 306 col. a, b–c (Am Hof V): "1471 Hs., das weil. war Robijns vom Wolsacke, und sind 2 Gaddamen . . . 1395 das nächste Hs. . . . und war weil. Robyns vom Wolsacke . . . 1361, 1475 Hs., das weil. war Robyns vom Wolsacke gegenüber Salecgen" [a house located across the street on Am Hof I – cf. 1: 200 col. b, 1–2]; 2: 274 col. b, c (Eintrachtstrasse I): "1305 domus et area secus antiquum fossatum retro s. Virgines ex opposito putei, in quo quondam Richolfus Buntebart morabatur durch Jutta, vidua de Wolsacke an Joh. Scharreman in Erbleihe gegeben. 1317 dom. apud fossatum iuxta puteum versus Renum, et vocatur domus de Wolsacke. 1336 dom. apud antiquum fossatum iuxta dom. domine de Wolsacke." Another "domus zum Wolsack" existed on Bechergasse I (see Keussen, *Topographie der Stadt Köln*, I, p. 105 col. a; I, p. 106 col. b, 7]. This house was named after a certain "Arnoldus Wollemengere," who is mentioned in 1231: "domus, in qua mansit Arnoldus Wollemengere, oppos. palatio archiepiscopi et stabulum adiacens." Later the house is referred to simply as: "domus zume Wolsack super Postibus in ordone under Rindshuderin." Here we have then a

and few, show how deeply integrated into the local life of the city the family was. Once again an *Anglicus* widow managed the family's estate after the death of her husband. Iutta was particularly active in her buying and selling of property, yet she did not alienate the family estate but even increased it before passing it on to her children. Her Christian name suggests that she was a Cologner and not English, so again we likely have a case of marriage between an Englishman and a Cologne woman.

Robinus' activities as a wool merchant in Cologne raise another important issue, since the standard accounts of the English wool trade have always focused on the Low Countries and on the role of foreign merchants (i.e. non-English). M. M. Postan has suggested that there might have been an English wool trade with Cologne, but he says this in the context of the cloth trade of the fourteenth and fifteenth centuries.[102] Of course one man does not make an industry, yet the appearance of an English wool merchant in Cologne – indeed one who even bore a name that signified his profession and who had highly placed connections (as seen in the placement of his son in Groß St. Martin) – recommends a reconsideration of just how early English merchants became directly involved in trade with the Rhineland and other parts of the empire.[103]

Each of the English families discussed thus far established multi-faceted contacts in Cologne, with personal and marriage ties linking them to local life. There is another instance of such ties that clarifies another important issue: how a Cologner could have borne the surname *Anglicus*. The answer appears in the case of Wilhelmus Anglicus and his son-in-law Teodericus, who lived in St. Columba parish. At the death of Wilhelmus Anglicus his four children and their spouses received equal portions of their father's estate. As was often the custom, relatives would exchange their portions in order to consolidate ownership in separate properties. We see this as Johannes, the son of Wilhelmus Anglicus, and his wife Cristina sell their quarter part of the family house on Drususgasse to Johannes' sister Sophia and her husband, Teodericus.[104] This entry clarifies the relationship between Teodericus and

clear connection between a wool merchant (Wollemengere) and the naming of his house after his trade.

[102] M. M. Postan, *The Medieval Economy and Society*, The Pelican Economic History of Britain, 1 (New York, 1975; rpt. 1984), p. 218.

[103] Another example is William Trente, an Englishman who spent several years in royal service as purchaser for the royal household. He was present in Cologne in 1296 purchasing wine for the king. In 1302 he became the king's butler and keeper of the exchanges under Edward II: Williams, *Medieval London. From Commune to Capital*, p. 119.

[104] 156 Berlici (St. Columba) fo. 1v: "Notum sit presentibus et futuris, quod Johannes et uxor sua

Wilhelmus Anglicus: Wilhelmus was the father-in-law of Teodericus. Another entry a few folios later further spells out the inheritance settlement.[105] The aforesaid sale by Johannes to Teodericus and Sophia was confirmed again, along with the grant of a plot of land nearby, and Sophia's sisters Margareta and Blanche foreswore any claims to said property. In return the remainder of the family house was given to Margareta, with her sisters Sophia and Blanche foregoing any further claims.

So far this was a commonplace of inheritance practices in Cologne, but there is something else going on here. In this entry (as well as in those following) Teodericus, the husband of Sophia and son-in-law of Wilhelmus Anglicus, is called "Teodericus Anglicus." Hence a Cologner bore the family name *Anglicus*, and did so from his marriage into an English family – something unnoticed by either Lau or von Winterfeld. In fact, von Winterfeld incorrectly identified this Teodericus Anglicus with a certain Teodericus, son of Teodericus dictus Sapiens of the Mühlengasse *Geschlecht*.[106] She surmised that the son took the name to distinguish himself from his father – a surname which would then prove his trading activities with England. This assumption is unfounded and does not correctly explain how a Cologner could have borne the surname *Anglicus*. We have, on the contrary, now seen how this was possible – through marriage to an English family and the taking of its surname.

Lau's family tree for the "Weise" (Sapiens) branch of the Mühlen-

Cristina remiserunt et contradiderunt Teoderico et uxori sue Sophye quartam partem domus, que sita in Berlico, que fuit soceri sue Wilhelmi Anglici et uxoris sie Methildis, retro domum Everardi Ganeweth, ubi eis iusta particione contigerit" (*c.* 1222). The location was Drususgasse II (see Keussen, *Topographie der Stadt Köln*, I, p. 307 col. a, 1–2). My thanks go to Dr. Manfred Groten for his assistance in unravelling this complex series of family connections.

105 156 Berlici (St. Columba) fo. 3r: "Notum sit presentibus et futuris, quod, legitima facta divisione inter Teodericum Anglicum et uxorem suam ex una parte et coheredes eorum ex altera, illa area totalis a mansione illa, que non est proxima puteo Everardi Ganeweg, scilicet secunda est a puteo usque ad finem platee retro iacentis, que vocatur Scurgegaszen, [i.e. Elstergasse] pro portione legitima eiusdem Teoderici et uxoris sue Sophye et portione empta a Johannem fratrem eiusdem Sophie pertinet ad eumdem [*sic*] Teodericum et Sophiam et effestucaverunt super eadem area Margareta, soror Sophie, et maritus eius Conradus pro sorore vero eius Blancheflors. Domini nostri non respondebunt, donec effestucaverunt.

Item notum sit presentibus et futuris, quod mansio illa, que contigue est curie Everardi Ganeweg et fuit quondam Wilhelmi Anglici, legitima divisione pertinet ad Margaretam, filiam Wilhelmi Anglici, et maritum suum Cunradum, iure et sine omni contradictione optinenda et effestucaverunt super eadem mansione Sophie, soror eiusdem Margarete, et maritus suus Teodericus et soror vero eius Blancheflor. Domini nostri non respondebunt, donec effestuca-verunt" (1222).

106 von Winterfeld, *Handel, Kapital und Patriziat in Köln bis 1400*, p. 37: "Auswärtige Handelsbeziehungen müssen die Weisen nach England und zum Oberrhein unterhalten haben. Denn um 1231/46 wurde ein Sohn Dietrichs des Weisen zum Unterschied von seinem Vater Theodericus Anglicus genannt."

gasse *Geschlecht* shows no son of Teodericus Sapiens by the same name,[107] and von Winterfeld gives no source for her conjecture. It is not difficult, however, to see how she could have confused the references. Teodericus Anglicus was in fact the son of a Teodericus dictus Sapiens, but this Teodericus Sapiens was also known by the surname "de Coggone" or "de Kocgen," which was the name of the family house on Breitestrasse.[108] To complicate matters even more, all three of these men named Teodericus (i.e. T. Sapiens von der Mühlengasse, T. Sapiens de Coggone and his son T. Anglicus) had wives named Sophia.

Teodericus Anglicus' relationship to his own family can be found in two entries concerning his inheritance from his father. In the first he sold his rent from the property on Drususgasse – obtained from his wife's family – as well as the entire inheritance from his father on Breitestrasse.[109] The entry clearly indicates the father–son relationship between a Teodericus Sapiens and Teodericus Anglicus, and perhaps von Winterfeld had based her conjecture on this entry. But the second entry clarifies who the father was.[110] Here Teodericus foregoes any claim to his father's house "ad Coggonem," which his brother Gerardus

---

[107] Lau, "Die Kölner Patriziat bis zum Jahre 1325," p. 128.

[108] The location was Breitestrasse VI (see Keussen, *Topographie der Stadt Köln*, I, p. 288 col. b; I, p. 289 col. a, 3–4).

[109] 156 Berlici (St. Columba) fo. 12v: "Notum sit presentibus et futuris, quod Henricus de Zabelo et uxor sua Margareta emerunt sibi erga Teodericum dictum Anglicum et uxorem suam Sophiam redditum . . . solidorum monete Coloniensium annuatim hereditario iure in domo et area, ante et retro subtus et superius, ita ibi iacet, que sita in platea Vogelonis [i.e. Drususgasse], in qua manent idem Teodericus Anglicus et uxor sua Sophia, in nativitate beate Marie virginis solvendorum quatuor septimanas post sine captione. [Quod si] Teodericus Anglicus et uxor sua Sophia vel eorum heredes terminum prescritpum neglexerint, pro pena solvent prescripto Henrico de Zabelo et uxori sue Margerete vel eorum heredibus duodecim solidos monete Coloniensium.

Item notum sit quod ex morte Teoderici dicti Sapiens et uxori sue Sophie [cessit supra ?] Teodericum due septime partes duarum mansionum sitarum sub uno tecto in lata platea [i.e. Breite Strasse] oppositas domui Wolcwitz [?] et septimam partem [in una mansione] in eadem platea, quarum due mansiones site sunt sub uno tecto oppositas domui Petri Mercenarii et est hec mansio versus murum. [Ita quod] potest Teodericus alienare et transferre, ad quoscumque voluerit.

Item notum sit presentibus et futuris, quod Henricus de Zabelo et uxor sua Margareta emerunt sibi erga Teodericum prescriptum, filium Teoderici dicti Sapienti, duas septimas partes duarum mansionum sub uno tecto [sitarum ?] in lata platea oppositas domui Wolcwiti [?] et septimam partem in una mansione in eadem platea, quarum due mansiones site sunt sub uno tecto oppositas domui Petri Mercenarii et est hec mansio versus murum. Ita quod predictus Henricus de Zabelo et uxor sua Margareta iure obtinebunt" (1245–6).

[110] 168 Campanarum (St. Columba) fo. 2r: "Notum sit Theodericus, filius Theoderici dicti Sapientis dicti de Coggone, super omni iure, quod ipse in domo ad Coggonem vocata habuit vel habere potuit, ad manus fratrum suorum, scilicet Ulrici et uxoris sue Gertrudis et Gerardi et uxoris sue Elizabet penitus effestucavit et ad hoc super omnibus, que dicti fratres sui nunc habunt vel umquam fuerint habituri, renunciavit. Actum anno Domini 1260."

would turn into a beguine house in 1276.[111] Nowhere do we see any of Teodericus' brothers or his father bearing the surname *Anglicus*. Thus we have a case where a Cologner – perhaps a younger son – removed himself from his own family's property and took the name of his wife's English family.

The practice of sons taking a surname from their mother's family was not uncommon in Cologne, and sons-in-law taking the surname of their wife's family was also a custom which the Schreinsbücher evidence.[112] But it was only advantageous for someone to do this if the family into which the man was marrying and whose name he was adopting represented for him a step up on the socio-economic ladder. Given this, we have learned something about the social status reached by the family of Wilhelmus Anglicus. Such evidence further confirms the upward social mobility achieved by some of the English in Cologne, as we have already seen in the case of Walterus Anglicus and Robinus Anglicus.

Teodericus Anglicus and his wife Sophia lived in the Anglicus family house, which was still called the "domus Wilhelmi Anglici."[113] Over the next few years he concluded a series of purchases in the vicinity of the house, thus consolidating a compact estate of property and rents on the block. Shortly after his purchase of the quarter portion of the house on Drususgasse he managed to gain full ownership of it from Margareta, leaving her one of the two adjoining *mansiones*.[114] Sophia's other sister Blanche and her husband, also named Teodericus, received the other

---

[111] Keussen, *Topographie der Stadt Köln*, I, p. 288 col. b, 11–12.

[112] Hagström, *Kölner Beinamen des 12. und 13. Jahrhunderts*, I, pp. 40–2 discusses families in which the sons took their mother's *Geschlechtsname*. He also mentions sons-in-law who took the surnames of spouses from the Mühlengasse (I, p. 43) and Overstolz (I, p. 48) families. Lau, "Das Kölner Patriziat bis zum Jahre 1325," p. 82 shows that a branch of the Crop von Lyskirchen Geschlecht bore the coat of arms of the Overstolz family after the marriage between Constantius Crop and Margareta Overstolz; he also lists (p. 104) numerous branches of the Hardevust family which, "infolge von Verschwägerung mit den H[ardevust] den Namen der letzteren angenommen haben." Taking matronymic surnames was common in England as well when the mother was the inheritor of family property: see for example Barbara A. Hanawalt, *The Ties that Bound. Peasant Familes in Medieval England* (Oxford, 1986), pp. 82, 175.

[113] 156 Berlici (St. Columba) fo. 3r: "Notum sit presentibus et futuris, quod Demudis post mortem mariti sui Volgelonis per sententiam scabinorum in iudicio obtinuit portionem, que Vogelonem filium suum post obitum patris . . . cum area sita ex obposito contra domum, que quondam fuit Wilhelmi Anglici" (1222).
156 Berlici (St. Columba) fo. 4v: "Notum sit presentibus et futuris, quod Demudis remisit et contradiderit Tirico Rozere marito suo dimidietatem domus cum area opposite domui Wilhelmi Anglici" (1224).

[114] 156 Berlici (St. Columba) fo. 4v: "Notum sit presentibus et futuris, quod Blanche et maritus eius Teodericus ad manus Sophie, sororis predicte Blanche, et mariti sui Teoderici Anglici effestucaverunt super domo et area sita in platea Vogelonis, in qua manent idem Teodericus Anglicus et Sophia.
Notum sit presentibus et futuris, quod Teodericus et uxor sua Sophia effestucaverunt super

117

mansio, but sold it a year later.[115] From this point on the house was called "domus Teoderici Anglici."[116] About the year 1231 he obtained from the monastery of Groß St. Martin a yearly rent of five shillings paid from the house itself as well as one of 33 pence from the two adjoining *mansiones* (in which Sophia's sisters lived) and an unspecified rent of 27 pence.[117] He had also obtained a rent of 12 shillings from three *mansiones* and a plot of land across the street from the Anglicus family house, which he sold in 1244 to a cathedral canon named Johannes de Sancta Katherina.[118] Two years later this canon gave the rent, along with others in the city, to the cathedral chapter.[119] The grant, which was part of a foundation Johannes had made for his own

mansione illa, que contigua est domui Teoderici Anglici versus ecclesia sancte Columbe, ad manus Teoderici et uxoris sue Blanche" (*c.* 1225).

[115] 156 Berlici (St. Columba) fo. 13v: "Notum sit presentibus et futuris, quod Conradus Graloc et uxor sua Margareta, Teodericus et uxor sua Blanche talem inter se fecerunt divisionem, quod Conradus Graloc et uxor sua Margareta unam mansionem, que sita est in platea Wogelonis, ante et retro subtus et superius, oppositam domui Teoderici Roscere et est mansio contigua puteo, ita quod Conradus Graloc et uxor sua Margareta iure obtinebunt. Et Teodericus et uxor sua Blanche obtinebunt aliam mansionem in eadem platea contiguam prescripte mansioni versus domum Teoderici Anglici. Salvo iure censu solvendo, sicut superius scriptum est. Et sciendum, quod ambe mansiones habebunt accessum ad privatum cum expensis ambabus mansionibus. Anno gratiae 1246.

Notum sit presentibus et futuris, quod Rigmudis, relicta Richolfi dicti Sclefere, emit sibi erga Teodericum et uxorem suam Blanche domum cum area, ante et retro subtus et superius, sitam in platea Wolgelonis oppositam [domui] Teoderici dicti Roscere contiguam domui Conradi Graloc versus murum veterem, eo iure censu solvendo, sicut superius scriptum est. Ita quod Rigmudis prescripta iure obtinebit. Anno gratiae 1247."

[116] 156 Berlici (St. Columba) fo. 5r: A house is mentioned, "contigua domui Teoderici Anglici" (1241).

[117] 156 Berlici (St. Columba) fo. 3v: "Notum sit presentibus et futuris, quod Teodericus Anglicus et uxor sua Sophia comparaverunt sibi erga abbatem et totum conventum Sancti Martini censum quinque solidorum annuatim solvendorum de domo et area, in qua manet idem Teodericus Anglicus, 33 denariorum de duabus mansionibus sub uno tecto contiguis domui predicti Teoderici versus ecclesiam Sancte Columbe, 27 denariorum, quas 27 denarios solvent in vigilia Omnium Sanctorum" (*c.* 1231).

[118] 156 Berlici (St. Columba) fo. 6r: "Notum sit presentibus et futuris, quod Johannes, canonicus maioris ecclesie, dictus de Sancte Katerina, emit sibi erga Teodericum Anglicum et uxorem suam Sophiam reditum duodecim solidorum monete Coloniensium de tribus mansionibus et areis, ante et retro subtus et superius, et area contigua adiacente versus latam plateam [i.e. Breitestrasse] et sunt hec mansiones site in platea Wogelonis [i.e. Drususgasse] oppositas domui Teoderici Anglici: in nativitate Christi sex solidos solvendos quindecim dies post sine captione et in nativitate sancti Johannis Baptiste sex solidos solvendos item quindecim dies post sine captione. Et sciendum est, si predictus Teodericus Anglicus et uxor sua Sophia vel eorum heredes aliquem de prescriptis terminis neglexerint, censu non persolvo sicut superius scriptum est, pro qualibus quindecim diebus tres solidos predicto Johanni pro pena persolvent. Salvo iure censu solvendo domui Sancti Spiritus, sicut superius scriptum est, scilicet duodecim solidorum. Anno gratiae 1244."

[119] *Ennen/Eckertz*, II, pp. 250–1 no. 249: "unam marcam annualem a Theoderico dicto Anglico de tribus mansionibus et una area sitis ex opposito domus iam dicti Th. Anglici" is listed among the rents given by Johannes to the cathedral chapter in May 1246. The text is also published in *UGN*, II, p. 157 no. 301.

and his family's memory, was confirmed ten years later,[120] and the memorial appears in the *necrologium* of the cathedral chapter on the day of Johannes' death (III Kal. of May).[121]

Teodericus disappears from the records by the middle of the century in the same fashion as several of the other *Anglicus* families. In 1253 he sold the family house with its two adjoining rooms, and never appears again.[122] The pattern of disappearing from the sources, which occurs with other *Anglicus* families, is peculiar since they had previously become so integrated into the life of their neighborhoods and of the city as a whole. Perhaps it is an indicator that they returned to England, or simply resettled elsewhere. In 1271 a certain "Thierius le Sage," together with Artelemus de Colonia, made an oath to the English royal officials as the "King of Almain's merchants of Cologne" that they would not trade their purchase of thirty sacks of wool with Flanders.[123] As this would have been too late a date for either Teodericus Sapiens von der Mühlengasse or Teodericus Sapiens de Coggone, perhaps it is this Teodericus Anglicus in England and involved in the wool trade under his father's family name.

The issue of a Cologner bearing the English surname occurs again in relation to the possible marital connections of another *Anglicus* family. This involves a certain Godefridus Anglicus, who was probably not the same as the son of Walterus Anglicus. Although the dates concerned make it possible, as Walterus' son was deceased by 1263, no heirs or widow appear for him in the inheritance settlements of his father.

---

[120] *Archiv für die Geschichte des Niederrheins*, ed. Theodor Lacomblet (Cologne and Düsseldorf, 1832–69), III, pp. 177–8: the confirmation of Johannes' foundation grant dated June 19, 1256 is published, including "redditus unius marce de domibus et areis ex opposito domus Th. dicti Anglici, quam solvunt michi fratres Minores singulis annis." The rent came from the Franciscans, on whose property the mansiones and the field were located.

[121] *Ennen/Eckertz*, II, p. 611: Item de redditibus unius marce de domibus et areis ex opposito domus Th. dicti Anglici, quam solvunt fratres Minores singulis annis." The editors suggest *c.* 1272 for the dating of this necrology.

[122] 156 Berlici (St. Columba) fo. 9v: "Notum sit presentibus et futuris, quod Albertus dictus Colnere et uxor sua Petrissa emerunt sibi erga Teodericum Anglicum et uxorem suam Sophiam domum cum area, ante et retro subtus et superius, cum duabus cameris adiacentibus sub uno tecto in platea Vogelonis, que fuit mansio predicti Teoderici et uxoris sue Sophie. Ita quod Albertus et uxor sua Petrissa possent alienare et transferre, ad quoscumque voluerint a eo iure, censu solvendo, sicut superius scriptum est. Anno Domini 1253." By 1279 the house had been renamed "Ad Lilium" and sold by Albertus to the Franciscans across the street: 157 Berlici (St. Columba) fo. 24r: "Notum, quod Albertus dictus Colnere tradidit et remisit unam domum cameris et areis, ante et retro subtus, [*sic*] prout iacent in Drusianegazzin, que ad Lilium vocatur, et Johannes filius suus, quodcumque iuris habuit in domo et cameris predictis, fratribus Minoribus. Ita quod fratres dictam domum cum cameris adiacentibus et areis, ante et retro subtus et superius, prout iacent in Drursianegazzin super angulum Randolfgazzin [i.e. Elstergasse], que quondam fuit Th. Anglici, iure obtinebunt et divertere poterunt, quocumque voluerint, omni iure, quod antedicti habuerunt" (1279).

[123] *CPR Henry III*, IV, p. 565.

Rather, it appears that he died young and without heirs. We begin with entries concerning the Windeck family, which lived on Lintgasse in St. Brigida parish. Hadewigis Windeck was the sister of Petrus Windeck, at whose death she received a portion of his property in the district of Niederich.[124] In addition she received half of the house called "Ad Renum" on Lintgasse, near the family "domus Windeck."[125] She willed this to her grandchildren in 1284, who were the children of Hadewigis' daughter Gertrudis and a Godefridus Anglicus.[126] When she inherited her brother Iacobus' share in the house at his death in 1292 she granted it also to these children.[127] To find some clues for the identity of the father of these children we shall have to return to Hadewigis' brother Petrus de Windeck.

Petrus had contacts with the English in Cologne. In 1279 he purchased a rent in the "domus Domicelli" on Martinstrasse from a certain Gobelinus Anglicus.[128] The domus Domicelli may have been an important point of contact for the English in Cologne. The house, originally the domicile of the *Burgraf*'s brother, had five *cubiculi*

---

[124] 240 Ad portam antiquam (Niederich) fo. 43r–44r dated 1283.

[125] The location was Lintgasse III (see Keussen, *Topographie der Stadt Köln*, I, p. 131 col. a, 9 – col. b, 14). The domus ad Renum and the domus Windeck were separated by the domus Sigeri, which by 1306 was known as the domus Overstolz.

[126] 58 Windeck (St. Brigida) fo. 29v: "Item notum sit, quod dicta Hadewigis aliam medietatem domus predicte, [i.e. ad Renum site in Lintgassen] prout eam possedit, tradidit et remisit Henrico et Winrico, nepotibis eius, pueris quondam Gertrudis, filie ipsius Ha[dewigis], et Godefridi dicti Anglici mariti sui, post mortem ipsius Ha[dewigis] . . . Actum anno Domini 1284."

[127] 58 Windeck (St. Brigida) fo. 33v: "Item notum sit universibus tam presentibus quam futuris, quod Hadewigis, vidua dicta de Windeck, tradidit et remisit nepotibus suis Henrico et Winrico, fratribus, pueris quondam Godefridi dicti Anglici et Gertrudis eius uxoris, duas marcas census hereditarii pro sua tercia parte ad ipsam ex morte quondam Jacobi fratris eius devolutas in domo et eius area sita in Lintgassin, que dicitur ad Renum. Ita quod dicti fratres prefatas duas marcas, videlicet quilibet eorum unam de domo predicta post mortem ipsius Hadewigis habeat, teneat et divertat, quocumque voluerit. Actum in vigilia beate Lucie anno Domini 1292."

[128] 84 Brandenburg (St. Alban) fo. 8r: "Notum sit, quod officialibus a scabinis de domo civium testificatum est, quod Petrus de Windecke scriptus sit in cartis scabinorum in domo civium, quod habeat in medietate domus, que dicitur domus Domicelli site ante portam Martis ex opposito domus, que dicitur Sewarscapelle, quatuor marcas et sex solidos singulis annis duobus terminis solvendos, quas comparavit erga Gobellinum dictum Anglicum, sicut proprie Gobellinus in sua habebat proprietate, tali condicione, quod dicto Petro singulis annis in festo pentecosten vel infra sex septimanas sine captione sequentes 27 solidii et in festo beati Martini vel infra sex septimanas sequentes 27 solidii de medietate domus predicte persolventur, hoc adiecto, quod si aliquis terminorum predictorum neglectus fuerit, censum debitum non solvendo, quod ad proprietatem medietatis domus Domicelli predicte, ante et retro subtus et superius, ubicumque ipsum in particione attingit, ascribi debet. Itaque ipsam medietatem domus predicte divertere poterit, in quascumque manus voluerit. Actum anno Domini 1279 crastino exaltacionis sancte crucis." In the following entry Petrus gives four marks and six shillings hereditary rent to the church of St. Brigida "pro remedio anime sue et parentorum suorum."

aurifabrorum attached to it.[129] Located on the corner of Martinstrasse and Oben Marspforten, it was literally thirty-five steps from the home of Walterus Anglicus *Aurifaber* on Oben Marspforten.[130] Hence we already have two Englishmen, one of whom we know was a goldsmith, in some contact with the house. Godefridus Anglicus, the father of Henricus and Winricus, could have been a relative of either Walterus Aurifaber Anglicus or Gobelinus Anglicus – in any case the possible relationship between goldsmiths in the area and the English is something to consider.

There is another conjecture concerning the identity of Godefridus Anglicus based on circumstantial evidence involving the Zudendorp family. The Zudendorp *Geschlecht* was a powerful and well-placed *ministerialis* family which prospered, eventually achieving free knighthood, through service to the archbishops of Cologne. They were often involved in activities with the English, representing the archbishop as envoys to the English court and counseling English envoys in Cologne.[131] The various branches of this family held a vast number of houses and other property throughout the city, one of which was on Martinstrasse and it bore the name "Ad Rufam Ianuam" or "zir Rodirdure." Originally a plot of land separated this house from the domus Domicelli, over which eventually some sort of storage facility (*lobium*) was built.[132] This *lobium* later functioned as *cubicula aurifabrorum*. Henricus Senior de Zudendorp, the patriarch of the family, had inherited the house Ad Rufam Ianuam from his father-in-law Sifridus de Nussia (Neuß)[133] and passed it down to his son and namesake.[134]

---

[129] Keussen, *Topographie der Stadt Köln*, I, p. 165 col. b–166 col. a.

[130] Extensive Schreinsbuch entries survive for Walterus Anglicus Aurifaber (not to be confused with Walterus Anglicus whom we have already discussed) and his connection to the Cologne goldsmith community, but we shall not consider him at length in this book.

[131] The next chapter studies this most important Cologne family and their English contacts.

[132] Keussen, *Topographie der Stadt Köln*, I, p. 165 col. b, 1–3.

[133] Schöffenschrein Karte 2 col. 11: no. 1: "Notum sit tam etc., quod pueri Sifridi senioris de Nusya et Beatricis in particione totius hereditatis eorum per sententiam scabinorum et per consensum Beatricis matris eorum ita convenerunt per electionem factam in iudicio: Henricus de Zudindorp et uxor eius Elyzabeth hereditario iure obtinuerunt domum sitam ante portam Martis, que dicitur zir Rodirdure, ante et retro, sicut eam Sifridus, pater Elyzabeth, in sua possedit proprietate."

[134] Schöffenschrein Karte 2 col. 6: no. 20: "Notum sit etc., quod Henricus de Zudendorp et uxor eius Elisabeth contradiderunt et remiserunt Henrico, filio suo, et uxori sue Gertrudi proprietatem domus et aree, que sita est ante portam Martis contigua domui Henrici Cleinegedanc, sicut eam in sua possident proprietate, ita quod iure et sine contradictione obtinebunt. Et sciendum, quod idem Henricus, filius Henrici et Elisabet, et uxor eius Gertrudis duas marcas annuatim in cubiculis eiusdem domus in antea recipient. Preterea in medietate eiusdem domus Henricus de Zudendorp et Elisabeth uxor eius usumfructum quamdiu vixerint iure et sine omni contradictione percipient" (c. 1205–14). Text published in *Kölner Schreinsurkunden des 12. Jahrhunderts*, ed. Hoeniger, II, 1, pp. 308–9.

There was an income of 2 marks from adjoining *cubicula* – perhaps they were rented to goldsmiths. Each of Henricus Iunior's four children inherited a portion of this house, but one of the sons – Gerardus Iunior, known as "miles de Novo Foro" – eventually reunited the portions and then sold the house in 1255.[135] The second son, who for a time held a portion of this house,[136] is our main focus: Godefridus de Zudendorp, for Godefridus also held propriety in a third of the domus Domicelli.[137]

How he came into ownership of this third we do not know, yet two things are noteworthy here. In this Schreinsbuch entry he has sold his share to Henricus de Windeck (Wintecgin), the brother of Petrus and Hadewigis de Windeck. In addition he is referred to here as *dictus Anglicus*.[138] This use of the surname is difficult to account for, as it is the only time that Godefridus is so called in the Schreinsbücher. The rest of the time he is simply referred to simply as "Godefridus, filius Henrici de Zudendorp." Yet it is clear that he knew the Windeck family: the families were acquainted and Godefridus de Zudendorp was married to a woman named Gertrudis, whose mother's name was Hadewigis.[139] Hence, it is possible that Godefridus de Zudendorp – if he were called Anglicus – was the husband of Gertrudis, the daughter of Hadewigis de Windeck, and the father of Henricus and Winricus.

If so, the only explanation for the surname Anglicus here would be

---

[135] 447 Schöffenschrein Generalis fo. 40v: "Notum sit tam futuris quam presentibus, quod Hildegerus dictus de Sterza et uxor sua Agnes emerunt sibi domum et aream, que vocatur Ad Rufam Ianuam, sitam proximam domui, que vocatur Birbon, versus portam Martis, ante et retro subtus et superius, prout iacet, erga Gerardum dictum Zudindorp, filium Henrici de Zudindorp Iunioris, sicut idem Gerardus in sua habebat proprietate. Ita quod dictus Hildegerus et uxor sua Agnes iam dictam hereditatem iure et sine contradictione optinebunt. Actum anno Domini 1255."

[136] 84 Brandenburg (St. Alban) fo. 2r: "Notum sit, quod Godefridus, qui filius fuerat Henrici de Zudendorp Iunioris et Gertrudis, de morte parentum suorum predictorum quintam partem domus site inter aurifabros, que dicitur Ad Rufam Ianuam, ante et retro, prout ibi iacet, ubicumque eum in partitione attingit. Ita obtinuit, quod iure et sine contradictione obtinebit." An entry below this on the same folio shows eight "cubiculorum aurifabrorum sitarum inter domum Domicelli et domum, que dicitur Ad Rufam Ianuam."

[137] 447 Schöffenschrein Generalis fo. 12r: "Notum sit tam futuris quam presentibus, quod Godefridus, filius Henrici de Zudindorp, dictus Anglicus, et uxor sua Gertrudis tradiderunt et remiserunt tertiam partem domus et aree site ante portam Martis, que dicitur Domus Domicelli, ante et retro subtus et superius, ibi iacet et cum omni iure, sicut in sua habebant proprietate, Henrico dicto de Wintecgin et uxori sue Elizabeth. Ita quod dictam hereditatem iure et sine contradictione obtinebunt. Actum anno Domini 1249."

[138] von Winterfeld, *Handel, Kapital und Patriziat in Köln bis 1400*, p. 7 has incorrectly attributed the surname Anglicus to Godefridus' father Henricus. However, as the passage above shows, Henricus is in the genitive case and the surname "dictus Anglicus" is in the nominative, thus belonging with Godefridus.

[139] 448 I Schöffenschrein Generalis fo. 16v: "Notum, quod Godefridus, filius Henrici de Zudendorp, cum Gertrude uxore sua, super omnibus bonis, [tam mobilibus quam immobilibus et suppellecti crossed out] que nunc habet Hadewigis, mater uxoris sue predicte, vel habitura fuerit ad manus eiusdem Hadewigis penitus effestucavit" (undated).

the family's unique role in serving the archbishops of Cologne in their negotiations with England. Perhaps Godefridus was even born in England and thus received the nickname in the same fashion as the Welf William (son of Duke Henry the Lion) who was born in Winchester and, although usually styled William of Winchester, is also recorded in the Pipe Rolls as "Willelmus Anglicus."[140]

Of course, the conclusion that Godefridus de Zudendorp was actually called *Anglicus* is based solely on circumstantial evidence – we must remember that no other Zudendorp family member bore the surname. Simply using the coincidence of first names can lead to error, as we have already seen in the case of Teodericus Anglicus. Godefridus de Zudendorp could very well have taken the name *Anglicus* through marriage to a daughter of an English family just as Teodericus Anglicus had; this would be quite plausible based on his family's thoroughgoing contacts with the English. In fact, the attribution of *Anglicus* to Godefridus de Zudendorp may even have been a scribal error – there were others with the surname who were involved in the domus Domicelli (i.e. Gobelinus Anglicus) – since nowhere else is he referred to with this surname, nor did any of his family bear it. In any case, this confusing array of possibilities leaves us with only uncertainty and too many men named Godefridus Anglicus.[141] We get no further clues from Henricus and Winricus, since they gave their rent in the house Ad Renum to their uncle Bruno (the brother of their mother Gertrudis) to be quit of a payment of wheat for their portions in said house, and then also fade from the record.[142] In any case we have no direct proof of a

---

[140] *Pipe Roll 32 Henry II*, PR, 36, p. 49: "Et pro acquietandis pannis Willelmi Anglici filii ducis Saxonie et nutricum suarum et lotricis sue et magistri sui viij l[ibri] et xviij s[olidi] et viij d[enarii] per breve Rannulfi de Glanuill." This entry is evidence of royal financial support for William, who spent many of his early years in England. J. H. Round considered this reference to William, "a curious coincidence in the case of the founder of the House of Brunswick" (p. XIX). A. L. Poole also noted this entry (in his article, "Die Welfen in der Verbannung," *Deutsches Archiv für Geschichte des Mittelalters* 2 (1938), pp. 129–48), but Jens Ahlers (*Die Welfen und die englischen Könige 1165–1235*) does not mention it.

[141] There are two other references to a Godefridus Anglicus, which occur in an archival transcript of a no-longer-existing citizen roll for St. Columba parish dated *c.* 1200–20: Stadtarchiv von Köln (Verfassung und Verwaltung C654a) 9 no. 88 (Extram Portam) and 19 no. 56 (Berlici).

[142] 58 Windeck (St. Brigida) fo. 35v: "Item notum sit universibus tam futuris quam presentibus, quod Henricus, filius quondam Godefridi dicti Anglici, nepos Hadewigis de Windecke, de ratihabitione Agnetis uxoris eius, unam marcam hereditarii census, quam habet in domo et eius area dicta ad Renum sita in Lintgassin, in omni modo et forma, prout sibi debitur et ad eam consriptus est, tradidit et remisit Brunoni, avunculo suo, filio dicte Hadewigis, et Marie eius uxori. Ita quod eam pure et sine contradictione optinebunt et divertere poterunt. Actum et conscriptum feria secunda post festum . . . anno Domini 1295.

Item notum sit, quod Bruno, filius Hadewigis de Windecke, de consensa et ratihabitione Marie uxoris eius, tercia maldra siliginis, que Henricus, filius quondam Godefridi Anglici, eius cognatus, sibi solvere tenetur pro parte sua de medietate domus ad Renum, in omni forma,

marriage between Gertrudis de Windeck and Godefridus de Zudendorp, nor do we have any concrete evidence explaining the one-time
attribution of the *Anglicus* surname to Godefridus in the municipal
records.

In conclusion, a brief survey of some of the English activities in the
lower Rhineland area is worth including here in order to give a broader
context for the English in Cologne. This has not been done before on
any scale, and while a short excursion is in no way exhaustive, it shows
the surprising breadth of activities in which the English appear. In the
witness list to a 1216 charter of Count Henry of Sayn to the abbey of
Heisterbach, in which he gives the monks two *mansi* of forest in
Witterschlick in lieu of two marks' rent for a grave plot in the abbey
church, the following men are listed:

Theodericus de Oitgenbach, Henricus de Dorendorp, Roricus de Styldorp,
Christianus de Blanckenbergh, Symon et Zacharias milites, Roricus de
Gevardeshagen dapifer, Gisilbertus de Seyne pincerna, Petrus Anglicus et alii
quamplures.[143]

The location of Petrus Anglicus' name in the list assures us that he was a
layman. The English were also active in Dortmund, where on May 15,
1334 the city council (*Rat*) granted to a Johannes *de Anglia* – called "our
citizen" – the office of inspecting the wool that came into the city
(*Woolwage*) for twenty years, and two years later granted him a sizeable
yearly rent from the *Lohhause* and the wine duty (*Wineaccise*).[144] A
Bertoldus *in Anglia* appears on a Dortmund list of new citizens of
1327.[145] We have already seen the high position reached by Christian
Anglicus in Ahrweiler, and a similar position was achieved even in
Lübeck, Cologne's trading rival in the early Hanseatic era, when
another Johannes de Anglia appears among the *consules Lubicenses* who

sicut conscriptus est, ad solutionem ipsorum tradidit et remisit eidem Henrico. Ita quod ipse
Henricus a solutione dictorum maldrorum est et erit liber et absolutus. Actum et conscriptum
anno Domini et die immediate prescriptis supra.

    Item notum sit etc., quod idem Bruno, filius Hadewigis de Windecke, de consensu Marie
uxoris sue predicte, tercia maldra siliginis, que Winricus, filius quondam Godefridi dicti Anglici
predicti, eius cognatus, sibi solvere tenetur pro parte sua de medietate domus dicte ad Renum,
in omni forma, prout ad eam conscriptus est, similiter tradidit et remisit eidem Winrico. Ita
quod ipse Winricus a solutione ipsorum est et erit liber et absolutus. Actum et conscriptum
anno Domini et die predicte." The alienation of Winricus' mark to Bruno is lacking here, but
his inclusion in the absolution from paying the three measures of wheat suggests his granting of
the mark rent as well.

143 *Urkundenbuch der Abtei Heisterbach*, ed. Ferdinand Schmitz, Urkundenbücher der Geistlichen
Stiftungen des Niederrheins, 2 (Bonn, 1908), pp. 139–40 no. 36.

144 *Dortmunder Urkundenbuch*, ed. Karl Rübel (Dortmund, 1881), I, 1, p. 350 no. 508 and
pp. 357–8 no. 525.

145 Ibid., I, 1, pp. 315–17 no. 456.

witnessed a charter of St. John's abbey in the city at the early date of 1232.[146]

Aachen, the city where Richard of Cornwall was crowned King of the Romans in 1257 and which lies so near Cologne, should be expected to have some Englishmen present, and we are not disappointed on this count. In 1288 the monastery of Arnstein purchased a series of yearly rents, among them "quatuor solidos denariorum Aquensium usualium" from the possessions of the knight Hermannus dictus Anglicus in the village of Quirnberg.[147] Bela, the daughter of a Hermannus Anglicus (perhaps this Hermannus) was in partial possession of the Cologne beguine convent of Klein Landskron on Große Sandkaule in 1329.[148]

There was also the case of a member of the Aachen gentry who married into an English family and took the name *Anglicus* as his new surname. We first meet the knight Gerardus de Altenfalkenburg on August 10, 1280 with his sons Engelbertus, Arnoldus, and Johannes, who oblige themselves to observe a settlement with the cathedral chapter over disputed property in Vaals.[149] Here the sons have no surnames. But on January 15, 1286 two of them confirmed an agreement for their purchase of the property at Vaals, and here they are called "Engelbertus *dictus Anglicus*" and "Arnoldus *dictus Mulart*."[150] Of course, no one else in their family bore such surnames, neither their father nor their brothers Johannes (probably deceased by this time) or Renardus (the deacon of the church of St. Servatius and notary of this latter charter). But we do know of many families who bore the name *Anglicus*, even some in the area of Altenfalkenburg. The unusual name *Mulart* was also the name of a *Geschlecht* in the area. An Arnoldus and a Bernhardus, both styled *Mulart*, were canons at the church of St. Maria in Aachen. In addition, Bernhardus Mulart held several other prebends, being at the same time in possession of canonries in Heinsberg and in the cathedral church of Liège and a vicarage at the church of St. Maria in Bamberg.[151] A Johannes Mulart was one of the *Schöffen* in Gülpen.[152] Our Arnoldus from Altenfalkenburg was present in Aachen on December 7, 1304 (as "dominus Arnoldus dictus Mulart") taking part in an enfeoffment settlement.[153] He was also involved in 1298 in a dispute with his peasants concerning the gathering of wood and payment for

---

[146] *LUB*, I, p. 62 no. 52.
[147] *Regesten der Reichsstadt Aachen*, I: 1251–1300, ed. Wilhelm Mummenhoff, PGRG, 47 (Bonn, 1961), p. 334 Nachtrag no. 137.
[148] Asen, "Die Beginen in Köln," *Annalen* 111 (1927), p. 123.
[149] *Regesten der Reichsstadt Aachen*, ed. Mummenhoff, I, pp. 196–7 no. 369.
[150] Ibid., I, p. 223–4 no. 415   [151] Ibid., II, nos. 329 and 331.   [152] Ibid., II, no. 642.
[153] Ibid., II, 17–18 no. 37.

the taking of swine from his manor at Huelhoven.[154] Thus it is quite plausible that these sons married into established families and took their surnames, a practice already identified.

This new archival evidence of the English in Cologne, although by no means a complete presentation of all the documentation, is nevertheless representative of the types of activities and social relations that the English maintained in Cologne. It has provided us with a clearer picture of the day-to-day interactions between the English and the Cologners: an interaction that was a living outgrowth of the commercial relationship existing between the two regions. Attention has hitherto been focused on the broader, impersonal aspects of Anglo-Imperial relations, that is on dynastic-alliance politics and on measuring the exchange of wealth and goods between the regions. Yet the Cologne Schreinskarten and Schreinsbücher give us a glimpse into specific families and their personal interactions. The evidence indicates that the English became quite thoroughly integrated into the life of the city. Whereas most of the other communities of foreign merchants clustered in geographical groupings, the English appear in every parish but St. Gereon, St. Peter, and St. Pantaleon. They married into some of the most powerful and prestigious Cologne patrician families (although they do not seem to have reached a patrician status themselves, except in the case of Christian Anglicus of Ahrweiler), purchased and mort-gaged houses and other property like the Cologners, and even placed their children into the religious community. We have learned also that the general lower Rhine area had a similar acquaintance with the English.

Such evidence of integration leaves us with the remaining problem of determining at what point in time these families should no longer be considered English. We unfortunately have no data that shows the first generation of emigrants from any of these English families, and so it is impossible to decide by how many generations we are removed from them when discussing certain households. Nor do we have any evidence concerning their continued ties (or lack thereof) to England and to other Englishmen and women in Cologne. The pattern of the sudden disappearance of *Anglicus* families from the sources in the years following the death of the patriarch, coupled with the selling off of the family estate, raises further questions about the length of stay by these

---

[154] Fahne, *Geschichte der Kölnischen, Jülichschen und Bergischen Geschlechter*, I, p. 99: "1298 ist Arnold M[ulart] mit den Hüffner seines Hofes Huelhoven im Streit. Gottfried von Heinsberg thut den Spruch, daß die Hüffner im Walde nur Douschout (dürres Holz) sammeln und die Schweine gegen 2 Denare für das Stück jährlich Bedungelt, zur Eichelmast, fructus quercnum et fagorum vulgariter Eykeyr, eintreiben dürften."

families. Was this a sign of their return to England? In any case, it complicates the decision concerning if and when these *Anglicus* families and individuals can no longer properly be called English. Perhaps the continued use of the surname *Anglicus* itself is the best evidence for determining whether these families identified themselves with their English heritage.

We have also found a plausible explanation for the presence of Cologners bearing the surname *Anglicus*: through marriage into an English family. The matter of Godefridus de Zudendorp is, however, not fully clear in this respect. Even this clarification complicates the picture, since we are thereby unable to distinguish absolutely between the English and those Cologners who married into such families and took their surname (except in cases such as those styled "de Anglia," and the "fratri dicti Anglici," who were more likely English than four brothers who had all married into English families). What is certain, however, is a link to an English family in all cases. Indeed the very existence of Cologners bearing the name *Anglicus* is the best evidence for the kind of intimate, daily interaction between peoples of the two regions.

Chapter 6

COLOGNE FAMILIES WITH ENGLISH CONNECTIONS: THE ZUDENDORPS

The Schreinsurkunden contain a rich store of material as well on many Cologne families that maintained intensive and enduring relations with England, either through trade or through diplomatic service. One such family and its history of diplomatic activity in England is the main focus of this chapter, and then in the following chapter we shall consider other Cologners who appear in English documents. When the Cologne municipal records are integrated with English royal documents the remarkable rise to prominence and surprising interregional activity of one particular Cologne *ministerialis* (i.e. *dienestman* or "unfree knight") household emerges. We have already met some members of this family, known by the surname "de Zudendorp," in the prior chapter. Yet there is a great deal more to be said about the family.

The Zudendorp *Geschlecht* was perhaps the most fascinating of all the Cologne families that maintained relations with England and the English during the twelfth and thirteenth centuries. Its members began their rise to prominence as *ministeriales* of the archbishops of Cologne and eventually, through service as ambassadors to the English court, became intimately involved in archiepiscopal negotiations with both the English and imperial courts. The wealth and high social status they achieved thereby is reflected in both the large number of houses and other property they accumulated in Cologne as well as in their marriage ties to many of the leading patrician families of the city. The archiepiscopal *ministeriales* of Cologne enjoyed an unusual status, in which they both lived among the burghers and participated in the leadership of the city while still serving either the archbishop or some other religious or noble house. Many eventually obtained the status of free knighthood.[1] Emblematic of this development, the Zudendorp *Geschlecht* is thus both of interest on a local level as well as on an inter-regional level.

---

[1] E. Ennen, "Kölner Wirtschaft im Früh- und Hochmittelalter," I, p. 127: "Minsterialität und

Important as they are for our understanding of contacts between England and Cologne, as well as of the relationship between the *ministeriales* and the burghers in Cologne itself, almost nothing has been said about this family to date. Friedrich Lau had promised at least a genealogical tree of the Zudendorps, but this never appeared.[2] Luise von Winterfeld suspected a *ministerialis* background for the family, but only devoted a short paragraph to them with only the most basic sketch of just four family members.[3] The remarkable rise to prominence this *Geschlecht* managed from a *ministerialis* origin to its final entry into the landed gentry needs to be told more fully because of the light it sheds on both Cologne's urban history as well as on Anglo-Cologne relations.

Since the family took their toponymic surname from a suburban village to the south of Cologne, this may be assumed to be their ancestral home. Although Zudendorp (or Zündorf) was under the lordship of the counts of Berg, there may have been some archiepiscopal possessions in the area.[4] The first documented appearance of a member of this family occurs in a charter granted by Emperor Frederick I Barbarossa to Archbishop Rainald of Dassel in 1167. Here a Richwinus de Zudendorp is recorded among the *viri honorati* who were with the imperial army in Italy and witnessed the grant to Rainald as a reward for his brave service against the Romans. The archbishop received the imperial court of Andernach with full regalian rights of mint, tolls, justice, fishery, mills, and bann (*bannus*), as well as the imperial court at Eckenhagen with its silver mines (*cum fodinis argenti*) and appurtenances.[5] Since Richwinus was in the service of Rainald of Dassel in 1167, he may have also accompanied the archbishop to Rouen and to the diet of Würzburg only two years earlier, where intense negotiations with the English court took place concerning the papal schism. If so, this family's role in negotiations with the English court began as early as the imperial efforts at gaining the support of Henry II of England against Pope Alexander III.

Other men styled "de Zudendorp" turn up in the twelfth-century

---

Bürgertum sind nicht klar voneinander abgegrenzt, sondern gehen ineinander über: Ministerialen erscheinen als burgenses. Wir beobachten sowohl ministerialische Herkunft als auch Eintritt in die Ministerialität." See also Knut Schulz, "Richerzeche, Meliorat und Minsterialität in Köln," *Köln, das Reich und Europa. MSAK* 60 (1971), pp. 149–72; W. Pötter, *Die Ministerialität der Erzbischöfe von Köln vom Ende des 11. bis zum Ausgang des 13. Jahrhunderts*, Studien zur Kölner Kirchengeschichte, 9 (Düsseldorf, 1967) and J. Ahrens, *Die Ministerialität in Köln und am Niederrhein* (Leipzig, 1908). For more in general on German *ministeriales* see Benjamin Arnold, *German Knighthood* (Oxford, 1985).

2 Lau, "Das Kölner Patriziat bis zum Jahre 1325," *MSAK* 25 (1894), p. 359.

3 von Winterfeld, *Handel, Kapital und Patriziat in Köln bis 1400*, p. 7.

4 Pötter, *Die Ministerialität der Erzbischöfe von Köln*, p. 68.

5 *REK*, II, p. 159 no. 900 dated August 1, 1167; also in *UGN*, I, p. 297 no. 426.

sources, but their relationship to the later members of the family remains uncertain. In the middle of the twelfth century Fortliph de Zudendorp appears both on the city's citizen roll[6] and on a guild list.[7] A certain Volcnant de Zudendorp appears on two separate guild lists as well.[8] Around the years 1193 to 1220 a Teodericus de Zudendorp purchased two quarter-portions of two separate houses near Heumarkt in St. Martin parish and then gave them to his wife Elizabeth.[9] None of these men, however, can be connected to the family with certainty.

A charter of Archbishop Engelbert I in 1218 gives us the first evidence of the family's knightly status. Here Engelbert takes a priory of Siegburg abbey located in Oberpleis into his special protection and itemizes their possessions, among which is mentioned "item agros emptos a Rychwino milite de Zudindorp iacentis in eadem parrochia, cum decima eorundem agrorum."[10] This same Richwinus was also a witness to a charter of Engelbert I dated July 1222 granting freedom from taxation to the city of Wipperfürth.[11] A kinship connection with the city of Wipperfürth may have existed, since a later member of the family would marry the daughter of a Godescalcus de Wuppelford.

The family only emerges from these hazy early references in the person of Henricus de Zudendorp the Elder (*Senior*) and his wife Elizabeth. Beginning with Henricus we learn of the family's growing involvement in the political intrigues of the English surrounding the imperial candidacy of Otto IV, the nephew of Richard I and John, who grew up at the English court. Henricus the Elder first appears in a charter of Archbishop Bruno IV dated March 19, 1206 among the witnesses "et alii ministeriales et amici nostri" who confirmed a charter granted to Abbot Otto of Siegburg.[12] The timing of this charter is important, since Bruno had just replaced Archbishop Adolf I of Altena only a few months before. Adolf had abandoned the Plantagenet-supported Welf Otto IV and gone over to the Staufer Philip of Swabia, thus incurring a suspension from ecclesiastical office by Innocent III. Adolf drew many of his vassals to the Staufen cause, yet the citizens of Cologne, mindful of their valuable economic ties with England, maintained steadfast support for Otto IV.[13] The Zudendorps had chosen to support the English–Welf cause along with the city and the new archbishop: this was not an easy decision, since it defied the former

---

[6] *Kölner Schreinsurkunden des 12. Jahrhunderts*, ed. Hoeniger, II, 2, p. 42.

[7] Ibid., II, 2, p. 56.   [8] Ibid., II, 2, p. 56.

[9] St. Martin Karte 21 [side 1] col. 3: nos. 12–15.   [10] *UGN*, II, pp. 43–4 no. 79.

[11] *REK*, III, 1, p. 64 no. 367; also in *UGN*, II, p. 59 no. 107.

[12] *REK*, III, 1, p. 3 no. 16.

[13] See Stehkämper, "England und die Stadt Köln als Wahlmacher König Ottos IV."

archbishop's lordship and was made only months before the city fell to the forces of Philip of Swabia.

Henricus the Elder's involvement in the Plantagenet–Welf cause deepened further, as three years later he was engaged in business with the English court. He sent a certain Gerardus to King John in order to inform the monarch about Otto IV's imperial coronation at the hands of Pope Innocent III, the crowning achievement of Anglo-Welf negotiations revived after the murder of Philip of Swabia. Otto had been crowned in Rome on October 4, 1209, news of which was anxiously awaited in England. Gerardus then reached King John at Mountsorel in Leicestershire with the news on November 12, five weeks and four days after the ceremony,[14] and he was generously rewarded for his efforts with 10 marks for expenses.[15] Gerardus may have been at the English court again a month later, since another grant of three pence was made to a messenger bearing a letter "de rumoribus imperatoris Romae" to the bishop of Winchester on December 12.[16]

Henricus the Elder apparently enjoyed such a status by this time that he had his own nuncios to represent him before the royal court. What role he played in these affairs, or whether he accompanied Otto to Rome, is unknown, but knowledge of him by name at the English court suggests ongoing contact preceding this particular instance. Also uncertain is the identity of the envoy Gerardus, although he may have been either Henricus the Elder's son or his son-in-law Gerardus de Belle, both of whom served as the Elder's messengers.

The following year, as diplomatic relations with the papacy were deteriorating for Otto IV, Henricus the Elder himself appeared before the English king, receiving ten marks as a royal gift.[17] The gift was granted to Henricus the Elder *de feudo suo*. It was not a money fief like those used by Richard I among the German princes and which King John attempted to revive in 1209.[18] An entry for the same year in the Pipe Rolls indicates that this was actually a land fief of the village of Laxfield (Suffolk), which Henricus the Elder received from Duke

---

[14] *The Great Roll of the Pipe for the Eleventh Year of the Reign of King John, Michaelmas 1209*, PR NS, 24 (London, 1948), p. xvii.

[15] *Rotuli de liberate ac de missis et praestitis regnante Johanne*, ed. Thomas Duffus Hardy, p. 138: "Rotulus Misae – Die Jov. in crastino Sancti Martini . . . Gerardo, nuncio Henrici de Suzentorp, qui prius tulit rumores de consecratione domini Othoni Imperatoris de dono X. marcas per rege" (1209).

[16] Ibid., p. 142: "Misae. Die Sabbata proxima ibidem . . . Cuidam nuncio eunti cum litteris de rumoribus Imperatoris Romae ad episcopum Wint. iij. d."

[17] Ibid., p. 156: "Henrico de Zudentorp militi de feudo suo X. marcas per regem."

[18] A. L. Poole, "Richard the First's alliances with the German princes in 1194," pp. 90–9.

Henry of Lotharingia.[19] Duke Henry, also known as the duke of Brabant or alternately as the duke of Louvain, had received the Honor of Eye in Suffolk through his wife in 1198 in exchange for his support of the Welf imperial candidacy. In fact, Otto IV was engaged to the daughter of Duke Henry, who was named Mary, at the time of his royal coronation in Aachen in the same year.[20]

The Pipe Roll entry declares that Henricus the Elder owed the king four mewed goshawks (*austurcos*) for the royal confirmation of this grant – an interesting aside regarding the personal dimension of medieval governance and diplomatic negotiations. His debt of the four goshawks continued to be recorded in the Pipe Rolls during the next two years until he was declared quit of it by royal letter.[21] Henricus had certainly come a long way; beginning as a local German ministerial he was now serving two monarchs as well as his archbishop, and held a fief in a foreign land as the subtenant of the duke of Lotharingia. Such wide-ranging contacts are impressive to say the least. This is also the first time that we find Henricus the Elder referred to as *miles*.

He remained in the Plantagenet–Welf camp through the remaining years of Otto IV's viable kingship. On January 1211 he was among the witnesses who confirmed a charter of Archbishop Dietrich I (successor of Bruno IV),[22] and on November 30, 1212 he was one of the witnesses listed on Otto IV's charter to the city of Cologne confirming the citizens' freedom from the imperial toll at Kaiserswerth and reducing their tolls at Boppard and Duisburg.[23] In addition, he is mentioned

---

19 *The Great Roll of the Pipe for the Twelfth Year of the Reign of King John, Michaelmas 1210*, PR NS, 26 (London, 1950), p. 30: "Henricus de Suthentorp debet iiii osturos mutarios et bonos pro habenda confirmatione regis de rationabili donatione quam Henricus dux Louanie dominus honoris de Eye ei fecit de villata de Laxefeld." Laxfield was about ten miles due east from the borough of Eye, and virtually at the mid-point between the boroughs of Eye and Dunwich on the coast.

20 The Honor of Eye was given by king Richard I to Maud, wife of duke Henry of Lotharingia (Lower Lorraine), who had some heritable claim to it, as reward for the duke's support of Otto's kingship. Duke Henry used this honor in his title: "Henricus dei gratia dux Lotharingie marchio Romani imperii et dominus honoris Eye." See *The Great Roll of the Pipe for the Tenth Year of the Reign of King Richard I, Michaelmas 1198*, PR NS, 9 (London, 1932), p. xvii. For the marriage of Otto and Mary see Roger of Wendover, *Flores historiarum*, ed. Henry G. Hewlett, RS, 84 (London, 1886–9; rpt. 1965), I, p. 272 and MPHA, II, p. 65.

21 *The Great Roll of the Pipe for the Thirteenth Year of the Reign of King John, Michaelmas 1211*, PR NS, 28 (London, 1953), p. 23 (Norfolk/Suffolk Roll): "Henricus de Swinetorp [debet] iiii osturos mutarios sicut continentur in rotulo precedenti"; *The Great Roll of the Pipe for the Fourteenth Year of the Reign of King John, Michaelmas 1212*, PR NS, 30 (London, 1955), p. 177 (Suffolk Roll): "Henricus de Swintorp debet iiii osturos sicut continentur in rotulo precedenti. Set postea habuit quietantiam pre breve regis." Either a scribal error or simply some difficulty in rendering a Germanic place-name accounts for the corruption of the surname from Suthendorp to Swinetorp.

22 REK, III, 1, p. 17 no. 89.

23 UGN, II, pp. 21–2 no. 40; also in *Böhmer*, V, p. 142 no. 491.

twice in 1212 at the English court. On July 3 he was at Westminster, and received a two-and-a-half mark advance from the income of his English fief.[24] On October 25 one of his sons named Ricardus was given an additional payment from the fief on his behalf.[25] This entry is valuable since it is the only surviving reference that mentions Ricardus as Henricus' son. We shall return to this Ricardus later, as he appears elsewhere in England in the service of the archbishop of Cologne. The passage also indicates that the actual amount of the fief was 20 marks, of which Ricardus received half at this time.

Although the Plantagenet–Welf coalition was shattered at Bouvines, Henricus the Elder continued to serve the new archbishops in affairs involving England. Only four months after the debacle at Bouvines, a certain Henricus de Colonia, envoy of Otto IV, took part in an embassy to the English court in London.[26] He later witnessed a charter of Archbishop Engelbert I (in May 1221),[27] and was also active in Cologne in 1224.[28] Henricus was also entertained at Westminster, along with Conrad de Wilre (the seneschal of the Welf Otto IV) and a member of the German Hospitalers, from November 19 to 21, 1222 as envoys of the archbishop of Cologne. They were given 25 marks, 19 shillings, 1 penny for their expenses and each received a goblet from the king at a cost of 5 marks apiece.[29]

The high point of Henricus' involvement in diplomacy between the empire and England, however, occurred in the year 1225. At this time Henry III of England began a protracted and ultimately frustrated attempt to secure an English marriage union with either Emperor Frederick II or a high-ranking German prince – in this case duke Leopold of Austria. As always the archbishop of Cologne was involved in any imperial negotiations with England. In fact, these negotiations intensified in early 1225 when Bishop Walter of Carlisle traveled to Cologne to expedite the affair. Bishop Walter wrote the first of several

---

[24] *Rotuli litterarum clausarum in turri Londinensi asservati*, ed. Thomas Duffus Hardy (London, 1833–4), I, p. 119: "Liberate de thesauro nostro . . . Et Henrico de Sumenthorp duas marcas et dimidietatem de praestito super feodum suum de eodem termino" (Westminster, July 3, 1212).

[25] Ibid., I, p. 125: "Item liberate de thesauro nostro Henrico de Sundestorp decem marcas de feodo xxti marcarum per manum Ricardi filii sui" (Westminster, October 25, 1212).

[26] Ibid., I, p. 177: "Liberate de thesauro nostro Henrico de Colonia nuncio domini Ottonis Imperatoris x. marcas et presbitero de Placenc. nuncio ejusdem Imperatoris c. solidos et magistro Jacobo ejusdem domini Imperatoris nuncio v. marcas de dono nostro. Teste me ipso apud Novum Templum London. xvii die Novembris" (London, November 17, 1214). Also mentioned in *Böhmer*, V, p. 1602 no. 10781.

[27] *REK*, III, 1, pp. 57–8 no. 322.

[28] He appears in the witness list of a charter: *UGN*, II, p. 65 no. 121, where Lacomblet has rendered Henricus the Elder with the surname "de Zudedre."

[29] *Rotuli litterarum clausarum*, ed. Hardy, I, p. 522. Here he is referred to as Henricus Cudinthorp.

letters to his king around February 10 to inform Henry of his initial progress. The account of his arrival in Cologne informs us of Henricus the Elder's role in the negotiations.[30] Even before the arrival of Bishop Walter and his entourage (on February 1, the eve of the feast of the Purification of the Virgin) Henricus the Elder and an English cleric named Johannes had gone to the imperial diet at Ulm in order to seek the return of Archbishop Engelbert I. The archbishop returned "ad eorum igitur instantiam," and met the English envoys at his castle of Altenberg. Thus Henricus the Elder received the English embassy at Cologne in the absence of the archbishop, which is a strong statement about his status in both the archiepiscopal as well as in the English court.

Another letter by a fellow envoy of Bishop Walter (namely Henry de Cornhill, the chancellor of London) to the Bishops Jocelin of Bath, Richard of Salisbury, and Ralph of Chichester reveals that Henricus the Elder was known by many of the magnates of England as a central figure in these negotiations and was well paid for his involvement.[31] The chancellor confidentially discusses the grave difficulties caused by the lack of money for the marriage project and declares that he doesn't expect to return "de partibus remotioribus" until at least Easter week,

---

[30] *Royal and other Historical Letters Illustrative of the Reign of Henry III*, ed. Walter Shirley, RS, 27 (London, 1862; rpt. 1965), I, p. 250: "Venimus itaque Coloniam, in vigilia Purificationis beatae Virginis, ibique dominum Henricum de Zudenthorpe et Johannem clericum nostrum invenimus, qui nuper de domini archiepiscopo redierant, de quodam colloquio quod dominus rex Alemanniae cum pluribus principum suorum apud Ulmam in Suevia celebraverat, et fere in itinere illo omnes equos suos amiserant. Ad eorum igitur instantiam dominus archiepiscopus ad partes Coloniae accessit, et die mercurii proxima, ad quoddam castrum suum, quod distat a Colonia per duo millearia, venit; quo statim nuncium nostrum ad eum destinavimus, adventum nostrum et qualiter sine sociis nostris venimus ei significantes." Also in *Diplomatic Documents Preserved in the Public Records Office. Vol. I: 1101–1272*, ed. Pierre Chaplais (London, 1964) 109–11 no. 160 and *Historia Diplomatica Friderici Secundi*, ed. J. L. A. Huillard-Bréholles (Paris, 1852–61), II, pp. 833–9.

[31] *Royal and other Historical Letters Illustrative of the Reign of Henry III*, ed. Shirley, I, pp. 254–8 (dated *c.* February 10, 1225) and *Diplomatic Documents*, ed. Chaplais, 112–13 no. 163 (dated March 1225). Bishop Walter, in his first letter indicates that both Henry de Cornhill and a certain Nicholas de Molis had arrived in Cologne after his initial meeting with the archbishop. *Rotuli litterarum clausarum in turri Londoniensi asservati*, ed. Hardy, II, pp. 20–1 contains payments of 60 marks each made to Bishop Walter of Carlisle, master Henry de Cornhill, chancellor of London, and to Nicholas de Molis for their expenses during the embassy. Then follows a payment to Henricus de Zudendorp of 40 marks for his expenses – this series was dated February 27 and witnessed by the Justiciar and Bishop Jocelin of Bath. Hence we can place Chancellor Henry de Cornhill in Cologne at the time of this letter and can understand why it is addressed in part to Bishop Jocelin, who was privy to the negotiations. Henry de Cornhill and Nicholas (or Colin) de Molis were still in Cologne with the bishop of Carlisle in June, as a reimbursement to a certain Henricus Lupus of Groningen was ordered on the 24th of this month for the £40 he had loaned to Bishop Walter of Carlisle and Nicholas de Molis and the 20 marks loaned to chancellor Henry de Cornhill (*Rotuli litterarum clausarum*, ed. Hardy, II, p. 46). The chancellor was, however, back in England by the end of June, as confirmed in a letter of Bishop Walter of Carlisle (*Diplomatic Documents*, ed. Chaplais, p. 117 no. 172).

citing two reasons: the first is because of the long distance to be traveled, and the second is:

quia Henricus de Suynethorp, si forte ipsum comitem habere possimus, nullatenus sine conductu bono partibus illis se credet, sicut in literis domino nostro missis continetur. Ipse quoque Henricus sine socio suo milite nullatenus nobiscum veniet, quorum expensas per socium meum, quem curialem habeo, benignum et fidelem, et per me ministrari conveniet.

Hence the chancellor expected a delay in getting Henricus de Zudendorp to travel to these more remote parts, since Henricus was concerned about safe passage and therefore wished to travel with his associate; who this was is not stated here, except that he was a knight. All of Henricus' expenses, however, would be paid by the chancellor and his colleague, perhaps a reference to Nicholas de Molis. In addition, the chancellor mentions the existence of a letter sent by Henricus to King Henry III, to which he was privy. This is one of three such letters sent by Henricus personally to the king, and although we know nothing of this first one, the latter two survive.

We discover where these more remote parts were in letters from Henry III to Bishop Walter, Henry de Cornhill, and Nicholas de Molis, dated March 2, 1225.[32] In the first the king thanks Walter for his efforts amid many difficulties and regrets that Alan Martel, the master of the Templars in England, and the prior of the Hospitalers in England (both of whom had accompanied the bishop initially to Cologne) could not remain longer than Easter, as they had pressing affairs within their orders.[33] In response, the king entrusts Henry de Cornhill and Nicholas de Molis, along with a certain W. de Kirkeham now being sent, to assist the bishop. The king then tells Bishop Walter:

Quia vero audivimus quod H. de Zudenthorp circa agenda nostra se sollicitum exhibet quem in partes Austriae cum predictis Henrico cancellario et Nicholo sicut per eos accepimus proficisci necesse est non sine magnis laboribus et expenses [sic]: precepimus et ad opus suum apud Ipr. per dictum Henricum xl. marcas assignari.[34]

Once again we hear of Henricus de Zudendorp's reservations about going to the remoter parts and the king's resulting willingness to

---

[32] *Rotuli litterarum clausarum*, ed. Hardy, II, pp. 70–1 (dated March 2).

[33] Ibid., II, p. 71 records a letter delivered to the master of the Templars and the prior of the Hospitalers dated March 2 in which the king regretfully accepts the need for them to leave the embassy. The king had already confirmed letters of authorization to negotiate for these two, along with Bishop Walter, Henry de Cornhill, and Nicholas de Molis, for the duke of Austria and archbishop of Cologne on January 3: *CPR Henry III*, I, p. 558; *Rymer*, I, pp. 275–6; *Böhmer*, V, p. 1622 nos. 10931–3.

[34] This payment of 40 marks is no doubt that mentioned above in note 31.

subsidize his trip; only here the party of Henricus de Zudendorp, Henry de Cornhill, and Nicholas de Molis is more specifically described as going together *in partes Austriae*. Therefore, while the bishop of Carlisle busied himself with efforts directed toward the imperial court, which ultimately failed, Henricus de Zudendorp and the other envoys went to Austria, apparently in early March, to parley with the duke about a possible marriage union.[35] The Austrian initiative proved unproductive, since the duke wavered, declaring that the entire matter was in the hands of the archbishop of Cologne.[36] Although the trip proved disappointing, we have discovered yet another distant connection in Henricus de Zudendorp's far-flung and impressive diplomatic activities.

The negotiations dragged on throughout the summer months with little change. King Henry III wrote a letter to Walter of Carlisle of August 27, in which he exhorted the bishop to continue patiently in the negotiations. He also acknowledged the reception of letters from both the archbishop of Cologne and Henricus de Zudendorp, which have assured him of their on-going support.[37] Henricus had sent this second letter sometime during mid to late summer,[38] while the negotiations were becoming increasingly difficult and protracted. Henricus exhorted the king to continue the endeavor with the duke of Austria and

[35] *CRC*, p. 255: "Heinricus rex [of Germany] curiam habuit Frankinvort; ubi quidam episcopus missus a rege Anglie cum ceteris ipsius legatis affuit, laborans, ut ipse rex matrimonium contraheret cum sorore regis Anglie. Sed cum talis contractus displicuisset principibus nec potuisset habere processum, nuncii inacte revertuntur."

[36] The initial delay in departing for Austria is mentioned also by Bishop Walter in his first letter, as the party awaited the return of the archbishop from Saxony for further counsel before setting out. The duke of Austria wrote a brief letter to Henry III, mentioning the arrival of his envoys, and announced: "omnem hujus facti processum in domino Coloniensi archiepiscopo locavimus atque posuimus" (dated February–March 1225). See *Diplomatic Documents*, ed. Chaplais, p. 113 no. 164; *Böhmer*, V, p. 1622 no. 10933. The delay, and the ultimate failure of the venture, were both due to a lack of money, which Bishop Walter makes clear in his first letter: "Ideoque necesse est ut magnos viros ad partes illas destinetis qui multa possint expendere, ut ibi morentur donec negocia vestra perficiantur."

[37] *REK*, III, 1, p. 82 no. 512; also in *Rymer*, I, p. 282.

[38] Chaplais, *Diplomatic Documents*, p. 127 no. 189: "Excellentissimo domino suo, domino H[enrico] illustri regi Anglie, domino Hibernie, duci Normannie, Aquitanie et comiti Andegavie, suus fidelis et devotus Henricus de Zudenthorp, salutem et fidele servitium usque ad consummationem vite. Noverit excellentia vestra quod mora quam dominus Karl[eolensis] fecit Colon', licet negotium non sit adhuc perfectum, extitit et erit processu temporis vobis et heredibus plurimum fructuosa. Credo autem quod dictum negotium per dominum ducem Austrie, cujus consilio dominus imperator vult illud terminare, prorogatum est et celsitudini vestre supplico obnixe in bona fide consulens quatinus nullo modo omittatis quin negotium illud debito fine consumetis, ne confusionem amicis vestris et gaudium inimicis detis, si per vos vel per consilium vestrum, quod absit, deficiat. De omnibus siquidem bonis michi et meis a liberalitate vestra vestri gratia collatis gratias refero excellentie vestre quantas possum, supplicans quatinus libitum vestrum michi sicut ligio homini vestro significare dignemini. Valeat excellentia vestra in Domino."

concluded the letter by asking the king to consider him as a liege vassal. The language of this and a subsequent letter are of a very intimate and personal nature, which suggests a high level of trust developed through his continued close contact with the English court over at least fifteen years. When the entire process was aborted in November of the same year through the brutal murder of the archbishop of Cologne by Count Frederick of Isenburg, it was Henricus who wrote to the English king announcing the violent death of Engelbert. Henricus assured the king that, had Engelbert remained alive, the marriage union would have been accomplished. He also made certain to exhort the king to maintain their relationship even though the archbishop was gone:

Excellenti domino suo Henrico, Dei gratia regi Angliae, Henricus de Zudendorf, civis Coloniae, ratissimum ac fidelissimum in omnibus obsequium. Serenitati vestrae dolendo significandum duxi, dilectum dominum nostrum archiepiscopum a quodam proximo consanguineo suo esse interfectum. Propter quod vos scire volo, si hoc infortunium non evenisset, ipse de negotio vestro finem bonum, per Dei gratiam, imposuisset. Ego vero modo indigeo ut gratiam vestram mihi et meis exhibere curetis.[39]

The rhetorical flourish at the letter's end contains a noteworthy message. Henricus the Elder sought from the English king "gratiam vestram mihi et meis exhibere curetis." This phrase had already appeared in the earlier letter. Such a request indicates the presence of colleagues or members of his family in England, perhaps even at the royal court, who at this time of confusion and frustration were in a vulnerable situation. The years just preceding and following the beginning of Henry III's personal rule (1227) were marked by tension at court as Henry gradually asserted his own authority, and the failure of this extensive diplomatic effort must have created even more conflict. Henry would soon thereafter (1232) level a charge against the justiciar Hubert de Burgh that he had secretly hindered Duke Leopold of Austria from an alliance with England.[40] This topped the list of accusations of treason made by the young king against Hubert and so it was surely a festering point of contention for him. Henricus followed up his letter by sending an envoy to the English court by the name of

---

[39] *Royal and other Historical Letters Illustrative of the Reign of Henry III*, ed. Shirley, I, p. 274 no. 227 (dated November 7, 1225); also in Chaplais, *Diplomatic Documents*, p. 129 no. 193 and *Böhmer*, V, no. 10957.

[40] Roger of Wendover, *Flores historiarum*, III, p. 32; Walter Kienast, *Die Deutschen Fürsten im Dienste der Westmächte bis zum Tode Philipps des Schönen von Frankreich*, Bijdragen van het Instituut voor Middelleeuwsche Geschiedenis der Rijks-Universiteit te Utrecht, 16 (Utrecht, 1924 and Munich, 1931), p. 29.

Lambekin, who received half a mark for his expenses upon returning to Cologne on December 11.[41]

Thereafter, Henricus de Zudendorp the Elder remained active in further negotiations under the new Archbishop Henry I of Molenark. During 1227–8 the archbishop pursued a marriage union for Henry III of England with both the king of Bohemia and (once again) the duke of Austria. At Westminster on January 7, 1227 the king granted ten pounds to "Gerard de Colonia, the fellow of Henry de Zudendorp."[42] As we learn from another royal grant of 5 marks on April 11 to the same Gerard, he was the son-in-law of Henricus the Elder.[43] This had to be Gerardus de Belle, the *miles* and *advocatus* of Mundesdorp, who was married to Henricus the Elder's daughter Gertrudis. Gerardus de Belle's father was Otto, the *camerarius* of the archbishop and from another major Cologne ministerial family. Whether this Gerardus was the same man as the nuncio of Henricus the Elder in 1209 is impossible to say. But the de Belle *Geschlecht* had its own involvement in England, as we shall see later when we discuss this collateral branch of the Zudendorp family. The embassy was no doubt in connection with the renewed efforts at a marriage union with a German princess, since only two days later Henry III issued letters to the young King Henry of Germany, the archbishop of Cologne, and the duke of Bavaria indicating that he had received their nuncio, the Prior Conrad of Speyer, and was sending his own negotiators to them concerning a "confoederationem inter dominum regem Alemanniae et principes imperii et nos."[44] Henricus the Elder did not rely only on family members as his messengers to the English court, as we find Lambekin there again in June of the same year.[45] But these efforts were also in vain, and no marriage union resulted.

Although this second effort was also a failure, the Zudendorp family benefited from their involvement. Two days after Henry III sent Nicholas de Molis (who was involved in the first failed attempt in 1225) and a certain Walerandus Teutonicus *in partes transmarinas*[46] the following is recorded in the Close Rolls:

---

41 *Rotuli litterarum clausarum in turri Londoniensi asservati*, ed. Hardy, II, p. 88: "Liberate etc. Lamberto nuncio Henrici de Zudenthorp eunti versus partes suas dimidietatem marcam ad expensas suas de dono nostro" (Westminster, December 11, 1225).

42 *CLR Henry III*, I, p. 15.

43 Ibid., I, p. 27: "And to Gerard the Almain (Teutonico), son-in-law of Henry de Zudentorp, 5 marks, of the king's gift."

44 *Rotuli litterarum clausarum*, ed. Hardy, II, p. 210; *Böhmer*, V, p. 1628 nos. 10984–6; *Rymer*, I, pp. 292–3 dated at Westminster, April 13, 1227.

45 *CLR Henry III*, I, p. 36: "and to Lambekin, the envoy of Henry de Zudinthorp, 5s. for his expenses, of the king's gift" (Westminster, June 1, 1227).

46 *Rotuli litterarum clausarum*, ed. Hardy, II, p. 100.

Dominus Rex concessit Ricardo de Swinethorp quod habet usque ad etatem domini regis unum mercatum apud manerium suum de Laxfeld. singulis septimanis pro diem sabbati. Nisi etc. Et mandatum est vicecomiti Suff. quod mercatum illud clamari et teneri faciat sicut predictum est. Teste ut supra (Westminster, February 23, 1226).[47]

Here we find a remarkable situation in which Ricardus, the son of Henricus de Zudendorp who previously appeared in England (to receive a portion of the income from his father's fief of Laxfield in 1212), now obtained the right to have a weekly market in the village. Such information sheds new light on this enterprising son, who oddly enough never appears in the Cologne sources. He seems therefore to have resettled in Laxfield and dwelt on the manor, and based on this grant he was doing quite well. But we have not seen the last of his peculiar activities.

Ricardus appears again in a most unexpected situation on May 29, 1227, only a month and a half after the formal negotiations for a marriage union had begun in earnest.[48] Now we find him in the royal jail at Ipswich, held there by royal order because he had remained incorrigible under sentence of excommunication for over forty days. The king commanded that he give proper security (as he finally appeared ready to do) for appearing before an ecclesiastical court and that he be released on his own recognizance until such time. It is most unfortunate that there is no mention of why he had been excommunicated in the first place. We do know that Ricardus and his family were well known at the English court; Ricardus himself had even served as an envoy of the archbishop of Cologne in 1224 and sailed out of the Norfolk port of Lynn. Thus royal intervention was probably a result of the ties the family had to the royal court.[49] In fact, since he would have

---

[47] Ibid., II, p. 100. The corrupted spelling of the family name is the same as that used in connection with Laxfield in 1211–12.

[48] *Rotuli litterarum clausarum*, ed. Hardy, II, p. 187: "Rex Th. Norwic. Episcopo salutem. Ex parte Ricardi de Zudenthorp in prisona apud Gipeswic. detenti eo quod in sentencia excommunicationis ultra xl. dies incorrigibile permansit prout nobis per litteras vestras patentes es signastis est intimatum quod ipse paratus est et censure ecclesiatice parere et inde cautionem sufficientem prestare. Et ideo vobis mandamus quod aliquam personam ecclesiasticam ad dictum Ricardum mittatis qui ipsam cautionem ab eo accipiat et deliberari faciat. Quia dominus rex mandavit vicecomiti Suff. quod ex quo ipse Ricardus caucionem predictam exhibuerit eum incontinenti deliberet. Teste ut supra. Mandatum est vicecomiti Suff. quod ex quo Ricardus de Zudenthorp quem tenet in prisona domini Regi captum per preceptum domini regi eo quod in sententia excomunicationis permansit incorrigibilis ultra xl. dies illi quem episcopus Norwic. ad hoc mittat prestiterit cautionem de parendo censure ecclesiastice eum deliberari faciat. Teste ut supra" (Westminster, May 29, 1227). Ipswich is about 20 miles southwest of Laxfield.

[49] Ibid., I, p. 610 and I, p. 634: "Mandatum est ballivis portus de Lenn. quod navem in qua Ricardus de Sidinctorp et Ricardus de Alemannia nuncii Archiepiscopi Coloniensis applicuerunt ad partes suas abire permittant non obstante mandato de navibus arestandis. Teste ut

been in jail since at least April 20, perhaps the April embassy of Gerardus de Belle was concerned with this matter as well. Whatever his transgression, Ricardus made satisfaction since he was given a letter of royal protection from Portsmouth in April of 1230.[50]

Ricardus was perhaps the same person as the Richwinus de Zudendorp mentioned earlier. Von Winterfeld had speculated that he might have been a son of Henricus the Elder, but she gave no proof for this.[51] Yet the Close Roll entry for 1212 gives us certainty in this matter. We meet him once more in November 1235, where he received royal confirmation of his fief of Laxfield, as well as some rents from new property.[52] It is perhaps not coincidental that the king had confirmed the Cologners' trading privileges in his realm only sixteen days before this confirmation.[53]

Embassies from members of the Zudendorp family continue to be evidenced throughout the 1230s. A certain Gerard de Colonia was given one hundred shillings at the king's gift "for his expenses to his own parts" on February 30, 1230 (this was probably Gerardus de Belle again).[54] On April 20, 1237 a certain Gerardus de Zudenthorp was given 20 marks at Westminster.[55] This Gerardus, bearing the family surname, was probably the son of Henricus the Elder (thus the brother of Gertrudis de Zudendorp and the brother-in-law of Gerardus de Belle). He, too, was a familiar at the English court.

Henricus the Elder was certainly too old to continue traveling to

---

supra" (Bedford, July 9, 1224). Also in *REK*, III, 1, p. 75 no. 442; *HUB*, I, p. 54 no. 165 and *Böhmer*, V, p. 1621 no. 10923.

50 *CPR Henry III*, II, p. 361.

51 von Winterfeld, *Handel, Kapital und Patriziat in Köln bis 1340*, p. 7.

52 *CCHR*, I, p. 215: "Nov. 24 (1235) Rayne: Grant to Richard de Swinesthorp of the gift made to him by Henry, late duke of Lorraine, of the town of Laxfield, and the essarts of the old park which was in the soke of Laxfield, and the rents of Stodhaye, saving the foreign service which the township of Laxfield owes to the castle of Eye." I have been unable to locate Stodhaye, but presumably it was in the vicinity of Laxfield. The king had just confirmed possession of the honor of Eye on May 7, 1235 (*Rymer*, I, p. 340) and at Windsor on October 10, 1235 to the son of duke Henry of Lotharingia (*Treaty Rolls Preserved in the Public Record Office. Vol. I: 1234–1325*, ed. Pierre Chaplais [London, 1955], no. 83); this grant was also confirmed on February 6 and February 9, 1236 (*Treaty Rolls Preserved in the PRO*, ed. Chaplais, no. 94; *Rymer*, I, p. 352; *Böhmer*, V, p. 1654 no. 11177).

53 *CCHR*, I, p. 214; *HUB*, I, no. 268; *Böhmer*, V, p. 1654 no. 11172; *Ennen/Eckertz*, II, p. 152. The bailiffs of the fair of Hoyland were notified of this confirmation: *CPR Henry III*, III, p. 130; *Ennen/Eckertz*, II, p. 153; *Böhmer*, V, p. 1654 no. 11173; *HUB*, I, p. 89 – all dated November 8, 1235 at Daventry.

54 *CLR Henry III*, I, p. 169.

55 Ibid., I, p. 263: "To William Hardel. Contra breve to pay, out of the issues of the exchange of London, to Gerard de Zudenthorp 20 Marks, of the king's gift." This William Hardel, a London cleric, joined the Gascon seneschal Henry de Trublevill and the cleric John Mansel on an English military expedition in support of Frederick II against the Italian cities in 1238 (*MPHA*, II, p. 408 and *MPCM*, III, p. 485).

England by the 1230s. The last dateable mention of him is *c.* 1235–37,[56] which confirms that he, his two sons Henricus the Younger and Gerardus, as well as his father-in-law Sifridus de Nussia (Neuß), were all members of the *Schöffen* (*scabini*) college, the most powerful administrative body in the city by this time. Thus he and his sons were not only involved in foreign diplomacy but also played an important role in the administration of the city of Cologne. Henricus the Elder lived a very long life, as he appears on two separate citizen rolls dated some time in the second half of the twelfth century.[57]

Most of Henricus the Elder's wealth in the city of Cologne came through his marriage to Elizabeth, the daughter of Sifridus de Nussia (Neuß).[58] Elizabeth brought a number of houses into the family as a result of her inheritance. The first house, named "zir Rodirdure" or "Ad Rufam Ianuam," was located on Martinstrasse in St. Alban parish near Marspforte and has already been the subject of discussion regarding the English in Cologne.[59] The second house was probably on the street named Am Frankenturm in St. Brigida parish, right at the shore of the Rhine.[60] A third property, half of a house in which a Godefridus Vinzelin dwelt, was located on Salzgasse in St. Martin parish just off Heumarkt.[61] The fourth house was located on Lintgasse in St. Brigida parish and became one of three houses known as the "domus Zudendorp."[62] Finally, a "dimidietas hereditatis" was located on Spulmannsgasse in the district of Airsbach near Katherinengraben.

A separate entry elsewhere clarifies the nature of this *hereditas*: four *mansiones* under one roof, each with its own courtyard, located on the corner of Follerstrasse and Spulmannsgasse.[63] Henricus the Elder and Elizabeth gave this *hereditas* to their daughter Gertrudis and her

---

[56] Friedrich Lau, "Beiträge zur Verfassungsgeschichte der Stadt Köln I: Das Schöffen Collegium des Hochgerichts zu Köln bis zum Jahre 1396," *Westdeutsche Zeitschrift für Geschichte und Kunst* 14 (1895), p. 193 has Henricus de Zudendorp (the Elder), his sons Henricus Iunior de Zudendorp and Gerardus, and his father-in-law Sifridus de Nussia present at an election of *scabini* around 1235–7.

[57] *Kölner Schreinsurkunden des 12. Jahrhunderts*, ed. Hoeniger, II, 2, pp. 19 and 25.

[58] Schöffenschrein Karte 2 col. 11: no. 1 dated *c.* 1205–14.

[59] The actual location was St. Martinstrasse I (cf. Keussen, *Topographie der Stadt Köln*, I, p. 165 col. b, 1–3).

[60] The location was probably Am Frankenturm I (cf. Keussen, *Topographie der Stadt Köln*, I, p. 120 col. b, 13 where a "dom. in littore Reni prope domum Theoderici Slavi versus s. Afram" is mentioned).

[61] The location was Salzgasse V (cf. Keussen, *Topographie der Stadt Köln*, I, p. 72 col. a, 5).

[62] The location was Lintgasse II (cf. Keussen, *Topographie der Stadt Köln*, I, p. 130 col. a–b, 1–4). The house of Winandus Iunior was located on Rothenberg (I, p. 71 col. a, c).

[63] 311 Spitzbutgasse (Airsbach) fo. 15r: "Notum sit, quod Elisabeth, que filia fuit Sifridi Senioris de Nussia et Beatris, de morte predictorum parentum suorum dimidietatem quatuor mansionum sub uno tecto et arearum retro unum ortorum versus urbis murum sitorum in Volratzgasse in angulo, ubicumque eam in particione attingit. Ita obtinuit, quod iure obtinebit."

husband Gerardus de Belle, whom we have already met, and they sold it directly to a third party. The final part of the inheritance, a one-third portion of a courtyard, was located just off Alter Markt on Bechergasse in St. Brigida parish.[64] With only one exception (the property in Airsbach, which Henricus the Elder and Elizabeth gave to their daughter and son-in-law) all this property was located within easy walking distance of each other and either on the border or within the parish of St. Brigida at Alter Markt. Most of the houses were rented out to other occupants. The only additional purchase made by Henricus the Elder and Elizabeth was of two parcels located against the old city wall in St. Columba parish.[65] The description of the location is too vague to be certain where the property lay specifically, but it was somewhere along the old Roman city wall either at the north or the west end of the parish.

Henricus the Elder passed the house named "zir Rodirdure" to his eldest son and namesake Henricus, who was called the Younger (*Iunior*), and his wife Gertrudis.[66] The father, however, retained the use of one half of the house while living. He also sold the rents he received from two of the other houses. Around the years 1227 to 1232 he released the income of 10 shillings from the house on Am Frankenturm to a certain Godeschalcus de Wippinvorde and his wife Richmudis.[67] Godeschalcus either was, or was shortly to become, the father-in-law of Gerardus de Zudendorp, the son of Henricus the Elder. Hence perhaps this business relationship engendered a marriage bond between the families. Henricus the Elder also allowed a certain Hildebrandus Hosemengere to redeem the 1-mark rent he owed on the house in Salzgasse.[68] The house was sold shortly thereafter.[69] The "domus Zudendorp" on Lintgasse was also sold at some point during the subsequent years. Although the house retained the Zudendorp name for many years thereafter, the Schreinsbücher entries evidence other

[64] The location was probably Bechergasse II. The house of Cunradus Phenerator was on Grosse Neugasse IVa (cf. Keussen, *Topographie der Stadt Köln*, I, p. 143 col. a, 4).
[65] 156 Berlici (St. Columba) fo. 1r: "Notum sit presentibus et futuris, quod Henricus de Zudendorp et uxor eius Elysabeth emerunt erga Henricum Suendewine et Aleydim uxorem eius duas areas super murum. Datum est etc. (1221)."
[66] Schöffenschrein Karte 2 col. 6: no. 20 dated *c.* 1205–14. Text published in *Kölner Schreinsurkunden des 12. Jahrhunderts*, ed. Hoeniger, II, 1, pp. 308–9.
[67] St. Brigida Karte 4 col. 3: no. 10 dated *c.* 1227–32.
[68] 448 I Schöffenschrein Generalis fo. 6r. Text published in *Die Kölner Schreinsbücher des 13. und 14. Jahrhunderts*, ed. Planitz and Buyken, p. 173 no. 724, but they incorrectly identify the passage as 447 II Generalis fo. 6r. Furthermore they date the text as before 1250, but it could not be later than the early 1230s.
[69] 448 I Schöffenschrein Generalis fo. 7v mentions the purchase of a "terciam partem aree eidem domui retro adiacenti, que fuerat Henrici de Zudendorp et uxoris eius Elsabeth" located in *platea Salis*.

owners by the 1280s.[70] The sale was probably earlier though, as no mention of it occurs in the inheritance entries of Henricus the Elder.

Henricus the Elder also held property outside of the city. An entry in the Red Book of the parish church of Holy Apostles indicates that he held property in Brizenberg, from which he contributed 32 shillings each year to the church.[71] The family's relationship with Holy Apostles church and its canons will be more fully explained in connection with Henricus the Elder's grandson Gerardus Iunior de Zudendorp, who held a great deal of property around the church and also bore the surname "de Novo Foro" (Neumarkt). An earlier event may have been influenced by the family's patronage relationship to this particular church. In 1225 when Bishop Walter of Carlisle was in Cologne to further negotiations for a marriage union for King Henry III of England, he was asked to celebrate Mass at Holy Apostles Church and to consecrate a number of relics housed therein. This took place on July 15, 1225, and afterwards Bishop Walter issued a charter to confirm his actions, which he performed "de auctoritate domini Coloniensis archiepiscopi Engilberti et ad petitionem conventus sanctorum apostolorum in Colonia."[72] He even issued an indulgence of thirty days to any who would either come to revere the relics or contribute alms on this feast day of saints Felix and Audauctus. The bringing together of Bishop Walter and Holy Apostles church may very well have been the result of the ties which the Zudendorp family had with the church. This was the church to which the family made memorials for their souls after death.

Henricus de Zudendorp the Elder disappears from the records by the late 1230s, and we may safely presume that his long life had finally come to an end. His was a remarkable career, which linked him personally with five different archbishops, two kings of England, three claimants to the imperial throne, and the dukes of Lotharingia and Austria. Indeed at the point of closest cooperation between England and Cologne (during the Welf candidacy of Otto IV) Henricus the Elder was integrally

---

[70] 58 Windeck (St. Brigida) fo. 17v: "dim. domus et aree site in Foro Piscium ex opposito retro domum de Zundindorp" (c. 1267). Also mentioned on fos. 30r and 30v. 58 Windeck (St. Brigida) fo. 27v and fo. 29v: the Domus Zudendorp was sold by owners other than the Zudendorp family c. 1280–4). Keussen, *Topographie der Stadt Köln*, I, p. 130 col. a, b 104: "Gr. 1315 dom. et ar. vocatur Zudendorp in Luntgasse [Lintgasse II] . . . Wk 1383 dom. et ar. in L[int]g[asse], que quondam fuit Sifridi Senioris de Nussia, que dom. nunc vocatur Z[udendorp]., et camera adiacens."

[71] Historisches Archiv der Stadt Köln GA 16 (Liber ecclesiae SS. Apostolorum dictus Rubeus) fo. 45r: "De Brizenberg. Henricus de Zudendorp solvit in die sancti Nicolai 32 solidos de bonis, que habet [in] Brizenberg, de quibus dantur 20 solidi dominis [i.e. the canons] in cottidanis denariis, reliqui denarii sunt obedienciarii" (not dated).

[72] *Ennen/Eckertz*, II, p. 95 no. 87.

involved in the diplomatic network between the two regions and was known by name at the English court.

There are further connections with England and the English among Henricus the Elder's descendents, whom we shall discuss next. But first let us evaluate the basis of his wealth and status in Cologne. It appears that his propertied wealth came almost completely through marriage. He shows no commercial activity, although his acquired property was located in the heart of the merchant quarter. His income in the city seems then to have come from rents on his properties. As an archiepiscopal *ministerialis* and *scabinus* of the city he was extremely busy with official duties. Thus his administrative role, rather than a mercantile career, connected him to England and provided him with the social status of knight and *scabinus*.

In regard to his legacy, he gave the house Ad Rufam Ianuam to his son and namesake Henricus the Younger, and the property in the district of Airsbach to his daughter Gertrudis and her husband Gerardus de Belle. But the remainder of his property in St. Brigida and St. Columba parishes are no longer mentioned in the land registers. Therefore we do not know exactly if and when they passed out of the family's hands. It is clear though that by his death he had established a strong foundation of wealth and status both in Cologne and in England.

Henricus de Zudendorp the Elder and his wife Elizabeth had three sons and one daughter, each of whom we have already met. The eldest son, called Henricus the Younger, had already received the house "zur Rodirdure" from his father, and on this house he centered his activities in the adjoining parish of St. Laurence. Since St. Laurence parish was the location of the Jewish quarter, we naturally find Henricus the Younger involved in business with a Jew concerning the family house of his wife Gertrudis, who was of the *Geschlecht* known by the curious surname "Vetscholder," another prominent patrician family in Cologne. In 1237 he purchased a baker's house from a certain Jew named Seckelinus.[73] Subsequent entries indicate that this house used to belong to his wife's father, Godefridus Vetscholder, and that his children each inherited a seventh part of the house.[74] Such portions are difficult to account for, since only four children are ever mentioned in the sources: Godefridus, Gerardus, Blithildis, and later a Henricus. Perhaps

---

[73] 92 Per totam parrochiam (St. Laurenz) fo. 1v. Text published in *Das Judenschreinsbuch der Laurenzpfarre zu Köln*, ed. Robert Hoeniger, Quellen zur Geschichte der Juden in Deutschland, I (Berlin, 1888), p. 172 no. 381. The same entry is repeated in another Schreinsbuch: 103 Liber IV de domo Kusini (St. Laurenz) fo. 3r. The location was Unter Goldschmied VI (cf. Keussen, *Topographie der Stadt Köln*, I, p. 199 col. a, 2).

[74] 103 Liber IV de domo Kusini (St. Laurenz) fo. 2v.

the one-seventh portion is a subdivision of the mother's original inheritance portion in the house. Furthermore, the later exchanges of one-sixth portions and "two parts of two children" are odd combinations, but the final result was that Blithildis and her husband Gerardus obtained full ownership of the house. At the death of Gerardus the house was passed down to their only son Johannes. This son then sold the house to another Jew named Seligmannus and his wife Minna.[75] Why the Vetscholder family had sold the house to Seckelinus in the first place is unknown, but the subsequent transactions have given us a glimpse into Henricus the Younger's family. His daughter Blithildis was married to Gerardus Krieg (*Grecus*), a member of a wealthy family that appears quite often in the Schreinsbücher. We shall have much more to say about the other sons Godefridus, Gerardus, and Henricus. Little else survives concerning Henricus the Younger; two Schreinsbuch entries, one of which details his inheritance, are unfortunately too marred to yield additional information.[76] The inheritance passage only adds confusion, since the children received a one-sixth portion, suggesting that there were six children. Yet all the other entries mention only the four discussed above.

Just when Henricus the Younger died is difficult to estimate because of the scarcity of information about him. We are much better instructed about his sons. The first was Godefridus, who is important for our consideration of the family's continued English connections. Godefridus had received a share in the house of his grandfather Godefridus Vetscholder, which he gave to his sister Blithildis. He also received from his father a share in the house "Ad Rufam Ianuam" or "zir Rodirdure" on Martinstrasse,[77] which appears to have been the main dwelling of this branch of the family. Again we have the problem of the size of the children's' portions; here being a one-fifth part of the house, which does not match the number of children nor does it equal the amounts given to the children from the Vetscholder house. In any case

---

[75] 92 Per totam parrochiam (St. Laurenz) fo. 8v. This transaction is also recorded in 107 Liber Iudeorum (St. Laurenz) fo. 7r. Text published in *Das Judenschreinsbuch der Laurenzpfarre zu Köln*, ed. Hoeniger, pp. 34–5 no. 130; Hoeniger also records the sale of this house by Seligmannus and his wife: (p. 35 no. 132) *c.* 1270–5.

[76] 449 IVb Schöffenschrein Generalis fo. 18r. The only two houses which can be made out with certainty here are the Vetscholder family house ("domum que . . . Sancti Laurentii") and the house "Ad Rufam Ianuam" ("domum que . . . versus domum Birbon"). A third property was located "inter incisores pannorum," also known as Unter Hutmacher in the center of Heumarkt in St. Martin's parish (cf. Keussen, *Topographie der Stadt Köln*, I, pp. 35–42). 447 Schöffenschrein Generalis fo. 12r: Henricus de Zudindorp Iunior et Gertrudis are involved in a grant, but the MS is also too faded to read (*c.* 1249).

[77] 84 Brandenburg (St. Alban) fo. 2r. This house is described as "domus site inter aurifabros, que dicitur Ad Rufam Ianuam."

each of Henricus the Younger's four children must have inherited a portion of this house, but one of the sons, Gerardus (often called the Younger [*Iunior*] to distinguish him from his uncle), known *as* "miles de Novo Foro," eventually reunited the portions and then sold the house in 1255.[78]

Godefridus de Zudendorp appears only once more in the sources in connection with another house, of which Godefridus held propriety in a third. We have already considered Godefridus' sale of his share to Henricus de Windeck (this was the domus Domicelli sold to the Windeck family) in the prior chapter and noted that he is oddly and incorrectly referred to here as "dictus Anglicus."[79]

While we lack more detailed information on Godefridus de Zudendorp the same cannot be said for his brother Gerardus, who was styled "dominus Gerardus Iunior de Novo Foro." We have already encountered him alienating his inheritance in the Vetscholder house in favor of his sister Blithildis and selling the family house "Ad Rufam Ianuam." Diverging from his father's activities in St. Laurence parish, Gerardus the Younger concentrated his numerous holdings in the parishes of Holy Apostles and St. Columba, with the majority in the vicinity of Neumarkt and Holy Apostles church.

Gerardus the Younger purchased houses in St. Columba parish on Herzogstrasse in 1258[80] and Mörsergasse in 1282.[81] The former he eventually sold for a rent of 18s. in April 1277,[82] which he also sold four years later.[83] This latter entry identifies his wife Gertrudis' family. Here Gerardus is described as "generum . . . Slevere," that is a son-in-law of the family known by the unique surname "Dormitor" or "Schlefere." This family held much property in the area of Neumarkt and we shall learn more of them shortly. Two of the *mansiones* on Mörsergasse were sold for a rent of 62. 2d. in 1293.[84]

Gerardus the Younger and Gertrudis also owned a rent in St. Peter

---

[78] 447 Schöffenschrein Generalis fo. 40v.

[79] 447 Schöffenschrein Generalis fo. 12r: "Notum sit tam futuris quam presentibus, quod Godefridus, filius Henrici de Zudindorp, dictus Anglicus, et uxor sua Gertrudis tradiderunt et remiserunt tertiam partem domus et aree site ante portam Martis, que dicitur Domus Domicelli, ante et retro subtus et superius, ibi iacet et cum omni iure, sicut in sua habebant proprietate, Henrico dicto de Wintecgin et uxori sue Elizabeth. Ita quod dictam hereditatem iure et sine contradictione obtinebunt. Actum anno Domini 1249."

[80] 173 Litis Lupi (St. Columba) fo. 4r dated 1258. The location was Herzogstrasse III (cf. Keussen, *Topographie der Stadt Köln*, I, p. 325 col. b, 25–26).

[81] 157 Berlici (St. Columba) fo. 28v dated 1282. The house was purchased from the abbey of Burvenich, whose deed of this transaction also survives: Historisches Stadtarchiv der Stadt Köln, Columba 112. The location was at the intersection of Mörsergasse II and Auf der Ruhr I.

[82] 173 Litis Lupi (St. Columba) fo. 22r.

[83] 173 Litis Lupi (St. Columba) fo. 28 dated 1281. [84] 157 Berlici (St. Columba) fo. 43r.

parish on Caecilienstrasse.[85] But the bulk of their possessions was in Holy Apostles parish. The main living quarters for this branch of the family were situated at the east end of Neumarkt, where the house was known as the "domus Zudendorp."[86] Gerardus gave Gertrudis authority over the disposition of the family house should he predecease her.[87] An inheritance settlement which expressly excluded this house was later given to their daughter Gertrudis, who was a beguine.[88]

In addition, Gerardus made a number of purchases on Schildergasse, the largest of which was sizeable including three or four *mansiones*, a foundry (*fabrica*), and a work room (*camera*).[89] This was only one-third of the entire complex known as the *curia de Belle*. Gerardus apparently bought up all the remaining portions of the curia,[90] including an hereditary rent paid from the property.[91] The final portion of this inheritance came into the Zudendorp family in 1302, when relatives of Gerardus the Younger made the purchase.[92]

Gerardus de Mummersloch, a *Stadtvogt*, was married to Elizabeth (Bela) de Zudendorp, but no mention of her connection to the

---

[85] 121 Loergasse (St. Peter) fo. 13r. The location was Caecilienstrasse IIa (cf. Keussen, *Topographie der Stadt Köln*, I, p. 237 col. a, 28–30).

[86] 211 Novum Forum (St. Aposteln) fo. 15r. The location was Neumarkt VII (cf. Keussen, *Topographie der Stadt Köln*, I, p. 433 col. a, 7).

[87] 211 Novum Forum (St. Aposteln) fo. 51r: "Notum sit etc., quod Gerardus de Zudindorp et uxor sua Gertrudis concordaverunt inter se in hunc modum, videlicet quicumque alium supervixerit, habebit potestatem convertendi seu divertendi domum dictam de Sudindorp sitam in Novo Foro cum sua area, sicut ibi sita est, ante et retro, in usus quoscumque voluerit, que domus sita est iuxta domum, que dicitur Ad Turim" (c. 1300). Other entries mention the house also: 447 Schöffenschrein Generalis fo. 59r: A house mentioned "retro domum vocatam Zudendorp" (1290–3); 448 III Schöffenschrein Generalis fo. 9r: two *mansiones* mentioned "ex opposito domus, que Zudendorp appellatur . . ." (c. 1299).

[88] 451 I Schöffenschrein Generalis fo. 10r: "Item notum sit, quod Gerardus de Zundendorp [sic] miles et Gertrudis uxor eius peraverunt et dederunt post mortem eorum Gertrudi filii sue, becgine, in tota hereditate eorum, exclusa mansione, que ipsorum est ansedel, suam partem pueri, que post obitum ipsius Gert[rudis], begcine, ad proximos eius devolvetur. Actum anno Domini 1300 in vigilia Sanctorum . . . apostolorum."

[89] 211 Novum Forum (St. Aposteln) fo. 18r dated c. 1265. Text published in *Die Kölner Schreinsbücher des 13. und 14. Jahrhunderts*, ed. Planitz and Buyken, p. 189 no. 775. A subsequent entry states that there were four *mansiones* at this location: 211 Novum Forum (St. Aposteln) fo. 28v. The location was Schildergasse VIII (cf. Keussen, *Topographie der Stadt Köln*, I, p. 441 col. b, 1–6).

[90] 211 Novum Forum (St. Aposteln) fos. 33r, 33v, 44r dated c. 1283.

[91] 211 Novum Forum (St. Aposteln) fo. 29r.

[92] 212 Novum Forum (St. Aposteln) fo. 53v: "Notum etc., quod Drude, beginne, filie Engilberti dicti Bungisduvil, cessit sua pueri pars ex morte patris et matris in caminata lapidea sita in Novo Foro versus Bovem. Ita quod divertat, qua velit, eo iure, sicut pater et mater eam possidebant. Notum etc., quod Gerardus dictus de Mummersloch et Bela uxor eius et Johannes dictus de Zudindorp emerunt erga Drudam, begginam, filiam Engilberti Bunszduvil predicti, prescriptam pueri partem suam in lapidea caminata predicta sita in Novo Foro cum parte sue aree versus Bovem. Ita quod Gerardus et Bela uxor eius et Johannes de Zudindorp eam divertere, qua velint, eo iure, sicut ipsa pueri pars ad eos devenit. Datum anno Domini 1302."

Zudendorp family appears elsewhere.[93] She may have been the sister of Johannes de Zudendorp, who also appears in this transaction. Johannes is a rare name among the Zudendorps; it appears only once, signifying the son of Blithildis (the sister of Gerardus the Younger) and Gerardus Krieg. He was the one who obtained the Vetscholder house. Since their father had died years earlier, perhaps they gravitated to this branch of the family. The name of the *curia* (Belle) is identical to the family surname of Gerardus the Younger's uncle Gerardus de Belle, whom we have already met, though no certain familial connection is mentioned in the records.

Gerardus the Younger purchased another house on Schildergasse called "Ad Bovem."[94] The title given Gerardus in this entry, although it is too marred to read completely, may give us evidence concerning his administrative duties in this parish. As he was from a ministerial family, he would probably have served as an archiepiscopal functionary (*officialis*), or also perhaps as a *scabinus* within the parish. The house itself had been in the hands of the Dormitor family, the family of Gerardus the Younger's wife Gertrudis. It was adjacent to the *curia de Belle*, and the brother of Gertrudis, Simon Dormitor, had sold half of it previously to a Johannes Schönweder.[95] Therefore, Gerardus the Younger was buying back the half of a house that was once in the possession of his wife's family. About ten years later he sold this half of the house.[96] Simon Dormitor had retained ownership of the other half, since Gerardus the Younger declined any claim on the other half of the house (a claim he would have maintained through his wife) and in return Simon declined any claim he might have in the house adjacent to the house Ad Bovem (that is, the *curia de Belle*). In fact, Simon even paid Gerardus an hereditary rent of eleven pence as part of the deal.[97] What claim Simon would have had to the *curia de Belle* remains unclear, although this entire set of transactions is filled with familial connections. By 1290 Gerardus had already sold off one house from the *curia de Belle*.[98]

Gerardus the Younger gained an interest in two other pieces of

---

[93] Lau, "Die Kölner Patriziat bis zum Jahre 1325," p. 132.

[94] 211 Novum Forum (St. Aposteln) fo. 31v: "Notum sit, quod Gerardus de Zudendorp noster off[icialis ?] . . ." dated *c.* 1280–1.

[95] Keussen, *Topographie der Stadt Köln*, I, p. 442 col. a, 7–9.

[96] 211 Novum Forum (St. Aposteln) fo. 38r dated *c.* 1289–90.

[97] 211 Novum Forum (St. Aposteln) fo. 49r dated *c.* 1299.

[98] 179 Clericorum (St. Columba) fo. 35r dated 1290: this property is mentioned as lying "in termino Clericorum [*sic*] Clipeorum [i.e. Schildergasse] ex opposito domus, que Irregank vocatur." The domus Irregank was at one time a brewery as well as a bathing facility (Badestube) located on Schildergasse (cf. Keussen, *Topographie der Stadt Köln*, I, p. 373 col. a, 1; 374 col. a, 12; col. b. 16).

property in the vicinity of Neumarkt through his marriage into the Dormitor family. The first was half of a curia on the street named Rinkenpfuhl, which Gertrudis' son Constantinus Dormitor gave to her.[99] Since Constantinus bears the surname Dormitor and not Zudendorp it is likely that he was her son by a prior marriage. The language of the entry, which calls Gerardus the Younger the husband of Gertrudis and not the father of Constantinus, bears this out. Here we have a case, which often occurred in Cologne, where a male takes the surname of his mother or wife (since the surname Dormitor is maternal not paternal in the case of Constantinus). The entire Dormitor family then sold their interest in this property to members of the patrician Cleingedanc *Geschlecht*. The second inheritance was a rent of 5 shillings from a house on Spinmühlgasse, which Gerardus the Younger and Gertrudis, along with her sister Lora and husband Hartmannus, renounced in favor of their brothers Simon and Philippus.[100]

Gerardus the Younger may have also held one more piece of property. An entry dated *c.* 1251 mentions a "Gerardus filius Henrici . . . de Zudendorp" who gave the Franciscans a two-thirds part of a house in St. Columba parish on Hohestrasse called "de Veteri Libra."[101] It is interesting to note that the countess of Hochstaden, from whose family Archbishop Conrad (1238–61) also came, retained usufruct of the entire house for the remainder of her life. Here again we have a glimpse into the archiepiscopal–*ministerialis* world of the Zudendorp family. Gerardus de Zudendorp Miles, the son of Henricus the Elder and thus the uncle of Gerardus the Younger, may alternatively have been the Gerardus who was in possession of this property. We shall discuss his branch of the family shortly.

The close ties between the Zudendorp family and the church of Holy Apostles are reflected in the church's necrology and income book.[102]

---

[99] 223 Ovina Porta (St. Aposteln) fo. 12v: "Notum etc., quod Constantinus Dormitor renunciavit ad manus matris sue Gertrudis et Gerardi mariti sui dicti de Zudendorp medietatem curie iacentis iuxta ovinam portam prope murum versus portam piscine, que curia quondam fuit ave sue Megthildis. Ita quod ipsi Gertrudis et Gerardus maritus suus dictam medietatem divertere possunt, quocumque voluerint . . .

Notum etc., quod Hilderus dictus Clengedanc, filius Godefridi dicti Clengedanc, et uxor sua Greta emerunt erga Gerardum de Zudendorp et Gertrudim uxorem suam et erga Phillipum [Dormitor] et uxorem suam Elizabeth et erga Lutginum, Ceciliam et Johannem maritum suum et erga Symonem [Dormitor] patrem Lutgini et Cecilie usufructum, que habebant in curia predicta . . ." (c. 1286). The location was probably Rinkenpfuhl Ia, where a Henricus Slefere is evidenced (cf. Keussen, *Topographie der Stadt Köln*, I, pp. 436–7).

[100] 223 Ovina Porta (St. Aposteln) fo. 16v. The location was Spinmühlgasse II (cf. Keussen, *Topographie der Stadt Köln*, I, 3–5).

[101] 156 Berlici (St. Columba) fo. 15r. The location was Hohestrasse II (cf. Keussen, *Topographie der Stadt Köln*, I, p. 328 col. b, 3).

[102] Historisches Stadtarchiv der Stadt Köln GA 18 (S. Aposteln Nekrolog und Einkünfte Buch) 53

Here we find a great deal of detail concerning a grant made by Gerardus the Younger de Novo Foro for memorial Masses to be said for family members. To fund the Masses, Gerardus gave one-third of the property his father Henricus the Younger held in Dersdorp, further evidence of the family possessions outside the city. Since Gerardus gave only one-third of this property, the other two-thirds were probably in the possession of his brothers Godefridus and Henricus. Three sons of one of these two brothers had regained possession of the property in return for a yearly rent of 30 shillings. Since we know nothing of the children of either Godefridus (if he was not married to Gertrudis de Windeck) or Henricus, these children (Rolekinus, Gobelinus, and Gerardus) could be the sons of either brother. Three sons of Gerardus the Younger are mentioned: Lutginus, Gerardus, and Henricus. While Lutginus and Henricus are listed as sons from the marriage between Gerardus the Younger and Gertrudis, Gerardus is distinguished as the son only of Gertrudis. He was probably from the same earlier marriage which produced Constantinus Dormitor. Each of these sons have their own entries in the memorial book.[103] Memorials for both pairs of Gerardus

(March 10): "Obiit Gerardus de Novo Foro dictus de Zudendorp, civis Coloniensis, qui et uxor sua Drude contulerunt ecclesie Sanctorum Apostolorum pro remedio animarum suarum, suorum liberorum ac eorundem antecessorum terciam partem bonorum, que bona sita sunt aput Dersdorp, que bona integraliter possedit quondam Henricus miles de Zudendorp et Elyzabeth uxor eius, avi Gerardi predicti, sive fuit in vineis sive in agris sive in nemoribus sive censibus sive pratis sive piscinis cum area dictorum bonorum, quocumque sita sunt in Derstorp, quam terciam partem Gerardus, Rolekinus et Gobilinus, fratres, filii fratris Gerardi predicti, receperunt hereditarie ab ecclesia Sanctorum Apostolorum predicta ad annuum censum, videlicet 30 solidorum Coloniensium denariorum dicte ecclesie singulis annis in perpetuum in festo beati Martini hiemalis solvendorum. Ita quod, si non solverent termino supradicto, ipsa bona ad ecclesiam predictam libere revertentur. Qui triginta solidi dividentur in octo anniversarios secundum, quod inferius continentur, videlicet in anniversario Gerardi predicti, qui est hodie, quatuor solidi presentibus in choro et sex denarii sacerdotibus celebrantibus ad sex altaria infra monasterium in die anniversarii predicti. Tantumdem distribuetur in anniversario Drude, uxoris Gerardi predicti, qui immediate sequitur et ponentur in duobus anniversariis predictis quibusque (?) eorum quatuor honeste candele. Item in anniversario Lutgini, filii predictorum coniugum, qui est in die beati Petronille, distribuentur quatuor solidi presentibus choro et ponentur quatuor honeste candele. Item in anniversario Gerardi filii Drude predicte, qui est in die beati Magni Confessoris, dividentur quatuor solidi presentibus in choro et ponentur quatuor honeste candele. Item in anniversario Henrici, filii predictorum coniugum, qui est in die beati Amandi Confessoris, dividentur quatuor solidi presentibus choro et ponentur quatuor honeste candele. Item in anniversario Godefridi dicti Vethscolder et Gertrudis uxoris sue, qui est in die beati Clementis, dividentur tres solidi presentibus in choro, qui fuerunt avi Gerardi predicti. Item in anniversario Henrici de Zudendorp militis et Elyzabeth uxoris sue, avorum predicti Gerardi, qui est in vigilia beati Nycholai, dividentur tres solidi presentibus in choro. Item in anniversario Henrici et Gertrudis parentum Gerardi predicti, qui est in crastino beate Lucie, dividentur tres solidi presentibus in choro [in margin: Ista memoria scilicet Gerardi militis de Zudendorp vacat hic et fiet in die beati Johannis ante portam latinam, qui est nonas maii, sicut ibi plenius invenitur scriptum]."

103 Ibid., 96 (May 31): "Obiit Lutginus de Zudendorp, laycus de Novo Foro . . ."; 147 (Sept. 6):

the Younger's grandparents[104] as well as for his parents[105] are also included. The memorial for Gertrudis, the wife of Gerardus the Younger, was originally held on March 11,[106] but was later moved to February 23.[107] Gerardus' memorial had also been moved from March 10 to May 6.[108] Here he is called "sororius Dormitorum," a reference to his wife's family. The Dormitor family appears in this memorial book as well.[109]

As the sizeable amount of material presented above on Gerardus the Younger de Novo Foro has shown, he was the largest property holder of any member of the Zudendorp family. What role the *fabrica* on Neumarkt played in his mercantile activities is unknown, but he was involved in some sort of manufacturing as well as in the ministerial duties of his family. With regard to ministerial activities we have additional information. In April 1246 Gerardus de Zudendorp appears as a witness to a charter of Count Walram of Jülich for the abbey of Brauweiler.[110] On March 27, 1258 a Gerardus de Zudindor, along with an unnamed associate, were present at the English court at Westminster as envoys of the archbishop.[111] They each received a royal gift of a valet's robe as a reward for their service, which may have been in relation to Richard of Cornwall's activities in Germany as the new *rex Romanorum*. Richard had been in close contact with the archbishop of Cologne during the winter of 1257–8, since he had sojourned at Neuß and Siegburg. It is probable then that Richard had helped in the March 1258 settlement between the archbishop and the citizens of Cologne.[112]

"Obiit Gerardus, filius Drude de Novo Foro . . ."; 173 (Oct. 26): "Obiit Henricus, filius Gerardi dicti de Zudendorp, civis Coloniensis."

[104] Ibid., 195 (Dec. 5): "Obiit Henricus et Elizabeth uxor sua, avi Gerardi de Zudendorp . . ."; 188 (Nov. 23): "Godefridus Vetscolder et Gertrudis uxor sua, avi Gerardi de Zudendorp, in isto anniversario fiet sicut supra scriptum est in anniversario Gerardi de Zudendorp, civis Coloniensis."

[105] Ibid., 199 (Dec. 14): "Obiit Henricus et Gertrudis, parentes Gerardi de Zudendorp, civis Coloniensis."

[106] Ibid., 54 (March 11): "Obiit Druda de Novo Foro, uxor Gerardi de Zudendorp, civis Coloniensis . . . [in the margin: Hic vacat ista memoria et fiet in vigilia beati Mathie apostoli, sicut ibi plenius invenitur scriptum]."

[107] Ibid., 46 (Feb. 23): "Item eodem die obiit Druda, uxor Gerardi militis dicti de Zudendorp, civis Coloniensis, que contulit ecclesie nostre quatuor solidos et sex denarios singulis annis perpetuo solvendos de bonis sitis Derstorp."

[108] Ibid., 83 (May 6): "Obiit Gerardus miles dictus de Zudendorp, sororius Dormitorum, qui contulit ecclesie Sanctorum Apostolorum quatuor solidos singulis annis perpetuo solvendos de bonis sitis Derstorp."

[109] Ibid., 95 (May 29): "Obiit Phillipus de Novo Foro dictus Dormitor." This was probably Gertrudis' brother.

[110] *UGN*, II, p. 156 no. 299.

[111] *CCLR Henry III*, x, p. 207.

[112] J. Ferdinand Bappert, *Richard von Cornwall seit seiner Wahl zum deutschen König 1257–1272*

We should not regard as coincidental that the December 15, 1256 agreement reached between Richard of Cornwall and Archbishop Conrad of Cologne concerning Richard's coronation as *rex Romanorum* was signed in Zudendorp.[113] The Zudendorp family had been representing the archbishops of Cologne before the English court for half a century by this time.

As we conclude the discussion on Henricus the Younger's branch of the Zudendorp family there remains only the need to mention his third son and namesake Henricus – and mentioning him is all we can do, since he appears only once in the Schreinsbücher.[114] Fortunately, the passage refers to his wife and in-laws, so we are able to attach him to a powerful and prestigious Cologne patrician family known by the pleasant name of Schönweder.[115] He may also have been the Henricus de Zudendorp who in 1281 obtained a plot of land in Airsbach by default and then sold it (this could not be either Henricus the Elder or Henricus the Younger, as they were both dead by this date).[116] However, this Henricus could also have been the son of Gerardus the Younger. That is all we know about him, except that the sons mentioned in the Holy Apostles' necrology might have been his.

The next son of Henricus the Elder we have already discussed – Richardus de Zudendorp. He had resettled in the family's manor of Laxfield (Suffolk), which accounts for his absence in the Cologne sources. We have discussed his activities in England and no further comment concerning him is possible.

Now that we have considered the material on the branches of the family headed by Henricus the Younger and Ricardus, let us turn to the branch of their brother, who was simply known as "Gerardus Miles de Zudendorp" – we shall refer to him as Gerardus *Miles* to distinguish him from Gerardus the Younger *de Novo Foro*. He has only appeared thus far in the instances where the sources do not clearly distinguish him from his nephew Gerardus the Younger – hence he too could have been in England. The majority of property he held in

(Bonn, 1905), p. 25. Bappert speculates that Richard spent Easter (March 24) with Archbishop Conrad of Hochstaden.

113 *REK*, III, 1, p. 260 no. 1925; *UGN*, II, pp. 232–3; *Constitutiones et acta publica imperatorum et regum inde ab anno 1273 usque ad annum 1298*, ed. Jakob Schwalm, *MGH Leges* sectio IV (Hanover, 1904–6; rpt. 1980), pp. 481–4; *Böhmer*, V, p. 1733 no. 11771.

114 92 Per totam parrochiam (St. Laurenz) fo. 26r: "Item notum sit, quod supradicta Margareta et maritus eius Bruno, Richmudis [daughters of Gerardus Schonwedder and Elisabeth de Lyskirchen, as the previous entry on this folio states] et Henricus maritus eius de Zudendorp, donaverunt et remiserunt predictas tercias partes domus et aree" (c. 1263).

115 See Lau,"Das Kölner Patriziat bis zum Jahre 1325," 26 (1895), pp. 144–5 and von Winterfeld, *Handel, Kapital und Patriziat in Köln bis 1400*, pp. 30–1 for discussions on this family.

116 296 Porta de Pantaleonis (Airsbach) fos. 42r and 42v.

Cologne came to him by virtue of his marriage to Cristina, the daughter of Godeschalcus of Wipperfürth. Godeschalcus has already appeared in our study when he purchased a rent from Henricus the Elder de Zudendorp, the father of Gerardus Miles. Von Winterfeld states that the Wipperfürth family was involved in English trade, though she provides no specific evidence.[117] Gerardus Miles appears often in the sources with the Wipperfürth family. In August of 1257 he was present when Godeschalcus' widow Richmudis established a yearly memorial for her late husband at the abbey of Altenberg and had his name entered into their brotherhood book.[118] This abbey was near the archiepiscopal castle where earlier Henricus the Elder de Zudendorp had led the English envoys to meet with the archbishop in 1225. In September 1266 he, along with Theodericus de Wipperfürth (the son of Godeschalcus), represented the city of Cologne in its settlement of a dispute with Theodericus de Valkenburg, in which the sizeable sum of 1,000 marks was exchanged.[119] The other participant in this settlement, Winricus de Veissenich, was also the son-in-law of Gerardus Miles de Zudendorp.

The property that Gerardus Miles received through marriage into this family lay in St. Martin parish. The first house was located on Himmelreich and was known as the "domus ad Molendinum," of which he received half.[120] In 1240 Gerardus Miles mortgaged this half a house for 5 marks. A curious element in an otherwise standard transaction was the currency in which the mortgage was taken – Polish gold.[121] Either the mortgage was never taken out (the entire entry is crossed out) or it was redeemed, as they sold their propriety in the house sometime before 1260.[122] Two other houses came into this branch of the Zudendorp family from the Wipperfürths.[123] The first was a house on Turnmarkt somewhere between Rheingasse and Bruchenplätchen[124] and the other was known as "Ad Grisonem" on the street called Auf der Aar.[125] Gerardus Miles and Cristina eventually gained the portions of three of her siblings in the house on Turnmarkt,

---

[117] von Winterfeld, *Handel, Kapital und Patriziat in Köln bis 1400*, p. 7.

[118] *Urkundenbuch der Abtei Altenberg*, ed. Hans Mosler, Urkundenbücher der Geistlichen Stiftungen des Niederrheins, 3 (Bonn, 1912), I, pp. 155–6 no. 214. Richmudis was herself from an important patrician family – von der Mühlengasse (see Lau, "Das Kölner Patriziat bis zum Jahre 1325," 26 (1895), p. 128).

[119] *Ennen/Eckertz*, II, p. 541 no. 492.

[120] 448 I Schöffenschrein Generalis fo. 9r dated *c.* 1231. The location was Himmelreich V (cf. Keussen, *Topographie der Stadt Köln*, I, p. 32 col. a, 2–3).

[121] St. Martin Karte 23 col. 4: no. 4: ". . . auri de Polonia."

[122] 12 Cunradi (St. Martin) fo. 9r.   [123] 477 Schöffenschrein Generalis fo. 73r.

[124] See Keussen, *Topographie der Stadt Köln*, I, p. 88 col. b, a.

[125] The location was Auf der Aar III (cf. Keussen, *Topographie der Stadt Köln*, I, p. 4 col. a, 6–7).

and then sold the four-sevenths interest directly thereafter.[126] They also gathered the remaining three inheritance portions in this half a house and sold them in May 1277.[127] The same pattern of acquisition and sale holds true for the second house Ad Grisonem.[128] They sold their entire interest in the house in May 1277.[129]

In addition to these assets, each of which they eventually liquidated, Godeschalcus of Wipperfürth had left Gerardus Miles and Cristina 200 marks in moveable goods and a rent of 6 marks in the house called Ad Stellam at Heumarkt.[130] They, along with Cristina's other siblings, gave the 6-mark rent to their brother Theodericus in 1280.[131]

The only other major property held by Gerardus Miles, apart from the three houses in St. Martin parish, was located in St. Columba parish and was very close to his nephew Gerardus the Younger de Novo Foro's holdings at Neumarkt. The house, which probably comprised his main dwelling, was located on Gertrudenstrasse directly across the street from Holy Apostles church. This house (like his nephew's house on the east side of Neumarkt and his father's house in St. Brigida parish) bore the family name. It is described as having both a *curia* and a *mansio* or *domus*. The first mention of the house appears in an entry where Gerardus Miles lost possession of it to Heidenricus de Lintlo, the same man to whom he sold half of the house Ad Grisonem in St. Martin parish (one-seventh part in November 1275 and three-sevenths part in May 1277).[132] Since this loss of the house to Heidenricus de Lintlo occurred in October 1275 it could be evidence that Gerardus was having financial problems and sold the property in St. Martin parish to raise capital. Here the domus Zudendorp and its *curia* were forfeited by court judgment because Gerardus did not redeem a mortgage on the property of 70 marks. This was a sizeable amount of money and thus says something about both the value of the real estate as well as about the size of the financial dealings this family pursued. Whatever embarrassment this may have caused it was not until almost two years later (August 1277), with Heidenricus de Lintlo dead, that Gerardus Miles purchased the house back from Heidenricus' son.[133] At some point

---

[126] 13 Wolberonis (St. Martin) fo. 15v.

[127] 447 Schöffenschrein Generalis fo. 81r and 82v.

[128] They had obtained Theodericus de Wipperfürth's portion in 1275 but sold it directly: 6a Vogelonis (St. Martin) fo. 30v and 477 Schöffenschrein Generalis fos. 73v and 78r.

[129] 6a Vogelonis (St. Martin) fo. 31v.   [130] 447 Schöffenschrein Generalis fo. 6r.

[131] 16 Emundi (St. Martin) fo. 36r. The location of this house was Heumarkt V (cf. Keussen, *Topographie der Stadt Köln*, I, p. 19 col. a, 6–7).

[132] 173 Litis Lupi (St. Columba) fo. 18v. The location was Gertrudenstrasse III (cf. Keussen, *Topographie der Stadt Köln*, I, p. 314 col. a, 7).

[133] 173 Litis Lupi (St. Columba) fo. 22v.

154

Gerardus Miles had also obtained a rent of nine shillings from an adjacent house known as "Dune," which he subsequently sold in 1280.[134]

At the death of Gerardus Miles and Cristina their seven children each obtained an equal portion of the family house.[135] Here we learn some interesting things about his children. His eldest daughter Elizabeth was married to the knight Winricus de Veissenich, who had earlier assisted Gerardus Miles in the settlement with Theodericus de Valkenburg. In addition, there were two sons who shared the same name: Gerardus. In fact, the scribe had actually ceased writing the transaction entry and began a new one, perhaps out of concern that he had incorrectly duplicated the name. Another son, Winricus, bore the surname *"Scharre,"* probably to distinguish him from his brother-in-law. This name could also indicate his military service for the archbishop, as he is also called a knight.[136] Finally, there was the daughter and namesake of her mother, Cristina, who was a nun in Rheindorf.[137] These children all granted their propriety in the house to Elizabeth and her husband Winricus de Veissenich, who in turn sold the house to a certain Wickboldus and his brother the cathedral canon Wedekinus.

At that time Wickboldus was a *scholasticus* at the cathedral school, but ten years later he would become the archbishop of Cologne. No doubt we have yet another case of interaction between the family and the archiepiscopal court resulting from its ministerial service to the archbishops. Another English connection exists here as well: before becoming the archbishop, Wickboldus was the deacon of the Cologne cathedral and the prior of the church of Aachen. In this capacity he was intimately involved in Edward I's negotiations during the years 1294 to 1298 with Adolph of Nassau concerning a military campaign against France. He was even given the title of royal *familiaris* and *secretarius* by Edward I and promised a prebend in the church of Dublin worth at least 80 marks.[138]

---

[134] 173 Litis Lupi (St. Columba) fo. 27r. This house is mentioned before 1268: 162 Lata Platea (St. Columba) fo. 4r. Thus Gerardus Miles had possessed the Zudendorp house on this street at least since the 1260s. Other references to the "curia Zudendorp" occur, such as that of *c.* 1272: 162 Lata Platea (St. Columba) fo. 28v, where a house and courtyard "versus curiam, que Zudindorp vocatur" is mentioned.

[135] 180 Clericorum (St. Columba) fo. 28r.

[136] The word "scara" or "schara" meant military service and this term was used in the Cologne area. See J. F. Niermeyer, ed., *Mediae Latinitatis Lexicon Minus* (Leiden, 1984), p. 943.

[137] The charter of the convent of Rheindorf which confirmed Cristina's grant of her share to Winricus and Elizabeth survives: Historisches Archiv der Stadt Köln Columba 120.

[138] Correspondence between Wickboldus and Edward I has been published in the following: *Treaty Rolls*, ed. Chaplais, nos. 237, 242, 256, 434; *Rymer*, II, pp. 662, 678, 755–6; *CPR Edward I*, III, p. 103.

After the death of Archbishop Wickboldus in 1304 his other siblings passed their propriety in half of the house entirely into the hands of Wedekinus, who by this time had also become a *scholasticus* at the cathedral.[139] In addition, a brother and sister had also become the abbot and abbess of the monasteries in Brauweiler and Essen, no doubt through the influence of their archiepiscopal brother Wickboldus. Another brother, a Wilhelmus de Hulce, canon at Münster, gave his interest in the house to Wedekinus, who then possessed the entire house himself.[140] The following year Wedekinus sold the house to Franco de Cornu, who then sold it a year later to the convent of St. Gertrude, located next door to the house.[141] Throughout all these transactions the house is continually referred to as the "curia, que Zudendorp vocatur."

In addition to another possible house on Hohestrasse in St. Columba parish (see above, the domus de Veteri Libra, p. 149) Gerardus Miles also possessed a half of a house on Neumarkt. This house was around the corner from the curia Zudendorp and in partial possession of the convent of St. Gertrude.[142] A widow by the name of Richmudis de Hone eventually obtained Gerardus' rights in this house (known as domus Nirzhus) by virtue of her legal claim made on the house, which Gerardus apparently did not contest.[143] The details of this matter remain unexplained and so we cannot determine the relationship existing between Gerardus and Richmudis de Hone. This Gerardus could alternatively have been Gerardus the Younger de Novo Foro, who held most of his property around Neumarkt.

The final document involving Gerardus Miles de Zudendorp is very interesting on two counts. It is a charter confirming a settlement between the bailiffs of Sürth and the abbey of Altenberg – the same abbey with which he was involved because of his father-in-law God-eschalcus de Wipperfürth in 1257.[144] Here Gerardus Miles was engaged

---

[139] 179 Clericorum (St. Columba) fo. 53v.   [140] 179 Clericorum (St. Columba) fo. 54v.

[141] 179 Clericorum (St. Columba) fo. 55v.

[142] 179 Clericorum (St. Columba) fo. 5r dated 1267. The location was Neumarkt Vb (cf. Keussen, *Topographie der Stadt Köln*, I, p. 349 col. b, 16).

[143] 173 Litis Lupi (St. Columba) fo. 42r: "Item notum, [sic] medietas domus dicte Nirzhus in Novo Foro et aree ante etc. devoluta est Richmudi de Hone pro warrandia posita, ex cause tali, quia Gerardus de Zudendorp miles et uxor eius non fecerunt. Ita libamus, quod dicta Richmudis possit inscribi. Ita dicta Richmudis dictam medietatem domus sibi positam pro warrandia possidebit omni iure, quod antedicti habuerunt et divertere poterit, quocumque voluerit, ubi iusta divisione dabit" (1280). In the next entry on this folio the property is willed to Richmudis' son Hermannus at her death.

[144] *Urkundenbuch der Abtei Altenberg*, ed. Mosler, I, pp. 201–2 no. 288: "Universis presens scriptum visuris Gerardus miles de Zudendorp, advocatus in Palmersdorp cognoscere veritatem. Propter successiones vicissitudinum, quibus tempora permutantur, universis tam presentibus quam futuris notum facio per presentes, quod cum viri religiosi ac dilecti fratres ecclesie de Veteri–

in a jurisdictional settlement because he was the *advocatus* of Palmers-dorp (south of Cologne near Brühl). He, along with the auxiliary Bishop Winricus, affixed their seals to the settlement in order to secure lasting validity. The language of the charter makes it clear that this ministerial position of *advocatus* was the heritable right of Gerardus' family.

The second matter of note is the form of the Zudendorp seal.[145] In what may be more than a coincidence, the use of two leopards looks very much like the English royal coat of arms. An even more striking similarity occurs on the seal of Henricus the Elder de Zudendorp, which is preserved in a charter concerning his daughter Gertrudis, the sister of Gerardus Miles.[146] Henricus, along with the prior and *custos* of St. Severin, confirmed an agreement of his daughter Gertrudis' husband Gerardus de Belle concerning land held of him. I have seen the seals attached to this charter and there are in fact three cat-like animals in a row on the seal of Henricus the Elder de Zudendorp, the top one of which still has a curled tail much like the English royal lions. Thus there is a strong possibility that Henricus the Elder de Zudendorp imitated the Plantagenet royal emblem on his own family crest, a striking symbol of his own involvement in English affairs.[147]

monte racione quatuor bonorum suorum in Soreden curie in Palmersdorp tenerentur ad quatuor homines, qui dicunter hylude, qui tractatus ac placita, que vocantur Wisligdinc, tribus vicibus per annum, hoc est post pascha, post Johannem Baptiste et post nativitatem Domini in dicta curia Palmersdorp frequentarent, ego Gerardus predictus, advocatus de Palmersdorp, una cum sepedictis fratribus in presencia venerabilis viri domini Winrici, chorepiscopi ecclesie Coloniensis constitutus ad ipsius consilium, cui utrique consensimus in hac parte, acceptis ab eisdem fratribus tribus marcis ipsos absolvi a frequentacione predictorum hominum, qui vocantur hylude, ita ut magister curtis eorum in Soreden [i.e. Sürth], qui pro tempore fuerit, prestatutis temporibus exsequatur placita memorata. Et insuper pro duodecim denariis, quos de eisdem bonis in Soreden solverunt, hactenus dabunt duos solidos annuatim tali condicione, quod si advocacia de Palmersdorp a me et meis liberis alienata fuerit, tunc ego et dicti liberi mei tenebimur eisdem fratribus pretaxatam pecuniam integraliter restaurare et census addicio ad statum pristinum reverertur. Quod ego sepedictus Gerardus conscribi feci sub mei ipsius ac predicti venerabilis viri domini Winrici chorepiscopi Coloniensis sigillis pro perpetua firmitate. Acta sunt hec anno Domini MCCLX nono mense februario Colonie in domo predicti chorepiscopi" (February 1270).

145 Ibid., p. 202: "Or. Perg., 2 Siegel an Pressel. Links: Ganze Figur des Geistlichen mit Kirche und Stab: s·Winrici·choriepiscopi· col. Rechts: 2 Leoparden im Schild: [sigil]lum·gerardi·de·zudin[dorp]. Rückaufschrift: de duobus solidis quos damus Palmerstorp pro curia nostra Sorden. Andere Hand (13. Jahrh.); 'mutatum' [Altenberg Urk. no. 146]."

146 Historisches Archiv der Stadt Köln HUA 97A. The text is also published in H. Cardauns, "Rheinische Urkunden des 13. Jahrhunderts," *Annalen* 38 (1882), p. 14 no. 15. This is Cardauns' description of the seal: "An der kleinen Urk. hängen zwei Siegel an kurzen Pergamentsreifen. Das eine zeigt drei übereinanderstehende Thiere, umschrift fast ganz zerstört, das zweite einen Stab mit zwei gekreuzten Schlüsseln, umschrift: sigill·custodis·sci·severini·in colonia."

147 I wish to express my thanks to Dr. Manfred Groten, who pointed out this possibility to me: see Groten, *Köln im 13. Jahrhundert*, 84. Two other similar examples are noteworthy: (1) the coat of

We have already met the "de Belle" family, the in-laws of Gertrudis de Zudendorp, quite often. Gerardus de Belle, the husband of Gertrudis de Zudendorp, was often in England on behalf of his father-in-law. He and his wife also received from Henricus the Elder the four *mansiones* at the corner of Follerstrasse and Spulmannsgasse in Airsbach. We have also discussed the *curia de Belle* that Gerardus the Younger *de Novo Foro* possessed at Neumarkt. As previously noted, Gerardus de Belle's father Otto was the archiepiscopal *camerarius* and Gerardus himself was the *advocatus* of Mundesdorp; so the Zudendorps had married into yet another important ministerial family.

A settlement between Gerardus and Holy Apostles church reveals yet more interesting information about the family.[148] Gerardus de Belle sold allodial land in Mundesdorp to the chapter for 16 marks, and two of his sons renounced their claims to the property. However, as we could expect from this family, another son named Otto was in England and thus unable to perform his renunciation of the land. Therefore, Gerardus agreed to a fascinating arrangement. He would pay a fine of 20 marks (more than he had received from the sale itself) if Otto did not

---

arms of Emperor Otto IV, nephew of Richard I of England, was equally divided between the three English royal lions and the imperial eagle, and (2) Henry, the son of Emperor Frederick II and King Henry III's sister Isabella, had as his device likewise an equally divided shield with three leopards and a two-headed imperial eagle: see *MPHA*, II, p. 65 and III, p. 336, note 1 respectively.

[148] Historisches Archiv der Stadt Köln St Aposteln 1/22: "Omnibus ad quos hec littere pervenerint. Gerardus advocatus de Mundesdorp et uxor eius Gertrudis in Domino salutem. Notum esse volumus, quod nos capitulo Sanctorum Apostolorum in Colonia vendidimus viginti iugera de allodio nostro aput Mundesdorp constituto per 16 marcis et nos renuncivimus eisdem bonis et liberi nostri Henricus et Everardus adhibita debita sollempnitate promisimus eciam nos procuraturos, quod filius noster Otto, qui est in Anglia, infra biennium a pascha preterito veniet ad partes istas et renunciabit bonis pretaxatis debito modo. Eo adiecto, quod si infra predictum terminum eisdem bonis non renunciaverit, solvemus dicto capitulo viginti marcas et super hiis dedimus fideiussores dominum Hermannum Serphekin et Gerardum, filium domini Henrici de Zudendorp bone memorie, qui fide data promiserunt, quod si a predicto filio nostro Ottone non fuerit facta renunciacio infra terminum predictum, ipsi intrabunt domum, quam eis nominaverit capitulum infra muros civitatis Coloniensis et iacebunt ibi, sicut moris est, nunquam inde recessuri antequam capitulo sit satisfactum de viginti marcis. Insuper promisimus fide data, quod si dictum Hermannum, nostrum fideiussorem, de terra ista exire contigerit, loco eius alium dabimus fideiussorem idoneum et sufficientem. Dictum eciam capitulum eadem bona nobis iure hereditario concessit ad annuam pensionem, ita ut quolibet anno de bonis illi ei solvamus 5 maldra tritici et tria maldra siliginis in ecclesie estimationis in festo beati Martini vel ante, tali pena adiecta, quod si in mora denar. et sic de singulis duabus ebdomadibus 12 denarii solventur nomine pene donec plenaria solutio facta fuerit pensionis pretaxate et habebitur respectus pene ad prefata viginti iugera. Si autem in dubium hec possint devocari, hec pagina conscripta est et sigillum dicti capituli et domini G., prepositi monasterii et nostri communitatis. Acta sunt hec anno Domini 1236 mense aprili. Testes sunt: Henricus de Scaporten, Arnoldus de Erclenzen, Cristianus de Novo Foro, parochiarum nostri et Rigolfus de Foramine et filius eius Gorwinus."

return home and renounce his rights before the *biennium* after Easter.[149] To assure the payment of these 20 marks, two *fideiussores* (among whom was Gerardus Miles de Zudendorp, the brother-in-law of Gerardus de Belle) would take up residence in a house within the city chosen by the chapter and remain there until the payment was made. If Hermannus Scherfgin, a non-family member, should end his stay as *fideiussor*, another acceptable replacement would be found; however, no such replacement was contemplated for Gerardus Miles de Zudendorp. After all of these machinations the property was rented back by Gerardus de Belle in return for yearly payments in wheat, with appropriate penalties for late payment. Such sequestering of *fideiussores* was apparently a standard practice in Cologne, as the agreement was arranged *sicut moris est*. This entire arrangement was necessitated by the fact that one of the sons was in England.

There are only two other men styled de Zudendorp, whose relationship to the other Zudendorp family members remains a mystery. In the charters of the church of St. Severin there appears a certain Swykerus de Zudendorp. In 1293 he is listed among those who renounced possessions in Sürth in favor of the chapter of St. Severin's church.[150] Since Sürth is mentioned, where Gerardus Miles de Zudendorp was *advocatus*, there may be some relationship between the two men. Thirteen years earlier a Swikerus de Scuzendorf (called "filius quondam Engilberti militis de Lintlo") made a grant to Hermannus, the abbot of Groß St. Martin. Among the witnesses to this grant was a certain "Geuehardo de Sczudendorf" – was this either Gerardus Miles or Gerardus the Younger de Novo Foro?[151]

The final other man is the abbot who received the above-mentioned grant from Swikerus. It was made in 1280, the last year of the abbacy of Hermannus, who also bore the surname de Zudendorp.[152] Peter Opladen has recorded the main points of his otherwise undocumented abbacy: serving as abbot of Groß St. Martin from 1271 to 1280 he is mentioned only as mortgaging church property for 30 marks and as

---

[149] *Biennium* or *Biannum* was a "a duty of military origin exacted twice every year and consisting of castle repair service, later also of other labour or cartage services due to lords possessing high jurisdiction" (Niermeyer, *Mediae Latinitatis Lexicon Minus*, p. 97). This was apparently a set time of services done for the archbishop.

[150] *Die Urkunden des Pfarrarchivs von St. Severin in Köln*, ed. Hess, p. 55 no. 35 dated October 19, 1293.

[151] Historisches Archiv der Stadt Köln Severin 2/41.

[152] Helga Johag, *Die Beziehungen zwischen Klerus und Bürgerschaft in Köln zwischen 1250 und 1350*, Rheinisches Archiv, 103 (Bonn, 1977), p. 266 has Hermannus de Zudendorp in the list of abbots of Groß St. Martin. She lists his years in office as 1270 to 1280. Peter Opladen, *Gross St. Martin. Geschichte einer Stadtkölnischen Abtei*, Studien zur Kölner Kirchengeschichte, 2 (Düsseldorf, 1954), p. 172 lists Hermannus' years in office as 1271 to 1280.

traveling with the abbots of St. Pantaleon (Cologne), Gladbach, Deutz, Siegburg, Sauerland, Brauweiler and the deacon of Malmedy to the council of Lyon in 1274.[153] In addition he, along with the other abbots, priors, and clerics of Cologne, witnessed a declaration on September 25, 1270 rejecting a papal nuncio's sentence. Here he is called "Hermannus de Zudendorp electus in abbatem S. Martini."[154] Elsewhere he is simply referred to as Hermannus the abbot of St. Martin.[155] Since both Hermannus and Swikerus are names that appear nowhere on the Zudendorp family tree, these men may have simply come from Zudendorp and are not connected to the Zudendorp *Geschlecht* considered here. Though by the middle of the thirteenth century the name itself was synonymous with this *Geschlecht* in Cologne, and no other family appears in the records with the same surname. Unfortunately, we know nothing else about these last two men styled de Zudendorp, at least one of whom, as abbot of Groß St. Martin, held an important position in the city.

Such is the history of the Zudendorp family based on the surviving records. They were major participants in both the administration of Cologne and its environs as well as in the diplomatic and commercial contacts between the city and England, as they served the archbishops for at least a century and can be documented as ambassadors to the English court for at least fifty years in the thirteenth century. They even held feudal property in England. Their urban wealth was based on marriage ties made with such prosperous patrician families as Schönweder, Vetscholder, de Nussia, Dormitor, Mummersloch, Krieg, and de Wipperfürth. In addition, they maintained their ministerial influence and wealth in the countryside, with marriage ties to the de Belle family. Indeed, they eventually returned to their rural origins by entering the landed gentry in the fourteenth century.[156] Thus we have a family whose activities give us much information on such important areas of historical inquiry as the burgher–*ministeriales* relationship in German cities, land-holding and real estate customs in Cologne, prosopographical reconstruction of the city's major ruling families, and information concerning Cologner contacts with England and the English. In particular, we have benefited from knowledge of their behind-the-scenes activity in negotiations carried on between the empire and the English kingdom. Nowhere else in Cologne of the twelfth and

---

[153] Opladen, *Gross St. Martin*, pp. 33–4.

[154] *Ennen/Eckertz*, III, pp. 19–23 no. 27; *UGN*, II, p. 354 no. 603.

[155] *UGN*, II, p. 531 no. 892: "Hermannus abbas s. Martini Col."; 2: 303 no. 534: "Herman der abt van sente Mertine."

[156] von Winterfeld, *Handel, Kapital und Patriziat in Köln bis 1400*, p. 7.

thirteenth centuries does a family provide so much data on so many different areas of historical interest.

Although the Zudendorp family may be less typical than the many Cologne families which had English contacts, they are representative of the complex and lively activity that occurred between the two regions during this period, which has not received proper recognition in modern historiography. They are also exemplary of the depth of evidence surviving in such Cologne sources as the Schreinsurkunden as well as in the rich English sources. Their multifarious activities, which linked them to a wide variety of administrative, political, and economic power groups, underscore the value of studying those who functioned as liaisons between the groups which have traditionally received the attention of historical research. Relations between England and the empire were indeed vibrant and highly developed by this time, as the activities of such families as the Zudendorps make clear.

Chapter 7

COLOGNERS IN ENGLAND

Thus far we have seen considerable material on Anglo-Cologne social relations within the city of Cologne as well as on the diplomatic and commercial relations with England maintained by Cologne families. We have yet, however, to consider the other half of this equation: those activities of Cologne merchants and expatriates dwelling in England. Accounts of their affairs appear throughout English royal and municipal records and therefore we can complement the history of the English in Cologne with a similar study of Cologners in England. Unfortunately nothing as specific for our purposes as the Cologne Schreinsurkunden survives in England, so we must piece together the evidence scattered among the numerous surviving record collections. We can, though, characterize the wide variety of activities that Cologners pursued throughout England, and even reconstruct the careers of a few notable expatriates who achieved influential positions in the English realm.

The main business of most Cologners in England was trade. Here we shall put a human face on the statistical story of interregional commerce by discussing specific individuals who carried on this trade. Cologners could be found in every region of eastern England, from the cities of London, York, Boston, King's Lynn, Norwich, Yarmouth, Sandwich, Newcastle-upon-Tyne, Lincoln, and Stamford, to the lands of Suffolk, Huntingdonshire, and elsewhere. As early as 1176–7 a merchant of Cologne named Berengar appears in Lincolnshire.[1] References to Cologne trading vessels appear all along the eastern coast: two ships were among those released from confiscation by royal command in 1230 (at this time ships were being commandeered for use in Henry

---

[1] *Pipe Roll 23 Henry II*, PR, 26, p. 117: "Et de xx li. de Bereng. mercatore Colonie" (De exactis per justicias errantes for Lincolnshire).

III's failed attempt to regain Aquitaine),[2] and Peter of Cologne's ship, laden with wool, was likewise released from a Suffolk port.[3] In addition to the guildhall in London, Cologne merchants maintained houses in Boston[4] and even had contacts with Ireland.[5]

Rhine wine was the most important cargo the merchants brought to England, and the English kings were important customers throughout the thirteenth century.[6] But Cologne merchants provided the English court with a variety of other commodities, such as wax,[7] barley,[8] and even archery equipment.[9] The traditional skill of Cologne goldsmiths

---

[2] *CCLR Henry III*, I, p. 358: "Mandatum est Thome de Muleton' et sociis suis, custodibus portuum et costere maris in comitatu Linc', quod, non obstante mandato regis eis facto de navibus arestandis, duas cogas de Colonia et unam cogam de Grenig' et duas cogas de Stoverne, de quibus Petrus de Andwerp' ducit unam cogam de Colonia, et Gerardus de Flerching' aliam de Colonia, et Albertus de Grenig' cogam de Grenig', et Dodo de Staverne et Amisius de Staverne illas duas cogas de Staverne, permittant abire versus partes suas cum rebus et marcandisis suis in eis continentis. Teste S. de Sedgrave apud Stamf." (July 3, 1230).

[3] *CCLR Henry III*, I, p. 364; *HUB*, I, p. 80 no. 234: "Mandatum est W. comiti Warennie et sociis suis, custodibus portuum et costere maris in comitatu Suff', quod, non obstante mandato regis de navibus arestandis, navem Petri de Colonia carcatam lana et aliis mercandisis mercatorum Colonie, quam arestari fecerunt apud Orewell', sine impedimento permittant cum predictis catallis abire" (1230).

[4] *Calendar of Inquisitions Post Mortem and other Analagous Documents preserved in the Public Record Office* (London, 1906), II, p. 211 (dated 1280).

[5] *Rotuli de liberate*, ed. Hardy, p. 188: "Prestito. Die Lun. proxima ibidem ad proficiend. lib. marinell. qui sunt in coga Ernulfi de Colonia, in quam transfretavit Simon de Pateshull in adventu suo in Hibernia, x marcas lib." (dated 1210).

[6] *Rotuli litterarum clausarum*, I, ed. Hardy, p. 27; *Ennen/Eckertz*, II, p. 19 no. 14; *HUB*, I, p. 34 no. 71; Lappenberg, *Urkundliche Geschichte des Hansischen Stahlhofes zu London*, p. 7 no. 9: "Rex etc. Vic. Norf. etc. Fac habere Theobaldo de Colonia et Henrico mercatori socio suo xx marcas de firma tua pro duobus doliis vini captis ab eis ad opus nostrum et computabitur ad scaccarium" (London, April 13, 1205) – these payments are recorded in the Pipe Rolls (PR NS XIX): p. 241: "Et Teobaldo de Colonia et Henrico mercatori xx marcas pro duobus doliis vini per idem breve. Et in cariagio trium tonellorum vini a Lenn' usque ad Burgum viii s. per idem breve"; *CLR Henry III*, III, p. 366: "Liberate to Ernald de Colonia 30 li. 12s. for 17 tuns of wine bought of [him] for the king by Robert de Dacre" (Windsor, July 30, 1251); *CLR Henry III*, IV, p. 31: "To the sheriff of Kent. Contrabreve to pay 100s. of the king's gift to Ernald Colyn" (Canterbury, March 3, 1252); *CLR Henry III*, IV, p. 73: "To Ernald de Colonia . . . li. 16s. for 9 tuns [of wine]" (Windsor, September 28, 1252); *CLR Henry III*, IV, p. 134: "to Ern' de Colonia 138 li. 14s. for 63 tuns of wine" (Westminster, June 10, 1253); *HUB*, I, p. 132 no. 404: King Henry III orders payment to Ernald of Cologne of 30 li. 12s. for 17 casks of wine sold to Robert de Dacre at Boston market (Windsor, July 30, 1251).

[7] *CLR Henry III*, IV, p. 190; *HUB*, I, p. 170 no. 475: "To Frederick de Colonia 20 li. 10s. for 1,000 pounds of wax" (Westminster, January 12, 1255).

[8] *CFR*, II, p. 132: "Order to the collectors of the customs on wools, hides and wool fells in the port of Newcastle upon Tyne to cause Ingelram de Coloigne to have from the first issues of the custom 53 li., in which sum the king is held to him for 236 quarters of barley brought to him for the expenses of the household at Newcastle in April last; receiving from him letters of acquittance; and the king will cause them to have allowance thereof in their account" (York, May 18, 1312).

[9] *CLR Henry III*, V, p. 225: "To the same [William son of Richard, sheriff of London] contrabreve to let Marcmannus de Colonia and Bartholomew le Estreys, citizens of London, have 47s.

was known in England, and expatriate artisans were commissioned to fashion items for the royal court.[10] Cologne merchants were also active in the export of English wool, and several appear among those foreign merchants taking oaths not to take the wool to Flanders during Edward I's embargo of the county.[11] Supplementary to the series of trading privileges that the English kings granted to all merchants of Cologne

without fail for glue (fisco), cork (cortice), and feathers lately taken from them to repair the king's crossbows and quarrels in the tower" (Kenilworth, July 25, 1266).

[10] *CLR Henry III*, IV, p. 462; *HUB*, I, p. 185 no. 525: "Liberate to Hermann the goldsmith of Cologne 10 marks imprest on a cameo taken from him long ago to the use of St. Edward of Westminster, for which he demands (exigit) 100 li. and the king offered 100 marks. Cancelled 'quia aliter in rotulo anni xlv'" (Windsor, May 24, 1259); *CLR Henry III*, IV, p. 488: "Liberate with all speed to Herman de Coloyne 100 li. for a cameo long ago taken from him for the king" (Westminster, November 7, 1259); *CLR Henry III*, V, p. 6: "Liberate to Hermann the goldsmith of Cologne, from whom the king long ago bought a cameo (comahutum) for the shrine of St. Edward at Westminster, 10 marks of the king's gift for his expenses because of his poverty, as the king cannot at present satisfy him of the money due for the cameo" (Westminster, November 14, 1260). Henry III's difficult financial straits during these years cost Hermann a considerable sum of money for his services in this case.

[11] Edward I had placed an embargo on wool exports to Flanders in order to force the count of Flanders to cease his support of France during the war of 1294 to 1298. *CPR Henry III*, VI, pp. 557–66: among those taking oaths not to trade English wool with Flanders were: "Godschalk de Susad, for himself and Richard le Lytele, Woifard de Susad and Henry de Oke, his fellows, the king of Almain's merchants of Cologne, for 80 sacks of wool . . . Hermann de Susato, for himself and Gerard Quatremarc [a Cologner] and Elemann le White, his fellows, the king of Almain's merchant of Soest (de Susato), for 80 sacks of wool . . . [Westminster, September 20, 1271] . . . Artelemus de Colonia and Thierius le Sage, the king of Almain's merchants of Cologne, 30 sacks; Peter of Cologne, the king of Almain's merchant of Cologne, 20 sacks . . . Frank de Colonia and John de Uppelford, the king of France's merchants of Cologne [sic – perhaps this is a scribal error, as several French merchants are interspersed in this list] 60 sacks . . . Brunus de Colonia, Conrad Brysenck, Hermann de Herle, and John Fulplume, the king of Almain's merchants of Cologne, 80 sacks" (Westminster, July 29, 1271); *CPR Henry III*, VI, p. 686: among those taking the same oath: "Henry de Socese [i.e. Soest], John of Hasebergh, Peter de Colonia, merchants of the king of Almain" (Tower of London, January 28, 1272); *CPR Henry III*, VI, p. 702: "James de Colonia, merchant of Almain, 40 sacks" (Westminster, July 18, 1272); *CPR Henry III*, VI, p. 713: "Lewis de Colne, merchant of Cologne, 40 sacks" (Westminster, November 5, 1272); *Calendar of Various Chancery Rolls (Supplementary Close Rolls, Welsh Rolls, Scutage Rolls) Preserved in the Public Record Office (A.D. 1277–1326)* (London, 1912), p. 8: "To the bailiffs of Boston for John de Wickede of Cologne, for 40 sacks . . . to the bailiffs of Lynn for Henry de Colonia, merchant, for 60 sacks; Chancery Rolls 14: "Henry de Coloyne, merchant" and "John le Wyket, merchant of Cologne (dated 1277)." *CPR Edward I*, I, p. 25; *HUB*, III, pp. 405–7 and, *HUB*, Anhang I, p. 735 mention "Godfrey de Colonia, merchant of Coloyne (Colonia)" and "John de Stesnete, merchant of Coloyne (Colonia)" among the German merchants who obtained licenses to export English wool (Westminster, November 10, 1273). Apparently Cologne merchants were often suspected of ignoring Edward I's restriction on wool trade with Flanders and were therefore arrested. Hildebrand of Cologne was among those German merchants ("mercatorum ducis Brinneswik, de Lubek, de Dertmund") arrested in August of 1272, but released by the intercession of Queen Eleanore (*CCLR Henry III*, XIV, p. 516), and Conrad of Cologne was compensated for false arrest and confiscation of his ship and 50 quarts of oats in 1275 after giving evidence that his trading voyage had not originated in Holland or Seeland: *Hanseakten aus England 1271 bis 1472*, ed. Kunze, p. 34 no. 2.

(see chapter 1) many individual Cologners obtained royal writs of protection in order to assure unrestricted trade throughout England.[12] The king personally interceded on behalf of individual Cologne merchants several times when his bailiffs and sheriffs, especially those of London and Yarmouth, did not respect these royal privileges.[13]

We have already met several Cologners who were active at the English court as representatives of the archbishop of Cologne or of the German monarchs, but Cologners also served the English kings in other practical ways. Often merchants from Cologne, like Arnold Ungevuch and others, would offer the transportation services of their vessels for a

---

12 *CPR Henry III*, I, p. 446; *HUB*, I, p. 55 no. 168: "Johannes Vache de Doya habet litteras de conductu omnibus baillivis, ad veniendum ad terram Anglie cum nave sua et rebus et mercandisis suis, usque ad festum Sancti Michaelis . . . Eodem modo scribitur eisdem baillivis pro Baldewino de Gupil, Johanne le Baud, mercatore Rothomagi, Conrado de Colonia, mercatore" (dated 1224); *CPR Henry III*, II, p. 40; *HUB*, I, p. 65 no. 207: "Gerardus de Quatermares, mercator de Colonia, habet consimilem licenciam de nave sua et catellis et mercandisis suis, duraturas usque ad eundem terminum [ad Pascham]" (dated 1226); *CPR Henry III*, II, p. 373: among those with royal letters of protection: "Hyldebrandus de Colonia, Nicholaus de Colonia, cum nave que vocatur Welifare" (dated 1230); *CPR Edward I*, III, p. 570; *HUB*, I, p. 417 no. 1231: "Safe-conduct, for one year, for Ingelbert called 'Cole,' citizen of Cologne, trading" (Walsingham, February 3, 1297).

13 *Rotuli litterarum clausarum*, ed. Hardy, I, p. 617; Ennen/Eckertz, II, p. 92 no. 81; *HUB*, I, p. 55 no. 169; Lappenberg, *Urkundliche Geschichte des Hansischen Stahlhofes zu London*, pp. 10–11 no. 22: "Rex baillivis portus Jernem. salutem. Mandamus vobis quod omnes naves venientes in portu Jernem. cum mercandisis de Scotia et de Norweg. et Island et Frisland et de Colonia, de terra regis Dacia et de partibus illis orientalibus sine inpedimento abire permittatis et similter naves piscatorias de quacumque terra sint" (London, August 23, 1224); *CCLR Henry III*, II, p. 453: "Mandatum est majori et vicecomitibus London' quod occasione concessionis domini Regis eis facta ad claudendum civitatem Lond', nullam capiant consuetudinem vel exigant de mercatoribus de terra regis Alemannie vel archiepiscopi Coloniensis, set exactionem illam ponant in respectum donec dominus rex ad partes illas venerit et cum predictis majore et vicecomitibus locutus fuerit" (dated 1234); *CCLR Henry III*, III, p. 216: "Rex bailivis suis de Gernemuth' salutem. Sciatis nos quietos clamasse per cartam nostram pro nobis et heredibus nostris dilectos nostros cives de Colonia de omnibus consuetudinibus et demandis que pertinent ad nos per totam terram nostram Anglie, et concessimus eis salvum ire et salvum venire in totam terram nostram, et quod ii libere possint ire ad ferias per totam terram nostram et emere vendere in villa London' et alibi, salva libertate civitatis nostre London'. Et ideo vobis precipimus quod predictas libertates et quietancias predictis civibus a nobis concessas libere et sine impedimento habere permittatis, liii solidos et quatuor denarios quos nuper a predictis civibus contra easdem libertates cepistis, ut dicitur, eisdem civibus sine dilatione reddi facientes, ita quod clamor iteratus ad nos non debeat inde pervenire" (December 12, 1235); *CCLR Henry III*, III, p. 399: "Mandatum est ballivis de Jernemowe quod si, occasione libertatum quas habent homines de Colonia per cartam predessorum regum Anglie, vel per cartam Regis, quibus hucusque usi sunt, aliquid eis abstulerint contra libertates predictas, id ei (*sic*) reddi faciant" (dated 1236); *CCLR Henry III*, VI, p. 130: "Mandatum est ballivis de Jernemuta quod allec mercatorum de Colonia et de Brabancia, quod arestari fecerunt in portu suo ad opus regis, eisdem mercatoribus sine dilacione deliberari faciant, et ipsos mercatores pro voluntate sua inde disponere permittant. Et allec illud quod ad opus Regis capi precepit de mercatoribus terre Regis capi feciant" (Northampton, December 4, 1248).

fee, and others, like Bruno, provided loans for royal business.[14] In 1302 a certain Matthew of Cologne even received letters of safe conduct from Edward I so that he could deliver letters from the king of France.[15] The Zudendorps were not the only Cologners to receive a fief for their service at the English court. Lambert of Cologne, an envoy of Archbishop Adolf, served as liaison during Anglo-Cologne negotiations for Otto IV's kingship. As a reward for his diplomatic activities Richard I granted Lambert a pension of £20 from the manor of Brampton in Huntingdonshire. Payments of this pension are recorded in the Pipe Rolls for the years 1194–1201.[16] In 1199 a royal inquest was held concerning the lordship of Brampton manor after a certain Thomas, the parish priest, challenged Lambert's right to hold this manor as a royal fief.[17] In the end Lambert continued to enjoy his yearly

[14] *Rotuli litterarum clausarum*, ed. Hardy, I, p. 127; *HUB*, I, p. 39 no. 95: "Rex ballivis portus Sandwic. etc. Sciatis quod Arnoldus Ungenogh de Colonia fecit nos securos erit apud Lon. in media Quadrag. anno regno nostro xiiij. cum nave sua promittus ad eundem in servicium nostrum. Et ideo vobis mandamus quod si per vos transitum fecerit cum nave sua citra Natale anno regno nostro eodem ipsum non impediatis quominus ire possit ad negocium suum faciendum et mandatum est ballivis portus Jernem. ut predictum Arnoldum abire permittant cum nave sua in negocium suum" (Westminster, November 27, 1212). Seven months later King John commanded the archdeacon of Taunton to allow Arnold to leave Sandwich with his ship in order to visit the market of Hoyland under royal protection: *Rotuli litterarum clausarum*, Hardy, I, p. 137; *HUB*, I, p. 42 no. 104 (June 11, 1213) – we have already met Arnold Ungevuch in chapter 16. In 1210 Bruno of Cologne was paid for his services for transporting Simon de Pateshull to Ireland (*Rotuli de liberate*, ed. Hardy, p. 157), and he later loaned £30 to Bishop Walter Mauclerc of Carlisle to cover the prelate's expenses during an important embassy to the archbishop of Cologne in May 1225 (*Rotuli litterarum clausarum*, ed. Hardy, II, p. 38). A year earlier (May 1224) he had received a royal writ of trade protection in England (*CPR Henry III*, I, p. 460).

[15] *CPR Edward I*, IV, p. 25: "Safe-conduct, until Easter, for Matthew de Colonia, going to . . . with letters of the king of France" (Swaffham Market, April 1, 1302).

[16] *Pipe Rolls 6–10 Richard I*, PR NS, 5, p. 76; 6, p. 119; 7, p. 275; 8, p. 77; 9, p. 161 and *Pipe Rolls 1–3 John*, PR NS, 10, p. 153; 12, p. 163; 14, p. 120. In the final year Lambert only received 100 shillings as one quarter of the yearly rent. Lambert also collected Archbishop Adolf of Cologne's pension from the Cambridgeshire manor of Soham during the years 1195–6; otherwise it was collected by Adolf's butler Adam or by others.

[17] *Rotuli curiae regis*, ed. Francis Palgrave (London, 1835), I, p. 391: "Hunted. Dies datus est Thom. filio Thome petent. et Thom. clerico de Hunted. qui vocavit ad warantum Lambertum de Colonia qui se esson. de pl. ass. mort. antec. a die Sancti Johanni in xv dies et tunc veniat ass. Idem dies datus rec. in bancio" (June 14, 1199); *Curia Regis Rolls*, I, p. 80: "Hunted. Assisa venit recognitura si Thomas pater Thome fuit seisitus in dominico suo ut de feudo ut (*sic*) de iiii aeris prati et dimidia cum pertinenciis in Branton' die obiit, quam terram Thomas clericus de Hunted' tenet: Thomas clericus venit et vocat inde ad warantum Lambertum de Colon'. Habeat quod (*sic*) vocavit a die Pascha in iii septimanas; et tunc veniat assisa" (1199); *Curia Regis Rolls*, VII, pp. 349–50: "Robertus filius Ade, Robertus le Bonde, Henricus filius Roberti, Christianus filius Walteri, Sewardus de Hohton', Radulfus Clobbe Jonatha, Henricus filius Willelmi, Henricus prepositus, Andreas filius Roberti, Stephanus de Hocton', summoniti ad testificandum quod et quantum dominicum esset, debeat, et soleat in villa de Bramton' et quid et quantum homines ejusdem ville cognoverunt alias esse dominicum domini regis in eadem villa et quid et quantum tenuerunt ad firmam de vicecomitibus antequam eadem ville veniret in manus

pension for two more years, then King John ceased paying the foreign pensions that his brother had established. Strangely enough in 1203 Lambert appears in Rouen, but the enigmatic passage in the Norman Rolls leaves us only wondering what business he and his associates were involved in at the time.[18] A few years later, as John was trying to revive an alliance with his Welf nephew Otto, the pension was restored.[19] His name was misconstrued at times as Lambekin, as when the pension was restored to him in 1205,[20] and in the Red Book of the Exchequer he is recorded as still in possession of the restored pension in the years 1210 to 1212, with the rent now being paid from lands in Lincolnshire.[21] In any case Brampton was given by the king to Geoffrey de Nevill in 1216, and we can safely assume that Lambert was deceased by that time.[22]

The emigrants and merchants of Cologne were not always on the right side of royal justice, as we have already seen in the case of Ricardus de Zudendorp. They appeared in court often and faced their share of criminal charges. In 1210 a certain Segwinus and Marcmannus were charged with raping and robbing a woman named Wimarca, and their behavior after being arrested is most remarkable.[23] In response to the

---

Lamberti de Colon', dicunt quod Rex Henricus avus habuit ibi in dominico duas carucatas terre et quod ibi Rex fuit coronatus, et regina sua Matilda similiter, in capella quodam lignea que tunc temporibus ibi fuit: et de predictis duabus carrucatis terre dedit idem Rex Henricus avus et Regina ecclesie ejusdem ville unam carrucatam et fecerunt eam lapideam, et aliam carrucatam assignavit idem dominus Rex Henricus ad hospita baronum in adventu domini Regis in villam illam. Consideratum est quod summoneantur xij liberi . . . quatuor alii liberi homines de visneto quod sint in adventu justiciarorum in partes alias ad . . . veritatem" (Trinity term, 1199).

[18] *Rotuli Normannie in turri Londinensi asservati Johanne et Henrico Quinto Angliae regibus I: De annis 1200–1205, necnon de anno 1417*, ed. Thomas Duffus Hardy, (London, 1835), I, p. 80: "Robert de Veteri Ponte, etc. Mandamus vobis quod nullo modo dimittatis quin trahatis vadia Lamberti Colon' et sociorum apud Rothmag" (February 1203). The pledges or securities (vadia) offered by Lambert and his associates remain unexplained here.

[19] *Pipe Roll 9 John*, PR NS, 22, p. 105.

[20] *Rotuli litterarum clausarum*, ed. Hardy, I, p. 25: "Rex G. filio Petri. Mandamus vobis quod faciatis habere Lambekino de Colonia feodum suum ad terminos quos scitis illud sibi deberi" (Winchester, April 3, 1205).

[21] A Lambekin (Lambert) is listed along with Conrad de Weiler and Terricus Teutonicus, both of whom were involved in the Anglo-Cologne diplomatic connection (we shall be discussing Terricus shortly): *The Red Book of the Exchequer*, ed. Hall, II, p. 523 for Lincolnshire: "Cunradus de Wilere, xl marcatas in soca de Watham. Lambekin de Colonia, xx libratas ibidem. Terri Teutonicus, xx libratas ibidem."

[22] *Rotuli litterarum clausarum*, I, ed. Hardy, p. 246: "Mandatum est Vic. Linc. quod faciatis habere Gaufrido de Nevill. camerario domini Regis plenaram saisinam de tota terra que fuit Lamberti de Colonia cum pertinenciis suis in bailliva sua" (January 28, 1216).

[23] *Curia Regis Rolls*, VI, p. 54: "Lond. Segwinus et Marcman cives Colonie queruntur quod vicecomites Lond', scilicet Stephanus Crassus et Adam de Witebi, eos ceperunt et posuerunt in carcere cum latronibus, ita quod per unam noctem fuerunt cum eis in fundo carceris et eis non potuerunt valere littere domini imperatoris Ottonis quas ipsi habuerunt secum patentes, in quibus continentur quod ipse suscepit eos in protectionem suam et res suas; nec de carcere exire potuerunt quousque ipsi pacavissent eis iii marcas; et inde producunt sectam de hominibus terre sue. Et ipsi vicecomites veniunt cum latronibus et capcionem predictorum denariorum; set

hue and cry being raised, the London sheriffs seized the two Cologners and placed them in jail. But Segwinus and Marcmannus complained that they should not have been placed in a prison with common criminals, since they carried with them a letter of protection issued by the Emperor Otto IV. Perhaps they expected special treatment because Cologne was the bulwark of support for the English king's nephew. Yet the confidence they exhibited in asserting personal exemption from normal legal procedure, and their disdain at being placed in jail with the other "brigands," is astonishing. Either Segwinus and Marcmannus were exceptionally haughty or the privileges and powerful economic status that the Cologners enjoyed in England caused these men to expect better treatment. Unfortunately the case breaks off at this point and is never picked up again, so we are unable to determine whether Segwinus and Marcmannus were found guilty of the charges or not.

Just how violent life could be in London is further clarified by another incident.[24] A certain cleric named Lambert of Cologne was accompanying a friend's daughter home when he became involved in

dicunt quod quedam Wimarca, que manet in villa Lond', questa fuit quod, cum ipsa bene et in pace ivisset in vico domini Regis, predicti [*sic*] Segwinus cepit eam per pallium et fregit fibulas suas; et ei abstulerunt catalla sua, ut in anulis et firmaculis, ad valenciam x solidorum; et Segwinus tunc vi concubit eum ea, et in illa vi fuit ipse Marcman; et eo quod clamor et uthes levatus fuit et ipsa sanguinolenta fuit et affidavit sequi, ipsi vicecomites posuerunt loquelam in hustingo; et ad hustingum recordata fuit hec loquela; et quesitum fuit ab eis si invenire possent . . ." The passage breaks off at this point, with the words "loquendem cum Rege" in the margin (dated Michaelmas 1210).

24 *The London Eyre of 1276*, ed. Weinbaum, pp. 12–13 no. 39: "On Friday after the feast of St. Scholastica the Virgin [13 Feb.] in the ward of Laurence de Frowick [Farringdon ward], Lambert of Cologne and Walter esquire of Master Philip de Cancellis clerk were taking Philip's sister Alice home and when they came to the churchyard of St. Dunstan in the West (iuxta Novum Templum) they met Henry de Merston, a clerk of the chancery, and his servant Robert [de Kyngeston]. A quarrel ensued among them about the woman and Robert de Kyngeston, by Henry's order, stabbed Lambert with a knife below the right shoulder, so that he died on the third day after in the house of Master Henry the Versifier (Versificatoris). Robert at once fled and is suspended; because he is not of the City but of the county of Stafford, the sheriff of Stafford is ordered to have him exacted and outlawed in his own county. Henry is a clerk and lives in Bedfordshire in the diocese of Lincoln. Therefore the bishop of Lincoln is ordered to cause him to appear in three weeks from the Purification [23 Feb.]; and the sheriff of Bedford is to arrest him if he can be found. Walter and Alice and the others who were present when the incident occurred do not come and were not attached, so to judgement on the chamberlain and sheriffs not attaching them. The mayor and aldermen are asked if they suspect Walter and Alice of the death and they say that they do not, but that they were present. So they are in mercy. Afterward Henry comes, and asked how he wishes to clear himself of the incitement, says that he is a clerk and is not bound to answer here. Thereupon Richard de Berues minor canon of St. Paul's London comes and claims him as a clerk by virtue of letters of the bishop of London in which the bishop entrusted to him his authority for claiming clergy. Because it is provided by the king's council that no one is bound to answer a charge of incitement before the committer of the deed (factor) has been convicted, let Henry be handed over to the bishop to have him before the king or his justices on summons on penalty of £100." This Lambert of Cologne is, of course, not to be confused with the envoy of the archbishop of Cologne.

an altercation with a chancery clerk named Henry de Merston over the woman. The quarrel resulted in Lambert being stabbed and he died three days later from the wound. A judicial inquiry ensued, but Henry de Merston claimed benefit of clergy and thereby avoided being tried before the London Hustings court for the crime. After an investigation by the royal coroner was completed, Henry was apparently cleared of the charges.[25] He then made use of his connections at the royal chancery and obtained a pardon for his servant.[26] A similar case occurred in 1249, when Richard son of Gerard, Wydo of St. Edmund, and Stephan of Oxford were held in the royal jail of Lincolnshire for robbing and murdering a certain Gerard of Cologne.[27] Cologners were thus on both sides of crime in England: as victims and as perpetrators. Criminal behavior and Cologne citizens were the subjects of correspondence exchanged between Edward I and Archbishop Henry II of Cologne around the year 1306.[28] The archbishop assured the king that

---

[25] *CCLR Henry III*, VIII, p. 124: "Quia inquisicio nuper facta Lond' de morte Lamberti de Colonia minus sufficiens est, ut rex audivit, mandatum est majori et vicecomitibus Lond' quod in presencia Johannis de Gisorc', coronatoris Regis, secundem consuetudinem civitatis Lond' aliam pleniorem inde faciant inquisicionem per viros fide dignos per quos etc. et quid super hoc invenerit prout moris est inrotulari faciant."

[26] Ibid., VIII, p. 320: "Mandatum est majori et vicecomitibus ac aliis ballivis Regis Lond' quod litteras patentes, quas rex ad instanciam Henrici de Mercinton' concessit Roberto de Huntendon', vatletto ipsius Henrici, de perdonacione secte pacis Regis pro morte Lamberti de Colonia, clerici, interfecti Lond', unde idem Robertus rettatus est, in pleno hustengo suo legi; et eodem Roberto, quocumque cognomine vocitatus fuerit in inquisicione facta London' de morte predicta, firmam pacem Regis inde habere faciant" (October 29, 1254). Here we learn that there was some confusion about Henry's surname – either de Kingston or de Huntingdon.

[27] *CCLR Henry III*, VI, p. 198: "Ricardus filius Girardi et Wydo de Sancto Edmundo, capti et detenti in prisona regis Linc' pro morte Gerardi mercatoris de Colonia, unde rettati sunt, habent breve vicecomiti Linc' quod ponantur per ballium" (August 29, 1249) and p. 234: "Stephanus de Oxonia, captus et detentus in prisona regis Linc' pro morte Gerardi Colon' et pro roberia, habet litteras regis vicecomiti Linc' directas quod ponantur per ballium" (November 2, 1249).

[28] *Acta Imperii Angliae et Franciae ab anno 1267 ad annum 1313. Dokumente Vornehmlich zur Geschichte der Auswärtigen Beziehungen Deutschlands*, ed. Fritz Kern (Tübingen, 1911), pp. 109–10 no. 165 (April 5, *c.* 1306) and p. 114 no. 170 (August 13, *c.* 1306): "Magnifico ac excellenti domino, domino Edwardo Regi Anglie Domino Hibernie et Duci Aquitanie Henricus Dei gratia sancte Coloniensis ecclesie Archiepiscopus sacri imperii per Italiam archicancellarius salutem et paratam ad eius beneplacita quelibet voluntatem. Super hiis, que nobis scripsistis, quod dictus Euel the Yunge et Arnoldus eius frater et quidam eorum complices in dominio nostro, prout vobis relatum esse dicitur, servientes Willelmi Tollere burgensis et mercatoris vestri de Grymesby quadam magna pecunie quantitate, pannis et bonis aliis multis eorundem spoliarunt, vestram excellentiam scire affectamus, quod per Johannem marscalcum [*sic*] nostrum Westphalie per totam terram nostram Westphalie investigari fecimus, si que veritas in dicto spolio subesset, et hoc nobis referret. Qui hiis perquisitis dicit nemini in tota terra nostra predicta de dicto spolio constare et quod nomina ipsorum spoliatorum, sicut nobis in vestris litteris nominantur, sint ibidem ignota. Scripsistis etiam, quod ipsi raptores in villa Westphalen dicta bona abstulerint, cum non sit villa, sed terra multum spatiosa non solum tendens ad finem terre nostre ibidem, sed longe lateque sub dominio domini episcopi Monasteriensis et aliorum episcoporum, comitum et baronum ipsa terra Westphalie se extendit. Et nominastis illam villam, sicut eam 'villam' nuncupastis; de quo miramur, quis talis vobis retulerit. Quia nullus fluvius in tota terra

he could not find anyone fitting the description given him of the defendants. This case may have been nothing more than the confusion of Cologners with people of the region of Westphalia, but it was obviously not unthinkable to charge Cologne citizens with such crimes. In fact a similar case occurred in 1310, but those charged with the crime were eventually acquitted.[29]

We have already noted that Cologne artisans were known for their work as goldsmiths. They were also known for their abilities as coin manufacturers, since the archbishop had control of one of the oldest and most productive imperial mints. Some enterprising expatriates brought this skill with them to England and employed it in the manufacture of forged English coins. Recall that the three Cologners were charged in 1252 with forgery and were cast in the Tower of London;[30] or when Gocelin of Cologne publicly confessed that he was a forger after taking sanctuary in St. Paul's Cathedral.[31]

The merchants of Cologne also spent much time before the English courts defending their business investments and trading privileges from infringement. In 1270 a certain Gerard of Cologne appeared at the fair

Westphalie mare nominatur, non credimus premissa, sicut vobis sunt relata, ita esse nec vera esse. Unde consilium nostrum est, ut nomina spoliatorum et, in cuius domini districtu morentur, et, utrum in nostra terra vel non, ipse burgensis vester diligenter procuret investigari, et quidquid tunc, si inventum fuerit ipsos raptores in partibus terre nostre existere seu manere, per ius pro ipso burgensi vestro facere poterimus, expedite faciemus in hiis et in aliis rationalibus volentes vobis semper complacere." The second letter: "Magnifico principi et illustri domino Eduardo Regi Anglie Domino Ibernie Duci Aquitanie Henricus Dei gratia sancte Coloniensis ecclesie Archiepiscopus sacri imperii per Italiam Archiecancellarius paratum ad sua beneplacita voluntatem. Super ablatione rerum, de quibus Wilhelmus dictus Toller burgensis et mercator vester ville vestre de Grymtsby vobis est conquestus et nobis scripsistis, non reperimus aliquem in terminis nostris Westphalie, qui hoc nomine 'Euel the Junge de Westfale et Arnoldus frater eius' in littera vestra contenti nuncupantur, sed si hos vel quoscumque alios poterimus invenire in premissis culpabiles, taliter faciemus circa istud precibus sive mandatis sive aliis viis, quibus vestram efficere poterimus voluntatem, quod sentietis in hiis et aliis nostram promptam ubilibet voluntatem." The fact that the merchants of Westphalia were known as a group led the English to consider them incorrectly as from a city rather than a region. von Winterfeld, "Das Westfälische Hansequartier," II, 1, p. 266: "Dabei [in England] war der landsmannschaftliche Zusammenhalt unter den Westfalen gegen 1300 so fest, daß sie sich hier nicht nach ihrer Heimatstadt, sondern nur als 'Kaufleute aus Westfalen' zu bezeichnen pflegten. Hieraus entstand bei den englischen Beamten die irrige Meinung, 'Westfalen' sei – wie Lübeck, Hamburg, Kapmen, Stavoren – der Name einer Stadt." *REK*, IV, p. 650 dates these letters from August 14, 1311, which assumes that the King of England mentioned here was Edward II and not Edward I.

[29] *Calendar of Inquisitions Miscellaneous (Chancery) in the Public Record Office. Volume I: Henry III and Edward I* (London, 1916), p. 25 no. 11: "Writ to the sheriff of Norfolk and Suffolk. Berwick-on-Tweed. 6 July 4 Edward II [1310]. Inquisition: Saturday after St. Mary Magdelene 5 Edw. II Tideman de Affle and others (named), merchants under the power of the archbishop of Cologne, are not of the power or dominion of Westfale or other places (named) and took no part in the robbery at sea committed against Henry de Bello Monte."

[30] *CCLR Henry III*, VII, p. 277. See chapter 3 above.

[31] *The London Eyre of 1276*, ed. Weinbaum, p. 4 no. 11. See chapter 3 above.

court of St. Ives in order to obtain the return of two casks and one pipe of Rhenish wine from Peter Anger of Lynn and Tyleman the Easterling, who had illegally used the wine to pay a debt.[32] Gerard apparently had difficulty locating enough oath-helpers to verify his claim, as the case was given a continuance four times before disappearing from the court roll. He either settled out of court or needed to return to Cologne on other business. The following year two other Cologne merchants were arrested at the port of Lynn under suspicion of ignoring the ban on exporting English wool to Flanders.[33] Although they obtained a royal writ ordering the return of the confiscated wool, they were expressly ordered not to sell the wool outside England. Such a restriction was tantamount to a statement of guilt, since the purpose of possessing the wool was to export it for resale, and therefore the Cologne merchants were in effect still being punished. That they could sell the wool in England at a profit remains dubious at best A similar case occurred in 1297 when the ship of the Cologners Frederick Luyf de Cornu and his brother Herman was confiscated under suspicion that it was heading with 107 casks and 3 pipes of wine for either Flanders or Scotland –

---

[32] *Select Cases Concerning the Law Merchant. Volume 1: Local Courts (A.D. 1270–1638)*, ed. Charles Gross, Seldon Society, 23 (London, 1908), p. 5: "Gerardus de Colonia optulit se ad legem faciendem quod illa ii dolia et i pipe vini reneys per que Petrus Aungrede Lenn' et Tylemann le Estreys atachiati sunt ad respondendum Johanni le Corveyer de Lond' et non venit armatus sufficienter secundum legem mercatorum [i.e. he didn't have enough oath-helpers]. Quare datus est dies eidem Gerardo usque diem Lune prox' sequentem ad probandum dicta vina cum sexta manu [i.e. with five other oath-helpers] sua per plegium Derekan Selehorn, Warini de Sumptham et Roberti de Meldeburn', salva dicto Johanni de Lond' defalta facta in probacione sua isto die quam calumpniavit." The case is then continued: "Datus est dies ad Gerardo de Colonia usque ad crastinum de lege sua facienda Petro Angre de Len'" (p. 7) and again, "Datus est dies usque diem Sabbati Gerardo de Colonia veniendi ad probandum illud vinum renys esse suum quod Petrus Angre de Len' fecit hospitare et per que dictus Petrus atachiatus fuit ad respondendum Johanni le Correyer de Lond', et hoc cum sexta manu sua, et quod faciet ipsum Petrum quem dicit esse servientem suum venire ad dictam diem Sabbati" (p. 8) and finally "Loquela que tangit Gerardum de Colonia ponitur in respectum usque diem Sabbati" (p. 9). The record of the case ends here. The fair of St. Ives was on located on the manor of Slepe in Huntingdonshire.

[33] *CCLR Henry III*, XIV, p. 331: "Rex majori et ballivis suis de Lenn' salutem. Cum vos occasione contencionis habite inter nos et comtissam Flandr' quinquaginta saccos lane qui sunt Johannis Brunstayn de Colon' et Gerardi Quatremars socii sui infra villam vestram feceristis arrestari, ac iidem Johannes et Gerardus parati sunt ostendere quod non sunt de Flandr' nec quod aliqui de Flandr' partem habeant in eadem lana, et quidam ex parte ipsorum Johannis et Gerardi nos rogaverunt quod, si ita sit, dictam lanam deliberari jubeamus et eisdem Johanni et Gerardo concedamus quod comodum suum infra regnum nostrum Anglie inde facere possint, vobis mandamus quod, si vobis manifeste constare poterit quod non sunt de Flandr' nec aliqui de Flandr' partem habeant in eadem lana, tunc accepta sufficienti securitate, de qua vos ipsi volueritis respondere, quod ipsi lanam predictam vendent in regno nostro et extra illud eam non ducent, dictos quinquaginta saccos lane per vos, si ob causam predictam et non aliam eos arrestaveritis, dictis Johanni et Gerardo sine dilacione aliqua deliberari faciatis ad comodum suum inde faciendum in forma predicta" (Westminster, March 12, 1271).

both illegal entrepôts at the time for goods passing through English waters.[34] The Cologne merchants as a group issued a request to Edward I that he have the cargo released for shipment to Holland, which they claimed was its original destination. Either the ship had been confiscated directly off the mouth of the Rhine (a possibility since England was involved in hostilities with Flanders and therefore sought to blockade any English wool imports) or the cargo was clearly destined for Scotland as charged.

The merchants of Cologne made good use of the trading privileges that the kings of England had granted them. In 1298 three of them appealed to the Boston assize court about the royal purveyance of wine from their vessels; they employed the general grant awarded to the merchants of Cologne by King John and subsequently confirmed by Henry III as legal precedent for their exemption from such purveyances.[35] Their interpretation of the privileges could be disputed by this time, but unfortunately the conclusion of the case was not recorded and so we remain unclear about whether the claim was recognized as legitimate or not. Cologne merchants were not always defendants or plaintiffs in English courts; they also served as witnesses and jurors in

---

[34] *HUB*, I, p. 425 no. 1265. Frederick Luyf de Cornu was a member of a prestigious patrician family in Cologne (see Lau, "Das Kölner Patriziat bis zum Jahre 1325," *MSAK* 25 [1984], p. 366). The ship's name was *The Mariotta*. On November 6, 1257 Conrad of Cologne was compensated for the loss of 50 quarts of oats and half of a ship belonging to him, which was arrested in London because of an alleged Dutch origin, after he proved his origin was German: *Hanseakten aus England 1271 bis 1472*, ed. Kunze, pp. 3–4 no. 2.

[35] *A Lincolnshire Assize Roll for 1298 (PRO Assize Roll no. 505)*, ed. Walter Sinclair Thomson, Lincoln Record Society, 36 (Hereford, 1944), pp. 23–4: "Adhuc de Placitis apud sanctum Botulphum. Henricus Botermarkede, Galfridus de Coloyne, Hermannus Paramours mercatores Colonie querunter de Iohanne fil. Thome et Gerardo le Gauger quod ipsi attachiaverunt tria dolia vini de Rino quousque dicti mercatores fecerunt finem cum eis de sex m. etc. Iohannes venit, et Gerardus non venit, et Iohannes pro se dicit quod Matheus de Columbariis mandavit per litteras quas ostendit quod idem Iohannes caperet de qualibet navi continente viginti dolea vini; unum doleum de vini Rin' pro nichilo vel duo dolea pro lx s. et de qualibet navi continente viginti dolea vini de Vasconia; unum doleum pro nicholo vel duo dolea pro xl s. sicut semper usitatum est de capcionibus Regis, et quia predicti mercatores habuerunt duas naves, unde una continebat xxv dolea, ipse cepit simul cum Gerardo le Gauger de una navi duo dolea vini, et de alia navi unum doleum prout moris est de foedo pincerne Regis. Et postea ei vendidit predictis mercatoribus pro predictus sex m. allocans ei residuum argenti in feodo suo. Et quod nichil ad opus suum devenit nec maliciose cepit ponit se super patriam – Et mercatores dicunt quod cepit maliciose et quod devenit ad comodum ipsius Iohannes. [Et de hoc] ponunt se super patriam etc. Dicunt eciam quod dominus Henricus Rex pater domini Regis nunc concessit eisdem mercatoribus de Colonya per cartam suam quod quieti essent ab omni capcione et tallagio consuetudine et demanda que pertinet ad ipsum Regem per totum regnum Anglie pro illis duobus solidis quos solebant dare de Gildhalla sua London' quam quidem cartam dominus Rex nunc confirmavit quam quidem confirmacionem predicti mercatores ostendunt. Et dicunt quod predicti Iohannes et Gerardus non obstante predictis carta seu confirmacione . . . [case left uncompleted here] (1298)." Buttermarkt, the surname of one of these Cologne merchants, was the name of a street in the merchant quarter of Cologne.

cases involving foreign merchants and the crown. In a disputed case at the Norfolk *Curia Regis* in the Easter Term 1226 a group of Cologners attested that, although a ship confiscated at the port of Yarmouth was of Dutch origin, the cargo was indeed theirs.[36] In 1300 Cologners appear among the jurors who verified the native land of merchants from the province of the bishop of Liège, who were falsely sued for distraint as citizens of Brabant.[37] We get some picture here of how difficult it was for English magistrates to keep clear the identities of foreign merchants, many of whom were in business together. Those from different jurisdictions in Germany proved most difficult to distinguish in this regard before the 1303 *Carta Mercatoria* ended such distinctions.

As should be obvious by this point, the merchants of Cologne established themselves in England beyond London. We find them remarkably well integrated into the commercial communities of Norfolk and into the northeastern port city of Newcastle-upon-Tyne for example. Three individuals styled "de Colonia" (or "de Coloigne") appear along with others "de Alemania" on the Bede Roll of the Guild of Holy Trinity in King's Lynn (*c.* 1215–20), while Alexander Kello paid the guild 4 shillings on behalf of Gilbertus de Colonia – perhaps as an entry fine (1264). A truly interregional entry records Tyrus de Colonia in 1294 among the debtors in Lynn who owed allegiance to the king of France.[38] The Yarmouth court rolls of the 1280s are filled with references to Cologners along with other foreign merchants, of which one family's business is recorded at length. Henricus de Colonia and his

---

[36] *Curia Regis Rolls*, XII, p. 455 no. 2268. The confiscation of Cologner ships and merchandise is also mentioned in a case of the year 1228: *Curia Regis Rolls*, XIII, pp. 109–10 no. 472.

[37] *Calendar of Early Mayor's Court Rolls Preserved Among the Archives of the Corporation of the City of London at the Guildhall (A. D. 1298–1307)*, ed. A. H. Thomas (Cambridge, 1924), pp. 87–8: "Tuesday before the Feast of St. Michael [September 29] Stephen de Flete, Gerard de Hopstathe, Peter de Aske, John Teste, Gilbert Flemingg, John Fernus and Thomas de Dictfeld were summoned to answer Peter de Blakeneye, John de Dorking, John Beauflur and John Bussard in a complaint that John, duke of Brabant, had taken part of the plaintiff's goods when they were exposed for sale in the duchy of Brabant, for which reason the sheriff had been ordered to attach the goods of all Brabantine merchants until the duke made restitution, and that the defendants were under the dominion of the duke. The defendants denied this, and said that they belonged to the city of Malynges and held of the bishop of Leges [Liège], and that the bishop held of the church of St. Lambert and had nothing to do with the count [*sic*] of Brabant; and they demanded an inquest by foreign merchants who knew the said country. On Wednesday a jury of Theotard le Estreys, John de Eldchirk, Eylbrich, Henry Colle of Collon [Cologne], Godelin of Colon [Cologne], Tykimann the goldsmith, James Fisshe, Albridus de Dynaunt, Lambert Maulechyn, Peter of St. Vincent, John Saunterre, Baldewyn Chapun and Guy de Goly found a verdict for the defendants. Order was given to return their distraints, and the plaintiffs were told to sue distraints on men belonging to the duke's dominions" (September 27, 1300).

[38] These texts are published in Dorothy M. Owen, ed., *The Making of King's Lynn*, Records of Social and Economic History NS, 9 (Oxford, 1984), pp. 305, 309, 311, 314, 455.

wife (unnamed) brought suits against Willelmus de Stowe and Willelmus son of Adam of Norwich over disputed business transactions. They were also defendants before the court, as when Henricus and business partner Wynemer de Hardwick were sued by John Wyth over a loan of 36 shillings.[39] Although these particular transactions proved contentious, we find once again the extent of quotidian interaction with important members of the local community managed by Cologners such as Henricus and his wife, since Wynemer de Hardwick and John Wyth were both heads of major English merchant families in Norwich. Richard of Cologne owned a messuage in Norwich during the 1280s in the district of sheep shearers, which suggests participation in the wool industry.[40]

Ingelramus de Colonia dwelt with his wife Johanna (an Englishwoman?) as "merchant and burgess" in Newcastle-upon-Tyne. He was associated with Newcastle merchants in the export of wool to Flanders and in the sale of military wares and foodstuffs to the king. In 1308 he purchased a house and garden on the street called le Clos, which he sold six months later for a yearly rent of 10 shillings and a yearly income for the hospital of St. Mary de Westgate of 3 shillings. These transactions look curiously like real-estate practices in Cologne. Later in the same year he purchased another house in the close. Indeed he was a master of the hospital of St. Mary de Westgate and his only child, Katherine, eventually married an Englishman, Norman de Bidyk.[41] Several men from Cologne whose professions range from merchant, webster, and armorer to goldsmith appear on the York register of Freemen by the early fourteenth century,[42] and one Loteryngus de Coloyn "mercator de societate Bardorum" held a tenement on French Street from God's House in Southampton.[43] Cologners in England look every bit as integrated into their new homeland as the English expatriates in Cologne.

[39] Norfolk Record Office: Yarmouth Court Rolls 4/C4/6 membranes 1r, 5r; 4/C4/7 membranes 1r, 1v, 3r, 4r (dated from October 23, 1284 to January 1, 1285).

[40] Norfolk Record Office: Norwich Enrolled Deeds Case 1 Bundle 1 membrane 3v. His dwelling abutted others owned by familes styled "le Tundur," from the Norman-French *tondeur* (Latin = *tonsor*). These were sheep shearers (Sherman) who performed their work at Charing Cross (Shearing Cross): see John Kirkpatrick, *The Streets and Lanes of the City of Norwich*, ed. William Hudson (Norwich, 1889), pp. 54–5.

[41] These charters are published in Arthur M. Oliver, ed., *Early Deeds Relating to Newcastle Upon Tyne*, Surtees Society, 137 (London, 1924), nos. 20, 22, 24, 25, 328, 329. Also see note 8 above.

[42] *Register of the Freemen of the City of York. Volume 1: 1272–1558*, ed. Francis Collins, Surtees Society, 96 (London, 1897), pp. 14, 37, 47, 63, 87, 94, 98, 100.

[43] *The Cartulary of God's House, Southampton*, ed. J. M. Kaye, Southampton Record Series, 19 (Southampton, 1976), I, p. 111 and II, p. 377.

Amid the numerous references to Cologner activity in England a sizeable amount of information survives on the lives of three men in particular, whose expatriate careers during the thirteenth and early fourteenth centuries reveal the degree to which emigrants from Cologne could become integrated into English life. In fact, their lives mirror the same thoroughness of integration achieved by the expatriate English in Cologne. The first of the three men was Hermann le Heaumer, or Hermann the Helmeter.[44] Hermann was also known by the nickname Manekin, which was an English rendering of the German diminutive form of Hermann (*Mannchen*).[45] Hermann's trade, as his surname indicates, was that of an armorer. Cologne was famous throughout northern Europe for its arms industry,[46] and the Cologne longsword was praised in many *Chansons de Geste* of the time.[47] Matthew Paris mentions the Cologne sword in an implausible story about the uncovering of a Jewish plot to arm the Tartars in the year 1241,[48] and in 1263 such a sword was actually employed during an

---

[44] "Le Heaumer" is Norman French for "the Helmeter." See *Munimenta*, II, 1, p. 732 and R. Kelham, *A Dictionary of the Norman Old French Language* (London, 1978), p. 121.

[45] The same pattern occurs in the diminuitive form of Margaret: Gretchen. My thanks to Colin Taylor of the Museum of London, who pointed this out to me.

[46] E. Ennen, "Kölner Wirtschaft im Früh- und Hochmittelalter," p. 138: "Frankreich und England waren besonders wichtige Absatzmärkte des Kölner Waffengewerbes."

[47] Robert Dörner, "Das Sarwörter- und das Schwertfegeramt in Köln, von den ältesten Zeiten bis zum Jahre 1550," *JKGV* 3 (1916), pp. 1–60. Another example is that of Peter de Langtoft's "Chronicon Rhythmicon," *MGH SS*, XXVIII, p. 651: "Sire Jakes de Avennes, verray peleryn, | Sie signe de la croyce et prent sun chemyn | Sur la primere eschele, cum leverer sur mastyn. | Deus fez passa parmy et du braund asceryn | Tua paens saunz noumbre; més Calaphés Duryn | Coupa la jaumbre destre; Sir Jakes a l'houre s'encyln | Et dist: 'O ray Richard, je suy tun cosyn: | Le ray Henri, tun pere, en chastel Constantyn | Engendra ma mere sur dame Avelyn | Countasse de la Marche. Pur Deu et saint Martyn, | Venez venger ma mort sur ço Sarazyn!' | Jakes de rechef de l'espeye Coloyn | Assene sir Kalaphé aval du paitryn | . . ."

[48] *MPCM*, IV, pp. 131–3: "Sed cum in remotas partes Alemanniae pervenissent, et cum doliis suis quendam pontem transire pararentur, dominus pontis, ut moris erat, paagium pro transitu sibi reddi postulavit. Ipsi autem frontose respondentes, et postulata reddere renuentes, dixerunt, quod pro utilitate imperii, immo totius Christianitatis, his negotiis sollicitarentur, directi ad Tartaros, ipsos vino suo cautius potionaturi. Custos vero pontius suspectam habens Judaeorum assertionem, unum doliorum terebrando perforavit, nec inde ullus liquor eliquatus distillavit. Inde certior de fraude effectus, circulis ejectis illud dolium confregit, et apparuit armis diversis refertum. Exclamans igitur ait: 'O proditio inaudita! ut quid tales inter nos patimur conversari?' Et statim ipse et alii, quos stupor convocavit, alia omnia dolia, quae protinus confregerunt, plena gladiis Coloniensibus sine capulis et cutellis sine manubriis, ordinate et conferte reposits, invenientes, omnibus in propatulo monstraverunt fraudis inauditae laqueos absconditos Judaeorum, qui publicis mundi hostibus, qui, ut dicebatur, armis maxime indegebant, maluerunt subvenire, quam Christianis, qui inter se ipsos tolerant conversari et in venalibus communicare, cum immo etiam cum Christianis liceat eis ea de cause foenerari. Legitur enim, 'Non foenerabis Egiptio,' et subditur causa, 'quia colonum te et advenam in terra sua te Egiptii receperunt.' Traditi igitur sunt ipsi Judaei tortoribus, vel perpetuo carceri merito mancipandi, vel ipsis suis gladiis trucidandi."

assault in London.[49] Cologners skilled in fashioning these arms naturally brought their trade with them when resettling in England, just like the goldsmiths and minters introduced previously.[50]

We first find Hermann on April 2, 1298 in London when he, his mother Gertrude de Colonia, and brother Peter purchased a tenement in All Hallows Breadstreet parish (Bread Street Ward).[51] The house, named La Rouge Sale, was purchased for 200 marks and a yearly rent of 1 penny from Henry le Waleys, mayor of London during the years 1282–4 and again in 1299.[52] Not only does this deed indicate that

[49] *The London Eyre of 1276*, ed. Weinbaum, p. 42 no. 147: "Thomas Viel appeals Robert de Esture that when he was in the (ward?) (*via*) of Westchepe in Soperlane of the feast of SS. Simon and June 47 Henry III [28 Oct. 1263] Robert came up about the hour of curfew and wounded him in the left hand with a sword of Coloyne, so that he was maimed; that Robert did this wickedly and feloniously and with premeditation he offers to prove against him . . . [12 men of the ward declare, he was committed to jail to make satisfaction for the injury]."

[50] John de Colonia, armorer to the king, is mentioned several times, along with his wife Dulcia, in the CLRO Hustings Rolls for the years 1337 to 1353: 64 (76, 77); 71 (23), 80 (194, 195), 82 (10), and on May 18, 1335 John promised to provide the king military service in Scotland for forty days: *Calendar of Letter Books Preserved among the Archives of the Corporation of the City of London at the Guildhall. Volume 5: Letter Book E (c. 1314–1337)*, ed. Reginald Sharpe (London, 1903), p. 5.

[51] CLRO Hustings Rolls 27 (96); partially published in *Hanseakten aus England 1271 bis 1472*, ed. Kunze, pp. 23–4 no. 22: "Carta domine Gertrude de Colon', Petri et Hermanni filii eius [in left margin]. Dictus die et anno lecta fuit ista carta in hunc modum. Sciant presentes et futuri, quod ego Henricus le Galeys civis London' dedi, concessi et hac presenti carta mea confirmari domine Gertrude de Colonia, Petro et Hermanno filiis suis, civibus London' illud tenementum cum omnibus suis pertinentiis, quod habui in parochia Omnium Sanctorum de Bredestrate London' una cum porta et solario superedificato in aquilonari parte eiusdem tenementi, vocatum la Rouge Sale, et situm est inter tenementa quondam Hugonis Motum ex parte orientali et tenementa quondam Alani Pistoris ex parte australi et tenementa quondam Anketini de Betteville et Walteri le Waleys ex parte occidentali et tenementa quondam Johannis le Seour, Walteri de Bredstrate, Ricardi Scot et vicum regium ex parte aquilonis; videlicet quicquid ibidem habeam vel habere potui seu debui . . . mihi seu heredibus meis accedere potent quocumque modo vel iure ut . . . edificus gardinis clausturum lignis lapidibus long-itudine latitudine altitudine et profunditate absque aliquo retenemento vel aliqua diminucione habendum et tenendum totum predictum tenementum cum omnibus et singulis suis pertinenc-tiis prefatis Gertrude, Petro et Heremanno et heredibus et eorum assignatibus quibuscumque de me heredibus et assignatibus meis libere quiete bene et in pace in feodo et hereditate inperpetuum redendo inde annuatim in heredibus et assignatibus meis unum denarium argenti ad festum pascham per omnibus aliis serviciis secularibus demandis et rebus civitatis. Et ego Henricus predictus heredes et assignates mei totum predictum tenementum cum omnibus suis pertinentiis . . . prefatis Gertrude, Petre et Heremanno heredibus et eorum assignatibus contra omnes gentes warantizibimus acquietabimus et defendemus per predictum servicium inperpe-tuum. Pro hec autem donatione, concessione, waranta, defensione, acquietacione et presentis carte mee confirmatione dederunt mihi predicti Gertruda, Petrus et Heremannus ducentas marcas sterlingorum per manibus ingres'. Et ut omnia permissa robur perpetue firmitatis optineant presentem cartam sigillium . . . Hiis testibus domino Johanne le Breoim milite tunc custod' civitatis Lond', Johanne de Scorteford et Willilmo de Scorteford tunc vicecomitibus Lond', Thome le Moyn tunc Aldermanno eiusdem warde . . . Datum London' secundo die Aprilis anno regni Regis Edwardi filii Regis Henrici vicesimo sexto."

[52] *Munimenta*, II, 1, pp. 240, 243.

Hermann's family had financial means and high social connections, but also that they held citizenship in London. This would prove important for Hermann in the coming years. Moreover, Gertrude is referred to as *domina*, which indicates some sort of recognized social rank. Hermann himself had business with at least the lower nobility, as the Recognizance Rolls for the same year mention: the knight Jacob de la Planche owed Hermann eight marks sterling as payment for some armor or weapons.[53]

Hermann and his brother Peter then fell afoul of the law in subsequent years. In 1300 Hermann was among a number of London defendants who were ordered by royal writ to appear in Gloucester in order to answer charges.[54] A delay in facing the unspecified charges was gained because of the jealously guarded rights of the London commune. After a second royal writ was issued on the same matter, the mayor responded that he had no responsibility in the matter since he held no charge of prisoners, and the sheriffs for their part stated that they could not arrest Hermann and Laurence le Puleter as citizens of London without infringing upon their rights; therefore they had released the two defendants on mainprise and ordered them to appear at the next assize of the Tower of London or before the justiciars of Newgate jail.[55]

Only five years later did Hermann actually face these charges *coram rege*.[56] At this point we discover that he had not only been involved

---

[53] CLRO Recognizance Rolls 5 membrane 5: "Eodem die Iune Jacobus de la Plannche miles de Corn' Northumper' recognovit se debere Manekino le Heumer de London octo marcas sterlingorum solvendorum eidem vel suo attornato, heredibus aut executoribus suis ad festum Omnium Sanctorum anno regni Regi Edwardi vicesimo septimo. Et nisi fecerit conced' ut supra" (Roll dated November 1298 to November 1299).

[54] *Munimenta*, II, 1, p. 134: "Rex majori et vicecomitibus Londoniarum, salutem. Praecipimus vobis, quod salvo et secure conduci faciatis Manekynum le Heaumer, Laurentium le Poleter, Robertum Clarel, Willelmum de la Chancelerie, Galfridum Lussher, Willelmum de Chalfhunte, Edmundum le Criour, Elyam de la Warderobe, servientem Johannis de Benstede, et Thomam Quartrosoz, quos nuper, per appellum Roberti Nurry, probatoris, in gaola nostro Gloucestriae detenti, capi fecimus et vobis liberari."

[55] Ibid., p. 134–5: "Ad brevia Willelmi Inge, Justiciarii gaolae Gloucestriae deliberandae assignati per Dominum Regem, Johannes de Armenters et Henricus de Fingrie, vicomites Londoniarum, anno Regis Edwardii, filii Regis Henrici, xxviii, tale dederunt responsum, ut subsequitur. Major respondet pro se, quod non habet custodiam alicujus prisonae in Londoniis, nec de prisonibus debet respondere, eo quod de eis non oneratur. Vicecomites respondent: Mannekynus le Heaumer et Laurentius le Poleter sunt liberi de civitate Londoniarum, et, ratione ejusdem libertatis, eos dimisimus per manucaptionem habendi eos ad primam assisam apud Turrim Londoniarum, vel coram Justiciariis ad Gaolam de Neugate deliberandam assignatis per dominum Regem, ad standum recto coram eisdem de roberiis et aliis eisdem impositis. Et ideo coram vobis eos ducere non possumus, sine offenso libertatis civitatis praedicte."

[56] *Calendar of London Trailbaston Trials and Commissions of 1305 and 1306*, ed. Ralph B. Pugh (London, 1975), p. 85 no. 161: "Manekin le Heaumer and Peter his brother are indicted *coram rege* for being common thieves, homicides, and robbers within the city of London and without and common vagrants by night, beating men against the peace, and because Manekin falsely

with Laurence le Puleter in a murder, but he had subsequently delivered Laurence over illegally to face the charges alone and then intimidated the witness, a fellow helmet-maker named Richard Deveneys, to prevent himself from being implicated! In addition to this case both Hermann and his brother Peter were charged with being "common thieves, homicides, and robbers within the city of London and without and common vagrants by night, beating men against the peace . . . and . . . common maintainers and supporters of ill-doers and of those who make assaults in the city." The brothers were obviously brutal ruffians, but they had important social connections and their expertise in arms and soldiering made them valuable men. They pleaded the king's pardon, and were supported in this by Henry de Lacy, earl of Lincoln, and others who were preparing for war. The next day the requested pardon was issued, and no doubt the brothers returned the favor through military service to the earl.[57]

By 1311 Hermann appears to have mended his ways, since we find him serving as the master to an apprentice named Clement Passemer.[58] Seven years later he was again in military service to the crown: this time in Scotland, where he and Roger de la Water commanded the London contingent of soldiers as the centurions.[59] For this he was publicly

procured the delivery of Laurence le Puleter who killed a man on Cornhill, and beat, wounded, and ill-treated Richard Deveneys, 'heaumer,' whereof Richard through fear of Manekin did not dare to complain, and because both are common maintainers and supporters of ill-doers and of those who make assaults (baterias) in the city. Taken they plead the king's pardon, dated Shene 2 Oct. 33 Edw. I [1305], granted at the request of Henry de Lacy, earl of Lincoln, and others going (cuncium) to arms. So quit quit."

[57] *CPR Edward I*, IV, p. 379: "Pardon, at the request of Henry de Lacy, earl of Lincoln, to Manekin le Heaumer of London and Peter his brother for trespasses against the peace whereof they were indicted before the king" (Sheen, Oct. 3, 1305) and repeated on p. 392: "Pardon, at the request of Henry de Lacy, earl of Lincoln, to Manekin le Heaumer of London and Peter his brother for all felonies which they are said to have committed and all trespasses against the peace whereof they are indicted before the king."

[58] *Calendar of Letter Books Preserved among the Archives of the Corporation of the City of London at the Guildhall. Volume IV: Letter Book D*, ed. Reginald Sharpe (London, 1902), p. 143: "The same day [May 6, 1311] came Clement, son of William Passemer, before the same [ante portam Latinam] and acknowledged himself apprentice of Manekin le Heaumer for a term of six years from Easter last. For his ingress 2s 6d."

[59] *Calendar of Letter Books Preserved among the Archives of the Corporation of the City of London at the Guildhall. Volume V: Letter Book E*, ed. Sharpe, p. 93: "Writ to the mayor, aldermen, and commonality of the city that they provide 500 foot-soldiers armed with 'aketons,' 'habergets,' 'bacinets,' and gauntlets (circotecis ferreis), to serve the King in Scotland for forty days. Witness the King at Notyngham, 12 Aug., 12 Edward II [1318]. Another writ to the same, enforcing obedience to the former writ. Dated at Notyngham 16 Aug., 12 Edward II." The mayor then summoned only 200 foot-soldiers to assist the king at the city's expense: "And be it known that the said soldiers were obtained in the following manner, viz., by every citizen of the more powerful and better class finding one armed soldier. Names of centurions Manekyn le Heaumer, Roger de la Water . . ." [a long list of citizens who found soldiers follows].

thanked by the king.[60] Hermann's expertise in weaponry was later called upon in a case of defaulted payment for a shipment of iron spearheads, the value of which he was asked to appraise.[61] He was also a witness to a grant of rents and properties in the following year[62] and was involved in a coroner's inquest in 1323.[63]

At some point early in his London career Hermann sold the family tenement (La Rouge Sale) for a rent to Richard de Bettoigne, a London merchant, and relocated appropriately enough on Cheapside Street in St. Mary Colchurch parish between Ironmonger Lane and Colchurch Lane (Cheap Ward).[64] He first rented a shop located on the south side of Cheapside facing St. Mary Colchurch from William de Bettone (Richard de Bettoigne's father?), who then quitclaimed the shop to Richard de Rokyngham, a goldsmith, in 1305. Hermann continued to lease the property and then sublet it to Richard de Bluntesham, a taverner. Hermann was later forced out of any renewal on his lease, however, because of a £6 debt which Rokyngham owed to the sublessor Bluntesham. As a result Rokyngham transferred the rental rights to Bluntesham in 1306 for two additional years after Hermann's lease ran out.[65] Hermann's association with Richard de Bettoigne continued for several years, and in 1322 Richard granted him a yearly rent for life from property across the street from the shop Hermann had originally sublet (this second property was located on Cheapside Street

---

[60] Ibid., pp. 98–9: "The King's letter of privy seal to the mayor, aldermen, and good men of the city, thanking them for the military aid sent towards Scotland under Roger de la Water and Manekyn le Heaumer, and commending the behaviour of officers and men. Dated at York, 24 Nov., 12 Edward II [1318]."

[61] Ibid., p. 132: "780 spearheads of iron and not gilt appraised by Mankin le Heaumer among others, for William de Croiden, 'cotiller,' who owed £30 to Adam de Masschebury. Thus these heads, along with other moveables belonging to William (e.g. knives, clubs) were sequestered. Dated June 24, 1320."

[62] Ibid., pp. 144–5.

[63] *Calendar of Coroner's Rolls of the City of London A.D. 1300–1378*, ed. Reginald Sharpe (London, 1913), pp. 75–6: "Mankin de [*sic*] Heaumer attached John Wynton' iunior on coroner's inquiry about a murder in the parish of St. Laurence in the Ward of Jewry (Nov. 30, 1323)."

[64] A 1338 transaction of Richard de Bettoigne indicates that he had purchased Hermann's family tenement in All Hallows Breadstreet at an earlier date: *Calendar of Letter Books Preserved among the Archives of the Corporation of the City of London at the Guildhall. Volume VI: Letter Book F*, ed. Reginald Sharpe (London, 1904), p. 20: "Indenture touching defeasance of a bond in the sum of £100 entered into by Richard de Bettoigne, conditioned on Nicholas Crane, merchant, enjoying peaceable possession of a certain tenement formerly belonging to Herman le Heaumer and demised by the said Richard to the said Nicholas, situate in the parish of All Hallows de Bredstrate. Deeds of conveyance of the said tenement by the said Herman to Richard, as well as by Henry le Waleys to Dame Gertrude de Colon' and to Peter and the aforesaid Herman her sons, are deposited with the said Nicholas. Dated Tuesday before the Feast of the Ascension [May 21], 12 Edward III [1338]."

[65] Derek Keene and Vanessa Harding, eds., *Historical Gazeteer of London before the Great Fire. Part 1: Cheapside* (Cambridge, 1987), pp. 102–3; location: 105/9E.

between the church of St. Thomas of Acre and Ironmonger Lane), as well as from Richard's properties in the parish of St. Antonin and the old family tenement in All Hallows Breadstreet (La Rouge Sale), which had earlier been sold to Richard by Hermann.[66] In this grant we have the only mention of Hermann's wife, who was named Margery (an Englishwomen). Hermann's relocation from Breadstreet to Ironmonger Lane was in keeping with his livelihood and became therefore the center of his business activities.

Hermann le Heaumer's life, what little we know of it, shows the remarkable level of integration that was possible for foreigners in London. He had, along with his mother and brother (no mention of his father appears), obtained citizenship, purchased property and rents in the city, and even established important social and political connections by virtue of expertise in weapon-making. Indeed by the late 1320s, after a remarkably violent youth, his role in legal proceedings as one of the "liberi de civitate Londoniarium" and his training of apprentices within the armorer's guild creates the same dilemma for us previously noted with regard to the English in Cologne – can we still consider him a Cologner or a true Englishman and Londoner? By the later adult years of his life it seems the latter would be more correct.

The same must be said for the second individual whose career can still be traced, Terricus Teutonicus (Dietrich the German) of Cologne. In fact, he was so integrated into English life that he eventually bore the surname Terricus de Stamford (or sometimes Terricus de Colonia burgensis de Stamfordia) based on his mercantile activities in the town and his extensive property holdings in Stamford as well as in six surrounding villages.[67] This Terricus first appears in the surviving sources in 1218 as a "cambiator Regis Angliae," and by 1234 he had obtained a large wine cellar between the Thames and the royal mint (Queenhithe Ward) with the aid of the then mayor Andreas Buckerel and sheriff Ralph Eswy. He was also involved in royal service – following the model of the Zudendorp family of Cologne – with shipments, credit, diplomatic missions, and as royal bailiff of the trade fair at Stamford. There he enjoyed citizenship and was the largest distributor of cloth at the fair.[68]

There existed, however, another Terricus Teutonicus in the early part of the thirteenth century whose potential relationship to Terricus

---

[66] Ibid., p. 170; location: 105/16.

[67] Natalie Fryde has recently published her Habilitationsschrift (Trier 1987) on Terricus of Cologne: *Ein mittelalterlicher deutscher Großunternehmer. Terricus Teutonicus de Colonia in England, 1217–1247*, Vierteljahrschrift für Sozial- und Wirtschaftsgeschichte, Beihefte 125 (Stuttgart, 1997). See also Fryde, "Hochfinanz und Landesgeschichte im Deutschen Hochmittelalter," *Blätter für deutsche Landesgeschichte* 125 (1989), p. 1 note 1.

[68] Fryde, "Arnold fitz Thedmar und die Entstehung der Grossen Deutschen Hanse," p. 34.

of Cologne remains obscure yet whose career was equally phenomenal. This Terricus Teutonicus appears in English royal documents as early as 1199.[69] He was awarded a rent of 13 marks in the manor of Colemore in Hampshire. In 1200 the rent was increased to £4 6s 8d[70] or alternatively to £4 and half a mark.[71]

The means of Terricus' entry into English society remains unclear, but his royal appointment as warden to the daughter of William de Mandeville in 1201 secured not only his social and political standing, but also assured him access to a sizeable amount of landed wealth throughout England.[72] Adding to his favor the king released him from the sizeable fee due for the estates.[73] Not only was he freed from feudal dues for estates in Wiltshire, but also for those in Devonshire,[74] Norfolk/Suffolk[75] and the honor of Gloucester.[76] Eventually, however, the scutage due on the honor of Gloucester was maintained.[77] Wiltshire estates were granted to a third party in 1203,[78] yet Terricus was the recipient of further royal largess in the previous year when he was given the wardship of the lands and heirs of William Peverel, who had recently died in Palestine.[79] In 1203 he received a

---

[69] *Pipe Roll 1 John*, PR NS, 10, p. 2: "Et Terrico Teutonico xiii marcas per idem breve in eadem villa [i.e. Colemore in Hampshire]. For more on the manor of Colemore and Terricus' possession of it see *The Victoria County History of Hampshire and the Isle of Wight*, ed. William Page (London, 1911; rpt. 1973), IV, p. 136.

[70] *Pipe Roll 2 John*, PR NS, 12, p. 189: "Et Terrico Teutonico iiii li. et vi s. et viii d. in Colmere de eodem termino."

[71] Ibid., p. 190: "Et Terrico Teutonico iiii li. et dim. m. in Colemere de eodem termino."

[72] *Pipe Roll 3 John*, PR NS, 14, p. 82: "Teodericus Teutonicus debet ccc marcas pro habenda filia Willelmi de Mandevill' cum tota hereditate sua in uxorem que eam contingit."

[73] Ibid., p. 83; *Pipe Roll 4 John*, PR NS, 15, pp. 125, 128.

[74] *Pipe Roll 4 John*, PR NS, 15, p. 253.

[75] Ibid., p. 117.   [76] Ibid., p. 283.

[77] *Pipe Roll 5 John*, PR NS, 16, p. 43: "Terricus Teutonicus debet ii marcas de feodo i militis." This is continued in *Pipe Roll 6 John*, PR NS, 18, p. 231; *Pipe Roll 7 John*, PR NS, 19, p. 104; *Pipe Roll 8 John*, PR NS, 20, p. 19; *Pipe Roll 9 John*, PR NS, 22, p. 220.

[78] *Pipe Roll 5 John*, PR NS, 16, p. 75: "Matheus filius Hereberti debet ccc marcas pro habenda terra que fuit Willelmi de Mandevill quam Rex concessit Terrico Teutonico per plegium Ade de Port de c m. et Tome Basset et Gileberti Basset et Willelmi de Bocland' et Henrico filio Geroldi et Willelmi de Porte Audomari de cc m.. Set Thomas Basset quietus est de plegii per breve Regis." Cf. *Rotuli Normannie*, ed. Hardy, I, p. 51: "Sciatis quod Matheus filius Herberti finem fecit nobiscum pro terra de Hurlund' cum pertinentiis que fuit Willelmi de Mandevill' quam Terricus Teutonicus habuit" (June 17, 1202). The following entry occurs during the year 1218 in the Exchequer King's Memoranda Rolls 2, membr. 6d: "Wiltsera. Matheus filius Herberti debet ccc marcas de fine pro terra sua habenda quam Terricus habuit in custodia. Videatur quo tempore [sic] fecerit finem. Distringatur." This was apparently an investigation into the actual payment of the fine paid in 1202.

[79] *Rotuli de liberate*, ed. Hardy, p. 30: "Liberate. Rex etc. G. fil. Petri etc. Sciatis quod dedimus et concessimus Terrico Teutonico vadletto nostro custodiam terre et heredis Willelmi Peverelli, qui in partibus Jerusalem obiit ut dicitur et ideo vobis mandamus quod eidem Terrico custodiam terre predicti Willelmi cum herede suo sine dilatione habere faciatis, et nobis mandetis quid hoc fuerit" (Rouen, April 7, 1202).

royal grant of land[80] and a letter of royal protection throughout England, the latter suggesting some commercial activities on his part.[81] These documents reveal his status at the royal court: he is called a valet, a vague term for a young male courtier. In the following year, as negotiations between King John and his nephew, the German King Otto IV, were renewed, Terricus' German ties were called upon and he was sent as royal envoy "in Alemanniam."[82]

During the years 1206 to 1214 Terricus also enjoyed, along with the count of Salisbury, an income from the manor of Amesbury in Wiltshire[83] and his name appears as a royal official in transactions as far afield as Dorset/Somerset,[84] Norfolk/Suffolk,[85] Oxfordshire,[86] and Hertfordshire[87] throughout the year 1218. His role as an ambassador to Germany continued to evolve during this period. He had contact with Saxons,[88] and was deeply involved in Otto IV's visit to England in 1207 (he borrowed 100 marks from the merchant Walter Sproke of Gent for such expenses).[89] The reward for this service came in the form of a prebend that had belonged to none other than Stephan

---

[80] *Rotuli Normannie*, ed. Hardy, I, p. 70: "Terra data. Rex etc. ballivo de Faleis etc. Precimipum tibi quod sine dilacione facias habere Terrico Teutonico valleto nostro Sanctum Serninum cum pertinentiis que fuit Com. Rob." (January 22, 1203).

[81] *Rotuli litterarum patentium*, ed. Hardy, I, p. 1: "Terricus Teutonicus habet litteras nostras patentes de simplici protectione in Anglia" (June 4, 1203).

[82] *Pipe Roll 6 John*, PR NS, 18, p. 212: "Et pro conducta unius navis ad opus Terrici Teutonici et sociorum suorum euntibus [*sic*] in Alemanniam c s. per breve Regis" and *Rotuli de liberate*, ed. Hardy, p. 77: "Liberate. Rex etc. vic. Kent etc. Inveni navem bonam et securam Terrico Teutonico et aliis nuntiis nostris, quos mittimus in Alemanniam ad eundem sine percipio et co. etc." (1204). On this occasion Terricus' letter of royal protection was renewed: *Rotuli litterarum patentium*, ed. Hardy, I, p. 46: "Theodericus Theutonicus habet litteras patentes de simplici protectione" (September 21, 1204).

[83] *Pipe Roll 8 John*, PR NS, 20, p. 181: "Et Willelmo comiti Saresb' et Terrico Teutonico l li. bl. in Ambresberia per breve Regis"; *Pipe Roll 9 John*, PR NS, 22, p. 201; *Pipe Roll 10 John*, PR NS, 23, p. 192; *Pipe Roll 11 John*, PR NS, 24, pp. 81–2; *Pipe Roll 12 John*, PR NS, 26, pp. 76–7; *Pipe Roll 13 John*, PR NS, 28, p. 163; *Pipe Roll 14 John*, PR NS, 30, p. 147; *Pipe Roll 16 John*, PR NS, 35, p. 39.

[84] *Pipe Roll 10 John*, PR NS, 23, p. 111; *Pipe Roll 13 John*, PR NS, 28, p. 227; *Pipe Roll 17 John*, PR NS, 37, p. 97; *Pipe Roll 2 Henry III*, PR NS, 39, p. 74; and even in *Pipe Roll 14 Henry III*, PR NS, 4, p. 48: "Terricus Teutonicus debet xl marcas de eiusdem" ("De pluribus prestitis factis tempore Regis Johannis" for Somerset and Dorset).

[85] *Pipe Roll 11 John*, PR NS, 24, p. 36.

[86] *Pipe Roll 14 John*, PR NS, 30, p. 21.

[87] *Pipe Roll 16 John*, PR NS, 35, p. 13; *Pipe Roll 2 Henry III*, PR NS, 39, p. 74.

[88] *Rotuli de oblatis et finibus in turri Londinensi asservati tempore Regis Johanni*, ed. Thomas Duffus Hardy (London, 1835), p. 341: "Somerset. Hyldebrandus de Saxon' dat iii austurcos pro habendis litteris domini Regi patentis quod salvo et secura eat et redeat per terras domini Regis cum mercandisis suis. Terricus Theotonicus est pleg." (1206).

[89] *Rotuli litterarum clausaurm*, ed. Hardy, I, p. 82: "Liberate de thesauro nostro Waltero Sprot centum marcas quas ipse commodavit Terrico Theutonico per litteras dilecti et fideli nostri G. filii Petri Com. Essex. patentes ad ducendum Regem Ottonem in Angliam" (May 6, 1207).

Langton.[90] In 1211 he was again sent to Otto IV,[91] and in the following year to Henry, duke of Saxony (brother of the emperor and nephew of King John).[92] He was once again well rewarded for this service by receiving the wardship over the honor of Berkhamstead in Wiltshire.[93] It is clear that Terricus Teutonicus rose in stature at the English court by virtue of his German connections and his diplomatic service on behalf of the Anglo-Welf cause in the early thirteenth century.

Terricus remained in close contact with the royal court, serving as guardian of Queen Isabel of Angoulême and the royal princess, Joanna, on a trip into Gloucester in December of 1214.[94] This commission lasted well into the next year; in fact the royal family even stayed at Berkhamsted, and Terricus was thereafter referred to as the queen's seneschal.[95] Indeed it appears that the queen and her entourage remained at Berkhamsted during John's dark days at Runnymede preceding the issuance of Magna Carta. Patent letters sent to Terricus

---

[90] Ibid., I, p. 96: "Rex Roberto de Veteri Ponte etc. Mandamus vobis quod faciatis habere Terrico Theutonico valleto nostro prebendam que fuit magistri Stephani de Langeton" (November 8, 1207). *The Red Book of the Exchequer*, ed. Hall, I, p. 155; II, p. 489; II, p. 523 shows Terricus still in possession of the Honor of Gloucester and estates in Wiltshire and Lincolnshire during the years 1210–12.

[91] *Rotuli de liberate*, ed. Hardy, p. 238: "Prestito. Eadem die ibidem Terrico Teutonico eunti in nuncium domini Regi ad dominum Imperatorem xl marcas per Regem" (1211).

[92] *Rotuli litterarum clausarum*, ed. Hardy, I, p. 121: "Rex Henrico Duci Saxon. etc. mittimus vobis dilectem et fidelem nostrum Terricum Teutonicum. Rogantes quatinus fidem habeatis hiis que vobis dicet ex parte nostra. Mittimus autem vobis quod Philipp, vadlettus noster, feodum vestrum de anno integro s. quingent. marc." (Nottingham, August 6, 1212). Obviously the duke was as concerned with his own English money fief as with political affairs related to his brother the emperor.

[93] Ibid., I, p. 154: "Rex vic. Wyltesir. etc. Scias quod commisimus Terrico Teuthonico honorem de Berchansted. custodiend. quamdiu nobis placuerit. Et ideo tibi precipimus quod eidem Terrico plenaram saisinam de terra de Wynterlane in baillia tua que pertinet ad predictum honorem sine dilacione habere faciat" (Woodstock, November 4, 1213) and *Rotuli litterarum patentium*, ed. Hardy, I, p. 105: "Rex omnibus militibus et libere tenentibus de honore de Berkhamsted. etc. Sciatis quod commisimus Terrico Teutonico honorem de Berkhansted. custod. quamdiu nobis placuerit. Et ideo vobis mandamus quod ei tamquam custodi vestro sitis intendentes" (Woodstock, November 3, 1213). Peter Mauley apparently still had a legitimate claim to the honor, and a settlement was reached in Terricus' favor in the following year: *Rotuli litterarum clausarum*, ed. Hardy, I, pp. 162 and 172.

[94] *Rotuli litterarum patentium*, ed. Hardy, I, p. 124: "Rex Theoderico Theutonico etc. Mandamus vobis quod sine dilatione eatis usque Glouc. cum domina Regina et ibi eam custodiatis in camera in qua Johanna filia nostra nutritia fuit donec aliud inde precepimus. Mandavimus enim vic. Glouc. per litteras nostras ei directas quas vobis mittimus quod ipsam recipiat et ei et vobis necessaria inveniat" (Corfe, December 3, 1214).

[95] *Rotuli litterarum clausarum*, ed. Hardy, I, p. 189: "Rex baronibus de Scaccario etc. Comp. Therrico Theutonico custum quod posuit per visum et testimonium leg. hominium in domina Regina et familie sua apud Berkhamested. a die Mart. proxima ante Cathedr. Sancti Petri anno regno nostro xvj et custum quod ponet in eadem quamdiu ipsam ibidem moram faciet" (Tower of London, March 3, 1215).

from King John during the period of May 28 to September 14, 1215 reveal that he was ordered to enforce some of the clauses in Magna Carta by redeeming a hostage and returning lands previously confiscated by the crown.[96] We also see for the first time Terricus' contemporary Walerandus Teutonicus, who was also by now in the service of the king. The next year Terricus was further rewarded for his loyalty to John during the barons' revolt. He is mentioned as the queen's bailiff and seneschal[97] and received the wardship of St. Augustine's abbey in Bristol.[98] He entertained the king at Berkhamstead in early 1216 and was reimbursed for these expenses. Here the king refers to Terricus as the constable of Berkhamsted.[99] Later that year Terricus returned to the queen's entourage, she being now a widow.[100]

Terricus successfully navigated the transition from the death of King John to the minority of Henry III. He even managed to regain the

[96] *Rotuli litterarum patentium*, ed. Hardy, I, p. 142: "Rex Walerando Teutonico salutem. Sciatis quod bene volumus quod Hugo de Boues habet unam clavem de terri castri Berchamsted. et unam clavem de forinseco baillio. Et in hujus etc vobis mittimus" (Reading, May 28, 1215); I, p. 143: "Rex Regine Angliae salutem. Mandamus vobis quod sine dilatione liberari feciatis latori presencium Rogerum fratrem constab. Cest. obsidem. Et in hujus etc vobis mittimus. Teste ut supra. Idem mandatum est Theoderico Teutonico de eodem deliberando" (Runnymede, June 19, 1215); I, p. 216: "Rex Terrico Theutonico etc. Precipimus tibi quod si Radulfus Cheindeduit fuit injuste et sine judicio dissasitus de redditu xl. solidorum in Netteleg. per nos vel per baillivos nostros ipsum Radulfum de eodem redditu sine dilatione et sine difficultate seisies" (Runnymede, June 27, 1215); I, p. 155: "Rex Theoderico Teutonico salutem. Mandamus vobis quod de denariis nostris qui sunt in custodia vestra liberatis latori presencium xxx. marcas deferendas Walerando Teutonico ad liberaciones faciendas servientibus qui cum eo sunt in castro nostro Berchamsted. Et in hujus etc. vobis mittimus" (September 14, 1215).

[97] PRO E368: Exchequer Lord Treasurer's Remembrancer Memoranda Rolls 1, membranes 4d and 6.

[98] *Rotuli litterarum patentium*, ed. Hardy, I, p. 166: "Rex omnibus militibus et libere tenentibus de abbatia Sancti Augustini Bristoll. etc. Sciatis quod commisimus dilecto et fideli nostro Theoderico Teutonico abbatiam Sancti Augustini Bristoll. cum pertinentiis suis custodiendam quamdiu nobis placuerit" (York, February 18, 1216).

[99] *Rotuli litterarum clausarum*, ed. Hardy, I, p. 258: "Rex baronibus suis de Scaccario etc. Comp. dilecto et fideli nostro Terrico Teutonico constabul. de Berkhamsted. xxi marcas et quinque solidos quos posuit in expensis hospicii nostri quod Berkhamsted. die Sabbati proximi ante Floridum Pasch. et die Dominica sequenti scilicet ipsa die Floridi Pasch. anno regni nostri xvij" (April 4, 1216). The following day the king received several ecclesiastical gifts from Terricus and Cishop Hugo of Bath: *Rotuli litterarum patentium*, ed. Hardy, I, p. 174; and upon the departure of the king the next day Terricus was ordered to give full seisin to the new abbot of St. Augustine's at Bristol: I, p. 174 (Reading, April 6, 1216).

[100] *Rotuli litterarum patentium*, ed. Hardy, I, p. 192: "Rex Petro de Maulay etc. Mandamus vobis quod mittatis ad nos usque Bristollum Philippum de Kyma prisonem nostrum qui est in custodia vestra in conductu domine Regine et Theoderici Teutonici. Et in hujus etc. vobis mittimus" (August 9, 1216).

manors of Ringwood and Priors Dean in Hampshire[101] and a royal confirmation of all his holdings before the barons' revolt.[102] After taking a pilgrimage in 1221 to parts unknown[103] he remained in faithful service to the new king's regents until his death in 1223.[104] His office as constable of Berkhamsted was then transferred into the hands of his successor and countryman, Walerandus Teutonicus,[105] in spite of the fact that the justiciar, Hubert de Burgh, attempted to take the inheritance for himself.[106] Such was the strikingly successful career of this Terricus Teutonicus.

He obviously cannot be the same man as Terricus Teutonicus of Cologne/Stamford, as the dating of their respective deaths indicates. The question remains whether they were somehow related, perhaps father and son, yet too much can be made out of similar surnames. There are numerous men named Terricus throughout English and German sources, therefore fashioning a family out of this disparate collection of characters requires too much reliance on speculation rather than on any hard evidence.

This is a serious drawback when attempting to complete Terricus Teutonicus of Cologne/Stamford's career. Therefore we shall consider the evidence of his career using only those references that clearly

---

[101] *Rotuli litterarum clausarum*, ed. Hardy, I, p. 307: "Rex Willelmo Marescallo junioris salutem. Mandamus vobis quod sine dilatione plenam saisinam habere faciatis dilecto et fideli nostro Therrico Theutonico de manerio de Ringwode cum pertinentiis quod fuit Johelis de Meinill. quod dominus Rex Johannes pater noster ei dedit" (April 20, 1217). This grant was further confirmed on March 27, 1222 (I, p. 491): "Mandatum est vic. Sudhamt. quod talem saisinam habere faciat Terrico Teutonico de terra sua in Rincwud. qualem inde habuit ante preceptum quod dominus Rex ei fecit de dominicis et escaetis in man. domini R. capiendis unde dissaisitus fuit occasione ejusdem precepit. Et si inde ceperit postquam terram illam in manum domini R. cepit. Id ei sine dilatione reddi faciat" (Tower of London). Terricus had some difficulty maintaining seisin of Ringwood amid the claims of William Marshal the younger (later second Earl of Pembroke): see *The Victoria County History of Hampshire and the Isle of Wight*, ed. Page, IV, p. 607.

[102] *Rotuli litterarum clausarum*, ed. Hardy, I, p. 316: "Rex Henrico filio Com. salutem. Mandamus vobis quod sine dilatione habere faciatis dilecto et fideli nostro Terrico Theutonico talem saisinam qualem habuit in initio gwerre" (July 24, 1217).

[103] PRO E159: Exchequer King's Remembrancer Memoranda Rolls 4, membrane 8: "Cornubia. Rex vicecomiti. Scias quod dedimus Therico Theutonico ad peregrinacionem suam faciendam illas xii marcas et iii solidos et viii denarios qui asisi sunt super terram suam in comitatu Cornubie de fine quingentarum marcarum quas illi de comitatu Cornubie nobis debeant pro habenda libera eleccione vicecomitis sui. Per breve de magno sigillo." Here we learn that Terricus also held lands in Cornwall.

[104] PRO E368: Exchequer Lord Treasurer's Remembrancer Memoranda Rolls 3, membrane 1d; 3, membrane 3 (2) (dated 1221) and 4, membrane 1; 4, membrane 13 (1222). PRO E159: Exchequer King's Remembrancer Memoranda Rolls 5, membrane 14 (dated 1222).

[105] *Rotuli litterarum clausarum*, ed. Hardy, I, p. 534 (February 9, 1223); I, p. 541 (April 11, 1223); I, p. 555 (July 15, 1223).

[106] *Diplomatic Documents*, ed. Chaplais, pp. 88–9 nos. 128–9.

mention him with either the surname "de Colonia" or "de Stamford." This Terricus was definitely a money-changer (*cambiator*) at the royal mint in London in the year 1217,[107] a skill typical of Cologners, as we have already seen. He appeared at the *Curia Regis* in 1224 charging that Robert de Scaleford, after granting him a carucate of land in Watheringate (Northampton), subsequently ignored the agreement, destroyed a garden and mowed the meadow of the carucate to the cost of ten shillings.[108] Terricus of Cologne and his wife Beatrice produced two children. Their son Walter entered the priesthood and was assigned a prebend in the archdeaconry of Buckingham by Bishop Hugh of Lincoln in 1231, while their daughter Juliana married William Tikencote, a member of a leading Stamford family.[109] The reference to Walter's prebend informs us that Terricus also held citizenship rights in the city of London.

Terricus de Stamford was active in the ports of Boston and Lynn during the 1220s as an exporter of wool. He enjoyed royal protection for this commerce, and in recompense received a royal request in 1236 (addressed to "dilecto et fideli suo Therrico theutonico") for a loan of 40 marks in order to purchase horses at the Stamford market.[110]

We get the first mention of his economic activities in Stamford when he, along with other "*burgenses*" of the town, sent representatives before the *Curia Regis* to enter a plea against the prior of Durham in 1233.[111] The prior had appealed a case involving merchandise of the merchants of Stamford to the clerical courts in the hope of getting a better result,

---

[107] *Pipe Roll 17 John, Praestita Roll 14–18 John*, PR NS, 37, p. 20: "Compotus Cambii Lond. . . . Et in stipendiis et victu (Tercici) Terrici de Colonia cambiatoris ii marcas et dimidietatem."

[108] *Curia Regis Rolls*, XI, p. 354 no. 1777: "Northampton. Terricus de Colonia petit versus Robertum de Scaleford' quod warantizet ei i carucatam terre cum pertinenciis in Watheringhet', quam tenet etc. et unde cartam suam etc. et unde idem Terricus dicit quod contra cartam illam fregit gardinum suum et pratum suum falkavit etc., per quod dampnum habet ad valenciam x solidorum etc. Et Robertus venit et cognoscit cartam. Dies datus est eis a die sancti Michaelis in xv dies prece parcium."

[109] *Rotuli Hugonis de Welles episcopi Lincolniensis (A.D. MCCIX–MCCXXXV)*, The Canterbury and York Society Series, 3 (London, 1907–9), II, p. 92: "Tingherst. Walterus filius Terici de Colonia, civis Londoniensis, cui dominus episcopus ecclesiam de Tingeherst contulit, ad eandem ecclesiam admissus est, et in ea canonice persona institutus. Et mandatum est Matheo archidiacono Buckinghamiensi ut, etc." For Beatrice and Juliana see Fryde, *Ein mittelalterlicher deutscher Großunternehmer*, p. 80.

[110] *Rotuli litterarum clausarum*, ed. Hardy, I, pp. 559, 603, II, p. 60; *CPR Henry III*, I, p. 496; *CCLR*, I, p. 196; *CPR Henry III*, III, p. 9.

[111] *Curia Regis Rolls*, XV, p. 15 no. 65: "Ebor. Richardus Pecke et Therricus de Colonia et alii burgenses de Estaunford' per attornatos suos optulerunt se quarto die versus priorem Dunholm' de placito quare secutus est placitum in curia Christianitatis de catallis ipsorum que non sunt de testamento vel matrimonio contra prohibitionem etc.: et ipse non venit etc.; et prior attachiatus fuit per Walterum filium Thome et Henricum prepositum. Et ideo ponatur per meliores plegios quod sit a die Pasche in v septimanas; et primi etc."

and the merchants were seeking to reverse this turn of events. Terricus himself was brought before the royal court by the bishop of Bath as a result of a defaulted payment for wool in 1242.[112] These two court appearances confirm his involvement in the wool-cloth trade at Stamford.

Evidence for Terricus of Cologne's possession of a wine cellar in the parish of St. Peter the Little along the Thames river, a natural location for the import of Rhine wine from the environs of Cologne, comes from the London Eyre of 1244, where Terricus' warrant to hold this cellar was questioned. The cellar was originally a royal possession for the storage of wine, but Richard I had given the cellar to Robert le Herre of Saxony for a yearly rent of either a mark or a helmet.[113] Robert had subsequently enfeoffed Terricus with the cellar, but it was argued that any claim to the cellar should be forfeited since neither Robert nor Terricus had ever paid the aforesaid rent. After an appeal Terricus was apparently able to prove his rightful claim to the cellar and thus to retain it. Such a result before the royal court may suggest that Terricus had influential contacts in the royal entourage as in the cases of Hermann le Heaumer and Terricus Teutonicus. Terricus spent much time traveling

---

[112] Ibid., XVI, p. 5 no. 11: "Sumerset. Colonia. Terricus de Colonia venit in curiam domini Regis et cognovit quod emit a domino G. Bathoniensi episcopo totam ianuam suam de hac prima tonsione, scilicet quemlibet saccum lane pro x marcis, quotquot ibi fuerint etc. und reddidit ei per manibus arrarum nomine xxx marcas; et reddet ei ad hoc instans festum Pentechostes L marcas et totum residuum ad festum sancti Michaelis proximo sequens. Et ad solutionem istam faciendam sine fraude et dolo et secundum quod predictum est obligat se et omnia sua, tam mobilia et immobilia que in presenti habet et habiturus est . . . ubicumque fuerint, renuntiando privilegio fore, regie prohibitioni et omni juris remedio" (July 1242).

[113] *The London Eyre of 1244*, ed. Chew and Weinbaum, p. 89 no. 217: "Rex Ricardus dedit Roberto le Herre quoddam celarium in parochia Sancti [Petri] Parvi in quo idem dominus Rex solebat vina sua reponere, tendendum per servicium i marce vel i galee ad scaccarium per annum. Terricus de Staunford tenet modo celarium illud, nescitur quo warranto. Capiatur in manum domini Regis donec idem Terricus etc. Et super hoc Terricus profert cartam domini Regis Johannis que testatur quod idem dominus Rex dedit concessit et carta sua confirmavit Roberto le Herre de Saxonia quamdam domum cum pertinenciis in Londoniis in qua vina sua solebant reponi, tenendum ei et heredibus suis etc. reddendo inde annuatim unam galeam etc. Et profert aliam cartam per quam idem Robertus eum foeffavit. Et ideo inde loquendum coram domino Rege. Et dictum est vicecomiti quod interim permittat ipsum habere seysinam suam. Et habent etc. Et quia convictum est quod predictus Robertus toto tempore suo nichil solvit de predicta firma nec Terricus similiter, ideo capiantur pro arreragiis etc." and 119 no. 293: "Item quedam terra est in parochia Sancti Petri Parvi super Thamisiam in qua quondam fuit celarium domini Regis [ad] reponenda vina sua, quam vero terram dominus Rex dedit Roberto Here fabro unde dominus Rex debet habere per annum unum galeam de auratam vel . i marcam argenti; modo autem eam tenet Terricus Colonensis de Stanford qui postea tulit cartam domini Regis et habuit seisinam suam. Respice in dorso." Fryde's rendering of "galea" (helmet) as a "galeta" (tankard) in the shape of a "galley" ship seems too creative an alternative to a helmet (see Fryde, *Ein mittelalterlicher deutscher Großunternehmer*, 136). Cologners were well known for their skill in fashioning weaponry, and the one-mark alternative payment was even more in the custom of merchants.

between Stamford and London, the two poles of his economic activity and communities where he enjoyed citizenship. He appears as a witness to deeds issued in both locations,[114] and also paid a tallage along with other citizens of London in 1230.[115]

Fryde indicates that Terricus of Cologne died in 1247, and apparently he died a poor man with many debts. During the years 1249 to 1255 the lands and property of Terricus were frozen by distraint in the royal court, with much of it escheated into the hands of the crown.[116] Half of a messuage in Stamford, apparently held by Terricus of a Jew named Cok, was taken from his wife Beatrice because it fell under the royal right of escheat over the chattels of Jews deceased without legal heirs. The king granted this messuage to Nicholas, the messenger of Richard

---

[114] *A Descriptive Catalogue of Ancient Deeds in the Public Records Office* (London, 1890–1915), II, p. 395 no. B3361: "[N'hamp?] Sale by Richard Pek of Stanford, with the consent of Alice his wife, to Master Alexander son of Richard son of Seluf de Stanford, of his croft under Smithill with a croft without the gate of Scoftegate reaching to Smethell, for 37 marks. Witnesses: – Walter de Tikote, Terric de Colonia, and others." *Historical Manuscripts Commission Report of Wells Cathedral* (London, 1885), p. 206: "Charter of the Hospital of S. Bartholomew granting to Bp. Josceline a rent of 10s., which he used to pay on a tenement in s. Clements de Denissemanschirche on the south side of the Church toward the Thames. Test. Teric de Colonia; Stephan de la Strande; Richard fil. Edwardi, etc."; CLRO Bridgehouse Deeds A4: "Universis sancte matris ecclesie filiis presens scriptum inspecturis vel audituris custodes pontis Londoniarum salutem in Domino. Noverit universitas vestra quod nos dedimus et concessimus Nicholao Bat et heredibus suis vel suis assignatis quoddam gardinum quod situm est in parochia sancti Botulphi extra portam de Bischoppesgate tendendum et habendum de nobis et successoribus nostris libere, quiete, bene in pace reddendo inde nobis annuatim et successoribus nostris ad quatuor anni terminos iii solidi de domo Godwini celarii que est in parochia beate Marie de Abecherche videlicet ad natale xii denarii ad Pasche xii denarii ad festum sancti Johannis Baptiste xii denarii ad festum sancti Mikaelis xii denarii et domino episcopo Lond' xii denarii per omnibus serviciis demandis et querelis. Nos autem predicti custodes warantizabimus predicto N. Bat et heredibus suis vel suis assignatis predictum Gardinum cum pertinentiis suis contra omnes homines et feminas. Et quia volumus et hec donatio et concessio firma sit et stabilis preserveretur presens scriptum sigillorum virorum appositione roboravimus. Hiis testibus Mikaele Thom., Roberto de Cornelle, Roberto de Basinges, Johanne filio Pain, Terrico de Colonia et multis aliis."

[115] *Pipe Roll 14 Henry III*, PR NS, 4, p. 107: "Terricus de Colon' reddidit compotum de x li. de eodem" ("De tallagio civitatis London").

[116] PRO E368: Lord Treasurer's Remembrancer Rolls 23, membrane 6: "London. Distress of Terric de Colonia and others; money received from the issues of the mint (1249)," 24, membr. 7: "London. Money due from tenants of the lands of Terric de Colonia and others (1250)," 26, membrane 8d: "Surrey. The like [distress of heirs] against Terric de Colonia (1253)," 26, membrane 10d: "London. Distress of tenants of lands late of Terric de Colonia; issues of the mint (1253)," *CCLR Henry III*, VII, p. 451: "Rex vicecomiti Linc' salutem. Precipe Willelmo de Tikincote et Juliane uxori ejus quod reddant nobis medietatem unius mesuagii cum pertinenciis quod fuit Cok Judei in Stanford. Precipe Beatrici que fuit uxor Terrici de Colonia quod reddat nobis aliam medietatem ejusdem mesuagii cum pertinenciis in eadem villa, quod mesuagium debet esse in manu Regis tanquam escaeta de terris Judeorum et nis fecerint, summone eos quod sint coram nobis a die Pasche in xv dies etc. Per regem" (February 17–22, 1253).

of Cornwall, in 1255.[117] All in all not a glorious ending to the career of Terricus of Cologne, but a fascinating career it was for a citizen of no less than three different cities.

The final expatriate Cologner to be considered here was the most renowned of all, and was known by the name Arnold fitz Tedmar. His fame rests primarily on a chronicle of the city of London which he wrote, covering the period 1188 to 1274, and which has proven to be a valuable source for the events not only in London but also in England at large during this period.[118] Within the chronicle's early chapters he inserted a brief history of his own family, and also included himself in the chronicle's subsequent narrative. From this we learn of his Cologne origins and his rise to the aldermanship of a London ward. Arnold begins the family history with his grandparents: Cologne citizens named Arnold "de Grevingge" (perhaps Groningen?) and Ode. Modeling Abraham and Sarah in the Old Testament, they were pious and devout but were unable to conceive children. Hearing, however, of the great miracles wrought at the shrine of Thomas Becket at Canterbury, they set out on a pilgrimage to obtain the saint's assistance. At the tomb they swore a vow that if the child should be a male they would call him Thomas in honor of the martyr and commit him to Christ Church abbey as a monk. Unwilling to return to Cologne before visiting London, "de qua civitate tam nobili et famosa famam audierant in terra sua,"[119] they settled there and promptly conceived and delivered a son named Thomas. Ode soon conceived again and so a return to Cologne was further delayed. This time she bore a daughter named Juliana.

They then received news that Ode's mother had died in Cologne during their sojourn in England, and the couple decided to remain in London since no strong familial ties remained for them now in Cologne. Thomas, however, did not become the promised monk at Canterbury, but rather joined Richard the Lionheart and Philip of France on Crusade and died subsequently at Constantinople. Juliana, upon reaching marrying age, met a German merchant of Bremen

---

[117] *CCHR*, I, p. 451: "Gift to Nicholas, the messenger of Richard, earl of Cornwall, of all the houses in Stamford which the king deraigned in his court against William de Tykencot and Juliana his wife and Beatrice late the wife of Terricus de Colonia, as the king's escheat of the chattels late of Cok de Stamford, a Jew, to be held by the said Nicholas, his heirs and assigns, by the service due thence to the lords of the fee" (Westminster, October 18, 1255).

[118] Arnold fitz Tedmar, *De antiquis legibus liber. Cronica maiorum et vicecomitum londoniarum*, ed. Thomas Stapleton, Camden Society, 34 (London, 1846); and *Chronicles of the Mayors and Sheriffs of London (A.D. 1188–1274)*, ed. Henry Thomas Riley (London, 1863).

[119] Tedmar, *De antiquis legibus liber*, p. 238.

named Tedmar, to whom she was married and bore eleven children, six daughters and five sons. Although two daughters died before reaching adulthood, the other four were married into important London families: their husbands were no less than Ralph Eswy (sheriff 1234, 1239; chamberlain 1236; mayor 1241–43; royal sequesterer of London 1244), Walter of Winchester (sheriff 1228–9), John Gisors (sheriff 1240, 1245; chamberlain 1246; mayor 1246, 1258–9; royal butler 1236, 1253–6), and William fitz Richard (sheriff 1250; mayor 1257, 1259–60; bailiff 1265; royal sequesterer of London 1265). Ralph Eswy was the sheriff who aided Terricus de Colonia/Stamford in purchasing a large wine cellar; this reveals yet another Londoner–Cologner business network. From these marriages came male offspring who continued to fill such positions in the city (for example, Walter of Winchester's son Galfried was sheriff in 1248). The dowries required for such marriages say much about the wealth that Tedmar of Bremen had accumulated during his years of trade in England. It is also very likely that Tedmar and Juliana had met through the guildhall in London.

Of the five sons born to them, one died in childhood and three more around the age of twenty-four. The only surviving son was Arnold, born on August 9, 1201.[120] As sole male heir, Arnold came into possession of the family inheritance after his father's death. The London property gathered by Tedmar of Bremen was sizeable and located in a most important location – next to the Cologne guildhall. The extensive property, located in Dowgate ward between Windgoose Lane and Haywharf Lane to the west and east respectively and reaching the Thames wharves to the south, lay some 30 meters to the east of the guildhall and was separated from it by two other properties owned by Englishmen.[121] The entire property was almost twice the size of the guildhall, with the Thames Street frontage having a gate and five shops. Behind the shops were several cellars used as taverns. The main house lay behind this complex with its kitchen abutting Windgoose Lane. This large complex of buildings was later joined to the Cologne guildhall and became the Hanseatic Steelyard. Tedmar of Bremen was an extremely wealthy man who purchased prime real estate, and Arnold's continued use of the property speaks for the maintenance of the family's exceptionally large trading activities, no doubt with contacts in Cologne.

At some unspecified point in his career Arnold fitz Tedmar was

---

[120] In a rather self-promoting manner Arnold includes a dream-vision of his mother concerning him which preceded his birth: ibid., p. 239.

[121] Keene, "New discoveries at the Hanseatic Steelyard in London," pp. 23–4 with map on page 17.

elected alderman of a London ward.[122] Which one is never stated explicitly in the documents and so a reconstruction of the evidence is required in order to identify it.[123] An entry in the Bridgehouse Records provides us with an answer to this question.[124] Here Arnold fitz Tedmar appears among the witnesses to a 1261–2 grant of a rent located in the parish of St. Mary at Hill with Billingsgate to its immediate east. St. Mary at Hill parish was located within Billingsgate ward, and this rent was especially located near Billingsgate itself. Furthermore, Arnold is referred to in the list of witnesses as the "alderman of the ward." Hence the ward over which Arnold presided was Billingsgate ward.[125] A further confirmation of this can be found in another witness list dated *c.* 1243.[126] Here Arnold appears as "Ernald Tedmar, alderman of the ward" among the witnesses to a grant by William le Melkere, citizen of London, to the prior and the convent of Holy Trinity, London of his main dwelling in the parish of St. George Eastcheap. St. George Eastcheap was located within Billingsgate ward. In addition to his aldermanship Arnold held some sort of office in the city as custodian of the "chest of the citizens of London" wherein the valuable documents

---

122 He appears as alderman as early as *c.* 1243: *A Descriptive Catalogue of Ancient Deeds in the Public Records Office*, I, p. 205 no. A1744.

123 Tedmar, *De antiquis legibus liber*, p. viii: "That Fitz-Thedmar was an Alderman of London, we learn from several passages already alluded to [i.e. in the Chronicle]; but over which of the City Wards he presided, appears to be now unknown."

124 CLRO Bridgehouse Records Large Register: Card Calendar no. 148 (fo. 546 no. 550): "Grant by Emma, daughter and heiress of Ralph Sperling to Domino John de Breinford, chaplain of St. Paul's of 2 m. annual rent from the Quay and tenement of John Sperling in the parish of St. Mary de la Hulle, situated between Billingsgate on the E. and the lands which the abbot and convent of Waltham on the W., the which rent the aforesaid John Sperling gave to the said Ralph for the quit claim of the advowson of the church of St. Andrew Huberd; for the annual render of 4 d. to the grantor. Witnesses: Sir Thomas filius Thomas, Philip le Taillur and Richard de Walbroke, sheriffs, Arnald Thedmar, alderman of the ward, John Horn and many others" (1261–2). Arnold appears again as "alderman of the ward" in the witness list for the sale of this rent by John de Breinford to Richard de Karlton in 1269–70 (CLRO Bridgehouse Records Large Register: Card Calendar 149 [fo. 547 no. 551]) and for the subsequent grant of the rent by Richard de Karlton to the wardens of the Bridgehouse in 1271–2 (CLRO Bridgehouse Records Large Register: Card Calendar 150 [fo. 548 no. 552]).

125 Fryde, "Arnold fitz Thedmar und die Entstehung der Grossen Deutschen Hanse," p. 35 independently came to the same conclusion by comparing the election of Arnold's successor as alderman (CLRO Hustings Common Pleas Roll 2, membrane 9: "Homines de warda que fuit Arnoldi Thedmari eligerunt Wolmarum de Essex in Aldermannum suum et admissus est" [1274]) with the appearance of Wolmar of Essex in PRO Tax Roll E. 179/144/2 for the year 1295: "de warda Wolmari de Essex Billingsgate." She claims, "Nach Arnolds Ward suchte die deutsche wie die englische Forschung lange jedoch vergeblich," yet Alfred Beaven, *The Aldermen of the City of London* (London, 1908–13) had already identified Arnold's ward as Billingsgate (I, pp. 368, 373; II, p. 159). Nicholas Orme, "Lay literacy in England, 1100–1300," in *England and Germany in the High Middle Ages*, ed. Alfred Haverkamp and Hanna Vollrath (Oxford, 1996), p. 53 incorrectly identifies Arnold Fitz-Tedmar as alderman of Bridge Ward.

126 *A Descriptive Catalogue of Ancient Deeds in the Public Records Office*, I, p. 205 no. A1744.

of the city's archive were stored.[127] No doubt this was a rich source of material for his chronicle as well as a responsibility that drew him into hazardous involvement in the baronial revolt against Henry III.

Both his duties as alderman of Billingsgate ward and his personal ties with the leading families of London (by virtue of his sisters' marriages) drew him into the politics of both city and kingdom.[128] He was a member of the small yet wealthy party in London that supported Henry III against Simon de Montfort and the barons. As a result Arnold was disgraced by a 1258 inquisition into alleged abuses by the mayor and aldermen of London, which resulted in the revocation of his aldermanship. Indeed he and his fellow compatriots were forbidden to sell any property in the city; this may have been done to forestall efforts on the part of Arnold and his colleagues to lessen the calculation of their tallages due, which were under investigation.[129] He was reinstated the following year after proving his innocence – a fact he repeats emphatically in the chronicle.[130] It is worth noting that his brother-in-law William fitz Richard was mayor in 1259, the year in which Arnold fitz Tedmar was restored as alderman. He and his kin remained supportive of the royalist cause, and thus in 1265 he found himself, along with his brothers-in-law John Gisors and William fitz Richard, his nephew Galfried of Winchester, and others, marked for proscription and death by the mayor Thomas fitz Thomas and the constable Thomas de Piwelesdon. They were only saved by the royal victory at Evesham.[131]

A clear sign that Arnold and the royalist party had returned to a leading position in the city appears in Henry III's issuance of letters of safe conduct for Arnold and other aldermen so that they could travel to Windsor and there treat with the king concerning matters involving

---

[127] Tedmar, *De antiquis legibus liber*, p. 253: "In hoc folio continentur que carte fuerunt in scrinio civium anno Domini MCC septuagesimo, quod scrinium fuit tunc temporis in custodia Arnaldi Thedmari sub clavibus Roberti de Corenhelle et Roberti de Rikesle et Johannis Addrian Draparii" (1270).

[128] "Ernulph" son of Tedmar along with several notables of the city witnessed a royal confirmation charter for example: see *CCHR*, I, pp. 418–19.

[129] *CCR Henry III*, X, p. 298: "Quia rex intellexit quod Radulfus Hardel, Nicholaus filius Jocelini, Nicholaus Bat, Johannes le Mynur, Mathias Bokerel, Henricus Walemund, Johannes Tolusan et Arnulphus Thedmar proponunt vendere domos et tenementa sua que habent in civitate Lond', mandatum est majori et vicecomitibus Lond' quod eos hoc facere nullatenus permittant, ei, si quas domos vel tenementa sua jam vendiderint, ea sine dilacione capiant in manum Regis et salvo teneant donec Rex aliud inde preceperit" (Westminster, March 5, 1258). If Arnold was attempting to lessen his tallage valuation this would cast doubt on his claim to innocence concerning any unpaid tallages.

[130] Tedmar, *De antiquis legibus liber*, pp. 30–7, 43.   [131] Ibid., pp. 114–15.

London.[132] That they were to bring their entire households as well suggests that this was an important conference. It was held at great expense and must have lasted some time. In the following year Arnold and forty-eight other citizens of London were appointed by the king as "keepers and protectors" of the Jews for two years in order to provide them with protection after the "losses and enormities" suffered by the Jews during the recent "time of the disturbance in the realm" – a reference to the Montfortian regime and its defeat.[133] In 1273 we find Arnold safely on the side of Edward I in the conflict between the city leaders and the former mayor Walter Hervey.[134] He had good reason to oppose Hervey, who when mayor attempted to extort excessive tallages from him and was only defeated by royal writ.[135]

Although Arnold never makes mention of it, his activities in London went beyond serving as the alderman of Billingsgate ward and managing an apparently large business in trade: he was also the alderman of the Germans in the London guildhall. In this capacity he represented the German merchants as a liaison between them and the city government. He was perfectly placed to do this, since he maintained the trading ties of his father with Germany and had forged his own political standing as a citizen and municipal magistrate in London. Evidence of his service as the alderman of the Germans appears in two sources. The first comes from the year 1251, when he appears as a witness to the settlement between the brothers Nicholas and Walter Adrian and the merchants from Lübeck.[136] The Lübeckers, frustrated by Danish interference in their Baltic trade, had attacked Copenhagen, and in the process of demolishing Danish wares they also destroyed the goods of the brothers Adrian, who were English merchants. Here Arnold is called "Arnaldo Thedmar, aldermanno Teutonicorum." The second source appears nine years later, when William son of William Reyners sold a yearly income of 2 shillings from a piece of land lying to the east of the

---

[132] *CPR Henry III*, v, p. 457: "Safe conduct, until Tuesday next and for the whole of that day, for Stephen Bokerel, John Adrian, Robert de Cornehull, Arnulf de Tedmar, Reynold de Suff' and William son of Richard [i.e. Arnold's brother-in-law], and his own household which each will bring with him, coming to Windsor to treat with the king on matters touching on the city of London" (Windsor, September 27, 1265). The Battle of Evesham had just occurred on August 4, 1265.

[133] *CPR Henry III*, v, p. 577 (dated 1266).

[134] Tedmar, *De antiquis legibus liber*, pp. 164–6.

[135] Ibid., pp. 239–42. Henry le Waleys, the next mayor, continued this attempt to extract further payments from Arnold, but was again defeated by a royal writ of Edward I.

[136] *HUB*, I, p. 132 no. 405; *LUB*, I, p. no. 177 (dated July 31, 1251).

Cologne guildhall for 2 marks sterling.[137] He sold it to "Arnulpho filio
Thedmari aldermanno mercatorum Allemanie in Angliam veniencium
et eisdem mercatoribus." The German merchants were recovering a
rent from property they already held in the environs of the guildhall and
Arnold, as the alderman of the Germans, served as the broker for this
transaction. It is rather curious that Arnold never mentions any of his
activities as alderman of the Germans, since it was an important part of
both his political and business careers.

Throughout the years 1243 to 1272 Arnold fitz Tedmar appears in
several witness lists[138] and was still active in business as late as June
1274.[139] At this point he is listed with many other London citizens who
acknowledged that they owed 1,200 marks to Lucasius Natal' and
Opizo Malaspine, Italian merchants of Lucca, all of whom promised to
have a levy taken from their lands and chattels in the city of London
should they default on the loan. Shortly thereafter he apparently died,
because his successor Wolmar of Essex was elected as alderman of
Billingsgate ward.[140] Arnold's estate was then divided between his wife
(perhaps named Dionysia), his son John Tedmar, his brother-in-law
Stephen Eswy, and the monks of Bermondsey.[141] John Tedmar appears
in several documents from the period 1302 to 1313 and was married to
Cristina de Kancia.[142]

Nothing more can be said with certainty about the remarkable life of

[137] *HUB*, I, pp. 190–1 no. 540; Lappenberg, *Urkundliche Geschichte des Hansischen Stahlhofes zu London*, p. 13 no. 28: "Sciant presentes et futuri, quod ego Wilhelmus filius Wilhelmi Reyneri quietas clamavi et presenti carta mea confirmavi Arnulpho filio Thedmari aldermanno mercatorum Allemanie in Angliam veniencium et eisdem mercatoribus duas solidatas annui et quieti redditus, quas per annum recipere solebam de quadam particula terre cum pertinenciis in latere orientali gildhallie eorum, quam habent Londonie in parrochia omnium sanctorum . . . Pro hac autem remissione, quieta clamacione et presentis carte mee confirmacione dedit mihi prenotatus Arnulphus duas marcas sterlingorum."
[138] In addition to those already mentioned there are the following: *Cartulary of St. Bartholomew's Hospital*, ed. J. M. Kerling (London, 1973), p. 62 no. 563 (dated 1250–1) where a Thomas de Colonia also appears, p. 91 no. 902 (dated 1267), and p. 92 no. 904 (dated 1271); CLRO Bridgehouse Deeds C 11 (dated 1264); *A Descriptive Catalogue of Ancient Deeds in the Public Records Office*, p. 4: A7301 (dated Michaelmas 1270).
[139] *CCR Edward I*, I, p. 123 (dated Westminster, June 11, 1274).
[140] CLRO Hustings Common Pleas Roll 2, membrane 9.
[141] Tedmar, *De antiquis legibus liber*, pp. ix–x.
[142] *Cartulary of St. Bartholomew's Hospital*, ed. Kerling, p. 92 no. 911 (dated 1302–3); CLRO Hustings Rolls 33 (88) (dated 1305); *Calendar of Early Mayor's Court Rolls (A.D. 1298–1307)*, ed. A. H. Thomas (Cambridge, 1924), p. 173 (dated April 2, 1305) and pp. 250–1 (dated October 6, 1306); CLRO Bridgehouse Deeds F9 (dated 1305–6), F68 (dated 1311), and F17 (dated 1312–13). A William Tedmar appears in the 1292 London subsidy roll, and may well be a second son: see Eilert Ekwall, ed., *Two Early London Subsidy Rolls*, Skrifter Utgivna Av Kungl. Humanistika Vetenskapssamfundet I Lund, 48 (Lund, 1951), p. 165.

Arnold fitz Tedmar,[143] except to conclude that it is difficult to overstate the importance of his multi-faceted career as author, long-time alderman of both Billingsgate ward and the German merchants, and wealthy merchant with foreign affiliations. There is perhaps no better symbol of the diverse and profound connections that existed between Cologne and England during this period than the man Arnold fitz Tedmar. He was not only a product of the Anglo-Cologne connection, he also helped to perpetuate and enrich it.

The socio-economic connections between Cologners and the English reveal an entirely separate dimension of Anglo-Cologne relations: one which moves beyond the political and diplomatic activities of the aristocracy and provides us with a fuller picture of the interregional contacts between peoples of different parts of Europe. Primarily drawn from the merchant and artisan classes, this prosopographical approach has resulted in two major conclusions.

The first is that emigrants from both Cologne and England were able to achieve a remarkable level of integration in their new homeland. Through intermarriage, citizenship rights, property holding, and the freedom to pursue their trade (artisans such as Hermann le Heaumer entered the armorers' guild in order to practice their trade and take on apprentices) or business, these expatriates show us that interregional relations between England and Germany were as flourishing as those between England and France or elsewhere on the continent during the Central Middle Ages. Although still time-consuming and dangerous, travel between Germany and England had become highly developed at an early date, and by the late twelfth century the traffic was extensive. In the light of the evidence presented above it is reasonable to conclude that regions in western Europe were not as disconnected and unrelated as has often been assumed. This is particularly the case with Anglo-German relations, which have hitherto been relegated to an insignificant rank because their political and diplomatic relations bore such little fruit. The results of Anglo-German political history have sometimes

---

[143] Fryde's attempts [in "Arnold fitz Thedmar und die Entstehung der Grossen Deutschen Hanse," pp. 34–9 and *Ein mittelalterlicher deutscher Großunternehmer*, pp. 144–5] (a) to link Terricus of Cologne with Arnold fitz Tedmar either through kinship ties or by suggesting that Terricus preceded Arnold as the alderman of the Germans, (b) to create a high social status for Arnold's maternal lineage in Cologne, and (c) to link Arnold and his supposed royalist "Thedmar-Clan" to both Henry III's excessive favoritism of foreigners (actually Henry raised the ire of the English barons because of his favoritism to Provençal foreigners through his wife Eleanor, not because of favoritism to German merchants – they naturally supported the king since their trading privileges came from royal authority) and to the scheme to get Richard of Cornwall crowned King of the Germans are all unsubstantiated and remain unconvincing. So too is her conjecture that Terricus of Cologne asked Arnold's mother Juliana to be the godmother of his daughter (see *Ein mittelalterlicher deutscher Großunternehmer*, p. 142).

been generalized into the conclusion that relations between the two regions as a whole were ephemeral. This notion will, we hope, be laid to rest by the evidence cited in this chapter, and in future medieval Germany will be understood as part of western European history.

The second conclusion we draw from this study is that the English were involved in the Rhineland region at a much earlier date than has previously been assumed. Well before the Merchant Adventurers of Elizabethan times we find English merchants and emigrants in the environs of Cologne and northern Germany, and the record of their families indicates a thorough integration into local life.[144] Although we cannot say that English merchants were involved in the export of wool and the import of German products on a scale that the German merchants were, we still must grant more of a role for those merchants who traveled between these regions, often resettling in foreign parts, who were originally "de Anglia" but became "Anglicus." Once again we see the extensive traffic of people between England and Germany, which reinforces the conclusion that this was not an insignificant corridor of interregional activity in Europe.

[144] See Erich Weise, "Die Hanse, England und die Merchant Adventurers," *JKGV* 31/32 (1956–7), pp. 137–64.

Part III

Anglo-German religious and cultural life

Evidence for Anglo-German religious and cultural exchange is abundant, but is sequestered in a wide variety of little-used sources. So in this section more than elsewhere we shall be piecing together a fabric from many separate strands; but the resulting weave suggests a highly inter-connected world of piety, learning, and religious activism which united the Rhineland to the English kingdom yet which has seldom received much attention in modern historiography. To fill this gap in the record we shall range widely from hagiography and relics to monastic confratern-ities, pilgrims and crusaders, educational and evangelical associations, and expatriate clerics of all sorts as we gather evidence of the variety of religious and cultural exchanges between Cologne and the English kingdom.

Chapter 8

CONFRATERNITIES, EXPATRIATE MONKS, PIOUS LEGENDS, AND PILGRIMS

As in most cases, it was the monks who led the way in establishing such interregional ties. Our first surviving evidence comes from a single folio page of Harley MS. 1805 in the British Museum. This manuscript contains an Old Testament in Carolingian minuscule from the Tours school dated pre-820, and attached to it is a smaller parchment folio whose script dates from the early eleventh century and whose current function is to serve as the manuscript's front flyleaf.[1] On this folio there appears a list of Cologne churches along with 371 German names listed in two columns.[2] The names of prominent deacons and abbesses are inscribed among the many other members of these communities, no doubt in an effort either to establish or maintain a prayer confraternity with an English monastic house (or houses). The early date of this confraternity is striking, as it was probably established before the Norman Conquest.[3]

We know nothing about the English community to whom the prayer list was sent, but a later similar document tells us much more. In 1936 the names of monks from the Cologne abbey of Siegburg were discovered at the archive of Christ Church, Canterbury by the archivist P. W. Blore.[4] He identified a rectangular parchment leaf containing a twelve-line list of names of thirty-one deceased monks, for whom

---

[1] Wilhelm Levison, "Eine Kölner Namenliste aus dem elften Jahrhundert," *Annalen* 119 (1931), pp. 164–9; Rudolf Schützeichel, "Die Kölner Namenliste des Londoner Ms. Harley 2805," *Namenforschung. Festschrift zum 75. Geburtstag für Adolf Bach* (Heidelberg, 1965), pp. 97–126.

[2] St. Aposteln, St. Johannes, St. Gereon, St. Columba, St. Severin, Groß St. Martin, Sanctis Virginibus (St. Ursula), Klein St. Martin, St. Caecilia, St. Andreas, St. Alban.

[3] Aachen's earliest memorial book dates from the 1240s: E. Teichmann, "Das älteste Aachener Totenbuch," *Zeitschrift des Aachener Geschichtsvereins* 38 (1916), pp. 1ff.

[4] See P. W. Blore, *Tenth Annual Report of the Friends of Canterbury* (Canterbury, 1938), pp. 30–1; W. Holtzmann, *Historical Manuscripts Commission Report on Manuscripts in Various Collections, Volume I* (London, 1901), pp. 217f.; Wilhelm Wilbrand, *Mittelrheinische Landeszeitung* (December 31, 1936) and "Unbekannte Urkunden zur Geschichte der Abtei Siegburg," *Annalen* 137 (1940), pp. 73–97.

prayers were requested from the Benedictines at Christ Church, Canterbury. Indeed, the Siegburger community offered to send additional names of their deceased should those at Canterbury desire them.[5] This letter is an affirmative response to the English monks' attempt to establish a formal *societas* between the two communities. The script shows that this was established in the first quarter of the twelfth century, and given the abbots' names on the list it probably dates from before 1132.

Siegburg abbey was founded in 1064 by Archbishop Anno II with monks from St. Maximin near Trier. The first abbot, Wolfhelm, eventually transferred to the abbey of Brauweiler near Cologne a year later. After a trip to Italy in 1070, Anno brought back twelve monks from Fruttuaria to reform the monastery according to Cluniac custom and sent the older Benedictine monks back to St. Maximin. Siegburg abbey was thereafter used as the center for reforming other neighboring monasteries.[6] As part of its subsequent expansion of ties with other similar monasteries, Siegburg eventually established close relations with the French abbey of Grammont.[7] With due respect to its founder and patron, the Siegburg confraternity list begins with the name of Anno II, and continues with two abbots, three priors, fourteen monks, one deacon, three *conversi*, and two cloistered nuns. The list concludes with the names of two laypersons: Anno's father Walter and mother Engela. In each case, the feast day for each departed soul is indicated. Given that Anno II was one of the first Cologne archbishops to pursue a pro-English policy, it is no surprise to discover English monastic ties involving one of his monasteries.[8] These two obscure folios suggest that

---

[5] "Littere, quas audistis, o patres et domini, de componenda vobiscum societate, perorarunt: hec vero defunctorum nomina descripsimus, ut ad presens in exordio conventionis mutue apud vos pro testimonio recitentur. Quod si vobis placuerit, uti reliquorum fratrem [*sic*] nostrorum, qui ab initio fundate ecclesie nostre defuncti sunt, memoriam agatis, hoc ipsum nobis litteris declarate, et quecunque nostris impenditis, hec eadem vestris prompto animo rependemus."

[6] *Das Erzbistum Köln II: Die Benediktiner Abtei Siegburg*, ed. Eric Wisplinghoff, Germina Sacra NF, 9 (Berlin and New York, 1975).

[7] K. Corsten, "Eine Reise französischer Mönche nach Köln, Bonn und Siegburg im Jahre 1181," *Annalen* 116 (1930), pp. 29–60.

[8] *Vita Annonis minor, Die Jüngere Annovita*, ed. Mauritius Miller, Siegburger Studien, 10 (Siegburg, 1975), I, p. 44 lines 2–3: "Cuius [Anno] apud exteras quoque nationes quanta fuerit magnitudo nominis, hinc praeter alia estimandum est, quod Anglorum Danorumque regibus in amicicia iunctus, donis eorum et legationibus frequenter honorabatur." "Vita Annonis archiepiscopus Coloniensis, *MGH SS*, XI, pp. 478–9: "Praeterea cuius famae vel nominis vir tantarum inter suos virtutum apud exteras quoque barbarasque nationes fuerit, hinc aestimandum est, quod Anglorum Danorumque regibus in amicitia iunctus, donis eorum et legationibus frequenter honorabatur." This activity was no doubt in connection with his role as regent for the young Henry IV.

there were many more such confraternities between England and the Cologne environs than can now be demonstrated.[9]

Anglo-Cologne monastic confraternities may well have been stimulated by the remarkable period of Scottish monastic influence in Cologne from 963 to 1103. The prestigious Benedictine church of Groß St. Martin's was led during these many years by a series of Scottish abbots: Mimbrinus (963–75), Kilian (975–1003/4), Helias (1005–42), Maiolus (1042–61), Hezelin (1079–83/7), Isaak (1087–95), and Alvold (1095–1103). Scottish monks dominated the cloister for three-quarters of a century, among whom was Marianus Scotus, the author of a chronicle.[10] The Scots were then gradually replaced by German monks during the next half century until the Scottish contingent disappeared by the early twelfth century.[11]

Abbot Helias (or Elias) was the most important of these abbots, both for his long reign as well as for his reforming zeal. He was a close friend with Archbishop Heribert (999–1021), and thereby the abbey enjoyed many new benefices. But Heribert's successor, Archbishop Pilgrim (1021–36), did not consider so highly the Scot's legendary piety and spiritual rigor. Marianus Scotus tells us that Helias also became abbot of the Benedictine abbey of St. Pantaleon and tried to enforce his Scottish asceticism on this comfortable German community.[12] In one of several disputes between Helias and St. Pantaleon's cloister, the abbot threw a missal into a fire before the entire community because one of the monks had written it without his permission.[13] Helias brought in several Scottish monks and more conflict developed between the German and Scottish members. Eventually Archbishop Pilgrim stepped in and ordered Helias to remove the foreign monks within a specific

---

[9] Benno Hilliger, ed., *Rheinische Urbare: Sammlung von Urbaren und anderen Quellen zur Rheinischen Wirtschaftsgeschichte. I: Die Urbare von S. Pantaleon in Köln*, PGRG, 20 (Bonn, 1902), p. 55 contains a Memorialkalender dated to the tenth century with the following entry for August 26: "commemoracio fratrum Lubecensium et Lundoniacensium cum vigilia et missa et pulsatione." Anna-Dorothee von den Brincken, "Die Totenbücher der Stadtkölnischen Stifte, Klöster und Pfarreien," *JKGV* 42 (1968), p. 172 states that the latter (Lundoniacensium) is London, but I rather think it is the Cistercian abbey of Lond in Poland. Leonard Korth lists Lond among those areas colonized in the East with ties to the lower Rhine (see *MSAK* 10 [1886], p. 93).

[10] *MGH SS*, v, pp. 481–568.   [11] Opladen, *Gross St. Martin*.

[12] F. W. Oediger, *Das Bistum Köln von den Anfangen bis zum Ende des 12. Jahrhunderts*, Geschichte des Erzbistums Köln, I (Cologne, 1972), p. 353 rightly concludes that a reform of the cloister was included in the granting of the abbey to the Scots.

[13] *MGH SS*, V, pp. 556–7. The tensions are explained by Marianus Scotus: "Propter religionem districtam disciplinamque nimiam et propter aliquos Scottus, quos secum habebet Helias Scottus abbas, qui monasterium sancti Pantalionis et sancti Martini in Colonia pariter regebat." There seems to be no connection between the Scottish reformist regime and the Gorze reform movement in Lotharingia.

time.[14] Although Pilgrim died before the deadline was past (a fact noted by Marianus as indicative of divine disposition regarding the conflict), the reform movement had peaked. Helias himself died five years later in the odor of sanctity (he was canonized as a saint),[15] and subsequent Scottish abbots were restricted to Groß St. Martin's abbey. Since St. Pantaleon showed itself to be a strong supporter of Anno II's reforms at Siegburg abbey, the conflict was not so much over reform itself, but over personal conflicts about the Scottish regime. Yet to be fair, it must be said that the lengthy period of Scottish abbacy at Groß St. Martin's abbey was one of prosperity and cooperation. All in all, this must be considered a remarkable interregional exchange because of its early date and its lengthy institutional life. Once again, however, the lack of documentary evidence restricts us from knowing what was a much fuller story of Anglo-Cologne religious life.

Along with the exchange of monastic brothers both living and dead, one would expect an exchange of pious legends and hagiographical narratives. Monks and clerics used these along with prayers, relics, and visits to strengthen the bonds of brotherhood between communities. We are not disappointed on this count, and such stories tell us much about the impressions monks and clerics from either side of the Channel made on each other. Stories about ecclesiastical and secular politics abound in monastic chronicles,[16] but the transmission of pious legends also gives us insight into the world of Anglo-Cologne religious relations. The Cistercian Caesarius of Heisterbach (*c.* 1180–1240), for example, received his education in Cologne and was well informed about English affairs.[17] In particular he made mention of Thomas Becket's martyrdom, "qui nostris temporibus pro ecclesiae libertate usque ad mortem dimicavit."[18] Caesarius was quick to equate Becket's defense of the Church with the miraculous interventions of St. Anno II[19] and with

---

[14] Hans Joachim Kracht, *Geschichte der Benediktinerabtei St. Pantaleon in Köln (965–1250)*, Studien zur Kölner Kirchengeschichte, II (Siegburg, 1975), pp. 56–59.

[15] Rupert of Deutz records the mystical visions of Helias in his vita of St. Heribert: Peter Dinter, ed., *Vita Heriberti. Kritische Edition mit Kommentar und Untersuchung*, Veröffentlichungen des Historischen Vereins für den Niederrhein insbesondere das alte Erzbistum Köln, 13 (Bonn, 1976), pp. 74–6.

[16] *Urkundenbuch des Stiftes Kaiserswerth*, ed. Heinrich Kelleter, Urkundenbücher der Geistlichen Stiftungen des Niederrheins, I (Bonn, 1904), pp. 1–2 contains a portion of the vita Suitberti (692–713) in Bede's *Ecclesiastical History*, wherein Suitbert is ordained by Bishop Vilfrid.

[17] Caesarius of Heisterbach, *Dialogus Miraculorum*, ed. Joseph Strange (Cologne, Bonn, and Brussels, 1851), II, pp. 249–50 contains his account of Richard I surviving a storm at sea en route to the Holy Land. Here the prayers of the monks move God's hand to save the vessel, which in turn moves the hand of a grateful king to reward the monks with an alms house.

[18] Ibid., p. 139.

[19] Ibid., p. 140: "Simile habes de sancto Annone Coloniensi Archiepiscopo. Cui cum post mortem multi detraherent, dicentes eum ecclesiarum fuisse demembratorem, et civium suorum

Archbishop Engelbert II's political murder by his own nephew, Count Frederick of Isenburg,[20] as a result of a dispute between them over a monastery in Essen.[21] Caesarius even called upon Stephen Langton to legitimate the orthodoxy of transubstantiation; this reference came from a personal conversation between Stephen and Abbot Henry of Heisterbach.[22] Caesarius' knowledge of these events came not only from oral accounts, indicated by phrases like "Retulit mihi quidam abbas de ordine nostro"[23] and "Sicut didici a quodam abbate, nuper in Anglia"[24] but also from written texts, since he often says, "sicut legimus"[25] or "Unde legitur in Anglorum gestis."[26] Heisterbach abbey's location on the Rhine just north of Cologne made it a prime location for visitors passing between England and the German metropolis, and no doubt Caesarius was the beneficiary of manuscripts and stories told late into the night by these sojourners.

Episcopal saints were not the only ones to intervene in Anglo-Cologne history; St. Egidius saved the child of a merchant from drowning as he sailed a heavily burdened vessel from Cologne to

---

ex caecatorem, Dominus Deus in translatione illius, quantae sanctitatis esset, signis plurimis ostendit."

[20] *Die Wundergeschichten des Caesarius von Heisterbach*, ed. Alfons Hilka, PGRG, 43 (Bonn, 1937), I, p. 277: "Agnus Christi . . . tempore moderniori in sancto Thoma episcopo Cantuariensi occisus est propter libertatem ecclesie conservandam. Eadem causa mortis exstitit in presule nostro Engelberto. Occubuit ille pro libertate ecclesie Cantuariensis, iste vero pro defensione ecclesie Essendiensis [Essen]. Liberavit ille ecclesiam Anglicanam sanguine suo de gravi iugo regis Henrici; liberavit iste eque morete sua ecclesiam sue defensioni commissam de intolerabili exactione comitis Frederici. Et licet beatus Thomas ante passionem multa sustinuerit incommoda, dampna et exilia, que non sustinuit Engelbertus, in ipsa tamen passione plus doloris, angoris et confusionis certum est eum Thoma tollerasse." Engelbert was shortly thereafter canonized. See Wolfgang Kleist, *Der Tod des Erzbischofs Engelbert von Köln* (Münster, 1918).

[21] *REK*, III, 1, pp. 87–8 no. 569. A few months earlier Engelbert, at the command of both the pope and the emperor, had forced his nephew to cease interfering in the rights of the religious foundation in Essen, where Frederick held the office of bailiff. This dispute was the source of conflict between the archbishop and his nephew (*REK*, III, 1, pp. 82–3 no. 511). Engelbert's murder was noted in detail in the *Annales de Dunstaplia*, p. 96: "Eodem anno archiepiscopus Coloniensis, imperatoris justiciarius, interfectus a quodam consanguineo suo et vassallo in insidiis quia archiepiscopus dimittere noluit satellites illius militis, qui quoddam monasterium fuerant depraedati." Bernd Fischer has taken up Caesarius' comparison of Engelbert with Becket in "Engelbert von Berg (1185–1225). Kirchenfürst und Staatsmann (mit einer Gegenüberstellung zu Thomas Becket [1118–1170])," *Zeitschrift des Bergischen Geschichtsblätter* 94 (1989–90), pp. 1–47.

[22] *Die Wundergeschichten des Caesarius von Heisterbach*, ed. Hilka, III, pp. 22–3: "Eandem consuetudinem habet magister Stephanus archiepiscopus Cantuariensis (1207–28), qui nullo theologo huius temporis inferior scientia esse dinoscitur. Interrogatus a domino Henrico abbate nostro (1208–40), si post hec verba 'Hoc est enim corpus meum' statim fiat transsubstantio panis, scilicet in corpus Christi, respondit, 'Hoc credo, in hac fide moriar. Unde mox cum hostiam depono, supplex illam adoro.'"

[23] Caesarius, *Dialogus Miraculorum*, II, p. 5.   [24] Ibid., I, p. 138.

[25] *Die Wundergeschichten des Caesarius von Heisterbach*, ed. Hilka, I, p. 277.   [26] Ibid., I, p. 177.

England.[27] St. Norbert of Xanten, once a canon in Cologne, had a much less positive opinion of the English, however. He considered a certain Praemonstratensian novice "less devoted in confession, unsteady in word, restless in body, inconstant in his habits, tepid in prayer, and negligent in obedience." Why? . . . "*Anglicus enim erat.*"[28] Such attitudes were not uncommon, but at least the English novice was not charged with concealing a tail – another typical continental dig at the English.[29]

Caesarius of Heisterbach tells of an expatriate priest on English soil, who as a result of his passionate request to see the body of Christ physically was granted the private joy of embracing and kissing the Christ Child at the altar.[30] This priest "propter amorem celestis patrie patriam suam dimiserat, ut exul in divinis officiis liberius vacare posset." Caesarius also records an account of an English bishop from the Praemonstratensian order who taught a lesson about the value of frequent confessions by telling the priests at his death bed that he had nothing left to confess before dying.[31] Such clergy in England understood the importance of the sacraments.

English monastic writings also contain miracle stories gleaned from contacts with the region surrounding Cologne. In one instance a monk

---

[27] Petrus Guillelmus, "Miracula Beati Egidii," *MGH SS*, XII, pp. 319–20: "De quodam puero a profundo Reni fluminis vitae restituto. Institor quadam natione Theutonicus, Bruningo, de vico cui Neumaga vocabulum est – a civitate Colonie fere per quatuor miliaria seiungitur – a partibus Angliae veniens, navem sale onustam ducebat. Qui per Reni fluminis alveum ascendens, eandem navim cum sociis suis secus crepidinem alvei funibus trahens, gubernatore interius residente, filium suum, Ezelonem nomine, cum alio puero minoris aetatis intus reliquerat, ut aquam, quae intus perrimas forte patentes." St. Egidius thereafter saved the son at the distressed prayer of the boy's father.

[28] Roger Wilmans, ed., "Vita Norberti Archiepiscopi Magdeburgensis," *MGH SS*, XII, p. 684: "Cumque [Norbert] considerasset alterum eorum [two novices] minus devotum in confessione, levem in verbis, inquietum in corpore, inconstantem moribus, tepidum in oratione, negligentem in obenientia, Anglicus enim erat." (*c.* 1121).

[29] See Paul Meyvaert, "'Rainaldus est malus scriptor Francigenus' – voicing national antipathy in the Middle Ages," *Speculum* 66: 4 (October 1991), pp. 743–63; Ludwig Schmugge, "Über 'nationale' Vorurteile im Mittelalter," *DA* 38: 2 (1982), pp. 439–59; G. G. Coulton, "Nationalism in the Middle Ages," *Cambridge Historical Journal* 5 (1933–7), pp. 15–40. Early in the thirteenth century Jacques de Vitry described the national insults exchanged in the schools of Paris, among which the English were said to be heavy drinkers and have tails: *The Historia Occidentalis of Jacques de Vitry*, ed. John Frederick Hinnebusch, Spicilegium Friburgense, 17 (Fribourg, 1972), p. 92. Margery Kempe was told as much by German clerics when abandoned along the pilgrimage route from Danzig to Aachen: *The Book of Margery Kempe*, trans. Barry Windeatt (London, 1985), pp. 280–1: "Priests of that country came to her where she was lodged. They called her an Englishwoman with a tail and spoke many filthy words to her."

[30] *Die Wundergeschichten des Caesarius von Heisterbach*, ed. Hilka, I, p. 177: "Unde legitur in Anglorum gestis quidam fuisse presbiter religiosus valde." Once again we see Caesarius' concern with the physical body of Christ and Eucharistic transubstantiation.

[31] Caesarius, *Dialogus Miraculorum*, I, p. 138: "Sicut didici a quodam abbate, nuper in Anglia episcopus quidam defunctus est ordinis Praemonstratensis, vir bonus est et magnae religionis."

died without benefit of confession, but unlike the Praemonstratensian bishop he was in sore need of it (he was worldly minded and had fathered an illegitimate son). After the intercession of St. Peter, other saints and holy virgins, and finally Mary herself, Christ allowed the poor soul to return to earth in order to mend his ways and cleanse himself of sin.[32] This morality tale about the virtue of virginity took place in a monastery "sancti Petri quod apud Coloniam." Given the prominence of the Virgin and St. Peter in the story it is likely that the author conflated a monastery in the region with the Cologne cathedral church, whose patron saints were St. Peter and the Virgin (along with the Three Kings or Magi). Siegburg abbey, a possible source for the story given its ties to Canterbury and its location just outside Cologne, enjoyed the patronage of the Virgin, Archangel Michael, and St. Mauritius (of the Theban legion martyrs).[33]

William of Malmesbury's chronicles contain a marvelous collection of Cologne miracle stories. He describes Cologne as "a very great city, the capital of all Germany, endowed with markets [and] abounding in the patronage of the saints," and then begins to recount the harrowing adventure of repentance for a Cologner who had accidentally killed his brother.[34] The man was able to keep his deed a secret for many years, but his conscience was tormented as a result. Therefore, he confessed to Archbishop Anno II, "viro in primis severo," who imposed a brutal penance: the man was to be bound by iron chains, breastplate, and lance (which drew "kindred blood" at his every step), endure fasting and silence, and make pilgrimages throughout Christendom for seven years. The penitent obeyed, and trampled along in cleansing suffering to Rome and thence to Jerusalem (before crusaders had ever appeared), where the breastplate burst asunder before the Holy Sepulchre. Thereafter he wandered across Europe like Aeneas "tossed about by many dangers on land and sea" until he reached the monastery of Malmesbury, and there before the tomb of Edward the Confessor, he found his rest. In the midst of fervent prayer to heaven the remainder of his bonds were miraculously flung some fifteen feet away. This exquisite psychodrama is one part Virgilian epic, one part sacred redemption, and one

---

[32] *Miracula Sanctae Virginis Mariae*, ed. Elise Dexter, University of Wisconsin Studies in the Social Sciences and History, 12 (Madison, 1927), pp. 21–2: "In monasterio Sancti Petri quod apud Coloniam, erat quidam frater." See also R. W. Southern, "The English origins of the 'Miracles of the Virgin,'" *Medieval and Renaissance Studies* 4 (1958), pp. 176–216.

[33] *Das Erzbistum Köln II: Die Benediktinerabtei Seigburg*, ed. Wisplinghoff, p. 21. There was a parish church of St. Peter in Cologne.

[34] William of Malmesbury, *De gestis pontificum Anglorum*, RS, 52 (London, 1870; rpt. 1964), pp. 425–6.

part advertising which places Malmesbury abbey and its chief relic on a par with the Holy Sepulchre.

Elsewhere William recounts the Roman origins of Cologne, and then shifts the story from the deeds of emperors to those of an unidentified archbishop.[35] In the first episode, a terribly deformed rustic priest was saying Mass for the emperor disguised as a knight out on the hunt. During the Mass the emperor wondered how God could have created such a monster of nature and allowed him to administer the sacraments. But he was chastised during the service by the words chanted "Know ye that the Lord himself is God . . . He made us, and not we ourselves."[36] The monarch deemed the priest a prophet and promptly raised him to the archiepiscopal see of Cologne. Later this archbishop intervened in a case of abduction: a young virgin was taken as wife from a convent by a local nobleman while the archbishop was away in Rome. Upon his return the pastor demanded "that the sheep be returned to the fold," but the nobleman could not do without his mistress; after a second abduction he found himself under the archbishop's excommunication. Some time later upon his death bed, the archbishop heard the name of the sinful aristocrat, and groaned: "If that wretched man shall desert the accursed woman, he shall be absolved; but if he persists, let him be ready to give account before God on the following year, at the very day and hour on which I shall depart: moreover, you shall see me expire when the bell shall sound the sixth hour." Of course this prophecy was fulfilled entirely, and exactly a year after his death the nobleman was killed along with his mistress by a bolt of lightning. What God hath ordained – a prophetic priesthood – let no nobleman put aside.

Finally, William includes a lesson on the seriousness of the vow of obedience.[37] Here we find a first-person account of a trembling sinner named Ethelbert, who tells of the miraculous terror he experienced on Christmas eve "in a certain town of Saxony where there was a church of the martyr Magnus, and a priest by the name of Robert had begun the first Mass." Ethelbert was not observing Mass, however, but, rather in the churchyard with eighteen companions (fifteen men and three women), all of whom were singing "profane songs" and generally carousing. The noise of their merry-making repeatedly interrupted the

---

[35] William of Malmesbury, *De gestis regum Anglorum*, RS, 90 (London, 1887; rpt. 1964), I, pp. 204–5.

[36] Psalm 100: 3 (the Jubilate Deo). This echoes the story told by Odo of Cluny about Gregory of Tours, who recited this psalm in response to Pope Gregory the Great's surprise at his short stature: see Odo's tenth-century "Vita Sancti Gregorii," *Receuil des historiens des Gaules et de la France*, ed. Martin Bouquet (Paris, 1738), II, p. 24.

[37] William of Malmesbury, *De gestis regum Anglorum*, I, pp. 203–4.

priest in the midst of his sacred solemnities, and he finally cursed them saying, "May it please God and St. Magnus that you may remain singing thus for an entire year!" They remained so dancing and singing for a year without hunger or fatigue. A covering was placed above them as shelter from the elements, and miraculously even their clothing did not wear out. Instead they danced themselves into the ground up to their thighs. After a year of this forced merriment, Archbishop Heribert of Cologne freed the dancers from the curse and "reconciled us before the altar of St. Magnus." The three women, however, one of whom was the priest's daughter (!), died directly thereafter from the exhaustion while the others slept for three days and nights. Others died later and were famed for miracles, while the remainder betrayed their punishment by the constant trembling of their limbs. William tells us the point of the story: "Those who are bound by the vow of obedience should read this: how great a sin is the transgression of a command of a superior." He also informs us that the account was "given to us by the lord Pilgrim, the successor of blessed Herbert, in the year of our Lord 1013."[38] Although William's dates are off by a few years (Pilgrim was archbishop from 1021 to 36), this legend suggests a relationship between Malmesbury's monks and Cologne's archbishop which precedes the Norman Conquest.

The most astonishing legend of all was that of St. Ursula and her 11,000 virgin martyrs. Ursula was one of the most popular saints of the Middle Ages, whose cult spread all over Europe.[39] As a result, Cologne became a major pilgrimage site, where visitors venerated the relics of St. Ursula and her companions as well as those of the Three Kings (Magi). Yet according to the legend Ursula was not a Cologner, but a British princess. The historical basis of the *vita* is a carved stone dated *c.* 400, which commemorates the restoration by one Clematius of a ruined church in honor of some local virgin martyrs. Their names were not preserved, and not until a ninth-century sermon do we learn the local tradition that they were slain under the Emperor Maximian and were probably British in origin. A Corvey litany (*c.* 827–40), a *martyrologium* of Wandalbert (848), and a charter of Lothar II (867) all mention a "monasterium beatarum virginum," which fell into ruin during the Viking invasions.

---

[38] "Datae sunt nobis hae litterae a domino Peregrino, beati Herberti successore, anno Dominicae incarnationis millesimo decimo tertio."

[39] Wilhelm Levison, "Das Werden der Ursula-Legend," *Bonner Jahrbücher* 132 (1927), pp. 1–164 and Mary Tout, "The legend of St. Ursula and the eleven thousand virgins," *Historical Essays by the Members of the Owens College, Manchester*, ed. T. F. Tout and J. Tait (London, 1902; rpt. Manchester, 1907), pp. 17–56.

The martyred saints endured the invasions, and then extended their presence well beyond Cologne. In the tenth century the holy virgins appear in the liturgical calendars of Cologne, Paris, Würzburg, Munich, Freising, and Merseburg. It is no surprise that as the merchants of Cologne extended their European contacts during the commercial revolution of these centuries, their patron saints accompanied them. During the tenth and eleventh centuries names for the saints began to appear: Martha and Saula were soon joined by Paula, Brittola, Ursula, Sambatia, Saturnina, Gregoria, Pinnosa, Palladia, and Sentia. Thus the number of virgins was set at eleven.[40] Soon after their names and number were established in the early eleventh century the legend took an unexpected turn. As a result of misreading manuscript abbreviations, their number swelled from eleven to eleven thousand: "XI MV" was misread as "undecim millia virgines" instead of "undecim martyres virgines"! With so many relics to account for, it was propitious that an old Roman gravesite near the church of St. Cunibert was unearthed when the city walls were extended in 1106.[41] Here vast numbers of Roman-era bones were found, and a careful misreading of the Roman abbreviation "BM" (*bonae memoriae*) on the gravestones as "BM" (*beata martyres*) assured that substantial martyrs were accounted for. The cult of the 11,000 Virgins spread throughout the liturgies in Europe during the twelfth century (especially in the Low Countries, northern France, the Rhineland, and Venice), and a brisk business in relics soon followed. Even St. Norbert of Xanten came to Cologne relic hunting in 1121, and after fasting had a vision of one of the virgins, who explained where she was buried. The body was indeed found the next day as well as that of the patron saint, Gereon. Norbert promptly took the virgin along with other relics to Prémontre.

In 1155 Archbishop Rainald of Dassel, famous for his role in Frederick Barbarossa's papal schism, sought further spiritual patronage. He ordered a general excavation of the *ager Ursulinus* and hundreds of bodies were found in the subsequent nine years under the guidance of the entrepreneurial abbot Gerlach of Deutz.[42] One problem remained,

---

[40] These were often venerated separately. An eleventh-century psalter from Exeter includes "Sancta Pinnossa" in its litany: British Museum Harleianus 863 fos. 108v–111v, published in E. S. Dewick, *The Leofric Collectar I*, The Henry Bradshaw Society, 45 (London, 1914).

[41] Richerus monachus Walciodorensi, "Trium corporum sanctarum virginum Coloniensium e numero undecim millium," in *Acta Sanctorum Octobris*, ed. Joannes Bollandas (Brussels, 1858), IX, p. 239 tells of this discovery. A lawsuit ensued between the canons of St. Cunibert and the nuns of St. Ursula as to who had a better claim to the relics. They were on the land of St. Cunibert's, but were martyrs of St. Ursula.

[42] Rainald's sister, Gepa, was abbess of the convent of the Virgins. Thus her intervention must be considered as the initiative for the excavation.

however. How does one account for the fact that so many bones of men and children were also found in the Ursuline field? Luckily a series of small stone tablets were also discovered, on which were inscribed the names and dignities of the martyrs, male and female.[43] Ursula's body was then identified, neatly labeled "Ursula Regina." Male martyrs named on the tablets included: St. Sulpicius the archbishop of Ravenna, Pantalus bishop of Basel, several cardinals, St. Evergisius archbishop of Cologne, saints from as far afield as Ethiopia, Scotland, Ireland, England, Italy, Bohemia, Greece, Constantinople, Antioch, Jerusalem, several patriarchs, kings, dukes, the consul of Ancona, even a pope named Cyriacus (never mind that he could not be found on the list of popes).[44] Surely the abbots of Deutz had good sense for the European-wide marketing of their treasure.

The first *Passio* of St. Ursula was written during this period, and the mystic Elisabeth of Schönau, perhaps fed spurious information by the abbots of Deutz, received a series of visions that explained the existence of the new members of Ursula's entourage.[45] For example, Cyriacus had been pope only one year and eleven weeks, and had resigned to join St. Ursula. Therefore his name was expunged from the list of popes because of his resignation. When as a result of competition two bodies of Clematius were found, she explained that one had buried the virgins and the other had built the church in their honor. The presence of children's bones was explained by Ursula's fondness for children. Elisabeth's explanations were incorporated into the second *Passio*.

The legend eventually passed in altered form into Geoffrey of Monmouth's *Historia Brittonum*[46] (*c.* 1147) and into James of Voraigne's *Legenda Aurea*;[47] thereafter St. Ursula and her companions enjoyed European-wide fame.[48] The English ties to her legend and cult were

---

43 For the text see Th. J. Lacomblet, "Die Benediktiner-Abtei zu Deutz," *Archiv für die Geschichte des Niederrheins* 5 (1866), pp. 292–3.

44 Some of these inscriptions are quite remarkable for their mixture of naïveté and fraud. One, for example, reads: "S. Quirillus, qui vixit sex dies post martyrium suum."

45 F. W. Roth, ed., *Die Visionen und Briefe der Hl. Elisabeth . . . von Schönau* (Brünn, 1886), pp. 123–38.

46 Geoffrey of Monmouth, *The History of the Kings of Britain*, ed. Lewis Thorpe (Harmondsworth, 1966), pp. 141–3. Geoffrey does not mention Ursula by name in this account.

47 Jacobus de Voraigne, *The Golden Legend*, trans. and ed. Granger Ryan and Helmut Ripperger (Salem, New Hampshire, 1941; rpt. 1969), pp. 627–31. James includes a legend wherein the throng of virgins accompanied a monk to heaven after he had recited the Lord's Prayer eleven thousand times.

48 St. Ursula's legend inspired some of the greatest art of the Middle Ages: see G. de Trevarent, *La Légende de Sainte Ursule dans la littérature et l'art du moyen âge* (Paris, 1931); C. M. Kauffmann, *The Legend of St. Ursula*, Victoria & Albert Museum (London, 1964); Frank Günter Zehnder, *Die Hl. Ursula und ihre Elftausend Jungfrauen. Ausstellung des Wallraf-Richartz Museums in Köln 6. Juli bis 3. September 1978* (Cologne, 1978).

many. To begin with, she was herself a British Christian princess. As the story goes, she was betrothed against her will to a pagan prince yet obtained a three-year delay because of her desire to remain a virgin. This gave her time to spend on pilgrimage with ten noble female companions who shared her vocation, as well as time for the prince to convert to her faith. The term was spent at sea in ships: she and her ten colleagues sailed their own ship, each of which contained a thousand virgins who were also converted to Christianity (hence the 11,000 virgins). "A favorable wind" eventually drove them down the mouth of the Rhine, where they stopped at Cologne on their way as pilgrims to Rome via Basle (a path curiously familiar to English pilgrims in the twelfth and thirteenth centuries). After a meeting with the British Pope Cyriacus in Rome, he joined them (along with cardinals, *et alia*) for a return trip to Cologne. After their arrival they were martyred by the Huns for their faith, Ursula herself refusing to marry the Huns' chieftain.

In order to link Ursula's British origins to the Cologne tradition the first account of the martyrdom, the late tenth-century *Relatio de historia sanctorum Agrippinensium virginum*,[49] contains a prologue in which the author tells of a conversation he had with a certain "Count Hoolfus." The count claimed to have been sent as an ambassador to England by Emperor Otto the Great in order to secure a marriage with Edward the Elder's daughter Edith. During his mission Hoolfus visited Canterbury and spoke with the great reforming archbishop, St. Dunstan, who told him the story of the virgin martyrs. Although this chronology is impossible, the attempt to recreate a plausible narrative of origins for the legend that links Cologne to England is worth noting for its historical value.[50] In the same way as the export of Ursuline relics mirrors the growing commercial and ecclesiastical ties between Cologne and other European locales during the Central Middle Ages, so too does the prominent place of origin for the legend tell us something important about the preeminent status of Anglo-Cologne relations in particular during this period. Documentary evidence tells us that it was Archbishop Ceonwald of Worcester who took Princess Edith to Germany in 929 to marry Otto the Great, and as part of the venture he traveled with gifts "omnibus monasteriis per totam Germaniam." This included visits

---

[49] Generally known as *Fuit tempore* from its opening words. It was written some time in the last quarter of the tenth century and first published in full in 1884 in *Analecta Bollandiana*, III, p. 5–20.

[50] If this embassy had actually taken place, it would have been initiated by Otto's father Henry the Fowler, since Otto was still a child (he was not crowned emperor until 962 though the writer describes him as the emperor). Otto and Edith were married in 929, when Dunstan was only four years old (he became archbishop of Canterbury in 959).

as far south as Reichenau and St. Gall, where prayer brotherhoods were established between the English and German monks to strengthen ties begun with the marriage union.[51]

The Ursula legend was well known in England by the twelfth century. Indeed, collects appear under the entry *De Sanctis Virginibus Undecim* in the *Liber Missalis* of St. Augustine's abbey of Canterbury, which is dated around 1099.[52] Given the earlier confraternity between Siegburg abbey and the Canterbury monks it is not surprising to find the virgin martyrs here. Roger of Ford, a Norman monk at the Cistercian abbey in Devonshire, was another important avenue of transmission – indeed he is even said to have known Elisabeth of Schönau.[53] Geoffrey of Monmouth's *Historia Brittonum* assured a wide-spread familiarity with the story, and the popular *Legenda Aurea* only furthered knowledge of the legend. Caxton printed an English transla-tion of the *Legenda* at Westminster in 1483 and widened the circulation even more. By this time, however, the 11,000 virgin martyrs had been overshadowed by 15,000 male martyrs.[54] The cult of St. Ursula was of a limited but established variety in England. Her feast day occurs in the Sarum and other calendars on October 21, her proper feast day in Cologne, and a beautiful stained-glass window of her hangs in Holy Trinity church, York.[55] We know of both a hospital of St. Ursula in Leicester[56] and a London church dedicated to the Virgin Mary and St. Ursula's virgins known as St. Mary at the Axe in Lime Street Ward.[57] The church, located on St. Marie's street, served the Skinners of London until it was suppressed during the Reformation and turned into a merchant warehouse. Chevalier identified no less than 272 hymns and sequences dedicated to the praise of St. Ursula and her companions.[58] Such songs found vernacular expressions in England as well.[59]

[51] Gerd Althoff, *Amicitiae et Pacta. Bündnis, Einung, Politik und Gebetsgedenken im beginnenden 10. Jahrhundert*, MGH Schriften, 37 (Hanover, 1992), pp. 124–7.

[52] MS 270 of the Corpus Christi College Library, Cambridge, published in *The Missal of St. Augustine's Abbey Canterbury*, ed. Martin Rule (Cambridge, 1896), pp. 117–18. Rule concludes that the missal was completed in the summer of 1099 for the personal use of the newly consecrated abbot, Hugh of Fleury.

[53] Levison, "Das Werden der Ursula-Legende," pp. 160–4; Tout, "The legend of St. Ursula and the eleven thousand virgins," p. 43. The British Museum Cottonianus Otho A. XII manuscript contains a "Passio undecim mille virginum, a Rogero Fordonensi monacho scripta, anno 1181."

[54] Ibid., p. 47. Caxton's translation ends with the following passage: "Thus endeth the passion of Saynt Ursula, with enleven thousand vyrgyns and fyften thousand men al martirs."

[55] David Hugh Farmer, *The Oxford Dictionary of Saints* (Oxford, 1982), p. 387.

[56] Sir William Dugdale, *Monasticon Anglicanum* (London, 1830), VI, p. 765.

[57] John Stow, *The Survey of London*, ed. H. B. Wheatley (London, 1987), p. 145.

[58] U. Chevalier, *Repertorium hymnologicum. VI: Register* (Brussels, 1920), pp. 94ff.

[59] S. B. Liljegreen, "Four middle English versions of the legend of the eleven thousand virgins," *Englische Studien* 57 (1923), pp. 85–112.

Relics of the 11,000 virgins surely made their way into England. "Septem ossa de XI milibus virginum" are recorded arriving at Glastonbury abbey at the initiative of Bishop Henry of Winchester (1129–71), brother of King Stephan of Blois, for example.[60] Indeed, business in Cologne relics was so brisk that a black market involved illegitimate foreign exporters. We hear accounts of those who came to the city and looted relics, only to be punished by the martyrs themselves for their shoplifting. One Englishman experienced a Jonah-like storm during his return trip from Cologne to England, and was only able to pass safely across the sea after he fulfilled his vow to return the *sanctarum pignora* he had stolen from the tomb of the sacred virgins.[61] Such monastic cautionary tales were written to confront a real problem, since both monks and retailers understood the power of holy relics.

Kings and emperors also perceived the significance of having patron saints as members of the royal *familia*. During the years 1156 to 1157 Frederick Barbarossa negotiated in vain with Henry II of England for the return of a precious relic. Henry's mother Matilda, the widow of Emperor Henry V, had brought the hand of St. James, along with many other German treasures, back with her to England after the death of her husband. The relic was subsequently entrusted to the new royal abbey at Reading, where Henry I was buried. Barbarossa wanted the relic as part of his restoration of imperial rights, yet Henry II also saw the relic as part of his own heritage of royal prestige. His grandfather Henry I, the monarch whose royal prerogatives were so central to Henry II's vision of a restored kingship in England, was buried at Reading abbey along with his second wife and eldest son William. To lose the protection of the relic over his relatives was unthinkable both on a

---

[60] Thomas Hearne, ed., *Iohannis confraternis et monachi Glastoniensis Chronica* (Oxford, 1726), I, p. 20; II, p. 453; Levison, "Das Werden der Ursula-Legende," p. 57 note 2.

[61] Richerus monachus Walciodorensi, "Translatio trium corporum sanctarum virginum Coloniensium numero undecim millium," p. 239: "Alter denique, Anglus natione, ad littora maris descendens, navim scandit paratam; sed excitata ventorum procella, motu maris conteri navis periclitabatur, adeo saevissima tempestate orta, ut nec ad aridam navigare, nec ancoram ad sistendum figere possent. Ita nave undique crebra fluctuum collisione quassata, jam vita functos crederes. Anglus autem ille, velut Jonas, conscientiae reatu gravatus: Scio, inquit, scio quare mei causa mors haec ingruit repentina. Hoc enim opus meum, haec sanctarum pignora pertinaci sumere praesumpsi audacia, cujus praesemptionis me et vos ultio absorbebit insontes. Quod si earum, ait, intercessionibus Deus placatus, imminentem hanc mortem aut differe aut moderare dignetur; mox terris redditus, nulla diei vel noctis indulta quiete, ad tumulum sacrarum virginum regressus, digna satisfactione hujus sacrilegii expiabor contagione. Ad hanc compuncti cordis sponsionem, suffragiis (ut pie creditur) sanctarum virginum, insperata Dei adfuit clementia; quare aura mitiori tumultus aequoris mitigati sunt, et ad terram advecta navis. Emittitur Anglus, sponsione sua se liberaturus. Pauca itaque quae de earum revelatione ac miraculis diximus [quia cetera scriptorum incuria neglecta exstitere] nunc satis sint."

dynastic and personal level. And so St. James consorted with monarchs as well as pilgrims.[62]

Anglo-Cologne ties involving monks, relics, and saintly cults were joined by lay spirituality in the form of pilgrimages. Well before Margery Kempe departed from Ipswich in 1433 to pursue her arduous pilgrimage through Germany to Aachen[63] and before those in the mold of the Wife of Bath included Cologne on their itineraries in the late fourteenth century,[64] there was a high volume of pilgrims traveling between England and Cologne. Whereas English pilgrims pursued the Three Kings and St. Ursula's huge entourage in Cologne, those from Cologne made their way across the channel in search of the blessed Thomas at Canterbury.

Thomas' feast day of December 29 was duly observed in Cologne churches,[65] and he drew Cologners high and low to his tomb. In September 1184 Archbishop Philip of Cologne, accompanied by Count Philip of Flanders, came to England ostensibly for a pilgrimage to St. Thomas at Canterbury;[66] however, it is clear that the two had come on a diplomatic mission.[67] We do not know if this pilgrimage to the tomb of Thomas, who was murdered fourteen years earlier in Henry II's reign, carried with it any political implications. But there can be no doubt that the wily archbishop made a strong point by venerating a

---

[62] See Mayer, "Staufische Weltherrschaft? Zum Brief Heinrichs II. von England an Friedrich Barbarossa von 1157," pp. 265–78 and Karl Leyser, "Frederick Barbarossa, Henry II and the hand of St. James," *Medieval Germany and Its Neighbours (900–1250)* (London, 1982), pp. 215–42.

[63] Margery Kempe, *The Book of Margery Kempe*, pp. 271–82. Margery never mentions Cologne, but it is hard to imagine that she would visit the relics of Mary's birthing smock, Jesus' swaddling clothes, the cloth which held St. John the Baptist's head, and Jesus' loin cloth at Aachen without visiting the relics of the Three Kings and St. Ursula when Cologne was so near by.

[64] *Chaucer's Poetry. An Anthology for the Modern Reader*, ed. E. T. Donaldson (New York, 1958; rpt 1975), p. 21, lines 465–9: "And thries hadde she been at Jerusalem; She hadde passed many a straunge streem; At Rome she hadde been, and at Boloigne, In Galice at Saint Jame, and at Coloigne: She coude muchel of wandring by the waye."

[65] *Der Kölner Festkalendar*, ed. Georg Zilliken (Bonn, 1910), p. 124.

[66] Roger of Wendover, *Flores historiarum*, ed. Henry G. Hewlett, RS, 84 (London, 1886–9; rpt. 1965), I, p. 131: "Eodem tempore Philippus, archiepiscopus Coloniensis, et Philippus, comes Flandrensis, venerunt in Angliam vota orationum beato Thomae martyri soluturi, quibus rex Anglorum occurrens petiit ut Lundonias venirent visuri regiam civitatem; in quorum adventu, quod ante non erat visum, civitas coronata resplenduit, gaudium et tripudium per omnes plateas intonuit civitatis. Archiepiscopus vero Coloniensis et cum eo comes Flandrensis in ecclesia sancti Pauli suscepti sunt processione solenni; et die eodem simili honore sibi exhibito, tandem per quinque dies in palatio regis expensis sunt effusioribus hospitati, sed, an multis muneribus donati recesserunt, quaerere superfluum videretur."

[67] The Pipe Rolls show that Henry II was expecting the arrival of the archbishop and count: *Pipe Roll 13 Henry II*, PR, 33, p. 136: "Et pro xii tonellis vini emptis ad opus Regis contra adventum archiepiscopi Colonie et comitis Flandrie xxii li. et xiii s. et iiii d. per breve Regis" and p. 145: "Et Johanni de Morewic et Willelmo de Rudes servientibus Regis xxv li. et vi s. et iiii d. ad inveniendum quod necessarium fuerit in hospito Regis quando occurrit archiepiscopo Colonie et comiti Flandrie per breve Regis."

fallen champion of clerical rights before entering into negotiations with the English king. In any case Henry met the pilgrims at Dover and after their pilgrimage to Canterbury brought them to London, where they celebrated Mass at St. Paul's cathedral and then were received in splendor at Westminster.

Others sought power of a different sort from Thomas. We have already considered the pilgrimage of Arnold fitz Tedmar's grandparents, who asked the saint for children. The moving story of a Cologne woman's search for spiritual healing is also preserved among the miracles at the tomb.[68] A young women named Matilda "de partibus Coloniae" came to the shrine and was immediately labeled as demon-possessed because of her "mire insanientem." She tore her tunic (her only piece of clothing) into pieces and violently resisted anyone who tried to remove her. Fear that she might strangle a small child nearby was roused when Matilda dashed toward it, but she was prevented from touching it. She raved on before the martyr in like manner for some five or six hours before Thomas was said to have cast out the evil spirit. Having come to herself slowly throughout the night, Matilda told her story "idiomate suo, nobis vix intelligibili." She had seen the martyr in a dream that night, bloody and wearing pontifical robes. He revealed to her his own suffering, and promised her sanity and absolution from sin if she would go on pilgrimage either to "the home of the apostles" (Jerusalem) or to the church of Saint James (Compostella). When asked by the monks of Canterbury what had brought on such madness, she completed her confession: her brother had killed a youth who had loved her "heedlessly," and in horrified rage she struck her young child (conceived with the youth), who had been baptized only the day before. With her fists she had sought to do away with the baby. This was the madness for which she sought forgiveness and from which she sought release. The saint graciously shared in her suffering and restored her. "Therefore she departed from the martyr healthy and joyful, though anxious about her crime and pardon."

Caesarius of Heisterbach has three miracle stories involving Thomas, which range from the peculiar to the ridiculous. In the first, which he heard from a Cistercian abbot and which "nec in eius Passione legitur neque in libris Miraculorum eius reperitur," the archbishop had forbidden a priest in his diocese to perform the Mass. The priest was "idiota" and a "pauper et persona dispecta" as well, fully incapable of either saying the Mass or the Lord's Prayer properly. In sorrow the

[68] *Materials for the History of Thomas Becket*, ed. James Craigie Robertson and J. B. Sheppard RS, 67 (London, 1876; rpt. 1965), II, pp. 208–9 taken from Benedict of Peterborough's "Miracula sancti Thomae Cantuariensis" (book five, chapter 37).

priest cried out to the Virgin, who restored him to office through a secret sign to Thomas: his *cilicium* (hair-cloth garment) was repaired unannounced.[69] The second story further reinforces Thomas' intimate fellowship with the Virgin.[70] Here the youthful Thomas was "ab adolescencia sua castissimus" as a result of a vow made to Mary. But he struggled with this among his friends "like a lily among thorns," since they pursued youthful dalliances. One day these colleagues were recounting the gems they received from their *amicas* and in response he blurted out that a female friend had given him a gift surpassing all of theirs. When harassed by these friends to see it, he pleaded with the Virgin, who rescued him with the gift of a "pixidem parvulam valde et nimis pulchram" for all to see. Opening the box they found a purple chasuble inside, which foretold Thomas' future. When Archbishop Theobald of Canterbury (1130–61) heard of this, he promptly provided for Thomas' expenses and education in the priesthood. One wonders how closely this box resembled the reliquary for the martyr's blood that was fashioned by a Rhenish goldsmith in England (*c.* 1173–80).[71] This modified courtly love topos is joined by the final story, a bizarre account in which God rescues a small pet bird (*avincula*) from attack by a bird of prey (*milvus*), because the creature employed a phrase it had learned to imitate from its mistress: "Sancte Thoma adiuva me!"[72] Clearly St. Thomas and St. Ursula were the patrons of a vast Anglo-German *familia* of saints, sinners, and seekers, all of whom sought aid and comfort in their presence and exploits.

These varied religious artifacts and accounts widen our awareness of the Anglo-German spiritual and ecclesiastical nexus. Much of this evidence has been dismissed in the past as pious sentiments told *ut pie creditur*, however, there is much more of historical significance here. The forging of monastic brotherhoods between the regions signaled a new era of European expansion and growing interconnectedness. The subsequent written and oral transmission of miracle stories, the spread of saints' cults like St. Thomas of Canterbury and of relics like those of St. Ursula's legendary entourage, and the growth of pilgrimage sites like Cologne and Canterbury are all evidence of an ever-increasing integration of western Europe. Religious exchange is every bit as important as economic, social, or political activity for the historian who seeks evidence of trans-European intercourse in the Central Middle Ages.

---

[69] Caesarius of Heisterbach, *Dialogus Miraculorum*, II, pp. 5–6.

[70] *Die Wundergeschichten des Caesarius von Heisterbach*, ed. Hilka, III, p. 173.

[71] For a photograph of the reliquary see Carolyn Walker Bynum, *The Resurrection of the Body* (New York, 1995), plate 22.

[72] Caesarius of Heisterbach, *Dialogus Miraculorum*, II, pp. 255–6.

Indeed, the fact that monks, relics, sacred stories, prayers, and pilgrims accompanied the wine, wool, merchants, emigrants, and diplomatic embassies traveling between the Rhineland and the British Isles reminds us not only of the variety of medieval life but also of the abundant vitality of Anglo-German relations during this period.

Chapter 9

CLERICS, CANON LAW, CRUSADERS, AND CULTURE

Among the scattered references to Anglo-German cultural life we find many clerics who made use of this nexus to advance their careers in teaching and leadership within their religious orders. This sometimes brought them onto the political stage, where they proved themselves quite adept at making use of pan-European contacts for their own ends. As the age of regional cathedral schools gave way to that of universities comprised of *nationes* of foreign students, the confluence of English and German clerics naturally increased.[1] Since the educational goal of a German *scholasticus* was preparation for notarial service at the chanceries of bishops and emperors, few studied abroad in the twelfth and thirteenth centuries. Joachim Ehlers has found, for example, that of the approximately 646 German bishops from 1002 to 1197 only 25 had part of their formal education outside Germany.[2] Two of the most important archbishops of Cologne during this period, Rainald of Dassel and his successor Philip of Heinsberg, were among this select few. Hence until the early fourteenth century the direction of "the emigration of learning" ran generally from England to Germany.

Perhaps the most widely traveled expatriate scholar from England was Gervase of Tilbury (fl. 1211).[3] Born in Essex, he spent much of his youth in Italy. He studied and then taught law at Bologna for several years before returning to England in the *familia* of Earl Patrick of Salisbury. In 1177 he was present at the important meeting between Emperor Frederick Barbarossa and Pope Alexander III at Venice. Having befriended King Henry II's son and namesake during his

---

[1] Mineo Tanaka, *La Nation anglo-allemande de l'Université de Paris à la fin du Moyen Age*, Textes et documents sur l'histoire des universités, 20 (Paris, 1990).

[2] J. Ehlers, "Deutsche Scholaren in Frankreich während des 12. Jahrhunderts," in *Schulen und Studium im sozialen Wandel des hohen und späten Mittelalters*, ed. J. Fried, Vorträge und Forschungen, 30 (Sigmaringen, 1986), p. 114.

[3] See *The Dictionary of National Biography*, ed. Sir Leslie Stephen and Sir Sidney Lee (Oxford 1917–), VII, pp. 1120–1.

subsequent sojourn at home, he left England in sorrow after the young heir's drowning and served as a clerk in the *familia* of Archbishop William of Rheims (brother of the third wife of Louis VII, the father-in-law of the young King Henry). Some years thereafter he entered the service of William II of Sicily (son-in-law of Henry II of England) and then of the Plantagenet-raised Welf Emperor Otto IV of Germany, who made him marshal of the kingdom of Arles. While there he married a relative of the archbishop, Humbert of Arles, and dedicated a book to Otto IV entitled *Otio Imperialia*. This book is filled with references to natural history, geography, politics, and folklore reflecting Gervase's wide travels. The last we know of him was a friendship struck with Ralph of Coggeshall near the end of his life, when he was made a canon in England.

Gervase's remarkable career, much of which was passed in the territories of the German empire, is hard to surpass in its pan-European character and connections. But a certain Englishman named Savaric had already paved the way. He appears first in a curious letter of Emperor Henry VI to the prior and chapter of Canterbury in November/December 1191 while Richard I was on crusade.[4] Here the German monarch asked the chapter to elect as the archbishop someone who was satisfactory to him, and stated that "dilectus consanguineus noster et ecclesiae vestre devotissimus Savaricus archdiaconus" would convey to the chapter his wishes.

At this time Savaric was the archdeacon of Northampton, and related to both the emperor and to Reginald Fitz Jocelin de Bohun, the current bishop of Bath. Savaric had been appointed treasurer of Salisbury by Jocelin de Bohun before 1184 and then acquired the archdeaconry, hence he was clearly in the de Bohun *familia*. In 1186 his income from this prebend was sequestered because of debts. Thereafter, he went on some business to see Richard while the crusading king was wintering in Sicily and in return received a royal letter which decreed that he enjoyed Richard's consent for election to any bishopric which might be available.[5] Planning ahead, he forwarded the letter to his kinsman, Bishop Reginald, and went to Rome to gain papal support. When he had heard of the vacancy at Canterbury, the enterprising young cleric devised a plan which would advance both himself and his kinsman: Reginald would be elected archbishop and Savaric would then replace him at Bath. As a result of his further machinations both the emperor

---

[4] *Böhmer*, IV, 3, p. 79 no. 192.
[5] John T. Appleby, *England without Richard* (London, 1965), pp. 95–8. For the details on Savaric's career see *Chronicles and Memorials of the Reign of Richard I*, ed. William Stubbs, RS, 38 (London, 1864–5), II, pp. lxxxvii–lxxxviii.

and the king of France wrote letters of support for this proposal. We have the reason then for Henry VI's letter to the monks of Canterbury. Philip II also ·advised the monks to elect Reginald, whom Savaric had recommended, as he was a wise man and beloved by Philip's father Louis VII.[6] In an election disputed by the bishops who had supported Archbishop Walter of Rouen, the monks of Canterbury chose Reginald and he proceeded to settle affairs in Bath. After the archbishop-elect presented the royal letter of consent for Savaric's election to the chapter of Bath and personally recommended him, the convent duly elected his cousin as his successor. Reginald was not to enjoy his new pontificate, as he died on December 27 while on the way to Canterbury. Savaric, however, had succeeded and was now the bishop-elect of Bath and Wells despite his lack of ordination to the priesthood.[7]

Savaric's kinship ties with Emperor Henry VI (he claimed to be a cousin of Henry VI, which was perhaps possible through his mother Estrangia) soon drew him into intimate involvement with the negotiations for Richard I's release from German captivity. Savaric was consecrated bishop in Rome on September 19, 1192 and went directly thereafter to the imperial court. A letter from Archbishop Walter of Rouen to Bishop Hugh of Durham informs us that Savaric was busy treating with the emperor for a settlement.[8] Savaric was still present at the crucial Mainz conference on February 2–4.[9] When Richard was finally released, Savaric remained behind as a hostage for the balance of the ransom, along with Archbishop Walter of Rouen (who had disputed Reginald's election in 1191) and two sons of Henry the Lion, Otto and William, among others. Archbishop Walter was released after 10,000 marks were paid and he reached London on May 9, 1194. Savaric may have been released without payment by virtue of his kinship to the emperor.[10] During his time with Richard in Germany Savaric received two royal letters recommending him for the see of Canterbury; however, his next office was given to him by Henry VI. After his release as Richard's hostage he remained behind in Germany,

---

[6] "Epistolae Cantuarienses," *Chronicles and Memorials of the Reign of Richard I*, ed. William Stubbs, RS 38 (London 1864–5), II, pp. 350–1.

[7] *MPCM*, II, p. 395: "Eodem anno, Savaricus Norhamtoniensis archidiaconus electus est in episcopum Bathoniensem; qui Romam profectus, ibidem est presbyter ordinatus, et decimo tertio kalendas Octobris ab Albano Albaniensi episcopo munus consecrationis suscepit."

[8] Roger of Howden, *Chronica*, ed. William Stubbs, RS, 50 (London, 1868–71), III, pp. 196–7. In this letter Walter exhorts Bishop Hugh to take part in the upcoming Great Council at Oxford on February 28, 1193. Therefore Savaric had gone to Henry VI sometime between mid-September 1192 and early 1193.

[9] Roger of Howden, *Chronica*, III, pp. 231–3; Ralph de Diceto, *Ymagines historiarum*, II, pp. 112–13.

[10] *Pipe Roll 7 Richard I*, PR NS, 6, p. xvi.

becoming the imperial chancellor of Burgundy in 1196. He only returned to England after the death of the German monarch, passing his remaining days with the monks of Glastonbury and dying in 1205. Bishop Savaric of Bath, a man well placed with ties between Germany and England, played an integral role in the negotiations for Richard's release and led an amazing career with contacts throughout Europe. He is yet another example of the fascinating connections which existed between England and Germany during this era, and is surely evidence that Germany was in many ways integrated into the world of western Europe during the Central Middle Ages.

What of the Anglo-Cologne nexus in particular? While monastic ties seem to have been stronger than clerical ties during this period, there are two interesting examples of expatriate English clerics who found their way to the Rhenish metropolis. The first was the remarkable Gerard Pucelle, whose career was spent in England, France, and Cologne in the company of rival political and ecclesiastical powers.[11] Born around 1115 to 1120, Gerard was for many years a fellow philosophy student of John of Salisbury at the schools of France, where he taught as *magister* by the middle of the century. He lectured at Paris on theology as well as on both canon and civil law, and his pupils included the likes of Walter Map and Ralph Niger. He also enjoyed the patronage of Louis VII, but by the early 1160s he removed to the *familia* of the new archbishop of Canterbury, Thomas Becket, and when Thomas was exiled to France he accompanied his patron. The Alexandrine schism divided Europe during this period, and at the height of the conflict (in late 1165) Gerard Pucelle disturbed his friends and patrons by accepting a teaching post in Cologne, the episcopal city of Alexander III's arch-enemy Rainald of Dassel. Becket's secretary Herbert of Bosham sarcastically suggested that, exhausted from the stress of exile in Becket's entourage, Gerard desired a little peace.[12]

We are fortunate that John of Salisbury maintained correspondence with his old schoolmate during the latter's sojourn in Cologne, which affords us insight into the issues and machinations of the schism. We learn, for example, that Gerard had even invited John to join him among the schismatics in Cologne – a thought abhorrent to the

---

[11] See Stephan Kuttner and Eleanor Rathbone, "Anglo-Norman canonists of the twelfth century. An introductory study," *Traditio* 7 (1949–51), pp. 296–303 and Johannes Fried, "Gerard Pucelle und Köln," *Zeitschrift der Savigny-Stiftung für Rechtsgeschichte, Kanonistische Abteilung* 68 (1982), pp. 125–35.

[12] Herbert of Bosham, "Vita S. Thomae," *Materials for the History of Thomas Becket*, ed. Robertson and Sheppard, RS, 67 (London, 1876; rpt. 1965), III, p. 525.

Alexandrine partisan.[13] In his own distinctive prose style, John warned Gerard of the risks he was taking. Reminding Gerard of their "common father the archbishop of Canterbury" at the outset, he ironically compared his own Pauline plight with Gerard's comfortable situation in Cologne:

With God's help you have found grace among the Church's enemies . . . abundance of temporal goods . . . more or less supreme authority in scholarship . . . those barbarous people they regard as an oracle whatever you in your wisdom may have determined.[14]

All in all this is a blunt criticism of Gerard for exiling himself in Babylon in order to achieve worldly success and wealth. He also suggested that the benefice given to Pucelle in exchange for his services as cathedral *scholasticus* was substantial. John admonished Gerard to use his teaching authority in Cologne "to call back the wanderers from their schism" and compared him to Zerubbabel, "which is translated the prince or teacher of Babylon."[15] John's scruples about schismatic Cologne did not interfere, however, with his own desire to benefit from Gerard's presence there. He closed the letter with the following entreaty:

I have asked you before now, and now repeat my request: do send me as an old friend a fragment of the relics of the kings and virgins, with supporting letters from yourself.

By the autumn of 1166 the Becket affair had reached a dangerous pass, and John of Salisbury's concern for his friend's reputation is evident in the next missive.[16] In a lengthy letter John informed Gerard that Becket's power had been increased by papal confirmation of him as legate and primate of England, and then warned Gerard with many Old Testament tales of judgment not to succumb to the schismatics. We learn here that Gerard had actually obtained papal permission to go to Cologne, but danger still lay in other quarters:

Know, then, that there were various opinions as to your departure: many condemned, a few defended the journey you made. The crowd did not know what you had in mind, the compulsion you were under, the permission you

---

[13] *The Letters of John of Salisbury. Volume II: 1163–1180*, ed. W. J. Millor, H. E. Butler, and C. N. L. Brooke, Oxford Medieval Texts (Oxford, 1979), p. 99 (letter 167). In this letter to Master Raymond, chancellor of Poitiers cathedral, written just before Becket's annulment of the Constitutions of Clarendon at Vézelay (June 1166), John tells of Gerard's invitation and his response: "Vocat me magister Girardus ut, salva fide ecclesiae Romanae, Coloniam transeam; sed, auctore pio Iesu, pro nullo quaestu ponam cum scismaticis ad subversionem domus Domini scismatis portionem."

[14] Ibid., pp. 69–71 (letter 158). The English translations used here are those of the editors.

[15] Zerubbabel was a Hebrew prophet-priest in the pagan empire of Persia. See I Esdras (Ezra).

[16] *The Letters of John of Salisbury. Volume II: 1163–1180*, pp. 211–23 (letter 184).

had from the pope, the advantage the Church can receive from your decision. Their eyes are on the crime of schism, the wickedness of those to whom you have travelled, the danger of living among men excommunicated for good reason and in due form. They see you involved in the affairs of the damned, and they think you are acquiescing in their error.

What compulsion John speaks of here eludes us, perhaps a mission to function as a backchannel in negotiations between the European factions. In any case, clearly the price of such a venture had become dangerously high. John compared Gerard to St. Paul declaring Christ before the emperor (which proved to be costly for Paul), and then set before him an agenda: persuade Rainald of Dassel to speak to Henry II about bringing an end to the persecution of Becket, and soothe the anger of Louis VII, whose offense at Gerard's neglect to visit him *en route* to Cologne or to inform the king of his intention to leave the French kingdom had become known. Gerard was not merely like St. Paul before the emperor, but now stood before three powerful monarchs and two archbishops! In all this John had been active writing letters on behalf of Gerard to Becket and other bishops, as well as forwarding Pucelle's own letters. John was obviously the conduit between "Gerard in Babylon" and the Alexandrine party.

The two friends reveal their humanist bond again a few months later. After inquiring if Gerard knew whether Rainald of Dassel was to join Barbarossa's fateful expedition to Rome, John requested, "please tell me if you will of anything fresh you find in the book-cupboards you have pillaged."[17] He was looking in particular for the "visiones et oracula beatae illius et celeberrimae Hildegardis" – the writings of Hildegard of Bingen, in which he hoped to find a prophecy concerning the end of the schism. John also asked Gerard to protect the *res beati Remigii*; perhaps books which he had lent to Pucelle from the abbey library, or even the *curia* at Meerssen, where the monks had constant trouble with the lords of Heinsberg.[18] Since John was living at the abbey of St. Remigius in Rheims at this time he was well aware of the monks' affairs. Pucelle wrote back to the Becket party that Rainald was too ill to cross the Alps until after the winter of 1166–7.[19] No doubt everyone in the Alexandrine faction thought of the coming clash between

---

[17] Ibid., pp. 223–5 (letter 185).

[18] The Heinsberg dynasty was well placed in the Cologne archdiocese: Philip of Heinsberg was to be the successor of Rainald of Dassel as archbishop. Perhaps John expected Gerard to intervene personally to resolve the property dispute. See *MGH Diplomata* X, 1, p. 14 no. 8 (dated 1152) and *Papsturkunden in den Niederländen*, ed. J. Ramackers, Abhandlungen der Gesellschaft der Wissenschaften zu Göttingen. Philologisch-historische Klasse 3. Folge, 9 (Berlin, 1934; rpt. 1972), p. 249 no. 114 (dated 1165–6).

[19] *Materials for the History of Thomas Becket*, ed. Robertson, VI, Epistolae 234.

Barbarossa's army and Alexander III's partisans in Rome in apocalyptic terms, and they would not be disappointed. John's reply to Gerard's news about the archbishop shows increased anxiety about the current circumstances. He acknowledged Gerard's assertion that grain is mixed with chaff in life, and good men with bad, but exhorted him again to avoid casting his lot with the schismatics. In the most heated rhetoric to date, John conferred on Rainald of Dassel the following epithets: anathema, usurper, despiser of the church, blasphemer, and the "greatest among the locusts of the beasts, whose power is in their tongues and their tails."[20] Any hope that Gerard could affect the course of events was fading in the face of the upcoming showdown in Rome. John also referred to Gerard's relationship with the French king, a patron whose good graces were becoming increasingly indispensable to the Alexandrine party. John told Gerard not to blame the French king's anger on Becket and his circle, whom Pucelle clearly suspected were undermining his reputation. Rather, Gerard was told that he brought Louis VII's opprobrium upon himself by leaving France and accepting the patronage of Rainald, who Louis said "has the habit (so he has heard) of calling him a kinglet, with impudent buffoonery."[21]

Gerard's untenable situation finally gave way with the death of Archbishop Rainald, ironically of pestilence at the moment of Barbarossa's conquest of Rome in August 1167. The apocalyptic encounter with Antichrist had happened, and Armageddon was rescued by the Angel of Death, or so John of Salisbury and the Alexandrine party believed. John thereafter exhorted Gerard to exercise a prophetic role in Cologne to draw the emperor back into the fold:

For it may be that it was for the salvation of many that the Lord sent you to that barbarian land so that your intervention may restore the church of Cologne to the unity of the Catholic Church now the author of the schism [i.e. Rainald of Dassel] has perished. The emperor has retired in confusion from Rome, like a brand plucked from the burning. The stench of corpses has gone up from the camp to his nostrils, and the Lord has stretched forth his

---

[20] Revelation 9: 3, 10, 19.

[21] Rainald let loose his famous complaint that the *reguli* arrogantly claimed for themselves the authority of the Roman emperor to adjudicate the papal schism, after Louis VII had failed to meet Barbarossa at St. Jean-de-Losne on August 29, 1162 to settle the schism. See Ferdinand Opll, *Friedrich Barbarossa*, Gestalten des Mittelalters und der Renaissance (Darmstadt, 1990), pp. 76, 81–4; Walter Heinemeyer, "Die Verhandlungen an der Sâone im Sommer 1162," *DA* 20 (1964), pp. 155–89; Franz Josef Schmale, "Friedrich I. und Ludwig VII. im Sommer des Jahres 1162," *Zeitschrift für Bäyrische Landesgeschichte* 31 (1968), pp. 315–68; Walter Kienast, *Deutschland und Frankreich in der Kaiserzeit (900–1270). Weltkaiser und Einzelkönige*, Monographien zur Geschichte des Mittelalters, 9: 1–3 (Stuttgart, 1974–5), I, pp. 203–10 and T. Reuter, *The Papal Schism of 1159–1169, the Empire and the West*, PhD thesis, Oxford University (1975), pp. 80–101.

hand over him; yet still he would not see and admit the error of his ways. So let your spirit be roused to action, for Christ is conqueror, king and emperor.[22]

Gerard, however, chose not to play the prophet, but instead disappointed Becket's party once again by returning to England in the summer of 1168 and performing the oath of fealty to Henry II, which Becket's partisans refused to do.[23] In an extensive letter from John dated after May 1168, we learn the reasons for Pucelle's unexpected move.[24] John responded at length to Gerard's anger at Becket because of rumors he heard that the archbishop's followers had "spoken against your good name" at the French court. John asserted that Becket had not done so, but conceded that some of his party may have "inadvertently spoken against you or other folks, to curry favour with those they reckoned would welcome such remarks." Louis VII remained infuriated with Gerard, and thus the scholar had not only gambled away Becket and the French king as his patrons, but also lost the benefaction of the dead archbishop of Cologne, whom John called "the chief craftsman, inspirer, and standard-bearer of the whole schism." Where else could Pucelle turn for patrons except to Rome and the English king?

While those favoring Gerard in Becket's circle (including the archbishop himself) were actively seeking Louis VII's permission for Gerard's return to France, John admitted that others were "less than energetic in arranging your recall" before the pope, and that a complication had arisen over whether or not Pucelle had "sworn to the schismatic's error."[25] John's personal involvement in the rehabilitation of his old friend is testified to by his presence at the conversation when Becket obtained Louis VII's permission for Gerard's return, and by the participation of his *cognatus* (a former student of Pucelle named Master Richard) in the Roman mission; indeed, Richard had died of illness on the return trip. John also indicated that he had written letters of support to both pope and Becket. Perhaps these letters had initiated the entire process. Thus there was much activity surrounding the restoration of Pucelle, which proved difficult given his fraternization with the enemy and current position as client of Henry II. John concluded the letter by warning him not to remain "out of temper" with Becket or to plan departing from Cologne before the road to France was reopened.

---

[22] *The Letters of John of Salisbury. Volume II: 1163–1180*, pp. 395–7 (letter 226).

[23] Ibid., p. 579 (letter 275): in this letter to John of Canterbury, bishop of Poitiers, he informs the bishop of papal news that Gerard had done so "without seeing or saluting the archbishop of Canterbury, who made him a clerk and gave him his first benefice in the Church."

[24] Ibid., pp. 591–9 (letter 277).

[25] John indicates that a copy of a letter Gerard had sent to Louis VII asking permission to return had also been forwarded to Pope Alexander III by Becket.

Rather, making peace with the English king should not be done at the risk of an oath that would engender his salvation. Gerard thus should "tread warily" around the king and not forget Becket, his "first shepherd." Apparently Gerard could not wait for matters to settle with the papal–French faction and made his separate peace with the English king.

Thomas was not pleased in the least by Pucelle's reconciliation with Henry II, as we learn in a subsequent letter.[26] He was particularly angered that Gerard had been in communication with the archdeacon of Canterbury whom Becket had excommunicated. Gerard had written to the archbishop encouraging him to meet with the archdeacon and the bishop of Séez in Paris to resolve his dispute with Henry II. Once again we find Gerard functioning as a diplomatic backchannel in efforts to reconcile monarchs and ecclesiastics. Perhaps he did so out of necessity, or maybe we find here a consistent pattern of mediation which Pucelle felt called to perform as a scholar of both canon and civil law. In either case, he spent much time and energy in the fissures between temporal and spiritual power. John did not discourage such efforts in England (much as he had not before in Cologne), but counseled Gerard:

From now on do your negotiations more cautiously; take greater care to avoid intercourse with excommunicates, while working all the harder for their absolution – unless you wish yourself to be cut swiftly off from the Church and receive with them the portion of anathema.

This letter, written at the instance of Becket, was a cautionary response to Pucelle's offer to parley, and reveals what a dangerous and impossible task he had taken on in both Cologne and England.[27]

Papal intervention did more to restore Pucelle's good name than his own efforts at reconciling Becket and Henry II. Alexander III, perhaps seeing the diplomatic utility of showing favor to Gerard, wrote to Becket in June of 1168 and informed the archbishop that Gerard, "*suum recognoscens excessum,*" had been granted absolution. But this absolution was conditional: he was *nullo modo* to retain the *beneficium* given to him by the schismatics, unless the Cologne church returned to the Roman church and still desired to give it to him. Secondly, Gerard was to perform an oath designed for him and all others returning

---

[26] *The Letters of John of Salisbury. Volume II: 1163–1180*, pp. 685–91 (letter 297).

[27] John bluntly offers the archbishop's reply: "You promise kisses and embraces, if we comply with the man's wishes. He also who is the pattern for Christian men has heard the tempter say, 'All these things will I give unto you, if you will fall down and worship me.'"

a schismate.[28] We learn from Becket's letter commissioning the abbot and prior of de Valle to administer the oath to Gerard that the archbishop himself *per litteras et nuntios* had obtained this grant, which excused Gerard's departure to Cologne *sub praetextu licentiae* given him previously by the pope.[29] Thus Gerard's claim of papal permission to go to Cologne became the pretext for his restoration; but he was unable to avoid the taint of schism without exculpating himself with an oath.[30] The oath itself contains striking language which, while absolving Gerard of fraternizing with schismatics in Cologne, also directly contradicts his prior oath of fidelity to Henry II. Now he swears to be *obediens et fidelis* to Alexander and his successors.

The reward for this act of submission was restoration in France.[31] Alexander III also wrote to Louis VII, informing him that Gerard had repented of his association *cum delinquentibus* and was now worthy of the king's mercy; Louis was asked to allow Pucelle to dwell in France *sicut consueverat*. It appears that Gerard taught again in Paris for several years thereafter. Sometime in 1174–5, after the Becket crisis was ended by his murder, Gerard returned to administrative duties as the secretary of Thomas' successor, Archbishop Richard of Canterbury. He held this post until 1180, and was even sent by Richard to the Third Lateran Council in Rome in 1179. Yet the yearning to teach, as well as to regain his German benefice, did not fade during these years of service. In February 1178 Gerard was at the papal curia on archiepiscopal business, but he also obtained for himself two papal indulgences through the good offices of Archbishop Christian of Mainz. The first allowed him to retain his English benefices for four years should he return to teaching. In the following month Alexander permitted him to seek resumption of the German benefice he lost in 1168.[32] Apparently his renewed contact with German bishops at the papal curia and at the Third Lateran had induced him to return to Cologne, since he was again teaching as cathedral *scholasticus* from *c.* 1180 to 1182. His successor in Cologne, a certain Rudolf (under whom Caesarius of Heisterbach

---

[28] *Materials for the History of Thomas Becket*, ed. Robertson, VI, Epistolae 420.

[29] Ibid., VI, Epistolae 419.

[30] Ibid., VI, Epistolae 421 contains the oath: "Ego Girardus refuto et anathematizo omnem haeresim extollentem se adversus sanctam ecclesiam catholicam, et praecipue schisma et haerisim Octaviani et Guidonis Cremensis. Ordinationes quoque eorum irritas esse pronuntio, et amodo in antea obediens et fidelis ero domino papae Alexandro, ejusque successoribus catholicis. Sic me Deus adjuvet, et haec sancta Dei Evangelia."

[31] Ibid., VI, Epistolae 422.

[32] Fried, "Gerard Pucelle und Köln," pp. 129–30 and Kuttner, "Anglo-Norman canonists of the twelfth century," p. 302.

and Barbarossa's youngest son Philip had studied), conveniently went to Paris to teach during these years.[33]

It is quite surprising that Gerard Pucelle chose to teach in Cologne again instead of Paris at this stage of his career. The special arrangements whereby he could keep his English benefices while a member of the cathedral canons in Cologne (where residency was required for a benefice) and whereby Rudolf was shipped off to Paris to make room for Pucelle in Cologne, say a great deal about how much he desired to teach in the Rhenish metropolis. This was fortunate, for his contribution to the study of canon law in the Rhineland proved to be substantial, despite the interruption occasioned by the schism. A school of canon law emerged in Cologne, where a number of significant canonistic works were composed and copies of Gratian's *Decretum* were transcribed.[34] No doubt this school was patronized by Archbishop Rainald of Dassel and his successor Philip of Heinsberg, both of whom studied in France and subsequently sought to draw scholars from the French schools to Cologne.[35] Although few Cologne cathedral masters had gone to France for an education before Gerard's arrival, after his sojourn a series of *scholastici* learned in canon law appear. The influence of this English canonist and teacher on the spread of canon law literacy throughout the Rhineland had tangible results.[36] In fact, there is strong evidence that students from France and Italy came to Cologne during these years.[37]

With time running short on his papal indulgence for English benefices and himself advanced in years, Gerard made good use of his friendships among the papal *curia* and English episcopacy to gain the bishopric of Coventry in 1183. There he died a few months later with

---

[33] Fried, "Gerard Pucelle und Köln," p. 132.

[34] The outstanding *Summa Elegantius in iure divino* (or *Summa Coloniensis*), the *Distinctiones Monacenses*, and the *Hactenus magister Gratianus egit in personis* for example. Stephan Kuttner ("Anglo-Norman canonists of the twelfth century," p. 300) has concluded about the Cologne school of canon law: "If we add that the English Master Gerard was in Cologne while this Summa and other works on canon law were being written in that city, then the hypothesis of a special connection between the school of Cologne and the early English canonists becomes very suggestive."

[35] Caesarius of Heisterbach, *Dialogus Miraculorum*, I, pp. 84f. and 215 informs us that Philip of Heinsberg had a tutor (*magister et paedagogus*) in Rheims named Godfrey, who later became the master of the schools of St. Andrew in Cologne and an Augustinian canon until he joined the Cistercians in old age.

[36] Fried, "Gerard Pucelle und Köln," p. 135: "Die Rechtswissenschaft und das Interesse an ihr verbreiteten sich offenbar über die Schulen und die gelehrten Lehrer im Rheinland."

[37] See the "Annales Sancti Dionisii," *MGH SS*, XIII, p. 720 and Timothy Reuter, "John of Salisbury and the Germans," *The World of John of Salisbury*, ed. Michael Wilks, Studies in Church History, Subsidia, 3 (Oxford, 1984), p. 416. Clearly the schism did not hinder the traffic of students.

some suspicion that he had been poisoned.[38] His lengthy service to the archbishops of Canterbury was duly remembered when the cathedral monks celebrated his *obit* with rites usually reserved for an archbishop.[39]

For too long John of Salisbury's estimation of the Germans as wayward barbarians has served as a basis for modern Anglophone evaluations of the medieval *regnum Teutonicum*.[40] But even his hostile responses (no doubt fueled by personal dislike of Rainald of Dassel, a man whom he knew well) give the lie to modern dismissals of medieval Germany as beyond the pale of western European civilization. The very issue that angered John so, the pretensions of the German monarchy to direct the papacy, should be a clear indicator of the central place the *regnum Teutonicum* and its leadership held in Europe during the Central Middle Ages. One can disagree with the Teutons, but one cannot dismiss them altogether. Perhaps it would be better to take Gerard Pucelle's experience as a corrective to Salisbury's vituperative rhetoric. His interest in teaching at Cologne suggests that the city was not on the fringes of civilization (as defined by that which radiated from Paris in these years), and the fact that the Salisbury–Pucelle correspondence had only to pass through Lotharingia (from Rheims to Cologne) reminds us that the Rhineland was not that far East after all. The preference of such a cosmopolitan scholar as Pucelle for Cologne over Paris or England (often against tremendous pressure) is enough to recommend a reevaluation of our historiography when it comes to medieval Europe in general and Anglo-German relations in particular.

The second English cleric who can be documented in Cologne leaves us with a tantalizing possibility. Two strips of parchment in the Public Record Office preserve requests by a certain John "dictus de Garlandia" sent to the chancellor of England.[41] In the first John requests that his attorneys collect his rents, and in the second that "meos clericos et procuratores" might have portions "in rebus meis temporalibus et

[38] Gervase of Canterbury, *Chronicle of the Reigns of Stephen, Henry II, and Richard I*, ed. William Stubbs, RS, 73 (London, 1879; rpt. 1965), I, pp. 307–8.

[39] Obit list in British Museum Cotton MS. Nero C. ix, fo. 3v.

[40] For John of Salisbury's limited understanding of Germany and the German character see Timothy Reuter, "John of Salisbury and the Germans"; Horst Fuhrmann, "Quis Teutonicos constituit iudices nationum? The trouble with Henry," *Speculum* 69: 2 (April 1994), pp. 344–58; and J. Spörl, "Rainald von Dassel auf dem Konzil von Reims 1148 und sein Verhältnis zu Johann von Salisbury," *Historisches Jahrbuch des Görres-Gesellschaft* 60 (1940), pp. 250–7. For stereotypical representations of Germans see Ernst Dümmler, "Über den furor Teutonicus," *Sitzungsberichte der königlichen preußischen Akademie der Wissenschaften zu Berlin no. 9* (Berlin, 1897); Fritz Kern, "Der mittelalterliche Deutsche in französischer Ansicht," *Historische Zeitschrift* 108 (1911); Franz Böhm, *Das Bild Friedrich Barbarossas und seines Kaisertums in den ausländischen Quellen seiner Zeit*, Historische Studien, 289 (Berlin, 1936; rpt. 1965), esp. pp. 87–104.

[41] PRO SC1 vol. XVIII: 3 and PRO SC1 vol. X: 148.

spiritualibus in Anglia secundum tenorem litterarum domini regi Anglie per dictos clericos meos a me transmissarum." Both missives indicate Cologne as their point of origin, and are dated by the archivist as "early Edward I." The question immediately arises as to whether this was the famed teacher, poet, and musician John of Garland, who studied at Oxford and then taught at the Universities of Paris (where he gained his surname by teaching in the *Clos de Garlande*) and Toulouse from the 1220s onward. William Waite concluded that "the remainder of his life was spent in the environs of the University of Paris until his death sometime after 1272,"[42] while Louis Paetow lamented, "It is regrettable that we know so little about John of Garland's later years . . . there is no certainty about the place and year of his death" (though he too dates John's death after 1272).[43] A generally accepted post-1272 death fits nicely with the dating of the parchment strips in the Public Record Office, and no one knows his whereabouts late in life. In addition we know that John of Garland's treatise on rhythmic poetry had a profound influence on the thirteenth-century theorist Franco of Cologne.[44] The one mitigating factor placing the famous poet and musician in Cologne is the way in which John identifies himself here as "presbyter et canonicus de castello Tykehillie." The remains of the Norman castle of Tickhill can still be found in southern Yorkshire, south of Doncaster, but that the scholar John of Garland held a prebend there cannot be demonstrated.[45] At the least we have another instance of English clergy in Cologne (with apparently high connections with king and chancellor), and at best we might just have found the retirement home for John of Garland after his renowned teaching career.[46]

The coming of the friars in the thirteenth century added a new dimension to émigré life between England and Germany. With the arrival of the Franciscans in the region, new provinces were established and English leadership was imported into Germany. We have already encountered Bartholomaeus Anglicus, the Franciscan who studied and taught theology in Paris before being transferred to the province of

---

[42] William G. Waite, "Johannes de Garlandia, poet and musician," *Speculum* 35: 2 (April 1960), p. 181.

[43] Louis John Paetow, *Morale Scolarium of John of Garland, a Professor in the Universities of Paris in the Thirteenth Century*, Memoirs of the University of California, 4: 2 (Berkeley, 1927), p. 95.

[44] Waite, "Johannes de Garlandia, poet and musician," p. 182.

[45] There was an Austin friary established in Tickhill around 1260, but the existence of a canonry at the castle remains undocumented. See Nikolaus Pevsner, *Yorkshire: The West Riding*, The Buildings of England, rev. edn. Enid Radcliffe (Harmondsworth, 1959; rpt. 1967), pp. 518–21.

[46] The surname Garland can be demonstrated elsewhere in England: a John Garland was prebendary of St. Paul's in 1200 and another was sheriff of London in 1212 (see *Dictionary of National Biography*, VII, p. 877).

Saxony in 1231.[47] He taught at the Franciscan *studium generale* in Magdeburg until around 1250 and there wrote his famous *De proprietatibus rerum*.[48] No doubt Bartholomaeus was requested by the minister of the Saxon province, Simon of England (1230) or by his successor John of Reading (1230–2), and was joined in this mission by another English Franciscan, Johannes Anglicus.[49]

Peter of Tewkesbury successively held the office of warden of the London convent (1234), warden of the Oxford convent (1236–48), and vicar of the English province (appointed 1236) before moving to Cologne as the provincial minister of Cologne in 1250.[50] He returned after four years to become the provincial minister of England until 1258. Thomas of Eccleston tells of the tensions and confusion resulting from early expatriate Franciscan interactions. In 1237–8 the minister general Elias sent a certain Wygerius Alemannus – "vir valde famosus in peritia iuris et in omni honestate conspicuus et domino Ottoni cardinali, qui tunc erat legatus in Anglia, familiarissimus" – on a visitation of the English province. He possessed the power of excommunication to enforce obedience to the rule, and exercised it so stringently that the entire provincial chapter of England unanimously lodged an appeal against him. The *turbatio* spread to Scotland, where that chapter rebelled against his planned arrival. The crisis was resolved by having another brother visit Scotland on his behalf and report to him in Cologne.[51] Elsewhere we encounter Peter of Tewkesbury's remarkable response to the worldly nephews of cardinals sent him in Lyon by the pope. Thomas states that Peter did not reject them as candidates because they were unfamiliar with the *linguam Anglicanam*, but because they sought nothing *nisi temporalia*. When the curial advocate announced the nephews' refusal to accept the rigors of mendicancy by saying "canones hoc volunt," Peter replied "Immo, canes hoc volunt" and on bended knee before the youths beat his breast and tearfully lamented in English.

[47] The Franciscan province of Teutonia was divided into the provinces of Saxony and the Rhine in 1230, and the Rhine province split into those of Cologne and Strasbourg in 1247.

[48] Höfer and Rahner, *Lexicon für Theologie und Kirche*, II, pp. 9–10: "einer der ersten Enzyklopädisten des MA, gg. Ende des 12. Jh. in Alt-Engl., wahrsch. aus dem adligen Geschlecht de Glanville (lange mit einem Namensgenossen [1360] verwechselt); war Bacclaureus bibl. von Paris, als er 1231 ans Magdeburger Ordensstudium kam. Schrieb die naturwiss. orientierte, viel gelesene Enzyklopädie *De proprietatibus rerum* (wohl 1240–50 beendet)." For the text see *On the Properties of Things: John Trevisa's Translation of Bartholomaeus Anglicus' De proprietatibus rerum. A Critical Text*, ed. M. C. Seymour et al., 3 vols. (Oxford, 1975–88).

[49] See John B. Freed, *The Friars and German Society in the Thirteenth Century* (Cambridge, Mass., 1977), p. 122 note 44 and *Dictionary of National Biography*, VII, p. 1289.

[50] *Fratris Thomas vulgo dicti de Eccleston Tractatus de Adventu Fratrum Minorum in Angliam*, ed. A. G. Little (Manchester, 1951), pp. 91, 201 and *A Biographical Register of the University of Oxford to A.D. 1500*, ed. A. B. Emden (Oxford, 1959), III, p. 1857.

[51] *De Adventu Fratrum Minorum in Angliam*, ed. Little, pp. 38–9.

Completely confused by this display, the youths departed with the advocate in silence![52]

The Franciscans and Dominicans arrived within months of each other in Cologne during the year 1221, and soon overcame the institutional resistance to their new orders.[53] The Franciscans especially enjoyed the patronage of several patrician families, whose wealth was built on commercial ties with England. The Quartermart family, for example, gave the Franciscans property in St. Severin's parish for the building of an oratory.[54] Eventually the convent removed to St. Columba parish, where they built a new church and consecrated it in 1260. As a sign of the integration of the friars into city life, the adjoining street eventually took its name from the church, and is still known today as Minoritenstrasse. English Franciscans played a crucial role in the establishment of this community, as well as others in Germany. The Dominicans also became deeply intermeshed with the Cologne patrician families, as we saw in chapter 5 when Philippus Anglicus and his uncle Ricolfus Cleingedanc appear as members of the *ordo Praedicatorum* in the early 1290s.

We cannot end our consideration of the Anglo-Cologne mendicant connection without mention of its best-known member, the Franciscan John Duns Scotus. After having lectured at Oxford and Cambridge and finally receiving his degree from the University of Paris in 1305, he lectured there for an additional two years before being sent to Cologne by the order. Here the *doctor subtilis* lectured on theology for a short time until his untimely death in 1308 at the age of forty-two. His work in Cologne as an educator was briefer than Gerard Pucelle, but he is better remembered there. His body remains interred in the Minoritenkirche, where he is venerated by the Franciscan order and considered an equal to the other great mendicant theologian of Cologne, the Dominican *doctor universalis* Albertus Magnus.[55]

The reverse flow of Cologne students and clergy to England was later

---

[52] Ibid., pp. 91–2: "Item dixit fratri Johanni de Dya, quod provideret sibi sex vel septem idoneos clericos de partibus suis, quos posset beneficiare in ecclesia sua; qui scilicet, quamvis nescirent Anglicum, exemplo praedicarent. Unde constat, quod non recusavit eos quos papa instituit, et nepotes cardinalium, quia nesciebant linguam Anglicanam, sed quia non quaerebant nisi temporalia. Unde cum diceret ei advocatus in cura: 'Canones hoc volunt,' respondit: 'Immo, canes hoc volunt.' Surrexit et confessus est Anglice, flexis genibus, coram pueris praesentatis a cardinalibus sibi, et tundebat pectus suum cum fletu et eiulatu, et sic confusi recesserunt." The event is dated 1250.

[53] See the chapter on the friars of Cologne in John Freed's *The Friars and German Society in the Thirteenth Century.*

[54] *Ennen/Eckertz*, II, no. 110.

[55] See Konrad Eubel, *Geschichte der Kölnischen Minoriten-Ordensprovinz*, Veröffentlichungen des historischen Vereins für den Neiderrhein, I (Cologne, 1906).

in coming. By the late thirteenth century we begin to see the early signs of emigration that would reach significant proportions in the fourteenth and fifteenth centuries. This late date reflects the rising status of Oxford and Cambridge *vis-à-vis* Paris rather than any hesitancy on the part of German students to travel to England.[56] The English universities, mendicant convents, and cathedrals (like St. Paul's in London) maintained many Cologne students, friars, and canons throughout the Later Middle Ages,[57] and once the University of Cologne was opened in 1388 English students could be found attending there.[58] Cologne clergy appear in Lincolnshire by the early 1290s but not until the early fourteenth century do we find them in any great number.[59] If we were to widen the net to include all German students and religious beyond Cologne the number of participants would increase but as a whole they would merely confirm the pattern. In this regard the Anglo-Cologne religious and academic nexus was more extensive in the Later Middle Ages than in the Central Middle Ages.

The crusading movement marks another type of Anglo-Cologne cooperation typical of the blended religious, political, economic, social, and cultural interests that bound the regions together. The fall of Edessa in 1144 stirred up renewed interest in crusading, and both Conrad III and Louis VI of France took the cross in the first real European crusade. While the Saxons preferred to stay near home and led a crusade against

---

56 See A. Budinsky, *Die Universität Paris und die Fremden an derselben im Mittelalter* (Innsbruck, 1924); William J. Courtenay, *Schools and Scholars in Fourteenth-Century England* (Princeton, 1987) and *Teaching Careers at the University of Paris in the Thirteenth and Fourteenth Centuries* (Notre Dame, Indiana, 1988), p. 18.

57 *A Biographical Register of the University of Cambridge to 1500*, ed. A. M. Emden (Cambridge, 1963), pp. 149–50; *Alumni Cantabrigienses. A Biographical List of All Known Students, Graduates and Holders of Office at the University of Cambridge from Earliest Times to 1900. Part 1: From Earliest Times to 1751*, ed. John Venn and J. A. Venn (Cambridge, 1922), I, p. 375; *A Biographical Register of the University of Oxford to A.D. 1500*, ed. A. B. Emden (Oxford, 1957), I, pp. 469–70; *A Survey of Dominicans in England Based on the Ordination Lists in Episcopal Registers (1268–1538)*, ed. A. E. Emden, Institutum Historicum FF. Praedicatorum Romae ad S. Sabinae. Dissertationes Historicae Fasciculus 18 (Rome, 1967), p. 311; *Fasti Anglicanae 1300–1541. Volume V: St. Paul's London*, ed. John Le Neve (London, 1963), p. 58. The most illustrious of these emigré students was the Augustinian friar Giso of Cologne, who received his doctorate in theology at Oxford around 1384 and went on to become the provincial prior of the Austin friars in Cologne and dean of the faculty of theology there in 1399 (see *A Biographical Register of the University of Oxford to A.D. 1500*, ed. Emden, I, pp. 469–70).

58 Hermann Keussen, *Die Matrikel der Universität Köln*, PGRG, 8: 1 (Bonn, 1928), pt. 2, p. 11: "Richardus Anglicus, magister in artibus, Dunelmensis diocesis" enrolled in 1389 for example.

59 *The Rolls and Register of Bishop Oliver Sutton*, ed. Rosalind Hill, Publications of the Lincoln Record Society, 69 (London, 1975), p. 48 where the Franciscan Baldwin of Cologne appears on an ordination list for Wycombe dated December 19, 1293; *The Victoria County History of the City of Cambridge and the Isle of Ely*, ed. L. F. Salzman (London, 1948), II, p. 306 where John de Colonia was prior of the hospital of St. John the Evangelist in Cambridge (1321) for example.

the Wends, in the lower Rhineland and Flanders participants chose to take the sea route around Europe to join the Second Crusade in 1147. Among these crusaders were Cologne burghers, who had been spurred to action by the preaching of Bernard of Clairvaux in their city.[60] Accounts of this venture appear in many chronicles, with the eyewitness description *De expugnatione Lyxbonensi* as our main source.[61] The largest contingent of German ships under the direction of Count Arnold of Aerschot, which had assembled at Cologne, left port in late April and arrived at the English harbor of Dartmouth on May 19. There they met Flemish participants under the leadership of Christian de Ghistelles and added to their number an English army from Norfolk and Suffolk under the leadership of Henry (or Hervey) Glanville, a prominent local landowner and constable in Suffolk. Henry also held a general authority over additional participants from Kent, London, Southampton, Bristol, Hastings, Normandy, and even from as far away as Scotland.[62] This massive flotilla is estimated to have comprised at least ten thousand crusaders.[63] At an average of 70 men per ship this required approximately 150 ships, which is close to Osbern's report of 164 ships. This amazing array of regional representatives certainly required a great deal of organization and coordination. Oaths of unity and peace were taken, priests were placed on each ship for hearing confession and dispensing

---

[60] *REK*, I, p. 76 no. 446 dated January 13, 1147, where Bernard also is reputed to have healed a blind child in the presence of Archbishop Arnold I. Prior to this visit Bernard had convinced Conrad III to participate in the crusade at the Frankfurt diet (November 1146): Gaufridus, "Vita et res gestae sancti Bernardi," *Recueil des historiens des Gaules et de la France*, ed. M. Bouquet (Paris, 1877), XIV, p. 378 and Odo of Deuil, *De profectione Ludovici VII in orientem*, ed. Virginia Berry (New York, 1948), p. 13.

[61] Osbern, "De expugnatione Lyxbonensi," *Chronicles and Memorials of the Reign of Richard I*, ed. William Stubbs, RS, 38 (London, 1864; rpt. 1964), I, pp. cxliv–clxxxii – this text has also been edited and translated by C. W. David in *De expugnatione Lyxbonensi*, Columbia University Records of Civilization, 24 (New York, 1936). For other accounts see *CRC*, pp. 84–6; "Annales de Waverleia," p. 232; Robert of Torigni, *Chronica*, p. 155; "Annales Magdeburgenses," p. 189; "Annales sancti Disbodi," pp. 27–8; "Gesta Alberonis Archiepiscopus auctore Balderico," *MGH SS*, VIII, pp. 254–5; "Chronicon montis sereni," *MGH SS*, XXIII, p. 147; Roger of Howden, *Chronica*, p. 210; Helmold of Bosau, *Slawenchronik*, ed. Heinz Stoob, Ausgewählte Quellen zur Deutschen Geschichte des Mittelalters, Freiherr von Stein-Gedächtnisausgabe, 19 (Darmstadt, 1973), p. 220 and a letter sent by a Cologne priest named Winand to Archbishop Arnold I dated March 21, 1148, in which the priest tells Arnold about the conquest of Lisbon: *REK*, II, p. 79 no. 460. See also Friedrich Kurth, "Der Anteil Niederdeutscher Kreuzfahrer an den Kämpfen der Portugiesen gegen die Mauren," *MIÖG Ergäzungsband* 8 (1911), pp. 131–252; Giles Constable, "A note on the route of the Anglo-Flemish crusaders," *Speculum* 28 (1953), pp. 525–6, and Christopher Tyerman, *England and the Crusades 1095–1588* (Chicago, 1988), pp. 32–5. For the development of crusading in Portugal see Carl Erdmann, "Der Kreuzzugsgedanke in Portugal," *Historische Zeitschrift* 141 (1930), pp. 23–53.

[62] Bernard also stimulated crusading fervor in England, though by letter rather than by his personal presence. See *Letters of St. Bernard of Clairvaux*, ed. B. S. James (London, 1953), no. 391.

[63] Kurth, "Der Anteil Niederdeutscher Kreuzfahrer," p. 135. The number has been estimated at 13,000.

the eucharist once a week, and weekly meetings among the lay and clerical leaders were held. For every 1,000 men there were two men sworn as *iudices et coniurati* to maintain law and order.

The fleet left Dartmouth on May 23 and passed the western tip of Brittany two days later. *En route* they encountered a storm and the ships were separated, with the English landing at Gijon in the Asturias and fifty ships of the Germans and Flemish arriving at Gozon, some fifteen kilometers west of Gijon. This second party waited for the others to reassemble, but not finding them set sail again on June 3, arriving at the mouth of the Tambre river, whence they made a pilgrimage to Santiago de Compostella to celebrate Pentecost on June 8. Upon their return they found the English contingent and set sail together on June 15. One day later they arrived at Oporto, the capital of the newly carved out "kingdom" of Portugal under the rule of Alfonso I (1129–85). Alfonso, the son of Count Henry of Burgundy, had founded the principality while himself on crusade and was negotiating with the papacy for recognition as a king by conquest.

Alfonso sought to use the good fortune of the crusaders' arrival as a means to conquer Lisbon from the Moors, and enlisted the aid of the bishop of Oporto to warm them to the idea. The bishop preached to the crusaders that if they desired to make battle with the infidel they need not go all the way to Palestine since there were Muslims already in the vicinity. He also enticed them with promises not only of spiritual merit but also of rich estates. The English, however, were reluctant at first and vowed to press on to Jerusalem. Such a detour could vitiate the emotional focus of pilgrimage to the Holy City that unified the fleet and gave the expedition a purpose. But clerical insistence that the act rather than the destination of crusading was the ultimate virtue led to the capitulation of constable Glanville, and thereafter of the entire English contingent. The ships sailed up the Tagus river while Alfonso brought his army by land and the siege of Lisbon began on June 28, 1147. The Moors valiantly defended the city, which only capitulated after four months (on October 24) when given assurances that their lives and property would be spared. Yet once the city gates were opened a massacre ensued, in which the English, congratulating themselves on their virtuous choice, took a minor part.[64] After the conquest of Lisbon

---

[64] The "Annales Magdeburgenses" are explicit about the actions of the Cologners and the English in the siege of the city: "Deinde Coloniensibus ex sua parte dimicantibus cum Sarracenis, Anglici minus caute suam turrim custodientes, hanc ex inproviso succensam igne extinguere non potuerunt. Interim Colonienses quadam machina murum suffodere ceperunt. Quod videntes Sarraceni, igne olio admixto eandem machinam in favillam redigebant, magistrum etiam machinae in fractura muri lapidabant. Preterea mortes innumeras tam magnellis quam sagittis ipsis inferentes, illi quoque simili modo morte multipliciter puniti sunt. Colonienses de

some of the crusaders continued on to Palestine, where they accomplished nothing. But many more stayed behind and settled with the favor of the new Portuguese monarchy. Indeed, this coalition's conquest of Lisbon hastened the rise of Portugal as an independent Christian kingdom.

This venture shows both the interregional cooperation and interaction created by crusading, as well as the dark side of the infusion of religious ideals into a military *milieu*. None seemed troubled by the treachery done at Lisbon; in fact the Cologne chronicle expresses conviction that the victory was of divine origin, occurring as it did on the feast day of the eleven thousand virgins, the special patron saints of Cologne.[65] Nonetheless, the joining of Cologne burghers, Anglo-Normans, Lotharingians, and Flemish in a far-flung common venture is reflective of the growing integration of the;e regions during the early twelfth century. We must also note that 1 iis flotilla of crusaders was made up of the middle ranks of medieva. society: small landholders, knights, burghers, and merchants. These minor political players were able to organize in a very sophisticated fashion and regulate their affairs with a high degree of harmony and cooperation often uncharacteristic of their aristocratic betters. Since large numbers of German princes began crusading in the Second Crusade, and English magnates did not begin to participate in crusading until the Third Crusade, it was actually those from the middling range of English and German society who reveal the growing interregional cooperation and integration that was becoming increasingly typical of western Europe. Whereas regional and local political exigencies limited the magnates' interregional activities, the small landholders and townsmen forged new channels of European cooperation and integration.

It should not escape our attention that the motive force bringing together a flotilla of European soldiers, remarkable for both their disparate origins and their numbers, was a religious one. Whatever we make of the religious fervor of the crusades, even when joined by economic and political motives, we cannot escape the fact that it was

---

iactura machinarum et suorum contricione aliquantisper fracti, set in misericordia divina sperantes, ingenia et machinas reparare ceperunt . . ." (p. 189). Steven Runciman, *A History of the Crusades* (Cambridge, 1954), III, p. 258 mentions only the participation of English, Flemish, and Frisian contingents, and Christopher Tyerman, *England and the Crusades, 1095–1588* (Chicago, 1988), pp. 32–5 refers to the German contingent only in general terms as from the Rhineland.

65 *CRC*, p. 86: "Consummata est autem haec divina, non humana victoria in ducentis milibus et quingentis viris Sarracenorum in festivitate 11,000 virginum. Quorundam christianorum corpora variis occisionibus exstincta, apud Ulixbonam sepulta, miraculis claruerunt." Thus those crusaders who died at the taking of Lisbon gave forth miracles in the same fashion as the 11,000 legendary virgins who had been buried in Cologne after their martyrdom.

the sense of religious calling that moved these thousands of northern Europeans to join in a corporate venture so far away from home. Understood on its own, albeit violent, terms, the Second Crusade is symptomatic of a turning point in European history. In a world where localism and regionalism still predominated, there were forces under way that were interweaving the history of regions and locales into a truly European context – a context that now included the territories of the German kingdom. No longer would the conflicts or events in one part of Europe have little or no impact on other Europeans. No longer would religious movements and controversies be restricted to the regions in which they originated, but now they would have consequences and repercussions elsewhere in Europe.

The growth of interregional activity and cooperation between the lower Rhineland and England was further strengthened by the Third Crusade, wherein a combined flotilla of crusaders from both regions once again followed the pattern of the Second Crusade and passed through the port of Dartmouth in 1189.[66] These crusaders also paused in Portugal, made pilgrimage to Santiago de Compostella, and entered into temporary service under the king (Sancho I). The crusading Cologne burghers, however, who were in the minority this time, were more interested in commercial activity, and they returned to their city laden with costly cloth and other items without ever reaching the Holy Land.[67] Once again the growing commercial economy of Europe during the Central Middle Ages provided as much zeal as the traditional crusading ideal. The Third Crusade in many ways exhibited the cooperation and interaction between the lower Rhine region and England which became characteristic of this period.

A third crusading endeavor brought the citizens of Cologne and

---

[66] Kurth, "Der Anteil Niederdeutscher Kreuzfahrer," pp. 171–72: "Aus Köln fuhren 4 Schiffe am 2. Februar 1189 ab, mit 1500 Menschen, wie die Kölner Königschronik übertreibend angibt, an Bord. Proviant auf drei Jahre und reichliches Waffenmaterial nahmen mit. Wir wissen, dass Lütticher sich ihnen, wohl an einer der Maasmündigen, anschlossen, vermutlich aber auch Kreuzfahrer aus anderen flandrischen Städten, wenn diese nicht erst im englischen Hafen Dartmouth hinzugekommen sind, wo auch viele friesische und dänische Schiffe sich nach und nach hinzugesellten. So konnte am 27. Februar eine Kreuzfahrerflotte von 55 Segeln in See gehen. Die Zahl der Teilnehmer wird höchstens 5000 betragen haben. Genau den Anteil der einzelnen Stämme und Städte zu bestimmen, ist nicht möglich. Doch überwogen, wie es scheint, die Friesen und Dänen. Im Verhältnis zu diesen waren Flanderer und Kölner – letztere stellten nur 4 Schiffe – bedeutend in der Minderheit." See also Runciman, *A History of the Crusades*, III, pp. 9, 26 and Tyerman, *England and the Crusades*, p. 66.

[67] Kurth, "Der Anteil Niederdeutscher Kreuzfahrer," p. 175: "Übrigens sind die kölnische Schiffe wahrscheinlich nicht mit nach Akkon gefahren, wenn die Quelle der Kölner Königschronik Recht hat. Danach sind Kreuzfahrer, die bei Alvor beteiligt waren, in grosser Zahl um Lichtmess (2. Februar) 1190 wieder in Köln eingetroffen, mit wertvollen Kleidern und anderen Kostbarkeiten, die sie bei der Eroberung jenes Ortes erbeutet hatten."

England into cooperative contact once more. Spurred on by exhortations from Pope Innocent III in 1213 and in 1216, and by Pope Honorius in January 1217, crusaders from Cologne and its province, along with many Frisians, left on May 29, 1217 with 112 ships and followed the usual crusading route to Dartmouth, where they arrived on June 1.[68] The leader of the German contingent was a certain Oliver, the master of the schools of Cologne cathedral.[69] Disembarking ten days later under the joint leadership of Count William of Holland and Count George of Wied they made the traditional pilgrimage to Santiago de Compostella and landed at Lisbon on July 14. Once again the king of Portugal convinced them to assist him against the Moors. Although many Frisians refused to delay their passage to Palestine, the others besieged Alcacer on behalf of the king and the city capitulated on October 21. After wintering in Lisbon the crusaders then continued on to the East.[70] This well-worn route had now been followed three times in seventy years, and burghers from Cologne, Flanders, and England thereby fulfilled their religious vows while extending valuable trading ties with Lisbon.[71] The practice of crusaders from northwest Germany stopping at Lisbon and the growing commercial ties between the regions were no mere coincidence; the same can also be said for the English.[72] Interregional cooperation on a grand scale such as this has too

---

[68] *Ennen/Eckertz*, II, p. 47 no. 42; II, p. 58 no. 50 (incorrectly dated 1215); II, p. 65 no. 55. Cf. Kurth, "Der Anteil Niederdeutscher Kreuzfahrer," pp. 215–45.

[69] Haverkamp, *Medieval Germany*, p. 249.

[70] *CRC*, pp. 339–48 has an extensive account of this crusading venture, and both Roger of Wendover, *Flores historiarum*, II, p. 226 and *MPCM*, III, pp. 32–3 tell of the participation of those from the province of Cologne: "Circa dies istos facta est motio maxima ex Coloniensium et Frisonum provinciis virorum fortium et bellatorum, qui a principio praedicationis crucis post generale concilium trecentas naves magnas magno studio fabricatas ingressi sunt, ut vota suae peregrinationis exsolverent Crucifixo, qui sulcantes aequora velis patentibus, major pars eorum cum magna bellatorum virtute applicuit Lissebonam, ubi inter eos est exorta dissensio in obsidione cujusdam castri fortissimi, quod Alchacia nuncupatur, quibusdam procedere cupientibus, aliis ibi volentibus hyemare; sicque classe divisa, pars apud Cajetam et Tornetum hyemavit, et pars altera duos habens capitaneos, Willelmum scilicet Houlandiae ducem et comitem de Weiz Georgium, Alchaciam obsedit, qui cum adhuc in obsidione essent, congregata est contra eos Saracenorum maxima multitudo, contra quam fideles viriliter decertantes virtute divina infideles vicerunt. Rex unus paganorum occisus est, et multi trucidati atque in captivitatem adducti; castellum vero tandem per Teutonicos captum est et a Christianis possessum."

[71] Kurth, "Der Anteil Niederdeutscher Kreuzfahrer," pp. 245–51 and A. H. de Oliveira Marques, *Hansa e Portugal na Idade Media* (Lisbon, 1959).

[72] Concerning the English in Portugal see D. W. Lomax, "The first English pilgrims to Santiago de Compostela," *Studies in Medieval History presented to R. H. C. Davis*, ed. H. Mayr-Harting and R. I. Moore (London and Ronceverte, 1985), pp. 165–79 and Anthony Goodman's essays, "England and Iberia in the Middle Ages," *England and Her Neighbours 1066–1453. Essays in Honour of Pierre Chaplais*, ed. Michael Jones and Malcolm Vale (London, 1989), pp. 73–96 and "Before the armada: Iberia and England in the Middle Ages," *England in Europe 1066–1453*, ed. Nigel Saul (New York, 1994), pp. 108–20.

often been overlooked in favor of the endeavors of aristocratic communities, but doing so not only discounts the broader dynamics of western European integration in general but also ignores the vitality of the Anglo-German nexus in particular.

Two final Anglo-Cologne cultural contributions should be noted in closing. Though Richard of Cornwall made little headway in establishing his royal authority throughout Germany after his coronation as *rex Romanorum* at the hands of the archbishop of Cologne, his reign was not wholly without interregional consequence. During his third trip through Germany in the summer of 1262, Richard traveled up the Rhine as far as Strasbourg, and then returned to Frankfurt by late autumn. Archbishop Engelbert of Cologne accompanied Richard in his travels, as evidenced by Engelbert's signature on one of Richard's charters issued at Boppard.[73] At the outset of this third *iter* Richard sojourned in Aachen, where he gave the imperial coronation insignia (a golden crown, royal vestments with his heraldic arms, a scepter, and an imperial orb) to the Marienkapelle for use in future coronations. This was one of Richard's few lasting contributions to kingship in Germany, yet the establishment of a royal coronation treasury proved to be of significant cultural value.[74] By mid-October reports of Henry III's failing health and rumors of Simon de Montfort's return to England spurred Richard back home, and after a short stay in Mainz (until December 3) he returned down the Rhine to his homeland. In a study of medieval Anglo-Cologne expatriates and emigrants, it is fitting to have a king suitable for such a community; and Richard of Cornwall is our man. He was the ultimate migrant monarch, whose royal election and person linked England and Cologne politically in conjunction with the manifold social, economic, religious, and cultural ties that bound the regions together.[75] The stamp of Cologne was so strong on

---

[73] *REK*, III, 2, p. 9 no. 2219 dated September 3, 1262.

[74] Armin di Miranda, "Richard von Cornwallis und sein Verhältniss zur Krönungsstadt Aachen," *Annalen* 35 (1880), pp. 65–92. This article began the speculation that the head on the famous Aachen bust of Charlemagne might actually be that of Richard. Furthermore there is discussion on the Rathaus used by Richard as his curia: "Aachen bekam durch die Freigebigkeit Richards von Cornwallis ein Rathaus, in dessen Hallen man den kleinen Staatskörper, das 'Aachener Reich,' später genannt, organisierte und für sein Wohlergehen sorgte" (pp. 76–7). The following articles continue the debate concerning Richard's role in the Aachen Schatzkammer: Albert Huyskens, "Der Plan des Königs Richard von Cornwallis zur Niederlegung eines deutschen Krönungsschatzes in Aachen," *Annalen* 115 (1929), pp. 180–204 contains the text of Richard's 1262 grant; Huyskens, "Noch einmal der Krönungsschatz des König Richard von Cornwallis," *Annalen* 118 (1931), pp. 136–43; Paul Kirn, "Mit welcher Krone wurde König Sigmund in Aachen gekrönt?" *Annalen* 118 (1931), pp. 132–6. Both Richard and his second wife Sanchia are listed in the necrology of the Marienkirche in Aachen: *Necrologium ecclesiae beatae Mariae virginis Aquensis*, ed. Christian Quix (Aachen, 1830), p 12.

[75] For more on the role of Cologne's archbishop in the election and kingship of Richard of

Richard's kingship that even his royal seal was similar to the city's municipal seal.[76]

Finally, there is strong evidence that a lasting architectural connection exists between Cologne and England: it is highly likely that the style of York Minster's nave was derived not vaguely from the French *Rayonnant* Gothic, but directly from Cologne's cathedral.[77] From its flying buttress design to its choir stalls, clerestory ornamentation, and façade program York Minster bears the likeness of its Cologne exemplar.[78] Here we have a classic example of the problem cited at the outset: the linkage between the two cathedrals has gone unnoticed precisely because of the overriding Anglo-French thinking of historians of architecture, which follows the same pattern for medievalists of all disciplines. Just as the over-riding Anglo-French orientation has limited learning and clarity of vision in this case of architecture, it has done so to other areas of research into the European Middle Ages. Thus Richard of Cornwall's royal seal, York's beautiful cathedral, and even the career of Gerard Pucelle should remind us of the vitality and diversity of Anglo-Cologne religious and cultural ties during the Central Middle Ages, rather than being set aside as conundrums of history that do not fit the Anglo-French mold.

Cornwall see Hugo Stehkämper, "Konrad von Hochstaden, Erzbischof von Köln (1238–1261)," *JKGV* 36/37 (1961–2), pp. 106–16; Roswitha Reisinger, *Die römische-deutschen Könige und ihr Wähler 1189–1273*, Untersuchungen zur deutschen Staats- und Rechtsgeschichte NF, 21 (Aalen, 1977), pp. 71–88; C. C. Bayley, "The diplomatic preliminaries of the double election of 1257 in Germany," *EHR* 62 (1947), pp. 457–83; Henry S. Lucas, "John of Avesnes and Richard of Cornwall," *Speculum* 23 (1948), pp. 81–101; Hans-Eberhard Hilpert, "Richard of Cornwall's candidature for the German throne and the Christmas 1256 parliament at Westminster," *Journal of Medieval History* 6 (1980), pp. 185–98.

[76] Toni Diederich, *Die alten Siegel der Stadt Köln* (Cologne, 1980), p. 54: "Interesse verdient trotz aller stilistischer Unterschiede vielleicht das auf 1257 zu datierende Siegel König Richards von Cornwall, das in der Umschrift gewisse Ähnlichkeiten mit dem Kölner Stadtsiegel zeigt. Es wäre noch zu untersuchen, ob dieses Siegel, das Kahsnitz (*Die Zeit der Staufer, Ausstellungskatalog*, Band 1: 41) für England in Anspruch nimmt, nicht doch vielleicht im Rhein-Maas-Gebiet entstanden sein könnte. Die Reise Richards nach Deutschland im Jahre 1257 (Krönung am Himmelfahrtstage dieses Jahres in Aachen) gäbe den Hintergrund für die Herstellung des Siegelstempels. Die von Kahsnitz festgestellten Übereinstimmungen mit dem 1248 am Niederrhein geschaffenen Siegel Wilhelms von Holland, des Vorgängers Richards, fänden so eine Erklärung. Für eine Entstehung des Siegels Richards von Cornwall im Nordwesten des Reichs spräche auch der Verzicht auf den englischen Typ des Münzsiegele, bei dem ein gleich großer Siegelstempel für die Beprägung der Siegelrückseite verwendet wird."

[77] Hans J. Böker, "York minster's nave: the Cologne connection," *Journal of the Society of Architectural Historians* 50: 2 (June 1991), pp. 167–80.

[78] Böker states that Cologne cathedral "must be taken as [York Minster's] main and perhaps only source of inspiration" (p. 167) and concludes, "It is, therefore, the apparently aberrant character of York Minster's nave that ultimately reveals its historical importance, showing its international connections and manifesting the ambitions of the successive groups responsible for the church" (p. 180).

Conclusion

A REAPPRAISAL OF
THE ANGLO-GERMAN NEXUS

Anglo-German relations during the Central Middle Ages were certainly not a peripheral element in western European history, although most modern accounts of this era have neglected to integrate this dimension into the more traditional preoccupation with Anglo-French and German–Italian interactions. This study is an attempt to achieve such an integration and to illuminate in particular the centrality of Cologne in this important yet underemphasized interregional connection. The apparent lack of fruit borne from medieval diplomatic relations between England and Germany has negatively shaped modern assessments of Anglo-German relations in general; but these frustrated diplomatic initiatives should be understood rather as evidence of the actual realities and limitations of medieval politics than as a failure to achieve modern geo-political goals. Indeed the absence of lasting political consequences does not invalidate our thesis, because extensive and crucial negotiations did in fact transpire and these activities were a result of more productive, interregional relations in the areas of economic, social, religious, and cultural contacts. The political importance of Cologne and its arch-bishops for England during the Central Middle Ages could never have existed in isolation from these other historical dimensions. Therefore, just as it always behoves the seafarer to anticipate a larger mass beneath the waters when the tip of an iceberg is sighted, we have looked for further evidence of interregional contacts and were not disappointed.

Cologne was the leader in the development of Anglo-German trade in the pre-Hanseatic era. Her merchants enjoyed unparalleled commercial and legal privileges in England which other Germans achieved only a century later. The Cologne guildhall stood as a symbol of the dominance of its merchants in England for many a year, and the Cologners continued to exercise an important role among the amalgamated Germans of the Hansa thereafter. The uniformity of Cologne *pfennig* and English sterling in purity and weight throughout the Central

Middle Ages is perhaps the best evidence for an integrated and coordinated commercial relationship between the two regions. Both coins circulated widely in the Rhineland, Westphalia, and the Low Countries, often serving as models for both legitimate imitations as well as forgeries. Indeed, the use of the English penny by Cologne family members in estate settlements and by beguines in their personal affairs is exceptional evidence for a close relationship between the city and England. The flow of silver between northern Germany and England, often via Cologne, was a major impetus to the growing trade in northern Europe from the late tenth century onward. The periodic political payments of the English kings to German princes contributed greatly to the recirculation of specie normally flowing into England. In this context it is worth reminding ourselves that Richard I's enormous ransom was paid "ad pondus Coloniensium."[1]

In the realm of social relations between Cologne and England we moved beyond the relations of the elite class and a general description of commercial activities and looked at specific emigrant and merchant families in both Cologne and England. These prosopographical studies provide us with much new and important information concerning the interregional movement and resettlement of people between the Rhineland and England. These emigrants achieved a remarkable level of integration into the power structures and societies of their adoptive homelands – complete with important kinship ties through marriage and the accumulation of wealth (both movable goods and real estate). Cologners wound up as aldermen in London or in the employ of the crown as money-changers, soldiers, provisioners, and envoys, while the English appear in the Rhineland (much earlier than previously supposed) as integral members of urban life in Cologne and elsewhere.

With all the weight of the evidence presented here it is certainly safe to conclude that Anglo-German social and cultural relations were vital and flourishing, even at a very early date. Not only did prayer confraternities exist between Cologne and English monastic communities, there was even an era of Scottish monks in Cologne. The legend of St. Ursula and other miracle stories reveal interesting links between Cologne and England, and the two great pilgrimage sites of Canterbury and Cologne drew many pilgrims across the English channel. English scholars such as Gerard Pucelle and Duns Scotus (and John de Garlandia?) dwelt in Cologne, and both mendicants and students made their pilgrimages between the regions by the early fourteenth century.

---

[1] Roger of Wendover, *Flores historiarum*, I, pp. 221–2 and Roger of Howden, *Chronica*, III, pp. 214–15.

Conclusion

Increasing numbers of English prebends fell to expatriate Cologners during the period as a result.

This case study of Cologne's role in Anglo-German relations has also yielded other results. We have, of course, discovered that Cologne was the linchpin to Anglo-German relations on almost every level. Yet its uniqueness here does not suggest exclusivity. The sizeable amount of surviving evidence concerning interregional activity, especially that from unpublished archival manuscripts, recommends further similar studies in such cities as Mainz and Trier as well as further exploration in other English cities. That our investigation proved fruitful confirms the viability of such research. In a broader sense the picture emerging here suggests that Europe was not as disconnected and regionalized as is generally assumed, especially during the earlier period of the late tenth and into the eleventh century. The freedom of movement and integration of peoples between regions which has been demonstrated here calls for a reappraisal of the modern intellectual borders which have been placed on historical investigation. From the prayers of monks and pilgrimages of the faithful, to kinship ties, commercial, crusading, and diplomatic activity, education, even York cathedral architecture, Cologne (and Germany by extension) was not "so far east" after all.[2] Finally, this study has confirmed the value of interregional comparative history. Such an approach allows the historian to make new connections across the grain of traditional histories and methodologies, because it allows him/her to ask new questions and to look at sources in a new way. The most beneficial aspect of this approach stems from its ability to unite the individual national histories of Europe and integrate them into a more complete view of medieval European history. The research presented here began with this conviction, and it has only been strengthened at the conclusion.

---

[2] Regarding the elimination of the modernist Anglo-French teleology as a yardstick to measure German history, John B. Freed offers sound advice in his article, "Medieval German social history: generalizations and particularism," *Central European History* 25: 1 (1992), p. 25 when he says: "In discussing and explaining the differences between France and Germany, or, for that matter, between Saxony and Bavaria, historians should not assume, in other words, that there is an ideal type of societal development against which all others are to be measured and found wanting. Modern democratic, capitalistic, pluralistic society is no more the teleological end of history than the Hegelian nation-state." In this he follows the German historian Johannes Fried, "Deutsche Geschichte im Früheren und Hohen Mittelalter: Bemerkungen zu einigen neuen Gesamtdarstellungen," *Historische Zeitschrift* 245 (1987), pp. 625–59.

THE ARCHBISHOPS OF COLOGNE

Bruno I of Saxony	(953–65)
Anno II	(1056–75)
Hildulf	(1076–8)
Sigewin	(1079–89)
Hermann III	(1089–99)
Frederick I	(1100–1131)
Bruno II of Berg	(1132–37)
Hugo of Sponheim	(1137)
Arnold I	(1138–51)
Arnold II of Wied	(1152–6)
Frederick II of Berg	(1156–8)
Rainald of Dassel	(1159–67)
Philip I of Heinsberg	(1167–91)
Bruno III of Berg	(1191–3)
Adolf I of Altena	(1193–1205) suspended
Bruno IV of Sayn	(1205–8)
Dietrich I	(1208–12) suspended
Adolf I of Altena	(1212–16) reinstated
Engelbert I of Berg	(1216–25)
Henry I of Molenark	(1225–38)
Conrad of Hochstaden	(1238–61)
Engelbert II of Falkenburg	(1261–74)
Siegfried of Westerburg	(1274–97)
Wickold of Holte	(1297–1304)
Henry II of Virneburg	(1304–32)

SELECT BIBLIOGRAPHY

PRIMARY SOURCES

Manuscripts

Historisches Archiv der Stadt Köln
  Columba 112
  Columba 120
  Domstift 3/599
  GA 16
  GA 18
  HUA 1/97A
  Schreinskarten Series
  Schreinsbücher Series
  St. Aposteln 1/22
  St. Severin 2/41
  Verfassung und Verwaltung C654a
Stadtarchiv von Lübeck
  Anglicana no. 4
Corporation of London Records Office
  CLRO Bridgehouse Deeds
  CLRO Bridgehouse Records Large Register
  CLRO Hustings Deeds and Wills
  CLRO Hustings Common Pleas
  CLRO Recognizance Rolls
Public Record Office
  PRO E 159 (King's Remembrancer Memoranda Rolls)
  PRO E 368 (Lord Treasurer's Remembrancer Memoranda Rolls)
  PRO E 372 (Pipe Rolls)
  PRO SC1 (Ancient Correspondence)
  Exchequer Transcript of Lord Treasurer's Memoranda Rolls
    (Typescript in Search Room)
Norfolk Record Office
  Yarmouth Court Rolls
  Norwich Enrolled Deeds

Select bibliography

British Museum
  Cotton. Vespasian BVIII
  Cotton. Otho A. XII
  Cotton. Nero C. IX
  Harley 2805
Cambridge University
  Corpus Christi College Library, Cambridge MS 270

Printed sources

Aachener Urkunden 1101–1250, ed. Erich Methuen, PGRG, 58 (Bonn, 1972).

Acta Imperii Angliae et Franciae ab anno 1267 ad annum 1313. Dokumente Vornehmlich zur Geschichte der Auswärtigen Beziehungen Deutschlands, ed. Fritz Kern (Tübingen, 1911).

Acta Imperii Inedita Saeculi XIII et XIV, ed. Edward Winkelmann, 2 vols. (Innsbruck, 1880–5; rpt. Aalen, 1964)

Acta Imperii Selecta. Urkunden Deutscher Könige und Kaiser 928–1398, ed. Johann Friedrich Böhmer (Innsbruck, 1870; rpt. Aalen, 1967)

Die Admonter Briefsammlung, ed. Günther Hödl and Peter Classen, *MGH Epistolae*: Die Briefe der Deutschen Kaiserzeit, 6 (Munich, 1983)

Alumni Cantabrigienses. A Biographical List of All Known Students, Graduates and Holders of Office at the University of Cambridge from Earliest Times to 1900. Part 1: From Earliest Times to 1751, ed. John Venn and J. A. Venn (Cambridge, 1922)

Ancient Charters, Royal and Private, Prior to A.D. 1200, ed. J. Horace Round, PR, 10 (London, 1888)

Ancient Laws and Institutes of England, ed. B. Thorpe (London, 1840)

The Anglo-Saxon Chronicle, ed. Benjamin Thorpe, RS, 23: II (London, 1861; rpt. 1964)

Annales Monastici, ed. Henry Richards Luard, RS, 36:I–V (London, 1864–69; rpt. 1965)

Annales de Waverleia in *Annales Monastici*, ed. Henry Richards Luard, RS, 36, pt. 2 (London, 1865; rpt. 1971), pp. 129–412

Archiv für die Geschichte des Niederrheins, ed. Theodor Josef Lacomblet, 7 vols. (Düsseldorf and Cologne, 1832–69)

Arnold fitz Tedmar, *Chronicles of the Mayors and Sheriffs of London, A.D. 1188–1274*, ed. Henry Thomas Riley (London, 1863)

  De antiquis legibus liber. Cronica maiorum et vicecomitum londoniarum, ed. Thomas Stapleton, Camden Society, 34 (London, 1846)

Arnold of Lübeck, *Chronica Slavorum*, ed. J. M. Lappenberg, *MGH SS rer. Germ.*, 14 (Hanover, 1868; rpt. 1978)

A Biographical Register of the University of Cambridge to 1500, ed. A. M. Emden (Cambridge, 1963)

A Biographical Register of the University of Oxford to A.D. 1500, ed. A. M. Emden (Oxford, 1957)

Books of Prests of the King's Wardrobe for 1294–1295 Presented to John Goronwy Edwards, ed. E. B Fryde (Oxford, 1962)

Bremisches Urkundenbuch, ed. D. R. Ehmck and W. von Bippen, 6 vols. (Bremen, 1873–1940)

Briefsammlung der Zeit Heinrichs IV, ed. Carl Erdmann and Norbert Fickermann, *MGH Epistolae*: Die Briefe der Deutschen Kaiserzeit, 5 (Weimar, 1950)

Select bibliography

Brunos Buch vom Sachsenkrieg, ed. Hans-Eberhard Lohmann, *MGH Deutsches Mittelalter*, 2 (Leipzig, 1937)

Caesarius of Heisterbach, *Dialogus Miraculorum*, ed. Joseph Strange, 2 vols. (Cologne, Bonn, and Brussels, 1851)

Calendar of Chancery Warrants Preserved in the Public Record Office A.D. 1244–1326 (London, 1927)

Calendar of the Charter Rolls Preserved in the Public Record Office, 6 vols. (London, 1903–27)

Calendar of the Close Rolls Preserved in the Public Record Office. Edward I, 5 vols. (London 1900–8)

Calendar of the Close Rolls Preserved in the Public Record Office. Henry III, 14 vols. (London 1902–38)

Calendar of Coroner's Rolls of the City of London A.D. 1300–1378, ed. Reginald R. Sharpe (London, 1913)

Calendar of Documents Preserved in France 918–1206, ed. J. Horace Round (London, 1899)

Calendar of Early Mayor's Court Rolls Preserved Among the Archives of the Corporation of the City of London at the Guildhall, A.D. 1298–1307, ed. A. H. Thomas (Cambridge, 1924)

Calendar of Entries in the Papal Registers relating to Great Britain and Ireland. Volumes. I–II, ed. W. H. Bliss (London, 1893–5)

Calendar of the Fine Rolls Preserved in the Public Record Office. Volume I: 1272–1307 (London, 1911)

Calendar of Inquisitions Miscellaneous (Chancery) Preserved in the Public Record Office. Volume I: Henry III and Edward I (London, 1916)

Calendar of Inquisitions Post Mortem and other Analogous Documents Preserved in the Public Record Office. Volumes I–IV: Henry III and Edward I (London, 1904–13)

Calendar of the Letter-Books Preserved Among the Archives of the Corporation of the City of London at the Guildhall, ed. Reginald R. Sharpe, 6 vols. (London, 1899–1904)

Calendar of the Liberate Rolls Preserved in the Public Record Office. Henry III, 6 vols. (London 1916–64)

Calendar of London Trailbaston Trials and Commissions of 1305 and 1306, ed. Ralph B. Pugh (London, 1975)

Calendar of the Patent Rolls Preserved in the Public Record Office. Edward I, 4 vols. (London, 1894–1901)

Calendar of the Patent Rolls Preserved in the Public Record Office. Henry III, 6 vols. (London 1901–13)

Calendar of the Plea Rolls of the Exchequer of the Jews Preserved in the Public Record Office and the British Museum, ed. J. M. Rigg (vols. I–II), Hilary Jenkinson (vol. III), and H. G. Richardson (vol. IV), Jewish Historical Society of England (London, 1905–72)

Calendar of Various Chancery Rolls (Supplementary Close Rolls, Welsh Rolls, Scutage Rolls) Preserved in the Public Record Office A.D. 1277–1326 (London, 1912)

Calendar of Wills Proved and Enrolled in the Court of Hustings, London A.D. 1258–1688 Preserved Among the Archives of the Corporation of the City of London at the Guildhall. Part 1: A.D. 1258–1358, ed. Reginald R. Sharpe (London, 1889)

Calendarium inquisitionum post mortem sive escaetarum, ed. J. Caley and J. Bayley, 4 vols. (London, 1806–28)

Calendarium rotulorum chartarum et inquisitionum ad quod damnum, ed. J. Caley (London, 1803)

Select bibliography

Calendarium rotulorum patentium in turri Londinensi, ed. T. Astle and J. Caley (London, 1802)

Cardauns, Hermann, ed., "Rheinische Urkunden des X.-XII. Jahrhunderts," *Annalen* 26/27 (1874), pp. 332–71

ed., "Rheinische Urkunden des XIII. Jahrhunderts," *Annalen* 38 (1882), pp. 1–49

The Cartae Antiquae Rolls 1–10, ed. Lionel Landon, PR NS, 17 (London, 1939)

The Cartae Antiquae Rolls 11–20, ed. J. Conway Davies, PR NS, 33 (London, 1960)

The Cartulary of God's House, Southampton, ed. J. M. Kaye, 2 vols. Southampton Record Series, 19 (Southampton, 1976)

The Cartulary of Holy Trinity Aldgate, ed. Gerald A. J. Hodgett, London Record Society, 7 (London, 1971)

Cartulary of St. Bartholomew's Hospital, ed. J. M. Kerling (London, 1973)

The Cartulary of Worcester Cathedral Priory (Register I), ed. R. R. Darlington, PR NS, 38 (London, 1968)

The Charters of Norwich Cathedral Priory. Part 1, ed. Barbara Dodwell, PR NS, 40 (London, 1974)

The Charters of Norwich Cathedral Priory. Part 2, ed. Barbara Dodwell, PR NS, 46 (London, 1985)

Chronica pontificum ecclesiae Eboracensis, ed. James Raine, RS, 71: II (London, 1886; rpt. 1965)

Chronica regia Coloniensis, ed. G. Waitz, *MGH SS rer. Germ.*, 18 (Hanover, 1880; rpt. 1978)

The Chronicle of Bury St. Edmunds, ed. Antonia Gransden, Nelson Medieval Texts (London, 1964)

Chronicon Henrici de Hervordia, ed. August Potthast (Göttingen, 1859)

Chronicon Sancti Michaelis Luneburgensis, ed. L. Weiland, *MGH SS*, 23 (Hanover, 1874; rpt. 1986), pp. 391–7

Chronicon vulgo dictum chronicon Thomae Wykes, ed. Henry Richards Luard, RS, 36: IV (London, 1869; rpt. 1965), pp. 6–354

Close Rolls (Supplementary) of the Reign of Henry III Preserved in the Public Record Office 1244–1266, ed. Ann Morton (London, 1975)

Codex Diplomaticus Lubecensis. Lübeckisches Urkundenbuch, Verein für Geschichte und Althertumskunde, 11 vols. (Lübeck, 1843–1905; rpt. Osnabrück, 1976)

Constitutiones et acta publica imperatorum et regum inde ab anno 911 usque ad annum 1197, ed. Ludwig Weiland, *MGH Leges*, 4: I (Hanover, 1893; rpt. 1963)

Constitutiones et acta publica imperatorum et regum inde ab anno 1198 usque ad annum 1272, ed. Ludwig Weiland, *MGH Leges*, 4: II (Hanover, 1896; rpt. 1963)

Constitutiones et acta publica imperatorum et regum inde ab anno 1273 usque ad annum 1298, ed. Jakob Schwalm, *MGH Leges*, 4: III (Hanover, 1904–6; rpt. 1980)

Constitutiones et acta publica imperatorum et regum inde ab anno 1298 usque ad annum 1313, ed. Jakob Schwalm, *MGH Leges*, 4: IV (Hanover, 1906–11; rpt. 1981)

Constitutiones et acta regum Germaniae, ed. Georg Heinrich Pertz, *MGH Leges*, 1: II (Hanover, 1837; rpt. 1965)

Curia Regis Rolls of the Reigns of Richard I and John and Henry III Preserved in the Public Record Office, 16 vols. (London, 1938–79)

A Descriptive Catalog of Ancient Deeds in the Public Record Office, 6 vols. (London, 1890–1915)

Diplomatic Documents Preserved in the Public Record Office. Volume I: 1107–1272, ed. Pierre Chaplais (London, 1964)

Select bibliography

Documents Illustrative of English History in the Thirteenth and Fourteenth Centuries, Selected from the Records of the Queen's Remembrancer of the Exchequer, ed. Henry Cole (London, 1844)

Dornbusch, J. B. ed., "Memorienbuch des Stiftes S. Ursula zu Köln," *Annalen* 28/29 (1876), pp. 49–85

Dortmunder Urkundenbuch, ed. Karl Rübel, 4 vols. (Dortmund, 1881)

Early Deeds Relating to Newcastle Upon Tyne, ed. Arthur M. Oliver, Surtees Society, 137 (London, 1924)

Ecclesiae metropolitanae coloniensis codices manuscripti, ed. Philip Jaffé and William Wattenbach (Weidmannos, 1874)

Eckertz, Gottfried ed., "Cronica presulum et Archiepiscoporum ecclesie Coloniensium," *Annalen* 4 (1857), pp. 181–250

Ekkehard of Aura, *Chronica*, ed. F. J. Schmale and Irene Schmale-Ott, Ausgewählte Quellen zur Deutschen Geschichte des Mittelalters, Freiherr von Stein-Gedächtnisausgabe, 15 (Darmstadt, 1972)

Ellenhardi Chronicon, ed. Ph. Jaffé, MGH SS, 17 (Hanover, 1861; rpt. 1987), pp. 118–41

Das Erzbistum Köln II: Die Benediktiner Abtei Siegburg, ed. Erich Wisplinghoff, Germina Sacra NF, 9 (Berlin and New York, 1975)

Fasti Anglicanae 1300–1541. Volume V: St. Paul's London, ed. John Le Neve (London, 1963)

Florence and John of Worcester, *Chronicon ex chronicis*, ed. Benjamin Thorpe, English Historical Society Publications, 2 vols. (London, 1848–9)

Foedera, conventiones, litterae et cuiuscumque generis acta publica inter reges Angliae et alios quosvis imperatores, reges, pontifices vel communitates ab ineunte saeculo duodecimo, viz. ab anno 1101 ad nostra usque tempora, ed. Thomas Rymer, 2nd edn. reedited by George Holmes, 20 vols (London, 1727–35)

Fratris Thomas vulgo dicti de Eccleston Tractatus de Adventu Fratrum Minorum in Angliam, ed. A. G. Little (Manchester, 1951)

Friedlaender, Ernst ed., "Rheinische Urkunden," *Annalen* 50 (1890), pp. 220–49

Frutolfs und Ekkehards Chroniken und die Anonyme Kaiserchronik, ed. Franz Josef Schmale and Irene Schmale-Ott, Ausgewählte Quellen zur Deutschen Geschichte des Mittelalters, Freiherr vom Stein-Gedächtnisausgabe, 25 (Darmstadt, 1972)

Gerald of Wales, *Giraldi Cambrensis opera*, ed. J. S. Brewer, J. F. Dimock, and G. F. Warner, RS, 21: I–VIII (London, 1861–91)

Gervase of Canterbury, *Chronicle of the Reigns of Stephen, Henry II, and Richard I*, ed. William Stubbs, RS, 73: I (London, 1879; rpt. 1965)

Gesta regum continuata, ed. William Stubbs, RS 73: II (London, 1880; rpt. 1965), pp. 106–324

Die Gesetze der Angelsachsen, ed. Felix Liebermann, 3 vols. (Halle, 1903–16; rpt. 1960)

Gesta regis Henrici secundi, ed. William Stubbs, RS, 49: 1–2 (London, 1867; rpt. 1965)

The Great Roll of the Pipe for the First Year of the Reign of King Richard the First, A.D. 1189–1190, ed. Joseph Hunter (London, 1844)

The Great Rolls of the Pipe for the Second, Third, and Fourth Years of the Reign of King Henry the Second, A.D. 1155–1158, ed. Joseph Hunter (London, 1844; rpt. 1931)

The Great Rolls of the Pipe for the 5th–34th Years of the Reign of King Henry II, PR, 1–2, 4–9, 11–13, 15–16, 18–19, 21–2, 25–34, 36–8 (London, 1884–1925)

Select bibliography

The Great Rolls of the Pipe for the 2nd–10th Years of the Reign of King Richard I, PR NS, 1–3, 5–9 (London, 1925–32)

The Great Rolls of the Pipe for the 1st–14th, 16th and 17th Years of the Reign of King John, PR NS, 10, 12, 14–16, 18–20, 22–24, 26, 28, 30, 35, 37 (London, 1933–64)

The Great Rolls of the Pipe for the 2nd–4th and14th Years of the Reign of King Henry III, PR NS, 4, 39, 42, 47 (London, 1927–87)

Hamburgisches Urkundenbuch, ed. Johann Martin Lappenberg, Hans Nirrnheim, and Jürgen Reet, 4 vols. (Hamburg, 1842; rpt. 1907–67)

Hanseakten aus England 1271 bis 1472, ed. Karl Kunze, Hansische Geschichtsquellen, 6 (Halle, 1891)

Hanserecesse. Die Recesse und andere Akten der Hansetage von 1256–1430. I: 1256–1370, ed. Karl Koppmann (Leipzig, 1870)

Hansisches Urkundenbuch, vols. I–III ed. Konstantin Höhlbaum (Halle, 1876–86); vols. IV–VI ed. Karl Kunze (Halle and Leipzig, 1896–1905); vol. VII ed. H.G. Runstedt (Weimar, 1939); vols. VIII–XI ed. W. Stein (Leipzig and Munich, 1899–1916)

Hardy, Thomas D., ed., *Syllabus of the Documents relating to England and other Kingdoms Contained in the Collection Known as Rymer's Foedera*, 3 vols. (London, 1869–85)

Hebräische Berichte über die Judenverfolgungen während der Kreuzzüge, ed. A. M. Neubauer, M. Stern, and S. Baer (Berlin, 1892)

Helmold of Bosau, *Slawenchronik*, ed. Heinz Stoob, Ausgewählte Quellen zur Deutschen Geschichte des Mittelalters, Freiherr von Stein-Gedächtnisausgabe, 19 (Darmstadt, 1973)

Henry of Huntingdon, *Historia Anglorum*, ed. Thomas Arnold, RS, 74 (London, 1879)

Heusgen, Paul, ed., "Der Gesamtkatalog der Handschriften der Kölner Dombibliothek," *JKGV* 15 (1933), pp. 1–78

Hilliger, Benno, ed., *Rheinische Urbare. Sammlung von Urbaren und anderen Quellen zur Rheinischen Wirtschaftsgeschichte I: Die Urbare von St. Pantaleon in Köln*, PGRG, 20: I–V (Bonn, 1902)

Historia Diplomatica Friderici Secundi, ed. J. L. A. Huillard-Bréholles, 6 vols. (Paris 1852–61)

The Historical Collections of Walter of Coventry, ed. William Stubbs, RS, 58: I–II (London, 1872–3; rpt. 1965)

Historical Manuscript Commission Report of Manuscripts of Wells Cathedral (London, 1885)

Hugh the Chanter, *The History of the Church of York 1066–1127*, ed. Charles Johnson, M. Brett, Christopher Brooke, and M. Winterbottom, Oxford Medieval Texts (Oxford, 1990)

Inventar des Archivs der Stadt Ahrweiler (1228–1795), ed. Theresia Zimmer, Veröffentlichungen der Landesarchivverwaltung Rheinland-Pfalz, 5 (Koblenz, 1965)

Issues of the Exchequer; Being a Collection of Payments made out of His Majesty's Revenue, from King Henry III to King Henry VI Inclusive, ed. Frederick Devon (London, 1837)

The Jews and the Crusaders. The Hebrew Chronicles of the First and Second Crusades, ed. Shlomo Eidelberg (Madison, 1977)

Das Judenschreinsbuch der Laurenzpfarre zu Köln, ed. Robert Hoeniger, Quellen zur Geschichte der Juden in Deutschland, 1 (Berlin, 1888)

Die Kaiserurkunden des 10., 11. und 12. Jahrhunderts, ed. Karl Friedrich Stumpf-Brentano (Innsbruck, 1865–83; rpt. Aalen 1964)

Keussen, Hermann and Leonard Korth ed., "Urkunden der Gymnasial-Bibliothek von 922–1375," *MSAK* 9 (1886), pp. 116–40

Select bibliography

Knipping, Richard ed., "Ungedruckte Urkunden der Erzbischöfe von Köln aus dem 12. und 13 Jahrhundert," *Annalen* 74 (1902), pp. 179–94; 75 (1903), pp. 112–42

Der Kölner Festkalender, ed. Georg Zilliken (Bonn, 1910)

Die Kölner Königschronik, ed. Karl Platner, 2nd edn. (Leipzig, 1896)

Die Kölner Schreinsbücher des 13. und 14. Jahrhunderts, ed. Hans Planit and Thea Buyken, PGRG, 46 (Weimar, 1937)

Die Kölner Schreinsurkunden des 12. Jahrhunderts. Quellen zur Rechts- und Wirtschafts-geschichte der Stadt Köln, ed. Robert Hoeniger, PGRG 1: 1–2 (Bonn, 1884–94)

Die Kölner Zunfturkunden nebst anderen Kölner Gewerbeurkunden bis zum Jahre 1500, ed. Heinrich von Loesch, PGRG, 22: 1–2 (Bonn, 1907)

Korth, Leonard ed., "Die Kölner Nekrologien im Stadtarchiv," *MSAK* 9 (1886), pp. 169–72

  ed., "Liber privilegiorum maioris ecclesie Coloniensis. Der älteste Kartular des Kölner Domstifts," *Westdeutsche Zeitschrift für Geschichte und Kunst, Ergänzungsheft 3* (Trier, 1886), pp. 101–94

  ed., "Urkunden aus dem Stadtarchiv von Köln," *Annalen* 41 (1884), pp. 72–108

Lacomblet, Theodor Josef ed., "Die Benediktiner-Abtei zu Deutz," *Archiv für die Geschichte des Niederrheins* 5 (1866), pp. 251–322

Lampert of Hersfeld, *Annales*, ed. Oswald Holder-Egger, MGH SS rer. Germ., 38 (Hanover and Leipzig, 1894; rpt. 1984)

Laws of the Kings of England from Edmund to Henry I, ed. A. J. Robertson (Cambridge, 1925)

The Letters of John of Salisbury, ed. W. J. Millor, H. E. Butler, and Christopher Brooke, Oxford Medieval Texts, 2 vols. (Oxford, 1979–86)

A Lincolnshire Assize Roll for 1298 (PRO Assize Roll no. 505), ed. Walter Sinclair Thomson, Lincoln Record Society, 36 (Hereford, 1944)

London Assize of Nuisance 1301–1431, ed. Helena M. Chew and William Kellaway, London Record Society, 10 (London, 1973)

The London Eyre of 1244, ed. Helena M. Chew and Martin Weinbaum, London Record Society, 6 (London, 1970)

The London Eyre of 1276, ed. Martin Weinbaum, London Record Society, 12 (London, 1976)

Magni rotuli scaccarii Normanniae sub regibus Angliae, ed. Thomas Stapleton, 2 vols. (London, 1890–4)

Mainzer Urkundenbuch, ed. Manfred Stimming and Peter Acht, 2 vols. (Darmstadt, 1972)

Materials for the History of Thomas Becket, Archbishop of Canterbury, ed. James C. Robertson and J. B. Sheppard, RS, 67: 1–7 (London, 1875–85; rpt. 1965)

Die Matrikel der Universität Köln, ed. Hermann Keussen, PGRG, 8 (Bonn, 1928)

Matthew Paris, *Chronica majora (MPCM)*, ed. Henry Richards Luard, RS, 57: 1–7 (London, 1872–3; rpt. 1964)

Matthew Paris, *Historia Anglorum sive historia minor (MPHA)*, ed. Frederic Madden, RS, 44 (London, 1866–9; rpt. 1970)

The Memoranda Roll for the Michaelmas Term of the First Year of the Reign of King John, 1199–1200, together with Fragments of the Originalia Roll of the Seventh Year of King Richard I, 1195–1196, the Liberate Roll of the Second Year of King John, 1200–1201, and the Norman Roll of the Fifth Year of King John, 1203, ed. H. G. Richardson, PR NS, 21 (London, 1943)

The Memoranda Roll for the Tenth Year of the Reign of King John, 1207–1208, together with the Curia Regis Rolls of Hilary 7 Richard I, 1196 and Easter 9 Richard I, 1198, a Roll of Plate Held by Hugh de Neville, 9 John 1207–1208, and Fragments of the Close Rolls of 16 and 17 John, 1215–1216, ed. R. Allen Brown, PR NS, 31 (London, 1956)

"Miracula Sancti Thomae Cantuariensis," Materials for the History of Thomas Becket, ed. William Stubbs, RS, 67: II (London, 1876; rpt. 1965), pp. 1–282

Miracula Sanctae Virginis Mariae, ed. Elise Dexter, University of Wisconsin Studies in the Social Sciences and History, 12 (Madison, 1927)

The Missal of St. Augustine's Abbey Canterbury, ed. Martin Rule (Cambridge, 1896)

Monumenta Welforum antiqua, ed. Georg Heinrich Pertz, MGH SS rer. Germ., 43 (Hanover, 1869)

Munimenta Gildhallae Londoniensis: Liber Albus, Liber Custumarum et Liber Horn, ed. Henry Thomas Riley, RS, 12, 3 vols. in 4 (London, 1849–62)

Necrologium ecclesiae beatae Mariae virginis Aquensis, ed. Christian Quix (Aachen, 1830)

Ninth Report of the Royal Commission on Historical Manuscripts Part 1: Report and Appendix (London, 1883; rpt. 1979)

Novum Repertorium Ecclesiasticum Parochie Londinense, ed. George Hennessy (London, 1898)

On the Properties of Things: John Trevisa's Translation of Bartholomaeus Anglicus' De proprietatibus rerum. A Critical Text, ed. M. C. Seymour et al., 3 vols. (Oxford, 1975–88)

Ordericus Vitalis, The Ecclesiastical History, ed. Marjorie Chibnall, 6 vols. (Oxford, 1964–81)

Osbern, De expugnatione Lyxbonensi, ed. William Stubbs, RS, 38:1 (London, 1864; rpt. 1964), pp. cxlii–clxxxii

De expugnatione Lyxbonensi, ed. C. W. David, Columbia University Records of Civilization, 24 (New York, 1936)

Otto of Freising and Rahewin, Gesta Friderici I. imperatoris, ed. G. Waitz, MGH SS rer. Germ., 46 (Hanover, 1912; rpt. 1978)

Gesta Friderici seu rectius Cronica, ed. Franz-Josef Schmale, Ausgewählte Quellen zur Deutschen Geschichte des Mittelalters, Freiherr von Stein-Gedächtnisausgabe, 17 (Berlin, 1965)

Otto of St. Blasius, Ottonis de Sancto Blasio chronica, ed. Adolf Hofmeister, MGH SS rer. Germ., 47 (Hanover and Leipzig, 1912)

Papsturkunden in den Niederlanden, ed. J. Ramackers, Abhandlungen der Gesellschaft der Wissenschaften zu Gottingen. Philologisch-historische Klasse 3. Folge, 9 (Berlin, 1934; rpt. 1972)

Peter de Langtoft, The Chronicle of Peter de Langtoft in French Verse, ed. Thomas Wright, RS, 47: I–II (London, 1866–8)

Chronicon Rhythmicon, ed. F. Liebermann, MGH SS, 28 (Hanover, 1888; rpt. 1975), pp. 647–62

Placita coram domini rege apud Westmonasterium de termino sancte trinitatis anno regni regis Edwardi filii regis Henrici vicesimo quinto, ed. W. P. W. Phillimore (London, 1898)

Placitorum in domo capitulari Westmonasteriensi asservatorum abbreviatio, temporibus Regum Ric. I, Johann., Henr. III, Edw. I, Edw. II, ed. W. Illingworth (London, 1811)

Pleas before the King and His Justices 1198–1202, ed. Doris Mary Stenton, Seldon Society, 67–8, 83–4 (London, 1952–67)

Quellen zur Geschichte des Kölner Handels und Verkehrs im Mittelalter, ed. Bruno Kuske, PGRG, 33: I–IV (Bonn, 1917–34)

Select bibliography

Quellen zur Geschichte der Stadt Köln, ed. Leonard Ennen and Gottfried Eckertz, 6 vols. (Cologne, 1860–79)

Quellen zur Rechts- und Wirtschaftsgeschichte des Archdiakonats und Stifts Xanten, ed. Carl Wilkes, Veröffentlichungen des Vereins zur Erhaltung des Xantener Domes, 3 (Bonn, 1937)

Quellen zur Rechts- und Wirtschaftsgeschichte der Rheinischen Städte C: Kurtrierische Städte 1: Trier, ed. Friedrich Rudolph, PGRG, 29 (Bonn, 1915)

Ralph de Diceto, *The Historical Works of Ralph de Diceto*, ed. William Stubbs, RS, 68: I–II (London, 1876; rpt. 1965)

Ralph of Coggeshall, *Chronicon Anglicanum*, ed. Joseph Stevenson, RS, 66 (London, 1875; rpt. 1965)

Records of the Wardrobe and Household. Volume 1: 1285–1286, ed. Benjamin F. Byerly and Catherine Ridder Byerley (London, 1977)

Receuil des actes de Henri II roi d'Angleterre et duc de Normandie concernant les provinces et les affaires de France, ed. Léopold Delisle and Elie Berger, Chartes et Diplômes Relatifs à L'Histoire de France, 7: Introduction and 3 vols. (Paris, 1909–27)

The Red Book of the Exchequer, ed. Hubert Hall, RS, 99: I–III (London, 1896; rpt. 1965)

Regesta Imperii 3: 1. Die Regesten des Kaiserreichs unter Konrad II. (1024–1039), ed. Johann Friedrich Böhmer, reedited with additions by N. von Bischoff and Heinrich Appelt (Vienna, Cologne, and Graz, 1951)

Regesta Imperii 3: 2. Die Regesten des Kaiserreichs unter Heinrich IV. (1056 [1050]-1065), ed. Johann Friedrich Böhmer, reedited with additions by Tilman Struve (Vienna, Cologne, and Graz, 1984)

Regesta Imperii 4: 2. Die Regesten des Kaiserreichs unter Friedrich I. (1152 [1122]-1190), ed. Johann Friedrich Böhmer, reedited with additions by Ferdinand Opll (Vienna, Cologne, and Graz, 1980)

Regesta Imperii 4: 3. Die Regesten des Kaiserreichs unter Heinrich VI (1165 [1190]-1197), ed. Johann Friedrich Böhmer, reedited with additions by Gerhard Baaken, 2 vols. (Vienna, Cologne, and Graz, 1972–9)

Regesta Imperii 5: 1–5. Die Regesten des Kaiserreichs unter Philipp, Otto IV, Friedrich II, Heinrich (VII), Conrad IV, Heinrich Raspe, Wilhelm und Richard (1198–1272), ed. Johann Friedrich Böhmer, reedited with additions by Julius Ficker and Eduard Winkelmann, 3 vols. (Innsbruck, 1881–1901)

Regesta Imperii 5: 4. Die Regesten des Kaiserreichs unter Philipp, Otto IV, Friedrich II, Heinrich (VII), Conrad IV, Heinrich Raspe, Wilhelm und Richard, ed. Johann Friedrich Böhmer, reedited with further additions by Paul Zinsmaier (Vienna, Cologne, and Graz, 1983)

Regesta Imperii 6: 1. Die Regesten des Kaiserreichs unter Rudolf I. von Hapsburg (1273–1291), ed. Johann Friedrich Böhmer, reedited with additions by O. Redlich (Innsbruck, 1898; rpt. 1969)

Regesta Imperii 6: 2. Die Regesten des Kaiserreichs unter Adolf von Nassau (1291–1298), ed. Johann Friedrich Böhmer, reedited with additions by Vincent Samenek (Innsbruck, 1933–48)

Regesta Regum Anglo-Normannorum 1066–1154. I: Regesta Willelmi Conquestoris et Willelmi Rufi 1066–1100, ed. H. W. C. Davis (Oxford, 1913)

Regesta Regum Anglo-Normannorum 1066–1154. II: Regesta Henrici Primi, ed. Charles Johnson and H. A. Cronne (Oxford, 1956)

Regesta Regum Anglo-Normannorum 1066–1154. III: Regesta Regis Stephani ac Mathildis

Select bibliography

Imperatricis ac Gaufridi et Henrici Ducum Normannorum 1135–1154, ed. H. A. Cronne and R. H. C. Davis (Oxford, 1970)

Die Regesten der Erzbischöfe von Köln im Mittelalter, PGRG, 21, vol. I (313–1099) ed. Friedrich Wilhelm Oediger (Bonn, 1954–61); vol. II (1100–1205) ed. Richard Knipping (Bonn, 1901); vol. III, 1 (1205–61) ed. Richard Knipping (Bonn, 1909); vol. III, 2 (1261–1303) ed. Richard Knipping (Bonn, 1913); vol. IV (1304–32) ed. Wilhelm Kisky (Bonn, 1915)

Regesten der Reichsstadt Aachen I: 1251–1300, ed. Wilhelm Mummenhoff, PGRG, 47 (Bonn, 1961)

Regesten zur Geschichte der Juden im Fränkischen und Deutschen Reiche bis zum Jahre 1273, ed. Julius Aronius (Berlin, 1902; rpt. Hildesheim and New York, 1970)

Regestum Innocenti III papae super negotio Romani imperii, ed. Friedrich Kempf, Miscellanea Historiae Pontificae, 12 (Rome, 1947)

Register of the Freemen of the City of York. Volume I: 1271–1558, ed. Francis Collins, Surtees Society, 96 (London, 1897)

Registrum statutorum et consuetudinum ecclesiae cathedralis Sancti Pauli Londoniensis, ed. W. Sparrow Simpson (London, 1873)

Rheinisches Urkundenbuch. Ältere Urkunden bis 1100. Erste Lieferung: Aachen-Deutz, ed. Erich Wisplinghoff, PGRG, 57 (Bonn, 1972)

Richerus monachus Walciodorensi, "Trium corporum sanctarum virginum Coloniensium e numero undecim millium," in *Acta Sanctorum octobris*, ed. Joannes Bollandus (Brussels, 1858), IX, pp. 239–40

Robert of Torigny, *Chronica*, ed. Richard Hewlett, RS, 82: IV (London, 1882; rpt. 1964)

Roger of Howden, *Chronica*, ed. William Stubbs, RS, 51:I–IV (London, 1868–71; rpt. 1964)

Roger of Wendover, *Flores historiarum*, ed. Henry G. Hewlett, RS, 84:I–III (London, 1886–89; rpt. 1965)

Roll of Divers Accounts for the Early Years of the Reign of Henry III; Account of Escheats for the Sixteenth, Seventeenth and Eighteenth Years of the Reign of Henry III; Wardrobe Reciept Roll and Fragments of Household Roll, 10 Henry III, ed. Fred A. Cazel, PR NS, 44 (London, 1982)

Rolls of the Fifteenth of the Ninth Year of the Reign of Henry II for Cambridgeshire, Lincolnshire and Wiltshire and the Rolls of the Fortieth of the Seventeenth Year of the Reign of Henry III for Kent, ed. Fred A. Cazel and A. P. Cazel, PR NS, 45 (London, 1983)

The Rolls and Register of Bishop Oliver Sutton, ed. Rosalind T. Hill, The Lincoln Record Society, 69: VII (London, 1975)

Roth, Francis, ed., *The English Austin Friars 1249–1538. II: Sources*, Cassiacum: Studies in St. Augustine and the Augustinian Order, 7 (New York, 1961)

Rotulus cancellarii vel antigraphum magni rotuli pipae de tertio anno regni regis Johannis, ed. Joseph Hunter (London, 1833)

Rotuli chartarum in turri Londinensi asservati. II: 1 Ab anno MCXCIX ad annum MCCXVI, ed. Thomas D. Hardy (London, 1837)

Rotuli curiae regis, ed. Francis Palgrave, 2 vols. (London, 1835)

Rotuli de liberate ac de misis et praestitis regnante Johanne, ed. Thomas D. Hardy (London, 1844)

Rotuli de oblatis et finibus in turri Londinensi asservati tempore Regis Johanni, ed. Thomas D. Hardy (London, 1835)

Select bibliography

Rotuli Hugonis de Welles episcopi Lincolniensis A.D. MCCIX–MCCXXXV, ed. W. P. W. Phillimore, The Canterbury and York Society Series, 3: I–III (London, 1907–9)

Rotuli hundredorum temp. Henr. III et Edw. I in turri Londinensi et in curia receptae scaccarii Westmonasteriensi asservati, ed. W. Illingworth and J. Caley, 2 vols. (London, 1812–18)

Rotuli litterarum clausarum in turri Londinensi asservati, ed. Thomas D. Hardy, 2 vols. (London, 1833–4)

Rotuli litterarum patentium in turri Londinensi asservati. I: 1 Ab anno MCCI ad annum MCCXVI, ed. Thomas D. Hardy (London, 1835)

Rotuli Normannie in turri Londinensi asservati Johanne et Henrico Quinto Angliae regibus. I: De annis 1200–1205, necnon de anno 1417, ed. Thomas D. Hardy (London, 1835)

Rotuli selecti ad res Anglicas et Hibernicas spectantes, ex archivis in domo capitulari Westmonasteriensi deprompti, ed. Joseph Hunter (London, 1834)

Rotulorum originalium in curia scaccarii abbreviatio, ed. H. Playford and J. Caley, 2 vols. (London, 1805–10)

Royal and other Historical Letters Illustrative of the Reign of Henry III, ed. Walter W. Shirley, RS, 27: I–II (London, 1862–8)

Rupert of Deutz, *Vita Heriberti*, ed. Peter Dinter (Bonn, 1976)

Select Cases in the Exchequer of Pleas, ed. Hilary Jenkinson and Beryl E. R. Formoy, Seldon Society, 48 (London, 1932)

Select Cases Concerning the Law Merchant. Volume I: Local Courts, A.D. 1270–1638, ed. Charles Gross, Seldon Society, 23 (London, 1908)

Select Cases Concerning the Law Merchant. Volume II: Central Courts, A.D. 1239–1633, ed. Hubert Hall, Seldon Society, 46 (London, 1930)

Select Cases Concerning the Law Merchant. Volume III: Supplementary Central Courts, A.D. 1251–1779, ed. Hubert Hall, Seldon Society, 49 (London, 1932)

Select Cases of Procedure without Writ under Henry III, ed. H. G. Richardson and G. O. Sayles, Seldon Society, 60 (London, 1941)

Select Civil Pleas I: 1200–1203, ed. William Paley Baildon, Seldon Society, 3 (London, 1890)

Select Pleas, Starrs, and other Records from the Rolls of the Exchequer of the Jews A.D. 1220–1284, ed. J. M. Rigg, Seldon Society, 15 (London, 1902)

Starrs and Jewish Charters Preserved in the British Museum, ed. Israel Abrahams and Herbert Loewe, 3 vols. (Cambridge, 1930–2)

Das Stift St. Georg zu Köln. Urkunden und Akten (1059–1862), ed. Anna-Dorothee von den Brincken, *MSAK*, 51 (Cologne, 1966)

Das Stift St. Mariengraden zu Köln. Urkunden und Akten (1059–1817), ed. Anna-Dorothee von den Brincken, *MSAK*, 57/58 (Cologne, 1969)

Stow, John, *The Survey of London*, ed. H. B. Wheatley (London, 1987)

A Survey of Dominicans in England Based on the Ordination Lists in Episcopal Registers (1268–1538), ed. A. M. Emden, Institutum Historicum FF. Praedicatorum Romae ad S. Sabinae, Dissertationes Historicae Fasiculus 18 (Rome, 1967)

Thomas of Eccleston, *Fratris Thomas vulgo dicti de Eccleston Tractatus de adventu fratrum Minorum in Angliam*, ed. A. G. Little (Manchester, 1951)

Three Rolls of the King's Court in the Reign of King Richard the First A.D. 1194–95, ed. Frederick W. Maitland, PR, 14 (London, 1891)

Treaty Rolls Preserved in the Public Record Office. Volume I: 1234–1325, ed. Pierre Chaplais (London, 1955)

Select bibliography

Two Early London Subsidy Rolls, ed. Eilert Ekwall, Skrifter Utgivna Av Kungl. Humanistika Vetenskapssamfundet I Lund, 48 (Lund, 1951)

Die Urkunden Friedrichs I. 1152–1158, ed. Heinrich Appelt, *MGH DD*: Die Urkunden der Deutschen Könige und Kaiser, 10: I (Hanover, 1975)

Die Urkunden Friedrichs I. 1158–1167, ed. Heinrich Appelt, *MGH DD*: Die Urkunden der Deutschen Könige und Kaiser, 10: II (Hanover, 1979)

Die Urkunden Friedrichs I. 1168–1180, ed. Heinrich Appelt, *MGH DD*: Die Urkunden der Deutschen Könige und Kaiser, 10: 3 (Hanover, 1985)

Die Urkunden Heinrichs des Löwen Herzogs von Sachsen und Bayern, ed. Karl Jordan, *MGH DD*: Laienfürsten- und Dynastenurkunden der Kaiserzeit (Weimar, 1949)

Die Urkunden Konrads III. und Seines Sohnes Heinrich, ed. Friedrich Hausmann, *MGH DD*: Die Urkunden der Deutschen Könige und Kaiser, 9 (Vienna, Cologne, and Graz, 1969)

Die Urkunden des Pfarrarchivs von St. Severin in Köln, ed. Johannes Hess (Cologne, 1901)

Die Urkunden Philipps von Schwaben und Ottos IV (1198–1212), ed. Paul Zinsmaier, Veröffentlichungen der Kommission für Geschichtliche Landeskunde in Baden-Württemberg Reihe B: Forschungen, Band 53 (Stuttgart, 1969)

Urkundenbuch der Abtei Altenberg, ed. Hans Mosler, Urkundenbücher der Geistlichen Stiftungen des Niederrheins, 3: I–II (Bonn, 1912)

Urkundenbuch der Abtei Heisterbach, ed. Ferdinand Schmitz, Urkundenbücher der Geistlichen Stiftungen des Niederrheins, 2 (Bonn, 1908)

Urkundenbuch des Stiftes Kaiserswerth, ed. Heinrich Kelleter, Urkundenbücher der Geistlichen Stiftungen des Niederrheins, 1 (Bonn, 1904)

Urkundenbuch des Stiftes St. Gereon zu Köln, ed. P. Joerres (Bonn, 1893)

Urkundenbuch des Stiftes Xanten I: 590–1359, ed. Peter Weiler, Veröffentlichungen des Vereins zur Erhaltung des Xantener Domes, 2 (Bonn, 1935)

Urkundenbuch für die Geschichte des Niederrheins, Theodor Josef Lacomblet, 4 vols. (Düsseldorf, 1840–58)

Urkundenbuch für die Geschichte des Niederrheins. Nachweis der Überlieferung. Bearbeitet von Wolf-Rüdiger Schleidgen, ed. Theodor Josef Lacomblet, Veröffentlichungen der Staatlichen Archive des Landes Nordrhein-Westfalen Reihe C: Quellen und Forschungen, Band X (Siegburg, 1981)

Urkunden und Regesten zur Geschichte der Rheinlande aus dem Vatikanischen Archiv, ed. Heinrich V. Sauerland, PGRG, 23 (Bonn, 1902–13)

Verzeichnis der Kölner Testamente des 13.–18. Jahrhundert, ed. Wilhelm Baumeister, MSAK, 44 (Cologne, 1953)

Die Visionen und Briefe der Hl. Elisabeth . . . von Schonau, ed. F. W. Roth (Brünn, 1886)

Vita Annonis archiepiscopi Coloniensis, ed. R. Koepke, *MGH SS*, 11 (Hanover, 1854), pp. 462–514

Vita Annonis minor, Die Jüngere Annovita, ed. Mauritius Miller, Siegburger Studien, 10 (Siegburg, 1975)

Vita Norberti Archiepiscopi Magdeburgensis, ed. Roger Wilmans, *MGH SS*, 12 (Hanover, 1856), pp. 663–703

von den Brincken, Anna-Dorothee ed., "Die Totenbücher der Stadtkölnischen Stifte, Klöster und Pfarreien," *JKGV* 42 (1968), pp. 137–75

Die Welfen Urkunden des Tower zu London und des Exchequer zu Westminster, ed. Hans Friedrich Georg Julius Sudendorf (Hanover, 1844)

Select bibliography

Westminster Abbey Charters 1066–c. 1214, ed. Emma Mason, London Record Society, 25 London, 1988)

Wilbrand, Wilhelm, ed., "Unbekannte Urkunden zur Geschichte der Abtei Siegburg," *Annalen* 137 (1940), pp. 73–97

William of Malmesbury, *De gestis pontificum Anglorum*, ed. N. E. S. A. Hamilton, RS, 52 (London, 1870; rpt. 1964)

De gestis regum Anglorum, ed. William Stubbs, RS, 90:I–II (London, 1887; rpt. 1964)

William of Newburgh, *Historia rerum Anglicarum*, ed. Richard Howlett, RS, 82: I (London, 1884; rpt. 1964)

William of Poitiers, *Histoire de Guillaume le Conquérant*, ed. Raymonde Foreville (Paris, 1952)

Die Wundergeschichten des Caesarius von Heisterbach, ed. Alfons Hilka, PGRG, 43: 1–3 (Bonn, 1937)

SECONDARY WORKS

Abulafia, David, *Frederick II* (London, 1988)

Ahlers, Jens, *Die Welfen und die englischen Könige 1165–1235*, Quellen und Darstellungen zur Geschichte Niedersachsens, 102 (Hildesheim, 1987)

Ahrens, J., *Die Ministerialität in Köln und am Niederrhein* (Leipzig, 1908)

Althoff, Gerd, *Amicitiae et Pacta. Bündnis, Einung, Politik und Gebetsgedenken im beginnenden 10. Jahrhundert*, MGH Schriften, 37 (Hanover, 1992)

Appleby, John T., *England without Richard (1190–1199)* (London, 1965)

The Troubled Reign of King Stephen (London, 1969)

Arnold, Benjamin, "England and Germany, 1050–1350," in *England and Her Neighbours 1066–1453. Essays in Honour of Pierre Chaplais*, ed. Michael Jones and Malcolm Vale (London, 1989), pp. 199–216

"Germany and England 1066–1453," in *England in Europe 1066–1453*, ed. Nigel Saul (New York, 1994), pp. 76–87

German Knighthood (Oxford, 1985)

Asen, Johannes, "Die Begarden und die Sackbrüder in Köln," *Annalen* 115 (1929), pp. 167–79

"Die Beginen in Köln," *Annalen* 111 (1927), pp. 81–180; 112 (1928), pp. 71–148; 113 (1929), pp. 13–96

"Die Klausen in Köln," *Annalen* 110 (1927), pp. 180–201

Bappert, J. F., *Richard von Cornwall seit seiner Wahl zum deutschen König 1257–1272* (Bonn, 1905)

Barlow, Frank, *William Rufus* (London, 1983)

Barrow, Julia, "Cathedrals, provosts and prebends: a comparison of twelfth-century German and English practice," *Journal of Ecclesiastical History* 37: 4 (October 1986), pp. 536–64

"Education and the recruitment of cathedral canons in England and Germany 1100–1225," *Viator* 20 (1989), pp. 118–37

"German cathedrals and the monetary economy in the twelfth century," *Journal of Medieval History* 16: 1 (March, 1990), pp. 13–38

Bateson, Mary, "A London municipal collection of the reign of John," *EHR* 17 (1902), pp. 480–511, 707–30

Select bibliography

Bayley, C. C., "The diplomatic preliminaries of the double election of 1257 in Germany," *EHR* 62 (1947), pp. 457–83

Beaven, Alfred B., *The Aldermen of the City of London*, 2 vols. (London, 1908–13)

Beelmans, Wilhelm, *Wörterbuch für den Rheinischen Sippenforscher*, Hilfsbücher zur Westdeutschen Familie- und Sippenforschung, 2 (Cologne, 1939)

Berg, Dieter, *England und der Kontinent. Studien zur auswärtigen Politik der anglonormannischen Könige im 11. und 12. Jahrhundert* (Bochum, 1987)

"Imperium und Regna. Beiträge zur Entwicklung der deutsch-englischen Beziehungen im Rahmen der auswärtigen Politik der römischen Kaiser und deutschen Könige im 12. und 13. Jahrhundert," in *Zeitschrift für Historische Forschung Beihefte 5: 'Bündnissyteme' und 'Außenpolitik' im späteren Mittelalter*, ed. Peter Moraw (Berlin, 1987), pp. 13–37

Berghaus, Peter, "Das Münzwesen," in *Hanse in Europa. Brücke zwischen den Märkten 12.–17. Jahrhundert. Ausstellungskatalog des Kölnischen Stadtmuseums 9. Juni–9. Sept. 1973* (Cologne, 1973), pp. 73–84

"Die Perioden des Sterlings in Westfalen, dem Rheinland und in den Niederlanden," *Hamburger Beiträge zur Numismatik* 1 (1947), pp. 34–53

Westfälische Münzgeschichte des Mittelalters, 2nd edn., Landesmuseum für Kunst und Kulturgeschichte (Münster, 1986)

Berghaus, Peter and Siegfried Kessemeier, *Köln, Westfalen 1180–1980. Landesgeschichte zwischen Rhein und Weser. Ausstellung des Kölnisches Stadtmuseum April 11–May 1981*, 2 vols. (Cologne, 1981)

Bickel, Hartmut, *Beiname und Familiennamen des 12. bis 16. Jahrhunderts im Bonner Raum*, Rheinisches Archiv, 106 (Bonn, 1978)

Bock, F., "Englands Beziehungen zum Reich unter Adolf von Nassau," *MIÖG Ergänzungsband* 12 (1933), pp. 198–257

Böhm, Franz, *Das Bild Friedrich Barbarossas und seines Kaisertums in den ausländischen Quellen seiner Zeit*, Historische Studien, 289 (Berlin, 1936; rpt. 1965)

Böker, Hans J., "York Minster's nave: the Cologne connection," *Journal of the Society of Architectural Historians* 50: 2 (June, 1991), pp. 167–80

Brisch, Carl, *Geschichte der Juden in Cöln und Umgebung aus älterer Zeit bis auf die Gegenwart*, 2 vols. (Mülheim, 1879; Cologne, 1882)

Broodbank, Sir Joseph G., *History of the Port of London*, 2 vols. (London, 1921)

Brooke, Christopher and Gillian Keir, *London 800–1216: The Shaping of a City* (Berkeley and Los Angeles, 1975)

Budinsky, A., *Die Universität Paris und die Fremden an derselben im Mittelalter* (Innsbruck, 1924)

Bungers, Hans, *Beiträge zur mittelalterlichen Topographie, Rechtsgeschichte und Sozialstatistik der Stadt Köln*, Leipziger Studien aus dem Gebiet der Geschichte, 3:1 (Leipzig, 1891)

Buszello, Horst, "Köln und England (1468–1509)," *Köln, Das Reich und Europa. MSAK* 60 (1971), pp. 431–67

Cardauns, Hermann, *Konrad von Hostaden, Erzbischof von Köln (1238–1261)* (Cologne, 1880)

Carpenter, D. A., *The Minority of Henry III* (Berkeley, 1990)

Cartellieri, Alexander, *Die Schlacht bei Bouvines* (Leipzig, 1914)

Carus-Wilson, Eleonora M., "Die Hanse und England," in *Hanse in Europa. Brücke*

Select bibliography

zwischen den Märkten 12.-17. Jahrhundert. Ausstellungskatalog des Kölnischen Stadtmuseums 9. Juni–9. Sept. 1973 (Cologne, 1973), pp. 85–106

Medieval Merchant Venturers, 2nd edn. (London, 1967)

Carus-Wilson, Eleonora M. and O. Coleman, England's Export Trade 1275–1547 (Oxford, 1963)

Chazan, Robert, European Jewry and the First Crusade (Berkeley, 1987)

Clark, John, Saxon and Norman London, Museum of London (London, 1989)

Colvin, H. M., ed., The History of the King's Works 1: The Middle Ages (London, 1963)

Conrad, Hermann, Liegenschaftsübereignung und Grundbucheintragung in Köln während des Mittelalters, Forschungen zum Deutschen Recht, 1: 3 (Weimar, 1935)

Constable, Giles, "A note on the route of the Anglo-Flemish crusaders," Speculum 28 (1953), pp. 525–6

Corsten, K., "Eine Reise französischer Mönche nach Köln, Bonn und Siegburg im Jahre 1181," Annalen 116 (1930), pp. 29–60

Cuno, Klaus, "Namen Kölner Juden," Rheinische Heimatpflege NF 11 (1974), pp. 278–91

Davis, R. H. C., King Stephen (1135–1154) (Berkeley, 1967)

Deeters, Joachim, Die Hanse und Köln. Ausstellung des Historischen Archivs der Stadt Köln zum 8. Hansetag der Neuzeit in Köln im September 1988 (Cologne, 1988)

Denholm-Young, N., Richard of Cornwall (Oxford, 1947)

de Oliveira Marques, A. H., Hansa e Portugal na Idade Media (Lisbon, 1959)

de Trevarent, G., La Légende de Sainte Ursula dans la littérature et l'art du moyen âge, 2 vols. (Paris, 1931)

Dibben, L. B., "Secretaries in the thirteenth and fourteenth centuries," EHR 25 (1910), pp. 430–44

Diederich, Toni, Die alten Siegel der Stadt Köln (Cologne, 1980)

Dörner, Robert, "Das Sarwörter- und das Schwertfegeramt in Köln, von den ältesten Zeiten bis zum Jahre 1550," JKGV 3 (1916), pp. 1–60

Dössler, Emil, Südwestfalen und England: mittelalterliche und frühneuzeitliche Handelsbeziehungen (Münster, 1989)

Dobson, Richard B., The Jews of Medieval York and the Massacre of March 1190, Borthwick Papers, 45 (York, 1974)

Dollinger, Philippe, La Hanse (Paris 1964); Die Hanse (Stuttgart, 1966); The German Hansa, ed. and transl. D. S. Ault and S. H. Steinberg (London, 1970)

Domsta, Hans, Die Kölner Außenbürger: Untersuchungen zur Politik und Verfassung der Stadt Köln von der Mitte des 13. bis zur Mitte des 16. Jahrhunderts, Rheinisches Archiv, 84 (Bonn, 1973)

Dugdale, Sir William, Monasticon Anglicanum, 6 vols. (London, 1817–30)

Ellmers, Detlev, "Die Entstehung der Hanse," HGB 103 (1985), pp. 3–40

Emden, A. B., ed., A Bibliographical Register of the University of Oxford to A.D. 1500. 3 vols. (Oxford, 1957–9)

A Survey of Dominicans in England Based on the Ordination Lists in Episcopal Registers (1268–1538), Institutum Historicum FF. Praedicatorum Romae ad S. Sabinae. Dissertationes Historicae Fasciculus

Engels, Odilo, Der Niederrhein und das Reich im 12. Jahrhundert, Gesellschaft für Rheinische Geschichtskunde, Vorträge Nr. 23; Sonderausdruck aus Klever Archiv 4 (Kleve, 1983)

Select bibliography

Ennen, Edith, "Erzbischof und Stadtgemeinde in Köln bis zur Schlacht von Worringen (1288)," *Gesammelte Abhandlungen* (Bonn, 1977) 1: 388–404. Reprinted from *Bischofs- und Kathedralstädte des Mittelalters und der frühen Neuzeit* (Cologne and Vienna, 1976)

"Europäische Züge der mittelalterlichen Kölner Stadtgeschichte," *Köln, Das Reich und Europa MSAK* 60 (1971), pp. 1–48

"Kölner Wirtschaft im Früh- und Hochmittelalter," in *Zwei Jahrtausende Kölner Wirtschaft*, ed. Hermann Kellenbenz, Rheinisch-Westfälisches Wirtschaftsarchiv zu Köln (Cologne, 1975)

Ennen, Leonard, *Geschichte der Stadt Köln*, 6 vols. (Cologne, 1860–79)

Erdmann, C., "Der Kreuzzugsgedanke in Portugal," *Historische Zeitschrift* 141 (1930), pp. 23–53

Eubel, Konrad, *Geschichte der Kölnischen Minoriten-Ordensprovinz*, Veröffentlichungen des historischen Vereins für den Niederrhein, 1 (Cologne, 1906)

Fahne, A., *Geschichte der Kölnischen, Jülichschen und Bergischen Geschlechter*, 2 vols. (Bonn, 1843–53)

Farmer, David Hugh, *The Oxford Dictionary of Saints* (Oxford, 1982)

Fichtenau, Heinrich, "Akkon, Zypern und das Lösegeld für Richard Löwenherz," *Archiv für Österreichische Geschichte* 125 (1966), pp. 11–32

Ficker, Julius, *Engelbert der Heilige, Erzbischof von Köln und Reichsverweser* (Cologne, 1853)

Fischer, Bernd, "Engelbert von Berg (1185–1225). Kirchenfürst und Staatsmann (mit einer Gegenüberstellung zu Thomas Becket [1118–1170]," *Zeitschrift des Bergischen Geschichtsblätter* 94 (1989–90), pp. 1–47

Flink, Klaus, "Köln, das Reich und die Stadtentwicklung im nordlichen Rheinland (1100–1250)," *Blätter für deutsche Landgeschichte* 120 (1984), pp. 155–93

Förstemann, E., *Altdeutsches Namenbuch*, 2 vols. (Bonn, 1913–16)

Freed, John B., "Medieval German social history: generalizations and particularism," *Central European History* 25: 1 (1992), pp. 1–26

The Friars and German Society in the Thirteenth Century (Cambridge, MA, 1977)

Fried, Johannes, "Deutsche Geschichte im Früheren und Hohen Mittelalter: Bemerkungen zu einigen neuen Gesamtdarstellungen," *Historische Zeitschrift* 245 (1987), pp. 625–59

"Gerard Pucelle und Köln," *Zeitschrift der Savigny-Stiftung für Rechtsgeschichte (kanonistische Abteilung 68)* 99 (1982), pp. 125–35

Fryde, Natalie, "Arnold fitz Thedmar und die Entstehung der Grossen Deutschen Hanse," *HGB* 107 (1989), pp. 27–42

"Deutsche Englandkaufleute in Frühhansischer Zeit," *HGB* 97 (1979), pp. 1–14

Ein mittelalterlicher deutscher Großunternehmer. Terricus Teutonicus de Colonia in England, 1217–1247, Vierteljahrschrift für Sozial- und Wirtschaftsgeschichte, Beihefte 125 (Stuttgart, 1997)

Furhmann, Horst, *Germany in the High Middle Ages (c. 1050–1200)*, transl. Timothy Reuter (Cambridge, 1986)

"Quis Teutonicos constituit iudices nationum? The trouble with Henry," *Speculum* 69: 2 (April 1994), pp. 344–58

Giesen, Josef, "Köln im Spiegel englischer Reiseschriftsteller vom Mittelalter bis zur Romantik," *JKGV* 18 (1936), pp. 201–37

Gittoes, G. P. and N. J. Mayhew, "Short-cross sterlings from the Rotenfels hoard," *British Numismatic Journal* 53 (1983), pp. 19–28

Select bibliography

Gottschald, Max, *Deutsche Namenkunde. Unsere Familiennamen nach ihrer Entstehung und Bedeutung* (Berlin, 1960; revised by E. Brodführer in 1982)

Greving, Joseph, "Protokoll über die Revision der Beginen und Begarden zu Köln im Jahre 1452," *Annalen* 7 (1902), pp. 25–77

Steuerlisten des Kirchspiels S. Kolumba in Köln vom 13.–16. Jahrhundert. MSAK 30 (Cologne, 1900)

Groten, Manfred, "Die Anfänge des Kölner Schreinswesens," *JKGV* 56 (1985), pp. 1–21

Köln im 13. Jahrhundert. Gesellschaftlicher Wandel und Verfassungsentwicklung, Städteforschung: Veröffentlichungen des Instituts für vergleichende Städtegeschichte in Münster, Reihe A: Darstellungen, Band 36 (Cologne, Weimar, and Vienna, 1995)

"Untersuchungen zum Urkundenwesen unter den Erzbischöfen Arnold I und Arnold II von Köln (1138–1156)," *JKGV* 50 (1979), pp. 11–38

Güttsches, Arnold, "Das Sogenannte Overstolzenhaus in den Kölner Schreinsbüchern," *Im Schatten von St Gereon*, Veröffentlichungen des Kölnischen Geschichtsvereins, 25 (Cologne, 1960), pp. 97–132

Hävernick, Walter, *Der Kölner Pfennig im 12. und 13. Jahrhundert*, Vierteljahrschrift für Sozial- und Wirtschaftsgeschichte, Beihefte 18 (Stuttgart, 1930; rpt. Hildesheim, 1984)

Hagström, Sten, *Kölner Beinamen des 12. und 13. Jahrhunderts*, Nomina Germanica, 8, 16 (Uppsala, 1949–80)

Hartmeyer, Hans, *Der Weinhandel im Gebiete der Hanse im Mittelalter*, Volkswirtschaftliche und Wirtschaftsgeschichtliche Abhandlungen NF, 3 (Jena, 1905)

Harvey, P. D. A., "The English trade in wool and cloth, 1150–1250: some problems and suggestions," in *Produzione commercio e consumo dei panni di lana nei secoli XII–XVII: atti della «seconda settimana di studio» (10–16 aprile 1970)*, Istituto Internazionale di Storia Economica «F. Datini» Pubblicazioni Serie II: atti delle «settimane di studio» e altri convegni, 2 (Florence, 1976), pp. 369–76

Haverkamp, Alfred, *Medieval Germany (1056–1273)*, transl. Helga Braun and Richard Mortimer (Oxford, 1988)

Haverkamp, Alfred and H. Vollrath, ed., *England and Germany in the High Middle Ages* (Oxford, 1996)

"Germany and England in the high middle ages: a comparative approach. Conference held at the German Historical Institute London, 1–4 July 1987," *Bulletin of the German Historical Institute of London* 10: 2 (May, 1988), pp. 23–6

Heinemeyer, Walter, "Die Verhandlungen an der Saône im Sommer 1162," *DA* 20 (1964), pp. 155–89

Heusgen, Paul, "Ursula-Bruderschaften in Köln," *JKGV* 20 (1938), pp. 164–75

Höfer, Josef and Karl Rahner, *Lexicon für Theologie und Kirche*, 11 vols. (Freiburg, 1957–67)

Höhlbaum, Konstantin, "Kölns älteste Handelsprivilegien für England," *HGB* 3 (1882), pp. 41–8

"Über die Flandrische Hanse von London," *HGB* 8 (1898), pp. 147–80

Holtzmann, W., *Historical Manuscripts Commission Report on Manuscripts in Various Collections, Volume I* (London, 1901)

Honeybourn, M. B., "The Fleet and its neighbourhood in early and medieval times," *London Topological Record* 19 (1947), pp. 13–87

Howell, Martha C., *Women, Production, and Patriarchy in Late Medieval Cities* (Chicago, 1986)

Select bibliography

Huyskens, Albert, "Der Plan des Königs Richard von Cornwallis zur Niederlegung eines deutschen Krönungsschatzes in Aachen," *Annalen* 115 (1929), pp. 180–204

"Noch Einmal der Krönungsschatz des Königs Richard von Cornwallis," *Annalen* 118 (1931), pp. 136–43

Ihl, H., *Die Münzprägung der Edelherrn zur Lippe. Münzstätte Lemgo* (Lemgo, 1991)

Ilisch, Peter, *Münzfunde und Geldumlauf in Westfalen im Mittelalter und Neuzeit* (Münster, 1980)

Irsigler, Franz, "Industrial Production, international trade and public finances in Cologne," *The Journal of European Economic History* 6 (1977), pp. 269–306

Jaeger, C. Stephen, *The Envy of Angels. Cathedral Schools and Social Ideas in Medieval Europe, 950–1200* (Philadelphia, 1994)

Jakobs, Joachim, "Verfassungstopographische Studien zur Kölner Stadtgeschichte des 10. bis 12. Jahrhunderts," *Köln, Das Reich und Europa. MSAK* 60 (1971), pp. 49–124

Jenks, Stuart, "Die *Carta Mercatoria*: Ein 'hansisches Privileg,'" *HGB* 108 (1990), pp. 45–86

Jesse, W., "Der Münzfund von Hildesheim vergraben um 1260," *Hamburger Beiträge zur Numismatik* 2 (1948), pp. 16–48

Johag, Helga, *Die Beziehungen zwischen Klerus und Bürgerschaft in Köln zwischen 1250 und 1350*, Rheinisches Archiv, 103 (Bonn, 1977)

Jordan, Karl, *Henry the Lion: A Biography*, transl. P. S. Falla. (Oxford, 1986)

Kallen, Gerhard, "Das Kölner Erzstift und der 'ducatus Westfalie et Angarie' (1180)," *JKGV* 31/32 (1956–7), pp. 78–107

"Philipp von Heinsberg, Erzbischof von Köln (1169–1191)," *Im Schatten von St. Gereon*, Veröffentlichungen des Kölnischen Geschichtsvereins, 25 (Cologne, 1960), pp. 183–205

Kauffmann, C. M., *The Legend of St. Ursula*, Victoria and Albert Museum (London, 1964)

Kedar, Benjamin Z., "Toponymic surnames as evidence of origin: some medieval views," *Viator* 4 (1973), pp. 123–29

Keene, Derek, "A new study of London before the Great Fire," *Urban History Yearbook 1984* (Bath, 1984), pp. 11–21

"New discoveries at the Hanseatic Steelyard in London," *HGB* 107 (1989), pp. 15–25

Keene, Derek and Vanessa Harding, *A Survey of Documentary Sources for Property Holding in London before the Great Fire*, London Record Society, 22 (London, 1985)

Historical Gazetteer of London before the Great Fire. Part 1: Cheapside (Cambridge, 1987)

Kellenbenz, Hermann, "Der Aufstieg Kölns zur mittelalterlichen Handelsmetropole," *JKGV* 41 (1967), pp. 1–30

"Die Juden in der Wirtschaftsgeschichte des rheinischen Raumes von der Spätantike bis zum Jahre 1648," in *Monumenta Judaica. 2000 Jahre Geschichte und Kultur der Juden am Rhein*, Ausstellungsbuch des Kölnischen Stadmuseums Oct. 15, 1963–Feb. 15, 1964 (Cologne, 1963), pp. 199–241

ed., *Zwei Jahrtausende Kölner Wirtschaft*, Rheinisch-Westfälisches Wirtschaftsarchiv zu Köln, 2 vols. (Cologne, 1975)

Keller, Hagen, *Zwischen regionaler Begrenzung und universalen Horizont: Deutschland im Imperium der Salier und Staufer, 1024–1250*, Propylaen Geschichte Deutschlands, 2 (Berlin, 1986)

Select bibliography

Keussen, Hermann, *Die Matrikel der Universität Köln*, PGRG, 8: 1 (Bonn, 1928)
　　Topographie der Stadt Köln im Mittelalter, 2 vols. (Bonn, 1910; Bonn, 1918; rpt. Düsseldorf, 1986)

Kienast, Walter, *Die Deutschen Fürsten im Dienste der Westmächte bis zum Tode Philipps des Schönen von Frankreich*, Bijdragen van het Instituut voor Middelleeuwsche Geschiedenis der Rijks-Universiteit te utrecht, 10 and 16 (Utrecht, 1924 and Munich, 1931)
　　Deutschland und Frankreich in der Kaiserzeit (900–1270). Weltkaiser und Einzelkönige, Monographien zur Geschichte des Mittelalters, 9: 1–3 (Stuttgart, 1974–5)

Kirkpatrick, John, *The Streets and Lanes of the City of Norwich*, ed. William Hudson (Norwich, 1889)

Kirn, Paul, "Mit welcher Krone wurde König Sigmund in Aachen gekrönt?" *Annalen* 118 (1931), pp. 132–6

Kisch, Guido, *The Jews in Medieval Germany. A Study of their Legal and Social Status*, 2nd edn. (New York, 1970)

Kluger, Helmuth and Edgar Pack, ed., *Series episcoporum ecclesiae catholicae occidentalis ab initio usque ad anno MCXCVIII. Series 5,1: Archiepiscopatus Coloniensis* (Stuttgart, 1982)

Klußendorf, N., *Studien zu Währung und Wirtschaft am Niederrhein vom Ausgang der Periode des regionalen Pfennigs bis zum Münzvertrag von 1357*, Rheinisches Archiv, 93 (Bonn, 1974)

Knipping, Richard, *Die Kölner Stadtrechnungen des Mittelalters mit einer Darstellung der Finanzverwaltung*, PGRG, 15: I–II (Bonn, 1897–8)

Knoll, Kurt, *London im Mittelalter*, Wiener Beiträge zur englischen Philologie, 56 (Vienna and Leipzig, 1932)

Kober, Adolf, *Cologne*, transl. Solomon Grayzel, Jewish Community Series (Philadelphia, 1940)
　　Grundbuch des Kölner Judenviertels 1135–1425, PGRG, 34 (Bonn, 1920)

Korth, Leonard, "Das Urkunden-Archiv der Stadt Köln bis 1396," *MSAK* 3 (1883), pp. 1–70; 4 (1883), pp. 1–50

Kracht, Hans Joachim, *Geschichte der Benediktinerabtei St. Pantaleon in Köln 965–1250*, Studien zur Kölner Kirchengeschichte, 11 (Siegburg, 1975)

Kunze, Karl, "Das erste Jahrhundert der deutschen Hanse in England," *HGB* 6 (1889), pp. 129–54

Kurth, Friedrich, "Der Anteil Niederdeutscher Kreuzfahrer an den Kämpfen der Portugiesen gegen die Mauren," *MIÖG Ergäzungsband* 8 (1911), pp. 131–252

Kuske, Bruno, "Die Märkte und Kaufhäuser im mittelalterlichen Köln," *JKGV* 2 (1913), pp. 75–133
　　Köln, der Rhein und das Reich: Beiträge aus fünf Jahrzehnten wirtschaftsgeschichtlicher Forschung (Cologne, 1936)
　　"Köln. Zur Geltung der Stadt, ihrer Waren und Maßstäben in älterer Zeit (12.-18. Jahrhundert)," *JKGV* 17 (1935), pp. 82–119

Kuttner, Stephan and Rathbone, Eleanor, "Anglo-Norman canonists of the twelfth century. An introductory study," *Traditio* 7 (1949–51), pp. 296–303

Lappenberg, Johann Martin, *Urkundliche Geschichte des Hansischen Stahlhofes zu London* (Hamburg, 1851; rpt. Osnabrück, 1967)

Lau, Friedrich, "Beiträge zur Verfassungsgeschichte der Stadt Köln I: Das Schöffen

Collegium des Hochgerichts zu Köln bis zum Jahre 1396," *Westdeutsche Zeitschrift für Geschichte und Kunst* 14 (1895), pp. 172–95

"Beiträge zur Verfassungsgeschichte der Stadt Köln 2: Das Kölner Patriziat bis zum Jahre 1396," *Westdeutsche Zeitschrift für Geschichte und Kunst* 14 (1895), pp. 315–43

"Haus Quattermart zu Köln," *Annalen* 20 (1869), pp. 218–48

"Das Kölner Patriziat bis zum Jahre 1325," *MSAK* 24 (1894), pp. 65–89; 25 (1894), pp. 358–81; 26 (1895), pp. 103–58

"Das Schöffenkollegium des Hochgerichts zu Köln bis zum Jahre 1396," *Mevissenfestschrift* (Cologne, 1895), pp. 107–30

L'Estrange Ewen, C., *A History of Surnames of the British Isles. A Concise Account of their Origin, Evolution, Etymology and Legal Status* (London, 1931)

Levison, Wilhelm, "Das Werden der Ursula-Legende," *Bonner Jahrbuch* 132 (1927), pp. 1–164

"Eine Kölner Namenliste aus dem elften Jahrhundert," *Annalen* 119 (1931), pp. 164–9

England and the Continent in the Eighth Century, 1943 Ford Lectures (Oxford, 1949)

Lewald, Ursula, "Köln im Investiturstreit," in *Investiturstreit und Reichsverfassung*, Vorträge und Forschungen 17 (Munich, 1973), pp. 373–93

Leyser, Karl, "England and the Empire in the Early Twelfth Century," *TRHS* 5th Series 10 (1960), pp. 61–83

"Frederick Barbarossa, Henry II and the hand of St. James," *Medieval Germany and Its Neighbours (950–1250)* (London, 1982), pp. 215–42

Medieval Germany and Its Neighbours 900–1250 (London, 1982)

Liebermann, Felix, *Über die Leges Anglorum saecolo XIII. ineunte Londoniis collectae* (Halle, 1894)

Liljegreen, S. B., "Four Middle English versions of the legend of the eleven thousand virgins," *Englische Studien* 57 (1923), pp. 85–112

Lloyd, Terrence H., *Alien Merchants in England in the High Middle Ages* (New York, 1982)

England and the German Hanse, 1157–1611 (Cambridge, 1991)

The English Wool Trade in the Middle Ages (Cambridge, 1977)

Löhr, P. Gabriel M., *Beiträge zur Geschichte des Kölner Dominikanerklosters im Mittelalter. Teil 1: Darstellung. Teil 2: Quellen*, Quellen und Forschungen zur Geschichte des Dominikanerordens in Deutschland, 16/17 (Leipzig, 1920–2)

Mate, Mavis, "Monetary policies in England 1272–1307," *British Numismatic Journal* 41 (1972), 34–79

Mayer, Hans Eberhard, "Staufische Weltherrschaft? Zum Brief Heinrichs II. von England an Friedrich Barbarossa von 1157," in *Festschrift Karl Pivec*, ed. Anton Haidacher and Hans Eberhard Mayer, Innsbrucker Beiträge zur Kulturwissenschaft, 12 (Innsbruck, 1966), pp. 265–78

Mayhew, Nicholas J., "The circulation and imitation of sterlings in the Low Countries," in *Coinage in the Low Countries (800–1500)*, ed. N. J. Mayhew, B. A. R. International Series, 54 (Oxford, 1979), pp. 54–8

Sterling Imitations of Edwardian Type (London, 1983)

Miranda, Armin di, "Richard von Cornwallis und sein Verhältnis zur Krönungstadt Aachen," *Annalen* 35 (1880), pp. 65–92

Select bibliography

Nightingale, Pamela, "The evolution of weight-standards and the creation of new monetary and commercial links in northern Europe from the tenth century to the twelfth century," *Economic History Review* 2nd Series 38: 2 (May, 1985), pp. 192–209

"The ora, the mark, and the mancus: weight-standards and coinage in eleventh-century England," *The Numismatic Chronicle* 143 (1983), pp. 248–57; 144 (1984), pp. 234–48

Norgate, Kate, *The Minority of Henry III* (London, 1912)

Oediger, Friedrich Wilhelm, *Das Bistum Köln von den Anfängen bis zum Ende des 12. Jahrhunderts*, 2nd edn., Geschichte des Erzbistums Köln, 1 (Cologne, 1972)

Opladen, Peter, *Gross St. Martin. Geschichte einer Stadtkölnischen Abtei*, Studien zur Kölner Kirchengeschichte, 2 (Düsseldorf, 1954)

Opll, Ferdinand, *Friedrich Barbarossa*, Gestalten des Mittelalters und der Renaissance (Darmstadt, 1990)

Stadt und Reich im 12. Jahrhundert (1125–1190), Beihefte zur J. F. Böhmer, Regesta Imperii 6 (Vienna, Cologne, and Graz, 1986)

Ortenberg, Veronica, *The English Church and the Continent in the Tenth and Eleventh Centuries* (Oxford, 1992)

Ostermann, F. W., *900 Jahre Kölner Stahlhof in London* (Cologne, 1950)

Otte, James K., "The life and writings of Alfredus Anglicus," *Viator* 3 (1972), pp. 275–92

Owen, Dorothy, ed., *The Making of King's Lynn*, Records of Social and Economic History NS, 9 (Oxford, 1984)

Page, William, *London. Its Origin and Early Development* (London, 1923)

The Victoria History of the County of Hampshire and the Isle of Wight. Volume IV (London, 1911; rpt. 1973)

Peters, Inge-Maren, *Hansekaufleute als Gläubiger der Englischen Krone (1294–1350)*, Quellen und Darstellungen zur Hansischen Geschichte NF, 24 (Cologne and Vienna, 1978)

Philippi, Friedrich "Die Kölner Richerzeche," *MIÖG* 23 (1911), pp. 87–112

Planitz, Hans, "Das Grundpfandrecht in den Kölner Schreinskarten," *Zeitschrift für Rechtsgeschichte, (germanische Abteilung)* 54 (1934), pp. 1–88

Pötter, Wilhelm, *Die Ministerialität der Erzbischöfe von Köln vom Ende des 11. bis zum Ausgang des 13. Jahrhunderts*, Studien zur Kölner Kirchengeschichte, 9 (Düsseldorf, 1967)

Pohl, Hans, "Zur Geschichte von Wollproduktion und Wollhandel im Rheinland, in Westfalen und Hessen vom 12. bis zum 17. Jahrhundert," in *La lana come materia prima i fenomeni della sua produzione e circulazione nei secoli XIII-XVII: atti della «prima settimana de studio» (18–24 aprile 1969)*, Istituto Internazionale di Storia Economica «F. Datini» Pubblicazioni Serie II: atti delle «settimane di studio» e altri convegni 1 (Florence, 1974), pp. 89–96

Poole, Austin Lane, "Richard the First's Alliances with the German Princes in 1194," in *Studies in Medieval History Presented to F. M. Powicke*, ed. R. W. Hunt, W. A. Pantin, and R. W. Southern (Oxford, 1948), pp. 90–9

"Die Welfen in der Verbannung," *Deutsches Archiv für Geschichte des Mittelalters* 2 (1938), pp. 129–48

Postan, M. M. *The Medieval Economy and Society*, The Pelican Economic History of Britain, 1 (New York, 1975; rpt. 1984)

Postan, M. M., E. E. Rich, and Edward Miller, ed., *Cambridge Economic History* (Cambridge, 1963)

Power, Eileen, *The Wool Trade in English Medieval History* (Oxford, 1941)

Powicke, F. M., *King Henry III and the Lord Edward*, 2 vols. (Oxford, 1947)

Prestwich, Michael, *Edward I* (Berkeley, 1988)

Purcell, Donovan, "Der Hansische 'Steelyard' in King's Lynn, Norfolk, England," in *Hanse in Europa Brücke zwischen den Märkten 12.–17. Jahrhundert. Ausstellungskatalog des Kölnischen Stadtmuseums 9. Juni–9. Sept. 1973* (Cologne, 1973), pp. 109–12

Reaney, Percy Hide, *A Dictionary of British Surnames*, 2nd edn. (London, 1976)

Reuter, Timothy, "Past, present and no future in the twelfth-century *Regnum Teutonicum*," in *The Perception of the Past in Twelfth-Century Europe*, ed. Paul Magdalino (London, 1992), pp. 15–36

"John of Salisbury and the Germans," in *The World of John of Salisbury*, ed. Michael Wilkes, Studies in Church History, Subsidia 3 (Oxford, 1984), pp. 415–25

Rigold, S., "The trail of the Easterlings," *British Numismatic Journal* 26 (1949), pp. 31–55

Runciman, Steven, *A History of the Crusades*, 3 vols. (Cambridge, 1954)

Salzmann, Louis F., *English Trade in the Middle Ages* (Oxford, 1931)

The Victoria County History of the City of Cambridge and the Isle of Ely (London, 1948)

Sartorius, G. F., *Urkundliche Geschichte des Ursprungs der deutschen Hanse*, ed. John Martin Lappenberg, 2 vols. (Hamburg, 1830)

Sawyer, P. H., "The wealth of England in the eleventh century," *TRHS* 5th Series 15 (1965), pp. 145–64

Schmale, Franz Josef, "Friedrich I. und Ludwig VII. im Sommer des Jahres 1162," *Zeitschrift für Bäyrische Landesgeschichte* 31 (1968), pp. 315–68

Schmugge, Ludwig, "Über 'nationale' Vorurteile im Mittelalter," *DA* 38: 2 (1982), pp. 439–59

Schneider, Friedrich, *Arnold II, Erzbischof von Cöln 1151–1156* (Halle, 1884)

Schönbach, Anton E., "Des Bartholomaeus Anglicus Beschreibung Deutschlands gegen 1240," *MIÖG* 27 (1906), pp. 54–90

Schönfeld, M., *Wörterbuch der altgermanischen Personen- und Völkernamen* (Heidelberg, 1911)

Schreiber, Albert, "Drei Beiträge zur Geschichte der deutschen Gefangenschaft des Königs Richard Löwenherz," *Historische Vierteljahrschrift* 26 (1931), pp. 268–94

Schützeichel, Rudolf, "Die Kölner Namenliste des Londoner Ms. Harley 2805," in *Namenforschung Festschrift zum 75. Geburtstag für Adolf Bach* (Heidelberg, 1965), pp. 97–126

Schulte, Aloys, *Der hohe Adel im Leben des mittelalterlichen Köln*, Sitzungsberichte der Bayerischen Akademie der Wissenschaft, Philosophisch-philologische und Historische Klasse, 8 (Munich, 1919)

Schulte, Hans-Jürgen, *Die Verschweigung in der Kölner Schreinsurkunden des 12. bis 14. Jahrhunderts* (Cologne, 1966)

Schulz, Knut, "Richerzeche, Meliorat und Ministerialität in Köln," *Köln, das Reich und Europa. MSAK* 60 (1971), pp. 149–72

Simon, André L., *The History of the Wine Trade in England*, 2 vols. (London, 1906–9)

Southern, R. W., "The English origins of the 'Miracles of the Virgin,'" *Medieval and Renaissance Studies* 4 (1958), pp. 176–216

Spörl, J. "Rainald von Dassel auf dem Konzil von Reims 1148 und sein Verhältnis zu

Select bibliography

Johann von Salisbury," *Historisches Jahrbuch des Görres-Gesellschaft* 60 (1940), pp. 250–7

Spufford, Peter, *Handbook of Medieval Exchange* (London, 1986)

"Le rôle de la monnaie dans la révolution commerciale de XIIIe siècle," in *Etudes d'histoire monétaire*, ed. John Day (Lille, 1984), pp. 355–96

Money and its Use in Medieval Europe (Cambridge, 1988)

Stacey, Robert C., *Politics, Policy and Finance under Henry III (1216–1245)* (Oxford, 1987)

Stehkämper, Hugo, "Der Kölner Erzbischof Adolf von Altena und die deutsche Königswahl (1195–1205)," in *Historische Zeitschrift Beihefte NF 2*, ed. Theodor Schneider, Beiträge zur Geschichte des mittelalterlichen deutschen Königtums (Munich, 1973), pp. 5–83

"Die Stadt Köln in der Salierzeit," in *Die Salier und das Reich*, ed. Stefan Weinfurter (Sigmaringen, 1991) III, pp. 75–152

"England und die Stadt Köln als Wahlmacher König Ottos IV," in *Köln, Das Reich und Europa MSAK* 60 (1971), 213–44

"England und Köln," *Vierteljahrschrift für die Freunde der Stadt* 3 (1965), pp. 1–5

England und Köln. Beziehungen durch die Jahrhunderte in archivalischen Zeugnissen Ausstellung im Historischen Archiv der Stadt Köln Mai–Juni 1965 (Cologne, 1965)

"Geld bei deutschen Königswahlen des 13. Jahrhunderts," in *Wirtschaftskräfte und Wirtschaftswege I: Mittelmeer und Kontinent. Festschrift für Hermann Kellenbenz*, ed. Jürgen Schneider, Beiträge zur Wirtschaftsgeschichte, 4 (Bamberg, 1978), pp. 83–136

"Konrad von Hochstaden, Erzbischof von Köln (1238–1261)," *JKGV* 36/37 (1961–2), pp. 95–116

Stein, Albert Gereon, "Das Kloster und spätere adelige Damenstift an der Kirche der heiligen 11,000 Jungfrauen zu Köln," *Annalen* 31 (1877), pp. 45–111

"Die heilige Ursula und ihre Gesellschaft," *Annalen* 26/27 (1874), pp. 116–96

Die Pfarre zur heiligen Ursula in Köln (Cologne, 1880)

Stein, Frederick, "Einige Bemerkungen zu J. Asens 'Die Beginen in Köln,'" *Annalen* 178 (1976), pp. 167–77

Stenton, F. M., "Norman London (with William fitz Stephan's description of London edited by H. E. Butler and a map of London under Henry II by Marjorie B. Honeybourne and E. Jeffries Davies)," *Historical Association Leaflets* 93/94 (London, 1934)

Stewart, Ian, "Some German coins overstruck with sterling types," in *Lagom. Festschrift für Peter Berghaus zum 60. Geburtstag am 20. November 1979* (Münster, 1981), pp. 205–10

Stewartby, Sir Ian, "German imitations of English short-cross Sterlings," *The Numismatic Chronicle* 155 (1995), pp. 209–60

Stow, Kenneth R., "The Jewish Family in the Rhineland in the High Middle Ages," *The American Historical Review* 42: 4 (October 1987), pp. 1085–110

Strait, Paul, *Cologne in the 12th Century* (Gainesville, 1974)

Tanaka, Mineo, *La Nation anglo-allemande de l'Université de Paris à la fin du Moyen Age*, Textes et documents sur l'histoire des universités, 20 (Paris, 1990)

Tengvik, Gösta, *Old English Placenames*, Nomina Germanica. Arkiv för Germansk Namnforskning utgivet av Jöran Sahlgren, 4 (Uppsala, 1938)

Thierfelder, Hildegard, *Köln und die Hanse*, Kölner Vorträge zur Sozial- und Wirtschaftsgeschichte, 7 (Cologne, 1970)

Select bibliography

Tout, Mary, "The legend of St. Ursula and the eleven thousand virgins," in *Historical Essays by Members of the Owens College, Manchester*, ed. T. F. Tout and J. Tait (London, 1902; rpt. Manchester, 1907), pp. 17–56

Trautz, Fritz, *Die Könige von England und das Reich 1271–1377. Mit einem Rückblick auf ihr Verhältnis zu den Staufern* (Heidelberg, 1961)

Twiss, Travers, *On the Early Charters Granted by the Kings of England to the Merchants of Cologne*, The Ninth Annual Conference for the Reformation and Codification of the Law of Nations (London, 1881)

Tyerman, Christopher, *England and the Crusades, 1095–1588* (Chicago, 1988)

Venn, John and Venn, J. A., eds., *Alumni Cantabrigienses. A Biographical List of All Known Students, Graduates and Holders of Office at the University of Cambridge from Earliest Times to 1900. Part I: From Earliest Times to 1751* (Cambridge, 1922)

Vogts, Hans, "Die Strukturwandlungen der Kölner Stadtteile von St. Severin und St. Alban im Verlauf von acht Jahrhunderten," in *Aus kölnischer und rheinischer Geschichte. Festgabe Arnold Gültisches*, ed. Hans Blum, Veröffentlichungen des Kölnischen Geschichtsvereins, 29 (Cologne 1969), pp. 335–67

von Brandt, A., "Das angebliche Privileg Heinrichs III. von England für Lübeck. Ein ergänzender Hinweis zu den Fälschungsmethoden des Lübecker Syndikus Dreyer," *HGB* 71 (1952), pp. 84–8

von Loesch, Heinrich, *Die Kölner Kaufmannsgilde im zwölften Jahrhundert*, Westdeutsche Zeitschrift für Geschichte und Kunst, Ergänzungsheft 12 (Trier, 1904)

von Looz-Corswarem, Clemens Graf, "Hausverkauf und Verpfändung in Köln im 12. Jahrhundert," *Zwei Jahrtausende Kölner Wirtschaft*, ed. Hermann Kellenbenz, Rheinisch-Westfälisches Wirtschafts-archiv zu Köln (Cologne, 1975), I, pp. 195–204

von Ranke, Ermentrude, *Rheinische-englische Beziehungen bis zum 17. Jahrhundert*, Separatabdruck aus der Rheinischen Monatsschrift *Die Westmark* (Cologne, 1922)

von Winterfeld, Luise, *Handel, Kapital und Patriziat in Köln bis 1400*, Pfingstblätter des Hansischen Geschichtsvereins, 16 (Lübeck, 1925)

"Das Westfälische Hansequartier," in *Der Raum Westfalen* (Münster, 1955), II, 1, pp. 257–352

Wagner, F., *Studien über die Namengebung in Köln im zwölften Jahrhundert. 1: Rufsnamen* (Göttingen, 1913)

Wand, Karl, "Die Englandpolitik der Stadt Köln und ihrer Erzbischöfe im 12. und 13. Jahrhundert," in *Aus Mittelalter und Neuzeit. Festschrift zum 70. Geburtstag von Gerhard Kallen*, ed. Josef Engel and Hans Martin Klinkenbert (Bonn, 1957), pp. 77–95

Warren, W. L., *Henry II* (Berkeley, 1973; rpt. 1977)

King John (Berkeley, 1961; rpt. 1978)

Wegener, Gertrud, *Geschichte des Stiftes St. Ursula in Köln*, Veröffentlichungen des Kölnischen Geschichtsvereins, 31 (Cologne, 1971)

"Zur Verbreitung des Kölner Stadtrechts," *Köln, Das Reich und Europa. MSAK* 60 (1971), pp. 173–212

Weinbaum, Martin, *London unter Eduard I. und II.*, Vierteljahrschrift für Sozial- und Wirtschaftsgeschichte, Beihefte 28/29 (Stuttgart, 1933)

"Stahlhof und Deutsche Gildhalle zu London," *HGB* 33 (1928), pp. 45–65

Weiner, A., "Early commercial intercourse between England and Germany," *Economica* 11 (1922), pp. 127–48

Weise, Erich, "Die Hanse, England und die Merchant Adventurers," *JKGV* 31/32 (1956–7), pp. 137–64

Select bibliography

Weweler, Paul, "Lippische Sterlinge," *Festschrift zur Feier des 25jährigen Bestehens des Vereins der münzforscher und Münzfreunde für Westfalen und Nachbargebiete*, ed. K. Kennepohl (Münster, 1939), pp. 41–53

Wilbrand, Wilhelm, *Mittelrheinische Landeszeitung* (December 31, 1936) and "Unbekannte Urkunden zur Geschichte de Abtei Siegberg," *Annalen* 137 (1940), pp. 73–97

Williams, Gwyn A., *Medieval London. From Commune to Capital*, University of London Historical Studies, 11 (London, 1963)

Zehnder, Frank Günter, *Die Hl. Ursula und ihre Elftausend Jungfrauen. Ausstellung des Wallraf-Richartz Museums in Köln 6. Juli bis 3. September 1978* (Cologne, 1978)

Ziegler, Heinz, "Die Kölner Mark in neuem Licht," *HGB* 98 (1980), pp. 39–60

Unpublished dissertations and theses

Reuter, Timothy, "The papal schism of 1159–1169, the empire and the west," DPhil thesis, Oxford University, 1975

Stein, Frederick, "The Religious Women of Cologne 1120–1320," PhD dissertation, Yale University, 1977

INDEX

Aachen, 11, 79, 125, 132, 238
Adolf of Nassau, king of Germany (1291–8), 155
Adolf I of Altena, archbishop of Cologne, 19–20, 130
Aethelred II, king of England (978–1016), 9
Albertus Magnus, 231
Albrecht, duke of Brunswick, 30–1
Alcacer, 237
Alexander III, pope (1159–81), 16, 129, 217, 223, 225–6
Alfonso I, king of Portugal (1129–85), 234
Alfred the Great, king of England (871–99), 12
Altenberg, 134, 156
Andernach, 129
Anglicus
    Adam de Gipswich (Ipswich), 83
    Albreth Anglicus, 83
    Christian Anglicus, 124, 126
    conventus Englant, 110–11
    definition of the surname, 70–81
    domus Englant, 84–5, 91, 95, 111
    Engelbertus Anglicus, 124–5
    English Jews, 78–80: Joseph Iudeus Anglicus, 79–80; Vives Iudeus Anglicus, 79–80
    family genealogies, xvii
    "fratres dicti Anglici" (Vortlinus, Walterus, Hermannus, Arnoldus), 85–7, 127
    Gobelinus Anglicus, 121, 123
    Godefridus Anglicus, 89, 92, 95–6, 119–21
    Petrus Anglicus, 124
    Philippus Anglicus and wife Cristina Cleingedanc, 88–110
    Robinus Anglicus de Wolsacke and wife Iutta, 111–14
    Teodericus Anglicus, 114–19, 123
    Turris Anglici, 90–1, 99, 101, 104–5
    Walterus Anglicus and wife Guda, 82

Walterus Anglicus and wife Richmudis, 85–99
Walterus Anglicus Aurifaber, 121
Wilhelmus Anglicus, 114–19
Wilhelmus Anglicus and wife Hadewigis, 83
Wilhelmus de Anglia, 83
Anno II, archbishop of Cologne, 4, 200, 202–6
Antwerp, 19
Aquitaine, 21
Arnold, count of Aershot, 233

Barons' Revolt, 30
Battle of Evesham, 30, 192
Berkhamsted, 183–5
Bernard of Clairvaux, 233
Bologna, 217
Boppard, 132, 238
Bosham, Herbert of, 220
Boston, 32, 162, 172, 186
Brabant, 46, 48, 173
Brampton, 162
Brauweiler, 151, 156, 160, 200
Bremen, 9, 13, 27, 190
Bristol, 184, 233
Brühl, 157
Bruno I of Saxony, archbishop of Cologne, 4
Bruno IV of Sayn, archbishop of Cologne, 130, 132
Brunswick, 22, 28
Buckerel, Andreas, mayor of London, 180

Caen, 18
Cambridge University, 5
Canterbury, 5, 189, 211, 214, 218–20
Carta Mercatoria, 39, 173
Charlemagne, 9
Christian, archbishop of Mainz, 226
Cnut, king of England (1016–35), 42
Coggeshall, Ralph of, 218

Cologne
  archbishops, *see* individual names
  beguines, 50–1, 98, 100, 107, 110, 113
  Benedictines, 112
  Bürgermeister, 96
  district of Airsbach, 85–8, 91, 99–100, 141–2,
    144, 152
  district of Niederich, 83, 100, 111
  Dominicans, 103, 107, 231
  Franciscans, 148, 231
  Holy Apostles parish, 143, 146–7
  inheritance law (*Wartrecht*), 68
  land law (*Bodenrecht*), 68
  ministeriales, 96, 121, 128–9, 138, 144, 149,
    151, 160
  mortgage law (*Grundpfandrecht*), 69
  parishes and districts, xvi
  Praemonstratensians, 204, 208
  Richerzeche (*Meliorat*), 93, 96, 106
  St. Brigida parish, 142, 144, 154
  St. Columba parish, 114, 142, 144, 146, 156,
    231
  St. Laurence parish, 83, 93, 104, 108, 144,
    146
  St. Martin parish, 82, 84, 88, 90, 96, 99, 104,
    130, 141, 153–4
  St. Peter parish, 110, 146
  St. Severin parish, 88, 93–4, 96, 99–100, 231
  scabini (*senatores*), 68, 93, 96, 109, 141, 144
  trade fairs, 10
Compostella, Santiago de, 234, 236–7
Conrad III, king of Germany (1137–52), 232
Conrad of Hochstaden, archbishop of Cologne,
  40, 152
Conrad, prior of Speyer, 138
Constantinople, 189
Copenhagen, 193
Crusades
  Second Crusade, 189, 233–6
  Third Crusade, 236
  1217 crusade, 237
currency
  Cologne pfennig, 44–50
  English sterling, 40, 45, 47, 49, 50–63
  monnaie blanche (*albus denarius*), 51–2
  monnaie noire (*niger denarius*), 51–2
  Saxon silver, 41, 43, 56
  sterling forgeries, 46–50

Dartmouth, 233–4, 236–7
de Burgh, Hubert, royal justiciar, 137, 185
de Colonia, Berenger, 162
de Colonia, Bruno, 166
de Colonia, Gerard, 169–70
de Colonia, Gertrude, 176–77
de Colonia, Gilbertus, 173

de Colonia, Gocelin, 49, 170
de Colonia, Henricus, 173
de Colonia, Hermann, 30
de Colonia, Ingelramus, 174
de Colonia, Lambekin, 138
de Colonia, Lambert, 166–7
de Colonia, Lambert, cleric, 168–9
de Colonia, Loteryngus, 174
de Colonia, Marcmannus, 167–8
de Colonia, Matthew, 166
de Colonia, Peter, 163
de Colonia, Peter, brother of Hermann le
  Heaumer, 176–8
de Colonia, Richard, 174
de Colonia, Segwinus, 167–8
de Colonia, Tyrus, 173
de Cornhill, Henry, 135
de Cornu, Franco, 156
de Cornu, Friedrich Luyf, 171
de Cornu, Herman, 171
de Garlandia, John, 228–9, 241
de Ghistelles, Christian, 233
de Lacey, Henry, earl of Lincoln, 178
de Mandeville, William, 181
de Molis, Nicholas, 135–6, 138
Denmark, 28
de Nussia (Neuß), Sifridus, 141
Dersdorp, 150
Deventer, 9, 46
de Wilre, Conrad, sensechal of Otto IV, 133
de Wuppelford (Wipperfürth), Godescalcus,
  130, 142, 153–4, 156
Dictum of Kenilworth, 30
Dietrich I, archbishop of Cologne, 132
Dortmund, 9, 37, 46–7
Dover, 214
Dublin, 155
Düsseldorf, 79
Duisburg, 132
Duns Scotus, John, 5, 231, 241
Durham, 186

Easterlings, 23, 26, 27, 29–30, 33–4, 37–8, 171
Eckenhagen, 129
Edgar, king of England (959–75), 12
Edward I, king of England (1272–1307), 13, 35,
  37–9, 48, 155, 166, 169, 193
Engelbert I of Berg, archbishop of Cologne,
  130, 133–4, 137
Engelbert II of Falkenburg, archbishop of
  Cologne, 4, 30, 203
English counties
  Devonshire, 181
  Essex, 217
  Gloucester, 177, 181, 183
  Hampshire, 181, 185

Kent, 18, 233
Norfolk, 173, 181
Suffolk, 181
Surrey, 18
Wiltshire, 181, 183
Yorkshire, 229
Elbing, 23
Essen, 156, 203
Eswy, Ralph, sheriff of London, 180, 190

fitz Adelm, William, 16, 25
fitz Jocelin de Bohun, Reginald, bishop of Bath
    and Wells, 218–19
fitz Thomas, Thomas, mayor of London, 192
fitz Tedmar, Arnold
    alderman of the Germans, 27, 29, 189, 193–5
    alderman of Billingsgate ward, 191, 193–5
    author of London chronicle, 189
    custodian of the "chest of the citizens of
        London," 191
Flanders, 23, 32, 42, 46, 164, 171–2, 213, 233,
    237
Frankfurt, 44, 238
Frederick I Barbarossa, emperor (1152–90), 4,
    129, 208, 212, 217, 222–3, 227
Frederick II, emperor (1215–50), 4, 14, 21,
    24–5, 34, 50, 55, 133
Frederick, count of Isenburg, 137
Frisia, 42

George, count of Wied, 237
German Hospitalers, 133
Gisors, John, sheriff and mayor of London,
    192
Glanville, Henry (Hervey), 233–4
Gotland, 26

Hamburg, 23, 27, 30–1, 34–5, 37
Hanover, 79
Hanseatic League, 1, 2, 14, 23, 27, 39
Hanseatic Steelyard Complex, 5, 32, 190
Hastings, 233
Henry II, king of England (1154–89), 14–16,
    19–20, 45, 129, 212–14, 217, 224–6
Henry III, king of England (1216–72), 23–5,
    28, 30–1, 34–5, 37–8, 49, 133, 135–8, 143,
    162–3, 172, 184, 192
Henry IV, emperor (1056–1106), 4
Henry V, emperor (1106–25), 55, 212
Henry VI, emperor (1190–7), 4, 19, 218–19
Henry I of Molenark, archbishop of Cologne,
    138
Henry II of Virneburg, archbishop of Cologne,
    169–70
Henry, bishop of Winchester, 212
Henry, count of Burgundy, 234

Henry, duke of Lotharingia (Lorraine), 132,
    143
Henry, duke of Saxony, 183
Henry the Lion, duke of Saxony and Bavaria,
    16, 123, 219
Heribert, archbishop of Cologne, 4, 201, 207
Hervey, Walter, mayor of London, 193
Hoyland, 25–6
Hugh, bishop of Durham, 219
Humbert, archbishop of Arles, 218

Innocent III, pope (1198–1216), 130–1
Ipswich, 83, 139, 213
Isabel of Angoulême, queen of England, 183
Isabella, daughter of Henry III of England, 14,
    25–6, 55

Jerusalem, 234
Jocelin, bishop of Bath, 134
John, king of England (1199–1216), 13, 20–1,
    25, 28, 38, 49, 55, 131, 167, 172, 182–4
Jutland, 23

Kaiserswerth, 132
Kempe, Margery, 213
King's Lynn, 139, 162, 171, 173, 186

Langton, Stephan, archbishop of Canterbury,
    183
Laxfield (Suffolk), 131, 139–40, 152
Leges Edwardi Confessoris, 10
le Heaumer, Hermann (Manekin), 175–80, 187
Leopold, duke of Austria, 133, 136–8, 143
le Waleys, Henry, mayor of London, 36, 176
Ley as Lorengs, 12–13
Lincoln, 162, 186
Lisbon, 234–5, 236–7
London
    Billingsgate ward, 32–4, 36–7, 191
    Bishopsgate ward, 32–3, 35
    Breadstreet ward, 176, 180
    Cheap ward, 179
    Cologne guildhall, 4, 12, 14–18, 20, 24,
        27–9, 32, 84, 163, 190, 193, 240
    commune, 177
    Dowgate ward, 12, 18, 35, 190
    mayors, 34, 36
    Queenhithe ward, 180
    sheriff, 34
    Vintry ward, 12, 18
    wards, xv
Lotharingia (Lorraine), 4, 12, 228
Louis VI, king of France (1108–37), 219, 232
Louis VII, king of France (1137–80), 220, 222,
    224, 226
Louvain, 20

Index

Lübeck, 4, 23–4, 27–9, 31–2, 34, 37, 39, 193
Lüneburg, 22, 46
Luxembourg, 46

Magdeburg, 230
Mainz, 21, 219, 238, 242
Malmesbury, William of, 10, 12, 205
manufacturing and trade
  archery equipment and armor, 163, 175–6
  cloth and linen textiles, 11–12
  fish, 11
  fustian, 12
  gold and silver ornaments, 12, 163–4
  grains, 11–12, 163
  lard and bacon, 12
  metal wares, 11–12
  spices, 12
  wax, 12, 163
  wine, 11–12, 14, 163, 187
  wool(raw), 11–12, 56, 114, 164, 171–2, 174,
    187
  woolen textiles, 11
  yarn and thread, 11
Map, Walter, 220
Margaret, countess of Flanders, 29
Matilda, daughter of Henry II, 16, 55
Matilda, empress and mother of Henry II of
    England, 15, 212
Merbode, Gerard, 36
monastic relations
  Anglo-Cologne confraternity, 199
  Caesarius of Heisterbach, 202, 214, 226
  monastic legends, 202–7
  Norbert of Xanten, 204, 208
  Siegburg Abbey– Christ Church Canterbury
    confraternity, 199–200
  Scottish monks in Cologne, 201–2, 241:
    Helias, abbot of Groß St. Martin and St.
    Pantaleon, 201–2; Marianus Scotus, 201
Mountsorel (Leicestershire), 131
Münster, 9, 37, 47
Mundesdorp, 138, 158

Netherlands (Holland), 46, 79, 172
Neuß, 141, 151
Newcastle-upon-Tyne, 162, 173–4
Niger, Ralph, 220
Normandy, 19, 42, 233
Northampton, 14–15
Norwich, 162, 174

Otto I, emperor (936–73), 4, 42–3, 210
Otto IV, emperor (1198–1215), 13, 20–2, 28,
    49–50, 55, 130–3, 143, 166–8, 182–3,
    218–19
Otto, abbot of Siegburg Abbey, 130

Oxford University, 5

Palmersdorp, 157
Paris, 19
Patrick, earl of Salisbury, 217
Peverel, William, 181
Philip I of Heinsberg, archbishop of Cologne,
    4, 43, 217, 227
Philip II, king of France (1180–1223), 21, 189
Philip of Swabia, king of Germany
    (1198–1208), 130–1
Pilgrim, archbishop of Cologne, 201, 207
Portugal, 234–6
Portsmouth, 140
Pucelle, Gerard, 5, 220–8, 241

Quattermart, Henricus, 51

Rainald of Dassel, archbishop of Cologne, 15,
    129, 217, 220, 222, 227
Ralph, bishop of Chichester, 134
Rhineland, 10, 17, 42, 46–7, 56, 124, 172, 196,
    208, 228, 233, 236, 241
Richard I, king of England (1189–99), 19, 21,
    25, 34, 27–8, 49, 55, 130–1, 187, 189,
    218–19, 241
Richard of Cornwall, king of Germany
    (1257–72), 28, 125, 151–2, 188–9, 238–9
Richard, archbishop of Canterbury, 226
Richard, bishop of Salisbury, 134
Richard de Lucy, 14, 16, 25
Riga, 23
Rouen, 12, 15, 18
Rostock, 23, 27
Runnymede, 183

Salisbury, John of, 220–8
Sandwich, 162
Savaric, bishop of Bath and Wells, 218–20
Saxony, 42, 187, 230, 232
Scotland, 171–2, 230, 233
Siegburg, 130, 151, 160, 200, 202
Siegburg Abbey, 202, 205
Simon de Montfort, 29, 33, 192–3, 238
Soest, 9
Sproke, Walter, 182
St. Ives, 171
St. Ursula and the 11,000 Virgins
    architecture, 211
    English liturgy, 211
    Ford, Roger of, 211
    Gerlach, abbot of Deutz, 208–9
    hymns, 211
    legend, 107–11, 213, 215, 241
    Historia Brittonum of Geoffrey of Monmouth,
    209, 211

Index

Legenda Aurea of James of Voraigne, 209
relics, 212
Schönau, Elizabeth of, 209
St. Dunstan, 210
Southampton, 174, 233
Stamford, 162
Stephan of Blois, king of England (1135–54),
212
Stralsund, 23
Strasbourg, 238
Sürth, 156, 159

Tedmar of Bremen, 190
Teutonicus, Terricus, 180–5, 187
Teutonicus, Walerandus, 138, 184
Teutonicus de Stamford, Terricus, 180, 185–90
Tewkesbury, Peter of, 230–1
Thomas Becket, archbishop of Canterbury,
15–16, 189, 202, 213, 215, 220–1, 224–6
Tiel, 9, 13, 24
Tilbury, Gervase of, 217
Trier, 200, 242

Ungevuch, Arnold, 165
Utrecht, 9

Visby, 23, 26

Walram, count of Jülich, 151
Walter, bishop of Rouen, 219
Walter Mauclerc, bishop of Carlisle, 133–6, 143
Westminster, 133, 140, 151, 214
Westphalia, 4, 9, 17, 19, 23, 26, 28–9, 33–4, 37,
46–9, 56, 79, 170
Wichbold of Holte, archbishop of Cologne, 94,
155–6
Wife of Bath, 213

William, archbishop of Rheims, 218
William, count of Holland, 237
William II, king of Sicily (1166–89), 218
Winchester, Galfried of, 190, 192
Winchester, Walter of, sheriff of London,
190
Wipperfürth, 130
Wismar, 27
Würzburg, 15, 129

Yarmouth, 26, 162, 165, 173
York, 12, 162, 174, 239, 242

Zudendorp, ministerial family
de Belle, Gerardus, 131, 138, 140–1, 148,
158
de Belle, Otto, 158
Blithildis, 144, 148
Elizabeth (Bela), 147
family genealogies, xviii
Fortliph, 130
Gerardus, 131, 138, 142, 152–3, 155–7, 159
Gerardus the Younger, "miles de Novo
Foro," 122, 143–51, 154–9
Gertrudis, 140–1
Godefridus, 122, 127, 144–6, 150
Henricus the Elder and wife Elisabeth, 121,
130–44, 149, 152–3, 157
Henricus the Younger, 122, 141–2, 144, 150,
152
Hermannus, 159–60
Johannes, 148
Richardus, 133, 139, 152, 167
Richwinus, 129
Swykerus, 159–60
Teodericus, 130
Volcnant, 130

Cambridge Studies in Medieval Life and Thought
Fourth series

Titles in series

1 The Beaumont Twins: The Roots and Branches of Power in the Twelfth Century
   D. B. CROUCH
2 The Thought of Gregory the Great★
   G. R. EVANS
3 The Government of England Under Henry I★
   JUDITH A. GREEN
4 Charity and Community in Medieval Cambridge
   MIRI RUBIN
5 Autonomy and Community: The Royal Manor of Havering, 1200–1500
   MARJORIE KENISTON MCINTOSH
6 The Political Thought of Baldus de Ubaldis
   JOSEPH CANNING
7 Land and Power in Late Medieval Ferrara: The Rule of the Este, 1350–1450
   TREVOR DEAN
8 William of Tyre: Historian of the Latin East★
   PETER W. EDBURY AND JOHN GORDON ROWE
9 The Royal Saints of Anglo-Saxon England: A Study of West Saxon and East
   Anglian Cults
   SUSAN J. RIDYARD
10 John of Wales: A Study of the Works and Ideas of a Thirteenth-Century Friar
   JENNY SWANSON
11 Richard III: A Study of Service★
   ROSEMARY HORROX
12 A Marginal Economy? East Anglian Breckland in the Later Middle Ages
   MARK BAILEY
13 Clement VI: the Pontificate and Ideas of an Avignon Pope
   DIANA WOOD
14 Hagiography and the Cult of Saints: The Diocese of Orléans, 800–1200
   THOMAS HEAD

15 Kings and Lords in Conquest England
   ROBIN FLEMING

16 Council and Hierarchy: The Political Thought of William Durant the Younger
   CONSTANTIN FASOLT

17 Warfare in the Latin East, 1292–1291★
   CHRISTOPHER MARSHALL

18 Province and Empire: Brittany and the Carolingians
   JULIA M. H. SMITH

19 A Gentry Community: Leicestershire in the Fifteenth Century, c. 1422–1485
   ERIC ACHESON

20 Baptism and Change in the Early Middle Ages, c. 200–1150
   PETER CRAMER

21 Itinerant Kingship and Royal Monasteries in Early Medieval Germany, c. 936–1075
   JOHN W. BERNHARDT

22 Caesarius of Arles: The Making of a Christian Community in Late Antique Gaul
   WILLIAM E. KLINGSHIRN

23 Bishop and Chapter in Twelfth-Century England: A Study of the *Mensa Episcopalis*
   EVERETT U. CROSBY

24 Trade and Traders in Muslim Spain: The Commercial Realignment of the Iberian Peninsula, 900–1500★
   OLIVIA REMIE CONSTABLE

25 Lithuania Ascending: A Pagan Empire within East-Central Europe, 1295–1345
   S. C. ROWELL

26 Barcelona and Its Rulers, 1100–1291
   STEPHEN P. BENSCH

27 Conquest, Anarchy, and Lordship: Yorkshire, 1066–1165
   PAUL DALTON

28 Preaching the Crusades: Mendicant Friars and the Cross in the Thirteenth Century★
   CHRISTOPH T. MAIER

29 Family Power in Southern Italy: The Duchy of Gaeta and Its Neighbours, 850–1139
   PATRICIA SKINNER

30 The Papacy, Scotland, and Northern England, 1342–1378
   A. D. M. BARRELL

31 Peter des Roches: An Alien in English Politics, 1205–1238
   NICHOLAS VINCENT

32 Runaway Religious in Medieval England, c. 1240–1540
   F. DONALD LOGAN

33 People and Identity in Ostrogothic Italy, 489–554
   PATRICK AMORY

34 The Aristocracy in Twelfth-Century León and Castile
   SIMON BARTON

35 Economy and Nature in the Fourteenth Century: Money, Market Exchange, and the Emergence of Scientific Thought
   JOEL KAYE

36 Clement V
  SOPHIA MENACHE
37 England's Jewish Solution: Experiment and Expulsion, 1262–1290
  ROBIN R. MUNDILL
38 Medieval Merchants: York, Beverley and Hull in the later Middle Ages
  JENNY KERMODE
39 Family, Commerce and Religion in London and Cologne: Anglo-German Emigrants, c. 1000–1300
  JOSEPH P. HUFFMAN

* *Also published as a paperback*